THE FIX IS IN

THE FIX IS IN

A History of
Baseball Gambling and
Game Fixing Scandals

by
Daniel E. Ginsburg

McFarland & Company, Inc., Publishers
Jefferson, North Carolina, and London

The present work is a reprint of the library bound edition of
The Fix Is In: A History of Baseball Gambling and Game
Fixing Scandals, *first published in 1995 by McFarland.*

LIBRARY OF CONGRESS CATALOGUING-IN-PUBLICATION DATA

Ginsburg, Daniel E., 1956–
    The fix is in : a history of baseball gambling and game fixing
scandals / Daniel E. Ginsburg.
      p.   cm.
    Includes bibliographical references and index.

    ISBN-13: 978-0-7864-1920-3
    softcover : 50# alkaline paper ∞

    1. Baseball—United States—Corrupt practices—History.
2. Baseball—Betting practices—United States.   3. Gambling—
United States.   I. Title.
GV863.A1G58   2004
796.357'0973—dc20   94-47547

British Library cataloguing data are available

Cover images ©2003 PhotoSpin and Comstock.

Manufactured in the United States of America

McFarland & Company, Inc., Publishers
  Box 611, Jefferson, North Carolina 28640
    www.mcfarlandpub.com

To the memory of Lee Allen

Preface

I have been a student of baseball history since my pre-teen years. My interest in baseball is not devoted to the statistics or the ball parks or specific teams, but to the people who actually give life to the game. Like American society, baseball is a melting pot, made up of people from many different backgrounds and with many different character traits.

Baseball gambling and game fixing scandals – games in which the outcome has been altered due to the efforts of dishonest players or umpires – is the dark side of baseball society. My interest in this subject was kindled by Eliot Asinof's *Eight Men Out*, a history of the 1919 World Series fix, and Lee Allen's *The Hot Stove League*, which contains an outstanding chapter on pre–1900 scandals. Over the years I have continued to follow the subject and build my knowledge base.

In the course of my research, I discovered that no one had ever written a complete history of the subject. While there are books on specific scandals, such as the 1919 World Series, and while gambling and game fixing scandals receive a certain amount of coverage in the more serious baseball histories, there is no one source covering all of the scandals. *The Fix Is In* was written to fill that void.

In the research for this book, my single best source of information has been the newspapers of the day, especially the *Sporting News*. I have also studied numerous books, articles, and collections, and learned a great deal through discussions with baseball historians and former players.

This book has been a labor of love for me. I hope that it will expand the knowledge base on the subject and encourage others to do further research.

Finally, I would like to acknowledge the following people and organizations, without whose help this book would not have been possible: Ray Allen, The Baseball Hall of Fame Library and Photo Collection, Jay Bennett, The New York Public Library, Rare Books and Manuscripts Division, Teresa Ohmit, Joe Overfield, Mark Rucker, and the Society for American Baseball Research.

And special thanks go to my agent, Robert Ducas.

Contents

Introduction

The Evils of Gambling

Baseball is more than a game to me, it's a religion.
— Hall of Fame umpire Bill Klem, 1949

Baseball holds a special place in American society. While football, and more recently basketball, have grown in popularity, they have never approached baseball in its role as an integral part of American culture. Even our language is filled with baseball terminology — to excel is to "hit a home run," to fail is to "strike out," and to be confused is to be "way off base."

Baseball is the glory and the triumph — Bobby Thompson's home run to win the pennant for the New York Giants in 1951; Kirk Gibson's dramatic home run in the 1988 World Series for the Los Angeles Dodgers; Carlton Fisk's dramatic home run in 1975 for the Boston Red Sox; Don Larson's perfect game in the 1956 World Series; and little-known pinch hitters Gene Larkin and Francisco Cabrerra providing key hits to propel their teams to victory in 1991 and 1992.

Baseball is also the anguish — the ground ball bouncing between Bill Buckner's legs to end the sixth game of the 1986 World Series; Fred Merkle failing to touch second base for the New York Giants in 1908, which helped the Chicago Cubs beat out the Giants for the pennant; Roberto Clemente being cut down in his prime by a plane crash while on a mission of mercy to Nicaragua; and farewells by great stars Lou Gehrig and Babe Ruth during their last days of terminal illnesses.

Behind all the triumph and tragedy, the winning and losing, there is the assumption, and indeed the firm assurance, that the players are giving their absolute best to win each time they take the field. So what happens when baseball players do not give their best when they take the field? What happens when the outcome of games has been tampered with? How often has it happened? Could it happen again? These are the issues that this book will explore.

To study the history of baseball scandals, it is necessary first to understand the true cause of the scandals: gambling. Most of the game fixing scandals

1

have been the result of gamblers' attempting to manipulate the odds in their favor and assure themselves financial rewards through fixing games.

Baseball gambling by its nature is a risky business. In making a wager, the gambler is betting on a hunch or expert knowledge about which team will win in an extremely unpredictable sport. But when the fix is in, the gambler has a "sure thing," a guaranteed win. When that happens, a scandal is created.

In examining this subject, it is important to understand that there has always been a link between baseball and gambling. Baseball initially became popular among "gentlemen"—members of the upper class playing for leisure and fun. As part of this activity, a wager was usually made—perhaps dinner, perhaps a small sum of money—all in a "sporting" fashion.

As the game grew in popularity, "sportsmen"—that is, gamblers—began to take an interest in the game. Baseball provided a good opportunity to make a friendly wager. Many people found watching games more enjoyable with a small wager, and this was often handled very privately. As time went on, however, gambling grew to the point where it threatened the survival of baseball, as the coming chapters will document.

Gambling on baseball and other sports is a big business. In Nevada, where sports gambling is legal, approximately $1 billion is bet on major sports each year. According to *Sport* magazine's Robert McGarvey (April 1989), throughout the nation over $25 billion changes hands yearly through sports gambling, despite the fact that it is illegal outside of Nevada. That makes sports gambling bigger than many major industries in the United States—and a very real threat to the integrity of professional sports.

Not all the scandals examined in this book relate solely to game fixing. In many cases the scandals involve players or managers associating with gamblers, or becoming involved with gambling activities that do not affect the outcome of the game. However, as we will see, history has shown that any relationship between baseball and gambling is an extremely dangerous one, and one that must be avoided at all costs.

Baseball gambling scandals have occurred throughout baseball history. This book will trace these scandals in chronological order, and to some extent thus serve as a brief overview of the history of baseball. In addition to recounting the events involved in the gambling scandals, this book will attempt to put the events in historical perspective and provide some insight into the lives of the men involved in these scandals.

We are now ready to begin our journey through the dark side of baseball history. We will start by going back to the beginning, to baseball's early days.

Chapter 1

The Early Days

The development of the game of baseball took place over a period of many years. The game that we know and love today evolved from early bat and ball games, most notably the English game of rounders, and other games dating back to ancient Egypt.

For all practical purposes, however, modern baseball was developed in 1845 by Alexander Cartwright and his New York Knickerbocker Club. The major adjustments Cartwright made to the game, including the distance of 90 feet between the bases, form the heart and soul of modern baseball.

In the early days, baseball was a sport of the upper classes. Matches were played between "gentlemen's" social clubs, including the Knickerbockers, the Brooklyn Excelsiors, and the Gotham Club. The games were major social events and were usually followed by a large banquet, at which the members of both clubs were entertained in lavish fashion.

Throughout the 1850s, the number of baseball clubs began to grow rapidly. While the original concentration of baseball was in New York City, social clubs throughout New England, Washington, D.C., and New York State took up the game. This led to the need for a more formalized structure, and on March 10, 1858, representatives of 22 New York area clubs met to form the National Association of Base Ball Players. This new association drew up a basic set of rules and by-laws, and by 1860 the National Association had expanded into a national organization.

It was during the Civil War that baseball truly began to become America's national sport. Baseball was an ideal recreation for soldiers (including Union prisoners of war, who spread the game to the South), and by the time the war ended the popularity of baseball was already booming. During the postwar period, baseball spread like wildfire, leaping to the forefront of the American sporting mind.

As the popularity of the game spread, baseball ceased to be a "gentlemen's game" and became a game for the masses. This change did not happen overnight—the grand social events of previous days were still observed before and after certain matches—but slowly and surely the game began to take on the character of "the common man." In writing about a game between the

3

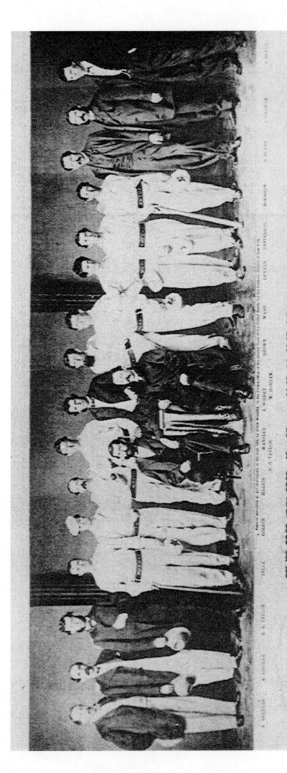

MUTUAL NINE, 1864.

Niagara Club of Buffalo, and the Ellicott Club of Jamestown, New York, which was followed by a 10-course meal at one of Buffalo's finest eating places, Joe Overfield, writing for the *Niagara Frontier*, stated:

> The Niagara-Ellicott game, and what followed, exemplified baseball as the gentlemen's game it was in its formative years. Baseball in the grand manner was somewhat of an anachronism in a period when gambling, hard drinking and corruption in government were patterns of the time. It was an anachronism that could not long continue.

And indeed it did not continue, for in 1865, baseball's first great scandal, the Wansley affair, took place.

Baseball in 1865 was, in theory, still an amateur sport played for enjoyment. In reality, a growing number of players, such as Philadelphia's Al Reach, were already accepting compensation to play baseball. Clubs wanted winning records, and they were willing to pay star players to ensure winning records. Bending the rules by paying players helped create an atmosphere in baseball that was conducive to dishonest play. If clubs were willing to pay players secretly to assure victory, it was not too great a leap for gamblers to pay players secretly to assure defeat!

Suspicion of "fixes" began early in the 1860s, as the game grew in popularity. By 1865, the rumors were becoming more frequent and more ominous. Much suspicion focused on the Mutuals of New York, whose president was the infamous Tammany Hall leader, William M. "Boss" Tweed. In 1865, the catcher for the Mutuals was William Wansley, who became the central figure in baseball's first scandal.

The Wansley affair began on the evening of September 27, 1865, when gambler Kane McLoughlin paid William Wansley the sum of $100 to see that the following day's game, between Wansley's Mutuals and the Brooklyn Eckfords, would be won by the Eckfords. In order to accomplish this, Wansley stated that he would bribe two other players on the Mutuals. Wansley first approached Mutuals third baseman Ed Duffy, who agreed to the plot if shortstop Tom Devyr would go along too. Lee Allen, writing in *The Hot Stove League*, reports the ensuing events as follows:

> Several hours before the players were to take the field, McLoughlin picked up Wansley, Duffy and Devyr in a wagon and drove them to the Hoboken Ferry. Wansley gave Duffy and Devyr $30.00 each, keeping $40.00 as his share. All these details were later freely confessed by Devyr.[1]

The result was a 23–11 victory by the Eckfords over the Mutuals. The Mutuals were leading 5–4 after four innings, when Wansley took over. The accounts

Opposite: **The 1864 New York Mutuals. Thomas Devyr and William Wansley, who a year later instigated baseball's first scandal, are standing sixth and tenth from right, respectively.** *Courtesy of Transcendental Graphics.*

of the game reported that "Wansley had a multitude of passed balls, and some of the infielders muffed easy flys and threw wildly. So, in the fifth, the Eckfords scored eleven runs." In fact, Wansley's play was so bad that during the fifth inning the manager moved him to right field, with right fielder McMahon moving behind the plate. While all three of the crooked players contributed to the fix, Wansley "distinguished himself" with six passed balls, and no hits in five at-bats.

A crowd of 3,500 attended the game, and soon after its conclusion rumors were rife that the game had been thrown. Reporting in the *New York Clipper*, the great chronicler of baseball, Henry Chadwick, who was to become one of the game's great reformers, wrote that "the comments on his [Wansley's] errors made him mad, and that is all there is to this talk of selling the game. Baseball has never yet been disgraced by any such thing, and never will, we hope."

But that hope turned out to be in vain. The Mutuals met after the game and charged Wansley with "willful and designed inattention," a flowery way of saying he threw the game. An investigation was undertaken, and on October 20, William Wansley appeared at the club's offices and made a confession in full. In the aftermath, Wansley, Duffy, and Devyr were all expelled from the National Association for their crooked play.

These expulsions turned out to be short-lived, however. In need of a shortstop, the Mutuals unilaterally restored Devyr to good standing in 1867. Two clubs then lodged protests against the Mutuals to the judiciary committee of the National Association. In his book *Playing for Keeps—A History of Early Baseball*, Warren Goldstein reports that

> The first was dismissed for want of evidence other than "newspaper reports, quotes and mere idle rumors," but the second was sustained; the committee held that the Mutuals had violated the Association's constitution in playing an expelled player and declared the game in question null and void.[2]

The question was taken up by the full National Association at their convention in Philadelphia on December 11. The convention voted overwhelmingly in the Mutuals' favor, recording a 451–143 decision to reverse the judiciary committee and reinstate Devyr. It was felt that Devyr's youth (he was only 18 at the time of his expulsion) was a contributing factor in this decision.

In 1868 the Mutuals began using Duffy, who had not been reinstated by the National Association. One of the Mutuals' opponents, the Actives, filed a complaint. On October 15 the judiciary committee of the New York State Association upheld the protest and declared all games that Duffy participated in null and void. The decision was appealed to the judiciary committee of the National Association.

On November 11 the New York state convention was held at Albany. The Mutuals were expelled for reinstating Duffy but were immediately reinstated and all was forgiven.

Finally, on November 30, 1870, the final convention of the amateur National Association was held. One of the issues before the convention was the reinstatement of William Wansley, the principal villain in the scandal. John Wildey, president of the Mutuals, moved that Wansley be restored to good standing, and the motion was passed.

Devyr and Wansley soon faded into obscurity. Duffy continued his career, playing with the Chicago White Stockings in the initial season of the National Association of Professional Base Ball Players, baseball's first major league. Duffy hit .231 and then left the professional game. He died in June of 1889.

In many ways it is quite fitting that baseball's first scandal was created by members of the New York Mutuals. The Mutuals had a reputation for involvement in "shady deals," and the club was closely connected with New York's Tammany Hall. John Wildey, mentioned earlier, was New York's coroner, and the infamous Boss Tweed joined the Mutuals' Board of Trustees in 1866. Perhaps the most corrupt politician in the history of the United States, Tweed's business methods soon began to permeate the operations of the club. As we will see in the next chapter, this helped make the Mutuals the center of many baseball scandals during the early 1870s.

The Wansley affair in many ways marked an end to the anachronism that Joe Overfield wrote about, an end to the age of baseball as a pure sporting event. While the honesty of baseball games in the past had occasionally been questioned, the Wansley affair, and the light punishments that the amateur National Association dealt out, brought more scrutiny to the game as a whole.

While rumors occasionally circulated about dishonest actions by the Mutuals and the Haymakers of Troy, New York (owned by famous gambler John Morrissey, the Arnold Rothstein of his day), the next baseball scandal of the amateur period surprisingly did not involve gambling at all. Instead, it involved a baseball tournament held in October 1866 in Auburn, New York. Prizes for this tournament included a $200 gold ball to the champion team and a $150 silver ball to the runner-up. The key game in the tournament pitted the Niagaras of Buffalo against the Excelsiors of Rochester, considered the two best clubs in the tournament. The game went into extra innings, with Rochester winning 28–26.

The importance of this game was soon overshadowed by the revelation that arrangements had been made to fix the outcome of some of the games in the tournament. It was revealed that the Excelsiors of Rochester and the Pacifics of Rochester had agreed to let the Pacifics win the game between the two clubs, thus assuring that the gold ball would go to the Pacifics, and the silver ball would go to the Excelsiors due to their win over the Niagaras. The plot then called for the clubs to return to Rochester, with the Excelsiors challenging the Pacifics, and winning the gold ball from them. This plot was revealed by some of the honest Excelsior players, and the Excelsior and Pacific teams both resigned from the tournament.

The 1871 Haymaker Club of Troy. Mike McGeary and Bill Craver, two major figures in early scandals, are hand-numbered 4 and 5, respectively. *Courtesy of Transcendental Graphics.*

The Niagaras were offered the gold ball, but they declined and accepted the silver instead. The scandal soon faded into oblivion, until the events were again uncovered many years later by Joe Overfield.

In contrast to this, the next scandal is one that is often recalled today because it involved a game with baseball's first openly all-professional team, the 1869 Cincinnati Red Stockings.

As the 1860s progressed, professionalism in baseball continued to rise. By the late 1860s, players were constantly changing clubs, and most of the major stars were receiving indirect compensation for their services. This compensation often included fictional jobs—for example, the star players on the Washington Nationals would often end up in government jobs, although their responsibilities in these jobs were extremely suspect.

In 1869 the Red Stocking Club of Cincinnati, led by President Aaron Champion and Captain Harry Wright, decided to openly proclaim themselves professionals and assemble an all-star nine. The team featured Hall of Fame brothers Harry and George Wright, as well as early stars Cal McVey, Doug Allison, and Asa Brainard.

During the course of the 1869 season, the Red Stockings played 65 games and won them all. They traveled nearly 12,000 miles by rail and boat and appeared before more than 200,000 spectators. While the financial results of the team were not impressive (they barely broke even), they established once and for all the superiority of an all-professional team, and their success doomed amateur baseball as a major force in the United States.

While the Red Stockings dominated the 1869 season, there were a number of other clubs to be reckoned with. Among the principal ones were the New York Mutuals, the Brooklyn Atlantics, and the Troy Haymakers.

As mentioned earlier, the Haymakers were owned by John Morrissey, and it was commonly acknowledged that the club had less than a sterling moral character. Morrissey's major interest was not wins and losses, but how he could profit from gambling on the games.

In the first match between Troy and Cincinnati, the Red Stockings prevailed by a score of 37–31. Encouraged by the closeness of the score, the Troy team decided that they could beat the Red Stockings in their return match. They also decided on a plan to maximize their profit from such a victory by manipulating the odds to heavily favor the Red Stockings. An early *Cincinnati Enquirer* account of the game went as follows:

> There is a little secret history connected with this affair that is worth relating. After our Red Stockings finished their triumphant eastern tour, the eastern people determined to organize a club to beat our champions, and after considerable discussion, the Haymakers were reorganized by procuring some of the finest players connected with other clubs. Such was the confidence of the Haymakers of their superiority that they deemed a blind necessary for procuring bets, and therefore, allowed the Eckfords, after their annihilation here, to beat them. After starting out on their tour, the Trojans were careful in their matches not to exhibit any very wonderful playing, so as to carry out the program and gain what they termed excellent bets.[3]

In addition to the Eckford game, it was rumored that the Haymakers' 25–11 loss to the Brooklyn Atlantics was also a fix in order to increase the odds.

Finally, on August 26, the Haymakers visited Cincinnati for the greatly awaited showdown. According to baseball historian Lee Allen, John Morrissey wagered $60,000 on the Haymakers to beat the Red Stockings, an astounding sum for that time (the equivalent sum in 1990 would have been well over $1,000,000). By manipulating the odds, Morrissey stood to make a fortune. However, if the Red Stockings beat the Haymakers, he stood to lose a fortune.

Exactly what happened has been obscured by the passage of time, but it appears that Morrissey instructed the players to assess their chances of winning early in the game. If uncertain of a victory, they were instructed to look for an opportunity when the game was tied or they had grabbed a lead to quit the game in order to protect Morrissey from losses. In those days of no gloves and high-scoring games, it was not unusual for the lead to see-saw back and forth a number of times before the final verdict was decided.

At the end of the fifth inning, the Troy Haymakers had tied the score at 17 all. The following account explains what happened next.

> McVey of the Red Stockings was the first man to bat in the sixth, and struck a foul ball which bounded and was picked up by Craver, the Troy catcher. Umpire Brockway ruled "not out" as the ball was not fielded on the first bounce in his opinion. At once, McKeon [the president of the Troy Club] rushed out onto the field and ordered his club to "stack your bats." Pitcher [William "Cherokee"] Fisher started to put the bats in the bag although some of the Haymakers wished to continue the game.
>
> As McKeon continued his clamor, the crowd rushed out upon the diamond greatly excited despite the efforts of the police to maintain order. Brockway was surrounded as he stood upon a chair and announced, "I decide the game in favor of Cincinnati because the Unions of Lansinburg [the Troy Haymakers] refuse to continue it." The forfeiture caused loud cheering. All this time, McVey stood coolly at home plate with bat in hand, ready to continue the game.[4]

After the game there was some controversy about whether it should be declared a Red Stockings victory, or a draw. Because the game was in Cincinnati, the Red Stockings immediately announced that they would retain all the gate receipts (receipts for the game exceeded $2,000). Some months later, the Haymakers offered a written apology and were then given their share of the gate receipts.

This incident received tremendous publicity across the country, and the newspapers of the time universally supported the position that the Red Stockings won the game by forfeit. However, some accounts of the Red Stockings' season show them with 64 victories and one tie, rather than the 65 victories they deserved. There is no question that the umpire's forfeiture of the game to the Red Stockings was justified, and that the Red Stockings deserved credit for the victory.

It is interesting to note that there were rumors that the Cincinnati pitcher, Asa Brainard, had been offered $500 to throw the game. After a rocky start, Brainard settled down to pitch well.

The success of the Red Stockings marked the beginning of the end in the battle between professionals and amateurs. In the years preceding 1869, writers such as Henry Chadwick had spent much of their time discussing the evils of professionalism. With professionalism now an accepted fact, the focus shifted to the evils of gambling and dishonesty in baseball. This was summed up in a *New York Times* editorial headlined "Baseball in Danger."[5] The editorial begins, "we are very sorry to hear the current stories relating to the enormous sums which are said to have changed hands in betting upon the exciting games of baseball which have recently taken place between a western nine and the championship clubs of New York and other Atlantic cities." The article warns that baseball must separate itself from the gamblers and remain a clean and honest game.

The next scandal, one that created overtones that lasted late into the 1870s, involved Bill Craver, catcher with the Chicago White Stockings, and the Troy catcher in the Troy-Cincinnati game. There is no doubt that Craver was one of the top players of his time. In an 1870 article, Henry Chadwick called Craver "the great North American catcher." He also remarked about Craver:

> He is at all times a safe, sure and reliable player behind the bat, standing close up to the striker, and facing the swiftest balls that can be sent in. His throwing is quick and accurate, one of his noble requirements being that of looking intently in one direction while he throws the ball to another. He is a tremendous hitter, his record of clean base hits always comparing favorably with those of any of his comrades or competitors in matches. When he chooses, he can make matters for his opponents uncomfortable whether they be at bat or in the field; about as uncomfortable as he wishes. He was connected last season with the Haymaker nine, and won for himself an enviable reputation.[6]

In August of that year, however, the Chicago club expelled Craver for gambling and general disobedience. On August 18, 1870, the following letter was sent to Craver by the Chicago Board of Directors:

> Dear Sir:
>
> We have been requested to forward to you the following minutes of the proceedings and copy of resolutions adopted by this baseball club last night: Whereas, William H. Craver, of the Chicago Nine, having violated his contract, made with the Chicago Baseball Association, showing the highest utter disregard of the rules adopted by them, from Rule No. 1 to 7 inclusive, and from Rule No. 9 to 12 inclusive and especially Rule No. 13 which reads: Gambling in any manner whatever, is prohibited at all times, and no player of the Club shall chance the games in which he plays, or try to induce others to do so. And said Craver, by disobeying such rules, having in some measure destroyed the confidence of the public in said "nine," and said Craver, as we are informed to believe, who received money as an inducement for not winning games; and having conducted himself in a manner unbecoming of a gentleman on many occasions since his connection with the Chicago Nine, in disregard of what that section of his contract that reads "The said William H. Craver from the signing hereof until the

expiration of said term promises and hereby agrees to deport himself in a quiet, gentlemanly, sober, and proper manner at all times." And said Craver, having been guilty of insubordination, and repeated disobedience of orders off and on the ball field, positively refusing to play in order to do so, and in other ways; and said William H. Craver, having disregarded and broken the rules and regulations of the Club contrary to his expressed contract, which reads: "The said William H. Craver further agrees to faithfully obey all orders which may be issued by said Club or the officers, and to hold himself subject to all rules and regulations which are now in existence, or may be hereafter established by said Club or its officers"; and said Craver having by his said actions and counsel apparently sought to create strife and confusion in the "nine" he contracted to help to sustain and build up; and said Craver having by his misconduct, misplay and disputes in a manner to induce people to think that the games were "tricked," it is hereby ordered and:

Resolved, according to the terms of said contract which reads: "a violation of any of the terms of this contract will nullify and destroy the whole if the said Club so desires and orders," that the said William H. Craver be, and he is hereby, "expelled" from the Chicago Baseball Club. Any contract made is hereby declared null and void. It is further:

Resolved that the Chicago Nine will forever refuse to play any baseball club which shall engage as a player William H. Craver, or seek to play him in their nine, he being indebted to this Club in the amount of several hundred dollars. It is further:

Resolved that the Club prosecute this action at the State Association and National Association so that said William H. Craver be expelled from both bodies.

By Order of the Board of Directors of the Baseball Club

Fred Erby, Secretary[7]

Craver completely denied the charges, stating that he had not done anything that other players had not done, and that he was being punished for refusing to play while sick. There is some justification to Craver's claim of hypocrisy by the Chicago organization—around the same time they expelled Craver, they acquired Ed Duffy to play shortstop from the Eckford club of Brooklyn. This is the same Ed Duffy who was expelled with Wansley and Devyr for throwing a game in 1865. The club members also included Fredrick Treacy, whose dubious exploits will be chronicled in the next chapter of this book.

At the close of the 1870 season, this matter was taken up by the amateur National Association convention. In its death throes, the convention was bitterly divided over a number of issues, including the Craver issue. After a great deal of debate, a resolution stating that "William H. Craver be expelled from all clubs belonging to this association" was adopted. Henry Chadwick commented on the situation:

> Craver was charged with discreditable conduct by the Chicago club and was expelled without a fair trial, he says. The expulsion was made on the basis of action taken by the so called National Convention, which is null and void in effect because of indirect violation of the Constitution. It will not change his playing

The 1870 New York Mutuals. The Mutuals were plagued with scandals throughout their existence. *Courtesy of Transcendental Graphics.*

status and should not. It is right and proper the club should have the power of expelling him for dishonorable conduct, but not unless this is done after a fair trial and proof of the charge conclusively shown. Unless this be done, the new rule of the game prohibiting expelled players from taking part in contests this season will not be applicable.[8]

As it turns out, Chadwick's prediction was correct. Craver was to return to the Troy Haymakers for the 1871 season, with the only protest coming from the Chicago White Stockings. Chicago announced that they would refuse to play Troy as long as Craver was with the club, and refused to accept a compromise offer from the Haymakers that Craver be benched during games with Chicago.

As time passed, the Craver incident was forgotten, and Craver continued among the ranks of players in good standing until the Louisville scandal in 1877, which will be chronicled later in this book.

Shortly after the Craver scandal, another controversy erupted in New York. On September 22, 1870, 6,000 patrons packed the Union grounds to watch the New York Mutuals play the Brooklyn Atlantics. This game had national significance because a Mutual victory would clinch the mythical "national championship" for the team. In addition to the honor of this championship, a gold ball was awarded to the national champion (shades of the Rochester-Buffalo scandal of 1866).

Before the game, Chicago papers reported that "on Thursday, the Mutuals and Atlantics will play for the championship, and the game will be thrown to the Mutuals, thus preventing the Chicago club going home with the gold ball as it is universally believed here they could have done. The Atlantics can beat the Mutuals."

As it turned out, the Mutuals won the game 10–4. Atlantic pitcher George Zettlein started off well but weakened as the game went on. Immediately after the game, urchins began selling photographs of the "Champion Nine Mutuals."

It will never be known for sure whether this game was played on its merits. The New York papers believed that it was, saying that "charges of the Atlantics throwing the game were dispelled by the style and steadiness of the players." Whatever the truth of the matter, it was a fitting swan song for baseball's first major organization, the amateur National Association of Baseball Players.

Chapter 2

The National Association

The success of the Cincinnati Red Stockings in 1869, and the rise of other all-professional teams in 1870, spelled doom for the amateur game in baseball. The Red Stockings' success removed the final veneer of amateurism from baseball and signaled a shift to the domination of the game by professional teams and players.

As this change occurred, the game was still being governed, in theory, by the National Association of Baseball Players, the old amateur association. The National Association's bylaws did not allow for professionalism, and the ruling forces behind the National Association continued to push for a return to a purely amateur game. This situation could not continue – and indeed it did not.

On March 4, 1871, representatives of 10 professional clubs met at a saloon located at 840 Broadway in New York and formed the National Association of Professional Base Ball Players, electing James N. Kerns, United States Marshal and representative of the Philadelphia Athletics, as their first president. Charter members of the league were the Philadelphia Athletics, New York Mutuals, Washington Nationals, Troy Unions, Boston Red Stockings, Chicago White Stockings, the Forest Cities of Rockford (Illinois), the Forest Cities of Cleveland, the Kekiongas of Fort Wayne (Indiana), and the Washington Olympics.

The league was loosely organized – the only requirement to join the league was the paying of a $10 annual fee. The champion at the end of each season would be awarded the "whip pennant," which would be purchased with the proceeds from the $10 membership fee. In addition, the National Association did not immediately draw up a constitution, rather choosing to utilize the amateur association's constitution, eliminating the sections that outlawed professionalism.

The debut of the league was a very positive one. In the first major league game ever played, Fort Wayne beat the Forest Cities of Cleveland by a score of 2–0, with star pitcher Bobby Mathews outpitching Al Pratt, Pittsburgh's first contribution to major league baseball. In those days of high-scoring games, a 2–0 game was unheard of and caused tremendous comment and excitement among sports fans around the country for weeks.

Henry Chadwick. A pioneer baseball writer, Chadwick was a leader in efforts to clean up the game. *Courtesy of Transcendental Graphics.*

Unfortunately, that triumphant first game was in many ways the high point of the National Association. The lack of organization in the league soon became a problem—in fact, clubs did not finish their set schedules, leading to uneven results. Also, the discipline of players was extremely poor. And most important, gambling ran rampant at National Association games, leading to corruption and, ultimately, the demise of the National Association.

As was discussed in the previous chapter, the practice of gambling on baseball games had gradually risen in popularity. From the gambler's point of view, the system was very loosely organized. Wagers were made with individuals, which often led to problems when losing bettors would deny having ever agreed to the wager. Therefore, a system called "pool selling" was devised.

The way pool selling worked was that rather than having bets between two individuals, all bets were made through a central pool, the forerunner of today's bookmaker or pari-mutuel betting system. Odds were widely quoted on each game, and bettors would put down their funds according to where they felt their best investment was. As money was pushed from one team to another the odds changed, reflecting the supply and demand curve.

The pool selling system served to organize betting and helped to eliminate the daily disputes between bettors. Unfortunately, however, it also led to the increased popularity of betting on games and vast increases in the amount of money bet on each game. While two individuals with a $100 bet were not likely to fix the game, the pool system put together many thousands of dollars' worth of bets on an individual game, allowing groups of gamblers to place large stakes and motivating them to tamper with games. Lee Allen, baseball's premier historian, described the situation as follows:

> The situation was especially bad in Brooklyn where the Atlantic club fostered so much open betting that one section of the grounds was known as the Gold Board, with activity that rivaled that of the stock exchange.
>
> Discovering that their salaries represented only a fraction of what they could make by dealing with the gamblers, the players travelled from city to city like princes, sporting diamonds, drinking champagne at dinner every night, and ostentatiously paying the tab by peeling off folding money from wads of the stuff that mysteriously reproduced themselves. Of course, this was the era of the Robber Barons, and compared to the really big business transactions that went on while Ulysses S. Grant sat benignly in the White House, the activity of baseball players was indeed of the small fry variety. But it served to furnish a sordid miniature of the nation's social and economic health.[1]

Historians of baseball tend to devote little attention to the National Association, other than to discuss its problems. One of the game's early historians, George Moreland, devoted only one paragraph to the National Association in his book *Balldom*. Moreland wrote that "bribery, contract-breaking, dishonest playing, pool-room manipulations and desertion of players became so shameful that the highly respectable element of patrons began to drop out of attendance, until the crowds that came to the games were composed exclusively of men who went to the grounds to bet money on results. The money was bet openly during the progress of the game."[2] This typifies the view of most baseball historians, who generally characterize the National Association as a stew of corruption, the darkest hour in the history of major league baseball.

Is this an accurate view of the National Association's history? There is no question that gambling ran rampant in the association, and there is also no question that there were a number of dishonest players, all of which will be chronicled in the following pages. But there is some evidence that the press during the 1870s overstated the corruption problem. In accounts of games from the period, many errors are treated with suspicion—and in those days before the advent of gloves, errors were quite frequent and a normal part of the game.

Discussing the National Association, Cap Anson states that

> Lots of men seem to forget that the element of luck enters largely into base-ball just as it does into any other business, and that many things may happen during a contest that cannot be foreseen either by the club management or by the field captain.
>
> An unlucky stumble on the part of the base runner or a dancing sunbeam that gets into a fielder's eyes at some critical time in the play may cost a game; indeed, it has on more than one occasion, and yet to the man who simply judges the game by the reports that he may read in the papers the thing has apparently a "fishy" look, for the reason that neither the sunbeam nor the stumble receives mention.
>
> If every sport and businessman in this world were as crooked as some folks would have us to believe, this would indeed be a poor world to live in, and I for one would be perfectly willing to be out it.[3]

The total extent of the corruption of the National Association will never be known. However, there is no question that corruption haunted the National Association from the beginning.

While the Wansley affair in 1865 and Craver's expulsion from Chicago in 1870 opened many people's eyes, there was a reluctance on the part of many fans to believe that there were dishonest baseball players. One who saw the corruption, and railed against it, was Henry Chadwick, baseball's first great sportswriter, inventor of the box score and the only writer to be elected to the Baseball Hall of Fame.

Chadwick was born in Exeter, England, in 1824. At the age of 13, he moved with his family to the United States, settling in Brooklyn. Chadwick's father had been a newspaper man, serving as editor of the *Western Times*. Chadwick followed in his father's footsteps.

In 1857 Chadwick joined the *New York Clipper*, a leading paper devoted to sports, theater, and leisure activities, serving as the paper's sports editor. He quickly became the leading expert on baseball, writing for the *Clipper* along with the *Brooklyn Eagle*. Chadwick also served as editor of many baseball guides, including *DeWitt's Baseball Guide*, *Beadle's Dime Book of Baseball*, and later *The Spalding Baseball Guide*.

From the time he joined the *Clipper* in 1857 until the time he died in 1908, Chadwick was the unquestioned leader in pushing for an end to corruption in baseball. Chadwick risked libel suits constantly as he worked to expose gambling-related corruption in the game and clean up the sport he loved.

During the 1871 and 1872 seasons, rumors abounded of baseball scandals, but few specifics were revealed. By the time the National Association had celebrated its first birthday, Chadwick was warning that corruption and the throwing of games were threatening the survival of the sport. Dishonest action by players was called "hippodroming," and Chadwick warned of its consequences. In an article appearing in January 1872, Chadwick discussed the "hippodrome business," and stated that corruption in baseball

> . . . leads us to look with some misgiving upon the announcement that the national baseball campaign of 1872 will be prosecuted with vigor. It is doubtful whether the pubic generally will not have more reason to congratulate itself upon the closing than upon the opening of another baseball season. All this mischief had been done by 2 or 3 clubs. It cannot be denied that hippodroming has prevailed or that rum drinking as well as pool selling and gambling has prevailed on some prominent ball grounds of the country during the past two years.[4]

Chadwick's rhetoric grew stronger as time went on. In an article in the *New York Mercury* after the close of the 1872 season, Chadwick surmised:

> Hitherto at the close of each season's campaign on the ball field of the country, *The Mercury* has had occasion to congratulate its readers in the fraternity, generally on the success of the season's play and the steady advance of the national game in popularity. This year there is no basis for any such congratulatory comments; instead of an advance movement the progress has been downhill, and the result is that at the close of the season of 1872 the only comments to be made on the season's play are those on the marked decline of the game in the estimation of its most reputable votaries, and the almost entire failure of professionalism as an institution meriting the support of the best members of the fraternity.
>
> It would appear as professional clubs were no longer amenable to any influence save that of the betting and pool selling business. Hence the steady decline in the popularity and loss of that prestige of playing games on the square which is the very life of a professional organization.
>
> No positive proof can be brought forward in support of any direct charges of collusion among players for fraudulent purposes, but not yet one man out of ten who witnessed the majority of the games of October last can be persuaded that the contests were fairly or honorably contested. In this respect, just one player of the nine can be guilty of the mischief, one club can do mischief enough to taint a reputation of a dozen. You may prove the fact plainly that honest play really pays best simply as regards investment; but there seems to be far more sweetness to a certain class in the stolen fruit of fraudulently obtained money than legitimate receipts of squarely played games. To teach this class that none but square games will pay is the only effectual remedy, and to do this, the only way is to cease to patronize contests marked by the pool selling and betting ring crowds.
>
> If the lessons of the season of 1872 are properly thought over and profited by, then we may look forward to 1873 for much desirable reformation. If not, then good-bye professional baseball playing. When the system of professional ball playing as practiced in 1872 shall be among the things that were, on its tombstone — if it have any — will be found the inscription "died of Pool Selling."[5]

The 1868 Baltimore Pastimes. Bobby Mathews (in the front row, second from left) was named in many National Association scandals, but a hero in 1876. *Courtesy of Transcendental Graphics.*

One early case of corruption in the National Association occurred on October 29, 1872, when the Lord Baltimore club beat the New York Mutuals by a score of 4–1. It was revealed that there had been heavy betting on the visiting Baltimore team. An investigation was called for, but none was forthcoming.

The first open scandal in the National Association occurred on July 24, 1873. On that day, the Lord Baltimore club visited New York to play against the New York Mutuals, the infamous organization headed by Boss Tweed. Umpiring that day was Bob Ferguson, the Brooklyn Atlantics captain, star player, and president of the National Association.

Ferguson had become fed up with the corruption brought on by the gambling element. Events of a game that had been played on July 4, when the New York Mutuals beat Ferguson's Atlantics 10–6, brought matters to a head. Ferguson was absolutely sure that some of his players had been tampered with by gamblers in this and succeeding games.

The fact that a player for the Atlantics was umpiring a game between the Mutuals and the Lord Baltimores will seem strange to modern readers. However, it must be remembered that baseball was much more loosely organized at that time, and no regular system of league umpires existed. While certain former players and other "sportsmen" were often used as umpires, on some occasions a player from another team, like Ferguson, whose honesty and integrity were unquestioned, would serve as the umpire.

It also may seem strange that a player served as president of the National Association. One must remember the full name of the National Association was the National Association of Professional Base Ball Players. While there were club owners, at least in theory the ball players were in control of the organization. This lack of management is often cited as causing many of the problems that the National Association experienced.

As he umpired the July 24 game, Ferguson reached the conclusion that the game had been fixed by gamblers. In what the papers described as "one of the most exciting scenes witnessed on our ball fields for the last ten years," at the conclusion of the game Ferguson charged into the stands and confronted the gamblers, vowing vengeance on those who were at the head of the conspiracy. Contemporary accounts reported that "this is the first instance on record that either a player or a captain of a ball nine or the manager of any professional club has had the moral courage to boldly and publicly denounce the gambling frauds who have brought such odium upon professional play."

Ferguson then went back down to the field to confront the players, specifically Mutuals third baseman John Hatfield and catcher Nat Hicks. Hatfield and Hicks began to accuse each other, and Hicks and Ferguson engaged in a shouting match. Ferguson then hit Hicks on the arm with a bat, breaking the arm of Hicks and putting him out for the year.

The quarrel between Ferguson and Hicks was patched up, and no action was taken against the Mutuals players. Ironically, some of the gamblers in the crowd accused Ferguson of having been bribed to umpire a dishonest game.

Scandals continued throughout the 1873 season. Shortly after the Ferguson-Hicks incident, two of Ferguson's Brooklyn players, catcher Tom Barlow and first baseman Harmon Dehlman, were publicly accused of dishonesty. Barlow and Dehlman took out advertising space in the New York papers to deny the charges against them and to demand a full investigation. No further action was taken against these players.

Another incident occurred on August 9, 1873, when again the New York Mutuals met the Brooklyn Atlantics. The betting odds before the game were 3–1 in favor of the Mutuals, but just before the game the odds suddenly shifted to only 5–4 in favor of the Mutuals. The Mutuals were a far superior team, finishing with a record of 29 wins and 24 losses, as compared to a record of 17 wins and 37 losses for the Atlantics, so the abrupt change in odds caused considerable speculation. As it turned out, the Atlantics scored four runs in the first inning and breezed to a 12–2 victory. Suspicion focused on Bobby Mathews, the Mutuals' star pitcher, who pitched an extremely poor game.

Unfortunately, these problems were more widespread than with just the New York Mutuals and Brooklyn Atlantics. In a tight pennant race, the Boston Red Stockings edged the Philadelphias by four games. The Philadelphia club was widely rumored to have thrown games during the season. In fact, in a play on words, the *Boston Advertiser* stated "the reason that the Philadelphia club loses so many games now is they have their bettors opposed to them." Many years later, Chadwick claimed in the *Spalding Baseball Guide* that Philadelphia lost the 1873 championship due to "crookedness in its ranks."

By this time, the problem of baseball scandals had come out into the open. Whereas earlier scandals tended to be confined to rumor and veiled reports, three seasons of problems had emboldened Chadwick and other reporters to print these rumors, leaving a trail for future historians.

The 1874 season was barely underway when rumors were afloat of a fix. In early May, the Philadelphia Athletics defeated the Chicago White Stockings by a score of 7–2. The Athletics benefited from six errors by Chicago third baseman Levi Meyerle. Newspaper reports claim "he could not have possibly done worse and it is charged that he assisted his old friends." However, Meyerle, the National Association's first batting champion, was a notoriously poor fielder throughout his career, which may well explain the six errors.

Not long after that, on June 16, 1874, the first-place Boston Red Stockings visited the New York Mutuals. Before the game, rumors circulated that Mutuals shortstop Tom Carey had sold the game. As it turned out, in spite of the fact that Carey put on a horrendous fielding exhibition, the Mutuals upset Boston by a score of 5–2. Contemporary reports stated that "Carey could not apparently throw the game all by himself."

Another scandal involving the Mutuals occurred in mid–July in a game against the Philadelphia Athletics. After five innings the Mutuals led the game by a score of 5–0. However, errors by Dick Higham and John Hatfield allowed Philadelphia to tie the score, and further errors led to a 6–5 Philadelphia victory. Despite an outcry from Chadwick, no action was taken against the Mutual players.

Unfortunately, baseball was ignoring the problem of corruption rather than dealing with it. While part of the blame for this can be laid on the doorstep of the poorly organized National Association, we will encounter a similar laissez-faire attitude when we examine events in the second decade of the twentieth century. In the early 1870s, baseball still had not learned the lesson that corruption left unchecked continues to grow, and indeed it nearly destroyed the game in its early years. This was a lesson that had to be relearned in the aftermath of the 1919 Black Sox scandal.

In August 1874, two major scandals were exposed to the public. Both scandals involved games played by the Chicago White Stockings, although the White Stockings were not the guilty party in either case.

The first scandal came to light on August 6, 1874, when the *Chicago Tribune* reported that "for the first time in the history of baseball in Chicago, the national game has been disgraced by a palpable and unbelievable fraud."

The story went on to report that the New York Mutuals had thrown their game of August 5 against the White Stockings. According to the report, an unnamed Mutuals player was seen associating with gambler Mike McDonald the

The 1871 Chicago White Stockings. The team included George Zettlein (bottom center) and Fred Treacy (upper left corner) — key figures in 1875 scandals — and Ed Duffy (below Treacy), a confederate of Wansley's and Devyr's. *Courtesy of Transcendental Graphics.*

evening before the August 5 game. The day of the game, McDonald bet heavily against the Mutuals, pushing the odds heavily in the White Stockings' favor. Considering the fact that the Mutuals had beaten Chicago in every game they had played that year, and the fact that the Mutuals had a far superior record to that of the White Stockings, these odds were hardly justified.

The suspicion during the game fell on a number of players. Bobby Mathews, the Mutuals pitcher, pitched the first five innings. In spite of one flagrant error on his part, the Mutuals led 4–2 at the end of that time.

At the end of the fifth, Mathews announced that he was not feeling well and left the game. He was replaced by John Hatfield, a strange choice in that this was the only game in his career that he ever pitched.

Chicago came back to win the game, strongly assisted by poor playing on the part of the Mutuals. Specifically implicated were shortstop Tom Carey and catcher Dick Higham. A "terrible wild throw" by Higham allowed Chicago to tie the game in the sixth, and three hits in the ninth gave Chicago the lead.

The Mutuals appeared ready to rally in the ninth. Outfielder Jack Remsen led off with a double. After Tom Carey failed to advance the runner, Dick Higham singled, with Remsen moving to third. According to newspaper accounts of the game, "Higham started on a slow steal from first, in fact so slow as to seem deliberate, and was put out easily, catcher Mallone to Meyerle, without giving Remsen any chance to score. Allison hit a high fly to Meyerle."[6]

The aftermath of the game created quite a controversy as newspapers investigated this flagrant hippodroming. Suspicion centered on Mathews and Higham. Reports circulated that some of the Mutuals players had become aware of the scandal but were powerless to prevent its consummation.

The excessive publicity was embarrassing to the Mutuals, who submitted an affidavit from a doctor certifying that Mathews had been in ill health. This did nothing to ease the minds of those trying to clean up the game, however. Shortly after that, the *Chicago Tribune* printed an anonymous letter alleging that three "outsiders"—that is, gamblers—were traveling with the Mutuals. The letter claimed that the gamblers had ties to Jack Nelson, the Mutuals' second baseman, as well as Mathews and Higham.

Unfortunately, no investigation was undertaken by the Mutuals or the Association regarding these charges. It was not to be the last scandal involving the Mutuals.

The next scandal erupted on August 20 when Billy McLean, a former boxer and frequent umpire of National Association games, charged that a game between Philadelphia and Chicago had been thrown by the Philadelphia club.

The essence of McLean's charges was that Philadelphia utility man John Radcliff had approached McLean before the game and told him that $350 was "up in his brother's hands; if McLean would make decisions in favor of Chicago, he should have half of it." Radcliff also told McLean that four other

The 1871 Philadelphia Athletics. John Radcliff is numbered 7, Fergie Malone 8, and George Bechtel 10. *Courtesy of Transcendental Graphics.*

players were in on the fix: pitcher Candy Cummings, early pitching star and inventor of the curve ball; second baseman Bill Craver, who had been implicated in the Troy–Cincinnati Red Stockings scandal in 1869 and "expelled for life" from the amateur association in 1870; catcher Nat Hicks, who had been earlier accused by Bob Ferguson of throwing a game; and first baseman Denny Mack.

The Board of Directors of the Philadelphia club met on September 1 to hear from Radcliff and McLean. The charges against Cummings, Craver, Hicks, and Mack were dropped on the grounds that the accusations were "hearsay"; however, the board did recommend the expulsion of Radcliff.

The stockholders of the Philadelphia club met on September 8 to discuss the issue. Just before a vote was taken, Billy McLean stated that he wanted to withdraw charges because he did not think it was fair for "Radcliff to bear the brunt of the odium." However, Radcliff was expelled by a vote of 26–15, and a motion was passed censuring the other players for loose play. The club offered a reward of $300 for "testimony sufficient to convict the other players." Radcliff vowed to appeal the expulsion to the judiciary committee of the National Association.

The judiciary committee heard Radcliff's arguments on March 2, 1875, at the annual convention of the National Association, and Radcliff was reinstated. According to Henry Chadwick, "Radcliff was reinstated, not on the grounds that the charges against him were not true, but that the complaint against him had not been properly brought against the committee." Obviously pleased with the outcome, Radcliff joined the recently formed Philadelphia Centennials for the 1875 season.

The Philadelphia Centennials team merits some mention. In addition to Radcliff, the team included Bill Craver, whose exploits have already been chronicled, as well as George Bechtel and Fred Treacy, both of whom would be involved in future scandals. The Centennials team was also notable because they were involved in the first player transaction in baseball history. Finding themselves short of funds, on May 26 the Centennials sold Bechtel and Craver to the Athletics for $1,500, and promptly disbanded.

It should be mentioned that although the National Association failed to take action against the players accused of dishonest play, it would be unfair to characterize the Association's attitude as one of total indifference. Article 10 of the National Association's rules stated that "no person engaged in a match, either as umpire, scorer or player, shall be either directly or indirectly interested in any bet upon the game." This rule was strengthened in 1874, when it was amended to read "all betting by players is prohibited, the penalty for their betting on games in which they are engaged being expulsion from the Association, and betting on other games suspension for the season." Unfortunately, this rule was not enforced.

The 1875 season proved to be the most scandal-ridden of all and helped lead to the downfall of the National Association. Even before the season started, the roster composition of certain clubs caused great comment. For example, the Chicago White Stockings signed Dick Higham, formerly with the New York Mutuals. This is the same Higham who was publicly implicated the previous year of being a party to throwing a game against the same White Stockings.

In early June, rumors were afloat that a game between the Boston Red Stockings and the St. Louis Brown Stockings had been fixed. Boston won the game 15–2, and gossip hinted that St. Louis shortstop Dickey Pearce "had received money from a prominent merchant to keep himself out of the way of ground balls." In the game, however, Pearce made only one error.

On June 24, another scandal erupted involving the Chicago White Stockings. The Philadelphia team won the game 5–2 in 12 innings. The game was marred by 21 errors, including five by Mike McGeary, third baseman for the Philadelphia club. As it turned out, the full story was a series of double crosses. According to newspaper reports, "a parcel of bunko men, low gamblers, and general disreputables made a pool of $300 to $500 and bought out some players [on the Philadelphia club]. They then bought all the pools on Chicago they could." However, as it turned out, one of the Chicago players, later discovered to be Dick Higham, found out about the plot and wanted a cut. When this was denied, Higham and other players decided to throw the game to Philadelphia to teach the gamblers a lesson.

The scandal was widely reported in the Chicago press, and on June 28 the Chicago club's board of directors met and suspended Higham and appointed John Glenn to replace him as captain. Pitcher George Zettlein was also named in the scandal but was exonerated. In addition, a reward of $500 was offered for evidence of crooked play. Higham's suspension, however, did not last long. By July 4, he was reinstated by the White Stockings.

Unfortunately, this was not the last scandal to rock the Chicago team in 1875. Throughout the year, pitcher George Zettlein's name kept coming up in connection with shady activity. Zettlein had been formally accused of throwing games in New York the previous year, but he had been exonerated. In July an article appeared in the *Chicago Times* quoting Chicago manager Jimmy Wood as accusing Zettlein of throwing a game to Boston. Wood denied the report, but as a result the former friendship between Wood and Zettlein cooled dramatically, and by August 3 Zettlein demanded and received his release from the Chicago club. He was quickly signed by the Philadelphia club. Scandal was to continue to follow both the Chicago club and Zettlein during the course of the year.

In early August, the Athletics of Philadelphia visited Chicago. In the first game, the Athletics won by a score of 8–4. The White Stockings made 15 errors in the game, including eight by Higham.

The next day the *Chicago Inter-Ocean* ran a story about Higham, saying:

> His play in yesterday's game caused ugly remarks. Many asserted that he sold the game. The basis of the accusations was: what was he doing with a Chicago character at Pratt's Billiard Hall waiting for the pool-selling, and when he found that there was to be none, why did he go to Foley's and there buy pools on the Athletics?[7]

As a result, Higham was suspended, and on August 18 he was released by Chicago. Despite Higham's horrible reputation, he quickly landed a job with his old team, the New York Mutuals.

In late August, another scandal involving George Zettlein occurred when the Hartford team visited Philadelphia. Hartford won the game 11–3. After the

The 1875 St. Louis Brown Stockings. Joe Blong, who was expelled from two clubs for dishonesty that year, is standing at the far left. *Courtesy of Transcendental Graphics.*

game, Zettlein and left fielder Fred Treacy were suspended by the team for crooked play. Their response was that they were innocent, and that Mike Mc-Geary was actually the perpetrator of the fix. On September 2, Philadelphia reinstated both Zettlein and Treacy.

The scandals of 1875 were not confined to the National Association. Early in the year, pitcher Joe Blong and utility man Trick McSorley were quietly expelled by the St. Louis Brown Stockings on suspicion of crooked play. Both landed with the independent Stars of Covington, Kentucky. On September 23, Blong was expelled by the Stars for throwing a game against a Cincinnati team. Despite all this, Blong was again signed by St. Louis at the end of the season and remained with that club until the end of 1877.

The National Association's final scandal occurred in Philadelphia on October 18. The Philadelphia Athletics were hosting the Chicago White Stockings, a relatively meaningless game since both teams were far out of the pennant race. Despite the apparent lack of interest in the game, there was heavy betting on Chicago to win. Newspapers reported the contest as a "disgraceful hippo-droming affair."

Chicago won the game by a score of 10–7. The game was sloppily played, with errors by McGeary and the recently reinstated Treacy leading to Philadelphia's downfall.

By the end of the 1875 season, the National Association was a shambles. The Boston Red Stockings had just won their fourth straight pennant, finishing with a record of 71 wins and eight losses and a 15-game lead over the second-place Philadelphia Athletics. Attendance had fallen each year, and the public was fed up with dishonest play. In addition, the association was racked by internal dissension. The block of eastern clubs controlled the league, with power concentrated in New York and Philadelphia. Any time there was a dispute, such as the famous Davy Force matter, in which both the Philadelphia Athletics and the Chicago White Stockings claimed Force, the decision always went to the eastern team.

As will be detailed in the next chapter, all these factors led Chicago owner William Hulbert to make bold moves both to improve his club and to found a new baseball organization based on strong, sound business management principles. That organization was the National League, still in existence today.

An article in the *St. Louis Globe Democrat* sums up the 1875 situation as follows:

> During the season there were more complaints of hippodroming than ever before, and from the appearance of things the charges were, in most cases, founded on fact. It was almost impossible to furnish proof positive that a game is not decided on its merits. Yet there were, doubtless, many of them thrown to benefit the gambling fraternity. The Philadelphia and Mutual Clubs, as they always have been, are looked upon as the black sheep in the flock, each particular organization being controlled by a coterie of sporting men. The Mutual team was not strong enough this season to successfuly hippodrome to a very great extent. Hicks, their catcher, it is said, could tell how many runs their opponents would make in each inning and his friends used to lay their bets accordingly.
>
> With the Philadelphia Nine it was different, its players being skillful enough to win when they pleased except when pitted against Boston or the Athletics. Hippodroming placed them next to last in the championship race, although their proper position should be third. Zettlein, the pitcher, only last week openly charged his associates with selling out, and retired in disgust. During the season half a dozen of the players have been frequently charged with crooked conduct, among them, Treacy, McGeary, Meyerle, and Zettlein.
>
> Of other clubs, it is overtly charged that Chicago lost her three final games to Hartford, allowing Hartford to beat St. Louis out of third place, which is about as probable as that Chicago and St. Louis arranged at the beginning of the season that each organization would win all games on its own grounds, which proved to be the case. Many there are who assert that they are confident this was the case.
>
> Though numerous players were accused of dishonesty, desertion and unfaithful conduct during the season, not a single member was expelled from the Association. On the contrary, they were all released from their engagements and by being at once hired by some rival club to the one they had left were tempted

further to sell out and revolve. Higham left Chicago and the Mutuals received him with open arms. Blong was expelled from the Reds and Stars to be affectionately received in the Brown Stockings fold. Latham went from Boston to New Haven, and then to Canada. Field skipped the Washingtons for the Ludlows, and others too numerous to mention skipped from one club to another with impunity. This has done more than anything else towards killing baseball. Unless the players to which class those mentioned belong are at once emphatically informed that their services are not desired, another year will show that baseball is assuredly played out.[8]

It is sad to note that the National Association today is remembered not as the pioneer baseball league, or as a place where great stars such as Al Spalding, Cap Anson, Jim O'Rourke, and Pud Galvin got their start, but as a cesspool of corruption and game fixing. To quote Henry Chadwick, "about half a dozen proved to be black sheep in the flock . . . this leaven of bad material must have the effect of bringing the whole fraternity into discredit."

Exactly who were these black sheep? Certain names have come up repeatedly in this chapter: Dick Higham, Mike McGeary, George Zettlein, and Bill Craver, among others. In fact, at the close of the 1875 season the *Brooklyn Eagle* chose an "all star" team of "rogues" consisting of George Zettlein, pitcher; Dick Higham, catcher; Bill Craver, first base; Mike McGeary, second base; John Radcliff, shortstop; Davy Force, third base; Fred Treacy, left field; George Bechtel, center field; Joe Blong, right field; and Dickey Pearce and Frank Fleet, substitutes. Left off the team were Nat Hicks, Bobby Mathews, and John Hatfield, all of whose names have come up more than once in these pages.

Who were these men? Were they really the rogues that the *Eagle* made them out to be? Were they really guilty of fixing games? Were they one-dimensional, evil characters? Because very few of the charges of corruption in the National Association were investigated, the whole truth will never be known. However, it is safe to say that at least a few of these men, most notably Dick Higham, earned their place in the *Eagle*'s hall of infamy.

Hal Chase, whose career will be covered in great depth later in this book, has been referred to as an evil genius, the master of baseball corruption. Chase's nefarious activities earned him that title, but Dick Higham, long forgotten by baseball historians today, could give Chase a good run for his money as the most corrupt player of all time.

Higham was born in England in 1852. He was a charter member of the National Association, beginning his career as a 19-year-old with the New York Mutuals in 1871. Higham then moved to the Lord Baltimores in 1872, then back to the Mutuals for the 1873 and 1874 seasons. He joined the White Stockings in 1875 and remained with that club until his expulsion; Higham finished his National Association career with the Mutuals. After the demise of the National Association, he continued his career in the National League, playing with Hartford in 1876, Providence in 1878, and one game with Troy in 1880.

Richard Higham. Higham was at the center of many nineteenth century baseball scandals. *Courtesy of Transcendental Graphics.*

Like many players in his day, Higham was extremely versatile. During his National Association career he played 107 games as a catcher, 74 as an outfielder, and 58 as an infielder. He was a strong hitter, with a .288 batting average for his National Association years and a .323 average for his National League years. His best season was with Providence in 1878, when he hit .320 and led the league in doubles and runs scored.

As the reader will have seen from the preceding pages, Higham was involved in many of the major scandals in the National Association. In spite of this, he was a good player and was always able to find a job (in this, he was similar to Hal Chase). In 1874, after the New York Mutuals got off to a slow start under Tom Carey, Higham was named manager of the team. His performance as manager was the highlight of his career, as the team won 23 of its last 30 games to finish second behind the perennially pennant-winning Boston Red Stockings. He was even hired as an umpire in the National League in 1881 — a story for another chapter.

While Higham joined the National Association as a youngster, George Zettlein was a veteran hurler by the time baseball's first major league began operation. Born in Brooklyn in 1844, Zettlein was one of 12 major league players involved in the Civil War, serving with Admiral David Farragut in New Orleans.

Zettlein started his baseball career with the Brooklyn Eckfords in 1865, before moving to the Brooklyn Atlantics for the 1866 season. Zettlein remained with the Atlantics through the end of 1870, and then he joined the Chicago White Stockings for the National Association's first season. He split the next season between the Brooklyn Eckfords and the Troy Haymakers, and then he moved on to the Philadelphia Athletics for the 1873 season. He was with the Chicago White Stockings in 1874 and the first part of 1875 before being released. He finished out the 1875 season with the Philadelphia team. Zettlein was active during the National League's first season with the Philadelphia club, and then he ended his baseball career.

Zettlein's career was remarkable in many respects. In 1870, pitching for the Brooklyn Atlantics, he ended the Cincinnati Red Stockings' phenomenal undefeated streak at 100 games. Known as one of the best in his profession, he had a record of 125 wins and 90 losses in the National Association but dropped to 4-20 in the National League in 1876. His greatest season was with Philadelphia in 1873, when he finished the year with a 36-14 record.

By all accounts, Zettlein was quite a personable man. His nickname was "the Charmer," and he was generally well liked by his fellow players. However, there is no escaping that he was closely linked with scandals, particularly in the 1875 season.

The other pitcher whose name was frequently mentioned in association with scandals was Bobby Mathews. Born in Baltimore in 1851, Mathews began his career at the age of 16 with the Maryland Juniors. During the following two seasons he worked with the "parent club," the Marylands.

When the National Association was formed in 1871, Mathews moved to the Kekiongas of Fort Wayne, Indiana. As mentioned earlier, his 2–0 shutout won the first game in major league history. Unfortunately, his club was a weak one, and he finished with a 6-11 record.

In 1872 he returned to his hometown to pitch for the Lord Baltimore team. Mathews had a very successful season, finishing with a 25-18 record. He then moved on to the New York Mutuals and pitched for that team during the rest of their tenure in the National Association and in 1876, their sole year in the National League.

Mathews compiled very impressive credentials in the National Association. His total of 132 wins in that league placed him third on the all-time list, behind Al Spalding and Dick McBride. In 1874 he enjoyed his finest season, with a record of 42-22.

After leaving the Mutuals in 1876, Mathews moved to the Cincinnati Red Stockings of the National League. He then proceeded to bounce around from club to club until 1883, when he moved to the Athletics in the American Association, then a major league. Mathews enjoyed great success with the Athletics, winning 30 games in 1883, 1884, and 1885, and leading the club to the American Association championship in 1883. He ended his career at the age of 36, posting a 3-4 record for the 1887 Athletics team.

As a pitcher, Mathews was known for his skill and control rather than overpowering speed. During his three 30-win seasons in the American Association, he walked only 137 batters while striking out 775. Despite lacking overpowering "stuff," he managed to strike out 16 batters in one game in 1884.

Mathews was an authentic baseball pioneer. While Candy Cummings is credited with inventing the curve ball (for this feat, Cummings is in the Hall of Fame), Mathews was acknowledged as one of its early practitioners. In addition, the great umpire Hank O'Day, a major league pitcher in the 1880s, credited Mathews with inventing the spitball. According to O'Day, "Mathews used to cover the palm of his left hand with saliva and then rub the ball in it, twisting the leather around until there was quite a spot on it as big as a silver quarter."[9]

After his playing career was over, Mathews did some umpiring in the American Association and in the Players' League until 1891. He then moved on to odd jobs and was in poor financial straits. Mathews died in 1898 in his hometown of Baltimore.

Mathews's case is an odd one from the standpoint of evaluating his honesty as a player. There is no question that he was a great pitcher and well liked by his contemporaries. Baseball historians portray him as a hard competitor and a great talent. Unfortunately, Mathews's name was brought up a number of times in connection with some of the New York Mutuals scandals. However, in 1876, Mathews turned into a hero, exposing a bribe attempt by a New York gambler, which will be discussed in the next chapter.

Another player who was a fixture in scandal rumors was Mike McGeary. Born in 1851 in Philadelphia, McGeary began his career with the Experts of that city in 1868 and 1869, before moving on to Troy in 1870. He remained with the Troy Haymakers during the National Association's inaugural season before returning to Philadelphia, first with the Athletics from 1872 to 1874, and then with the Philadelphias in 1875. After the breakup of the National Association, McGeary moved on to the St. Louis Browns in the National League in 1876 and 1877 and served with the Providence Gnats of the National League in 1879. He was traded to Cleveland in mid–1880 and remained with that team in 1881 while serving as manager. He finished his career with Detroit in 1882.

Like many players of his day, McGeary was extremely versatile. During his career he primarily played second base and shortstop, but he also saw extensive duty at catcher, third base, and the outfield.

During his career, McGeary was a solid, if unspectacular, player. His best season came in 1874, when he hit an impressive .362. His hitting fell off from that point and he never reached the .300 mark again.

Despite McGeary's checkered career in the National Association, there is no evidence that he strayed from the straight path during his National League days. In fact, an article disclosing his release by Detroit in 1882 praised him in his role as captain of the team, although it pointed out that his skills had deteriorated to the point where he could no longer help the club.

Little is known of what happened to McGeary after he left baseball. In fact, the date and place of his death are unrecorded.

John Radcliff was born in 1846 in Camden, New Jersey. He began his career with the Union club of that city as a catcher in 1866 and part of 1867. He then joined the Philadelphia Athletics, remaining with that team until the end of the 1871 season. He then moved to the Lord Baltimores for 1872 and 1873, to the Philadelphias in 1874, and to the ill-fated Philadelphia Centennials in 1875. His engagement with the Centennials was his last as a major leaguer.

Radcliff was primarily a shortstop during his career, and he was by no means a star. His lifetime batting average was .265, his best year coming in 1872, when he hit .283. However, he is best remembered for his involvement in National Association scandals, as well as an 1869 case wherein Radcliff, after accepting $65 as an advance payment from the Athletics, left the club to play with the New York Mutuals.

Radcliff lived to the age of 65, passing away in Ocean City, New Jersey, in 1911.

Bill Craver and George Bechtel were both involved in scandals in the early days of the National League, and they will be discussed further in the next chapter. Treacy, Blong, Hicks, and Fleet were relatively obscure players with limited impact on the game.

However, two of the players mentioned by *The Eagle*—Davy Force and

Dickey Pearce—are worth some comment. Both were early stars of the game, and in fact Pearce is often mentioned as a Hall of Fame candidate.

Davy Force was born in 1849 in New York City. He began his baseball career in 1867 with the Olympic Club and joined the National Association with that team. The year 1872 saw him playing both with Troy and Baltimore, and he remained with the Lord Baltimore club for the 1873 season. He then moved to Chicago in 1874, to the Athletics in 1875, and split the 1876 season between the Athletics and the Mutuals.

The well-traveled Force then moved to the St. Louis Browns in 1877 and finally found a home in Buffalo, staying with the Bisons until 1885. Force finished up his major league career with the Washington Nationals in 1886 and then played two years of minor league ball before ending his career in 1888.

Force was considered one of baseball's early stars. In 1872 he hit .406 to win the National Association's batting title in the organization's second year. His averages generally began to slip, and his National League average is an unimpressive .211. A great shortstop, Force also played second base, third base, and the outfield, and he even pitched three games in the National Association. Force's forte was fielding, and he was considered one of the best fielding shortstops of his era.

However, Force is best remembered not for his accomplishments on the field, but for the fact that he signed two contracts in 1874, touching off a controversy that contributed to the collapse of the National Association and the formation of the National League. Baseball historian Joe Overfield described the situation as follows:

> Force had batted .302 and starred in the field for the Chicago White Stockings in 1874. In September, before the season was over, he signed an 1875 Chicago contract. Later in the year, he received a better offer from the Athletic club in Philadelphia and signed a second contract, which was not an unusual practice in the pre–reserve clause days. The White Stockings management protested, and was upheld by the league's judiciary committee. Subsequently, the committee overruled the earlier decision, asserting the Chicago contract had been signed before the season was over, and was, therefore, invalid according to the league's bylaws. William A. Hulbert of the Chicago club was so infuriated that he resolved to bring the Association to its knees. In another year, the Association was dead and Hulbert had fathered the National League.[10]

In researching the period, the author has found no evidence that Force was guilty of any corrupt behavior. Perhaps his place on the "all rogues team" was a reflection of his lack of respect for contracts, rather than his dishonesty as a ball player.

Dickey Pearce was one of baseball's most famous early players. Born in 1836 in Brooklyn, Pearce began his baseball career with the Brooklyn Atlantics in 1856. According to some sources, he and James Creighton, baseball's first superstar, were probably the two earliest players to be paid for playing baseball.

The diminutive Pearce (he stood 5'3½") remained with the Atlantics through 1870 and moved to the New York Mutuals for the National Association's first two seasons. He went back to the Atlantics in 1873 and 1874 before moving to St. Louis for the 1875 and 1876 seasons. He finished his career in 1877 at the age of 41, splitting his time between St. Louis of the National League and the Rhode Island club in the minor league organization called the League Alliance.

Pearce's skills were legendary. He was considered an outstanding fielder and is credited with revolutionizing the shortstop position. When he began playing, shortstops tended to stay in one spot, but Pearce showed great natural ability and developed the shortstop position into the key defensive position of baseball. He was generally regarded as second only to George Wright as a great defensive shortstop in the early days of baseball.

In addition to revolutionizing the fielding aspects of the game, Pearce was also a pioneer with the bat. He is credited with inventing the bunt and was baseball's first really skilled place hitter.

Pearce was a prominent figure in many of the key events in baseball's early days. He was a teammate of George Zettlein's on the 1870 Brooklyn Atlantics, the team that broke the Cincinnati Red Stockings' 100-game winning streak. In fact, Pearce scored two runs in the contest, a dramatic extra-inning game won by the Atlantics with three runs in the bottom of the eleventh inning.

Other than one unsubstantiated rumor while Pearce was with the St. Louis Brown Stockings in 1875, and the fact that he was a member of the scandal-ridden New York Mutuals, there seems to be little evidence that Pearce was involved in foul play. He was well thought of by his contemporaries, and Henry Chadwick sang his praises.

After retiring as an active player, Pearce did some umpiring for the National League in 1878 and 1882. In 1890 he served as groundskeeper for the New York Player's League club in what would later become known as the Polo Grounds.

Pearce died at the age of 72 in 1908 in Onset, Massachusetts. Suffering from Bright's disease, Pearce caught a severe cold while attending a baseball old-timer's day, which led to his demise.

A number of baseball historians have made a case in recent years that Dickey Pearce belongs in the Baseball Hall of Fame. Despite the claim in the *Brooklyn Eagle*, there is no evidence that would suggest that Pearce committed any acts that would preclude his enshrinement in Cooperstown.

Chapter 3

The Louisville Scandal

A topic of great controversy among baseball fans is who should – or should not – be in the Baseball Hall of Fame. Countless baseball fans lobby for their favorites – Gil Hodges, Tony Oliva, Jim Bunning, and Vic Willis, to name a few – and question why players with relatively weak statistics, such as Rick Farrell and George Kelly, have been enshrined.

Perhaps the most inexplicable omission from the Hall of Fame is William A. Hulbert, the founder of the National League and one of the greatest of all baseball executives. Without Hulbert, it is quite possible that the problems of the National Association would have engulfed major league baseball, and it is also quite possible that professional sports would never have reached the prominence it has achieved in modern society without Hulbert's influence.

William Hulbert was born in 1832 in Burlington Flats, New York – a town, in fact, very near Cooperstown. Hulbert's parents moved to Chicago when he was two years old, and Hulbert became a dyed-in-the-wool Chicagoan. Hulbert once claimed that he would rather be a lamppost in Chicago than a millionaire in any other city, and much of his energies throughout his life were focused on enhancing Chicago's civic standing.

Hulbert achieved success in business early in life. He developed a successful wholesale grocery and coal business and later became a member of the Chicago Board of Trade. What is more important, perhaps, is that he was a great baseball fan and was instrumental in helping to bring Chicago back into the National Association in 1874 after a two-year absence due to the devastating effects of the 1871 Chicago fire. In 1875 Hulbert was named president of the Chicago White Stockings.

Hulbert was totally committed to making Chicago a winning team, but he faced great obstacles. One of the major obstacles was the eastern domination of the National Association, and Hulbert's frustration culminated in 1874 when Davy Force was awarded to the Philadelphia club, rather than Chicago, by the Philadelphia-dominated judiciary committee of the National Association.

Furious at this setback, Hulbert dedicated himself to overcoming these problems and building a great team. In June 1875, Hulbert met with Al Spalding, baseball's premier pitcher and a member of the champion Boston Red

William Hulbert. The father of the National League, Hulbert's firm stance during the Louisville scandal was a central factor in reducing corruption. *Courtesy of Transcendental Graphics.*

Stockings. Spalding was a native of Rockford, Illinois, and Hulbert put the following proposition to him:

> Spalding, you've no business playing in Boston; you're a Western boy, and you belong right here. If you'll come to Chicago, I'll accept the presidency of this club, and we'll give these fellows a fight for their lives.[1]

The result of this conversation was that Spalding signed a contract in June to play for the Chicago team in 1876. Spalding helped recruit Ross Barnes, Cal McVey, and Jim White from Boston, along with Adrian Anson and Ezra Sutton from Philadelphia. Because the rules of the National Association stated that a player could not sign a contract with another club during a playing season, an attempt was made to keep the signing secret. By the end of the month, however, the Boston papers were running the story, and Chicago's coup became common knowledge.

A great deal of pressure was brought on the players to back out of the Chicago deal, but only Ezra Sutton submitted to this pressure. However, the players played out the season with their teams, and it is interesting to note that the Boston team not only won the pennant, but also set an all-time record with an .899 winning percentage, showing that the players had no divided loyalties during the season.

After the season was finished, Hulbert and Spalding were concerned about what action might be taken by the National Association in retaliation for the contract signing. After some discussion, Hulbert stated to Spalding, "I have a new scheme. Let us anticipate the eastern cusses and organize a new association before the March meeting, and then see who will do the expelling." Thus the idea for the National League of Professional Baseball Clubs was formed.

Hulbert and Spalding first met with the owners of three key western teams, the Cincinnati Red Stockings, the St. Louis Browns, and the Louisville Grays. Hulbert explained the problems of the National Association, including gambling, and laid out the plan for the National League, which was to be a much more organized and businesslike entity than the National Association. Hulbert's proposal was met with enthusiastic acceptance by the western owners.

Hulbert's next step was to call for a meeting with the owners of the key eastern teams. The meeting took place in the Grand Central Hotel in New York City on February 2, 1876. Representatives from Philadelphia, Hartford, Boston, and New York attended the meeting to hear what Hulbert had to say. According to Spalding:

> One after another came until all had arrived. Then this aggressive Base Ball magnate from the West, who had never been present at a similar meeting in his life, went to the door of his room, locked it, put the key in his pocket, and, turning, addressed his astonished guests something after this manner:
> "Gentlemen, you have no occasion for uneasiness. I have locked that door simply to prevent any intrusions from without, and incidentally to make it

impossible for any of you to go out until I have finished with what I have to say to you, which I promise shall not take an hour."[2]

Hulbert and Spalding then laid out their plan designed to make baseball a respectable, honorable, and profitable business. After some discussion, the eastern owners agreed to the plan, and the National League was formed.

Hulbert suggested Morgan Bulkeley, president of the Hartford club, to be the first president of the National League. Bulkeley was a very prominent American and later a United States congressman and senator, governor of Connecticut, and president of Aetna Life Insurance Company. Bulkeley accepted after some persuasion and served as a figurehead president for one year. He was then replaced by Hulbert, who ran the league until his death in 1882.

One of the key reasons for the founding of the National League was to eliminate the gambling and crooked play that had ruined the National Association. However, plans for the new league were greeted with skepticism, particularly by the eastern powers such as baseball writer Henry Chadwick. Writing in the *New York Clipper*, Chadwick commented as follows:

> It is notorious among professional players and club officials that a great deal of what is called crooked play was indulged in during the season of 1875, especially in Philadelphia and Brooklyn—not exclusively in those cities, however. In view of this understood fact, what was there for those advocating reform to do? Neither more nor less than to put out of the power of the clubs in which this crooked business has been engaged in and naively sanctioned, as it were, the re-engagement of suspected or marked men to reenter the arena in 1876. Had this been done by the newly organized league? Certainly not. Again, part of the work of reform was to prevent the re-engagement of suspicious players and the adoption of rules rendering such players noticeable. Has this been the object accomplished by the league? We think not.[3]

While future historians tend to dismiss Chadwick's comments as sour grapes, since Chadwick was not involved in the formation of the National League, there is certainly some truth to his point of view. Most of the players suspected of crooked work—Dick Higham, George Zettlein, Bill Craver, Joe Blong, and the rest—were in the National League for the 1876 season. No action was taken against those suspected of crookedness, and at first glance it appeared that it would be business as usual.

During the early weeks of the 1876 season, events seemed to bear out the skepticism. On May 27 the New York Mutuals beat St. Louis by a score of 6–2. Mike McGeary, whom readers will remember from the preceding chapter, was charged with "selling the game." In the first inning the Mutuals scored three runs, primarily due to throwing errors by McGeary. McGeary added another error in the second inning, helping lead to three more runs. McGeary was suspended after the game.

The aftermath of the incident smacked of the bad old days of the National

Association. On June 1, 1876, the *Philadelphia City Item* published the following letter:

> It having been asserted, and published over the country, that the defeat of the St. Louis baseball club in Brooklyn last Saturday was due to the "crooked" playing on the part of Mr. McGeary, he was, in deference to the National League, suspended from play until the matter should be investigated. I immediately came to the city and have made careful inquiry into the matter. Justice to the accused requires me to say publicly through the press that there is no evidence, aside from the fielding errors made by him in that game, that McGeary was false to his club, and therefore he was reinstated today.
>
> To many people the mere restoration of Mr. McGeary to his former position in the club will not be any assurance of his innocence. I am authorized to say that the St. Louis club will pay a reward of $250 for any proof that he was directly or indirectly interested in any pool, wager, or money consideration on the game alluded to.
>
> Yours respectfully,
>
> C. O. Bishop, Vice President, St. Louis[4]

McGeary was reinstated and continued to play in the National League.

A few days after the McGeary scandal, another erupted involving George Bechtel of the Louisville club. This scandal was handled in a much different fashion and set a new tone for organized baseball.

Bechtel began his career with the West Philadelphia club in 1866, playing third base and first base and pitching. He played with other Philadelphia area clubs in 1868 and 1869, and in 1870 he was chosen as the tenth man for the powerful Philadelphia Athletics, ending the season as the regular left fielder. In commenting on his play during the 1870 season, Henry Chadwick stated: "At the commencement of the season, Bechtel's play in left field was equal to any player, but, as the season wore on, he grew careless, and from other causes unnecessary to mention, he played poorly."[5]

Despite this, Bechtel continued his career in the National Association, playing with the Athletics in 1871, the Mutuals in 1872, and with the Philadelphias in 1873 and 1874. In 1875, Bechtel started the season with the Philadelphia Centennials, and along with Bill Craver he was sold to the Athletics during the season.

On May 30, 1876, Bechtel appeared in right field for the Louisville team as it took on the New York Mutuals in New York. The *Louisville Courier Journal* reported on the game as follows:

> In the seventh inning, Booth and Mathews made base hits. Nichols' foul smash bounded to Gerhardt. Holdsworth and Start batted safe to right field. Bechtel let both go through his legs, and two runs were scored where otherwise the bases would only have been filled. Treacy and Hallinan hit to Fulmer, who threw straight and easy to Gerhardt, the latter muffing both times. Start and Treacy scored and the next two went out. Two of the five runs in this inning were earned.

The Louisvilles got their last run in the eighth inning. Hastings made a base hit, got caught between first and second, and in dodging around the base hit the top of his head and went out into right field, allowing him to get to third and then coming home on a wild pitch.

The Mutuals played a fine batting and short fielding game. The Louisvilles could not hit Mathews and made many inexcusable errors, Bechtel especially in allowing three balls to pass him.[6]

Louisville had a total of nine errors, three of which were by Bechtel. Bechtel had no hits during the game and only two putouts. After the game, the New York papers referred to Bechtel as "a much suspected man." Bechtel was suspended by the Louisville team after the game.

As if Bechtel was not in enough trouble already, on June 10 he sent the following wire to teammate Jim Devlin, who was with the team in Boston: "We can make $500.00 if you lose the game today. Tell John (manager John Chapman) and let me know at once. BECHTEL." Devlin refused the offer, responding, "I want you to understand that I am not that kind of a man. I play ball for the interest of those who hire me." Devlin reported this to the club's management.

Originally the Louisville management had presented Bechtel with the option of resigning or being expelled. Following the exposure of the June 10 telegram, Bechtel was expelled by the Louisville club. He was picked up by the Mutuals and played two games for them before being released.

Bechtel's case did not come before the National League as a whole until after the 1877 season. Bechtel appealed for a reinstatement, but his request was denied. Bechtel never again played in organized baseball.

Another blow at corruption was struck in July 1876. In this case, a National League player—Mutuals pitcher Bobby Mathews—was responsible for striking a strong blow against gamblers. Readers will remember that Mathews, inventor of the spitball, was mentioned prominently in a number of National Association scandals, but his performance in the National League merits only praise.

The situation started in June 1876, when Mathews received the following telegram while in Chicago with the Mutuals:

> I am in communication with Fred Seibert all day. If you want to say anything to him let me know; he has requested me to let you know it.
> Yours, D. H. Louderbeck[7]

Mathews immediately took the telegram to his manager, William Cammeyer, and a plot was hatched to entrap the gamblers.

On Cammeyer's instructions, Mathews sent the following message to Fred Seibert in New York:

> Write to me at the Washington Avenue Hotel, St. Louis, full particulars. All will be right.[8]

Seibert was somewhat suspicious, but after a series of telegrams back and forth, Seibert sent the following telegram to Mathews on June 26, 1876:

> Friend Mathews:
> Your two telegrams received. First one surprising because I did not understand it. I am perfectly willing to do anything you wish me to do provided it is confined to myself. Do not want to pay for one thing and have others have the benefit of it. If you wish me to go ahead I will do so and every game we have that you will give us straight will be worth $200.00. I enclose a cipher you can use. Telegraph me giving me plenty of time.
> We want a surety. If we are successful in this and you confine your business to us alone, you will find that no one will be wiser for it and that you will be dealt squarely with. Of course, when you wish us to, we will play the Mutuals for a winner. Don't make a mistake in the cipher, and be sure to get it to us early. We can do well for you and in all ways with yourself. Here are the cipher words:
> > Mutuals . . . Anderson
> > St. Louis . . . Bertram
> > Cincinnati . . . Chayletown
> > Louisville . . . Darling
> If you want to buy St. Louis just say "buy Bertram"; if you want us to buy St. Louis to win in 2 innings say "buy Bertram to win in 2 innings."
> Address all messages to George Howard, New York Turf Exchange, New York and sign them Robert. Don't forget.
> Yours, F. H. Seibert[9]

Armed with Seibert's reply, William Hulbert went public, releasing all the correspondence to the *New York Herald* for publication. While Seibert was not prosecuted for violating any laws, there is no question that this exposure made many gamblers nervous and sent a strong message to players that things were changing.

Unfortunately, the Mathews incident did not end baseball corruption. On September 13, in New York, the weak New York Mutuals team was made a 2–1 favorite against a stronger Louisville team. As it turned out, Louisville won by a score of 9–4 in a poorly played match. Bill Craver committed seven errors to help assure the Louisville victory. No proof was uncovered of corruption, and no action was taken.

In September, another scandal erupted, this one involving the Hartford Dark Blues club. Hartford pitcher Tommy Bond, one of the great pitchers of early baseball, quit his team, charging that Bob Ferguson, the team's captain, was throwing games. Ferguson, readers will remember, while president of the National Association was one of the few people to take action against gamblers and crooked players, including breaking the arm of Nat Hicks. However, Ferguson was accused of being involved in corruption on occasion during the National Association days.

Ferguson suspended Bond and countercharged that Bond was involved in crooked play. Bond then withdrew his charges against Ferguson, and the whole matter was dismissed at the league meeting after the season. Based on the evidence, the charges and countercharges seemed to have had more to do with personal dislikes than they did with dishonesty.

The 1877 season proved to be a turning point in baseball's battle against crooked play. The year started off relatively ominously when on February 3 longtime pitcher William "Cherokee" Fisher admitted that he was paid $100 to lose a game in 1876 while pitching for the West End club in Milwaukee. It may be remembered that Fisher was the pitcher on the Troy Haymakers team in 1869 that forfeited a game to the Cincinnati Red Stockings rather than risk having their gambling backers lose their wagers if the game was played to its conclusion. Fisher's action with the West End team was not under the National League's jurisdiction, so no action was taken against him by the National League. Fisher's career was in decline, and after the 1876 season he appeared in the National League only one more time, pitching one game for Providence in 1878.

The early part of the 1877 season was relatively free of rumors of corruption, and many contemporaries were beginning to think that the strong action in the Bechtel and Mathews cases had the right effect. Unfortunately, this was not to be the case.

The first scandal of 1877 occurred on August 1, when umpire Dan Devinney charged that St. Louis manager George McManus offered him $250 to help the St. Louis club beat the Louisville Grays. McManus denied the charges, and no action was taken.

The main event in 1877, however, was the famous Louisville scandal, baseball's greatest scandal until the Black Sox in 1919. The exposure of the scandal proved to be a pivotal event in the history of baseball, and one in which William Hulbert's strong leadership helped save the game.

The Louisville team took a strong stance against corruption before the 1876 season and backed it up with their expulsion of George Bechtel for crooked play. Despite this, during the winter of 1877 Louisville management brought Bill Craver, whose earlier exploits have been detailed in these pages, to Louisville to take over the shortstop duties from departed manager Chick Fulmer.

The key characters in the Louisville scandal were four players: Craver, star pitcher Jim Devlin, outfielder George Hall, and substitute Al Nichols. Craver, a Civil War veteran, began his career in 1869 with the Troy Haymakers. Involved in scandal almost from the start, Craver moved to Boston and Chicago in 1870, survived expulsion from the old amateur National Association, and returned to Troy at the end of the 1870 season. He remained in Troy for 1871, moving to Baltimore in 1872 and 1873 and to Philadelphia in 1874, remaining in Philadelphia in 1875, splitting his time between the Centennials and the Athletics. He spent the 1876 season with the Mutuals before moving over to Louisville in 1877.

Jim Devlin began his career in the National Association in 1873, playing primarily at first base with Philadelphia. He moved over to Chicago in 1874 and became a pitcher with the White Stockings in 1875. Devlin then moved to Louisville with the founding of the National League in 1876. He had a record of 30-35 with the fifth-place Grays in 1876, leading the league in complete games, innings pitched, and strikeouts, and finishing with an earned-run average of 1.56. He became recognized as a star in 1877, compiling a record of 35-25 and an earned-run average of 2.25.

George Hall was one of the great early sluggers in baseball history. A native of England, Hall began his baseball career in 1868 with the Cambridge (New York) Stars. He moved to the Brooklyn Atlantics in 1870 and entered the National Association with the Washington Olympics of 1871. He moved to Baltimore for the 1872 and 1873 seasons before joining Boston in 1874. He then moved to the Athletics, where he spent 1875 and 1876, joining Louisville for the 1877 season.

Hall was known as a strong batter. His greatest success came in 1876, when he became the National League's first home run king with five, a respectable total in those days of the dead ball. He also batted .366 that year, finishing second only to Ross Barnes of the White Stockings in the batting race. Hall also finished second in the league in triples, total bases, on-base percentage, and slugging percentage. In 1877 he slipped to .323 but still managed to finish among the league leaders in runs, doubles, triples, total bases, bases on balls, and slugging percentage.

Much less is known of Al Nichols, an obscure substitute. He began his major league career in 1875 with the Brooklyn Atlantics, batting an unimpressive .159 in 32 games. He then spent the 1876 season with the New York Mutuals, batting .179 in 57 games.

Nichols began the 1877 season with an independent team in Pittsburgh. In August, after Louisville third baseman Bill Hague developed a painful boil in his left armpit, George Hall strongly recommended Nichols to fill Hague's place, and Nichols was employed. When Nichols joined the club, the Grays were in first place in the National League. That, however, was about to change.

Much of the testimony about the scandal is conflicting, and to this day no one has a clear picture of exactly what happened. However, it appears that the problems were triggered by a Brooklyn man named Frank Powell, who was George Hall's brother-in-law. According to Hall's later testimony, Powell had been urging Hall for over a year to increase his income by throwing games. At first Hall steadfastly refused, but finally, during the 1877 season, he began to weaken and proposed to Devlin that they work together.

At the same time Devlin had been approached by a New York gambler named McCloud. McCloud offered Devlin money to throw games and told him that if he was ever willing to do so he should send a telegram to McCloud containing the word *sash*.

The first game that was thrown was an exhibition game in Cincinnati. It was common in those days for National League teams to supplement their income and fill up their schedule by playing nonleague games around the country.

Devlin received $100 from McCloud and gave $25 to Hall. He told Hall that McCloud had sent $50, and that he and Hall would split the proceeds 50-50.

The next game thrown was an exhibition at Indianapolis. Devlin was paid $100 for this game but ended up giving none of it to Hall. Louisville lost this poorly played game, 7–3. Hall and Nichols then conspired to lose an exhibition at Lowell, Massachusetts—Devlin was apparently not involved in this one.

In addition to the throwing of these nonleague games, there is strong suspicion that some of the league games were also thrown by the players. Before a game against Hartford, club president Charles E. Chase received an anonymous telegram to "watch your men!" Louisville lost badly to Hartford that day, primarily through errors by Hall, Craver, and Nichols.

Chase received a telegram before the next game predicting that Louisville would lose again, and when this prediction came true it raised the suspicions of Chase. At the same time, *Louisville Courier Journal* sportswriter John Haldeman began to become suspicious from watching the play of the Grays. An investigation was quickly launched.

One of the key tipoffs for Chase was the fact that substitute Al Nichols was receiving a tremendous number of telegrams. President Chase confronted Nichols, demanding permission to read these telegrams. Nichols indignantly refused, but relented after Chase said that refusal was an admission of guilt. While the telegrams were vaguely worded, two from P. A. Williams, a Brooklyn pool seller, raised a great deal of suspicion.

At this point, the investigation began to pick up steam. Haldeman then expressed carefully worded suspicions in the *Louisville Courier Journal*, and Chase prepared to confront the players.

Chase's first target was Devlin. According to Chase, he told Devlin that he knew that he had been throwing games, and "I want a full confession. I'll give you until 8:00 P.M. to tell me the whole story."

Before Chase could hear back from Devlin, George Hall approached him offering to confess. According to Chase, Hall explained, "I know I have done wrong, but as God as my judge, I have never thrown a league game. If I tell you all I know about this business, will you promise to let me down easy?"

Chase responded, "I know everything you have done, and I can't make any promises."

Hall took this to mean that Devlin had confessed, and Hall did likewise. He admitted throwing the exhibition games and named Nichols as the prime culprit. In reality, it appears that Nichols was merely following Hall and Devlin's lead and serving as a go-between from the players to the gamblers, which accounts for the large volume of telegrams.

The entire team was then summoned to a meeting at Chase's office and all the players were requested to sign an order giving the directors permission to inspect all telegrams sent or received by them. Chase said that there was no reason not to grant this request, and that refusal to go along with this order would be construed as an acknowledgment of guilt.

All the team agreed to sign this order with one exception—Bill Craver. Craver had been under suspicion for his play throughout the year, and his past record certainly did nothing to inspire the confidence of the Louisville management. There is an interesting side note. Craver told Louisville management that "you can [open the telegrams] if you will pay me the two months salary you owe me." As Lee Allen wrote, "the wires were not opened: Devlin, Nichols, and Hall had not set such a condition on the reading of theirs."[10]

Hall's confession took place on October 27, 1877. On October 30, a meeting of the Louisville directors was held and the following resolutions were adopted:

> *Resolved.* That, for selling games, conspiring to sell games, and tampering with players, A. H. Nichols, by a unanimous vote, the ayes and noes being called, be and is expelled from the Louisville club.
>
> *Resolved.* That W. H. Craver, because of disobedience of positive orders, of general misconduct and of suspicious play, in violation of his contract and the rules of the league, be and hereby is expelled from the Louisville club.
>
> *Resolved.* That, for selling games, conspiring to sell games, and tampering with players, George Hall be and hereby is expelled from the Louisville club.
>
> *Resolved.* That, for selling games, conspiring to sell games, and tampering with players, James A. Devlin be and hereby is expelled from the Louisville club.
>
> *Resolved.* That any sums to the credit of players expelled for cause be and the same are hereby declared forfeited.[10]

While it was proved that Hall, Devlin, and Nichols threw games, no real proof in this case was ever brought against Craver. In fact, other than his refusal to let the Louisville club open his telegrams, the only evidence against Craver was a statement by Nichols and his teammate George Schaffer that Craver's play caused him (Schaffer) to make errors, and Schaffer's repetition of a conversation with Nichols in which Nichols implied that he "thought some of the players were not working on the square. I understood him to mean Craver."

Craver then issued an immediate denial. Craver wrote the following letter:

> To The Editor of the Courier Journal—Louisville, November 4, 1877—Believing as the Editor of this paper as well as the President of the Louisville Baseball Club, in your efforts to purge that Club of those guilty of betraying their positions, you would not willingly or knowingly do an act fatal or even prejudicial to any member; I confidently submit the following statement in vindication of any conduct as one of the parties embraced in and affected by the series of resolutions passed by the Board of Directors of the Club, and published in yesterday's issue of your paper.

1 – I deny unequivocally any and every allegation or charge preferred against me, or in with which my name has been associated in this matter.

2 – I have never had an opportunity to confront, in the presence of the Board of Directors, the party or parties alleging, as the resolution of expulsion states, disobedience of the causative orders, of general misconduct, and suspicious play, on my part as a member of the said club.

3 – The cowardly attempt of the guilty parties, upon their own confessions, to identify others as participants in their infamy, to say the least, is a feeble foundation upon which the Board of Directors of this club should base said conclusions to deprive another member not only of his means to earn a livelihood, but likewise marking his character, blackening his reputation and prevent any opportunities to allow a fair and impartial investigation.

4 – In justification of this view of my case, I submit herewith and as part of this, separate statements of Joseph Gerhardt and George W. Latham in my behalf, and demand of the aforesaid Board of Directors a full complete and searching investigation touching on any and every act or thing done or influenced by me as a member of the Louisville Baseball Club, and appeal to you as a fair minded man to secure for me that which the humblest citizen, even though like myself a stranger in your midst, has a right to ask and receive, to-wit: an opportunity to confront his accusers and to be heard.

If the Board of Directors is not a Star Chamber organization or a remnant of the inquisition, my demand will be acceded too. If, under the circumstances, my reasonable request is unheeded, its performances merit the contempt and scorn of all who make the least pretense to honesty of purpose.

Very respectfully, W. H. Craver

Louisville – November 8, 1877 – This is to certify that the statement in the Courier Journal of November 3, stating that W. H. Craver was responsible for my errors playing baseball is false. Signed Joseph Gerhardt.

This is to certify that the statement of the Courier Journal of November 3, stating that W. H. Craver was responsible for my errors in playing baseball is false.

Signed George W. Latham[11]

Craver's letter is very impressive, particularly his statements from Gerhardt and Latham. Unfortunately for Craver, the *Courier Journal* reported that

> Immediately after signing the above certificate, Gerhardt took it to the President of the Louisville club and showing it to him said: "Craver bothered me so much about it, that I attached my signature to what he had written merely to get rid of him."
>
> "But Joe," the officer replied, "you certainly acknowledged before all the Louisville directors that which you have now denied."
>
> "I know I did," said Joe, "and I only signed the certificate to get rid of Craver."[12]

The scandal received tremendous play throughout the nation, and it was the first time that proof positive had been produced against players who were then forever expelled from the game. While some observers predicted that the exposure would destroy the game, the Louisville scandal was a turning point in cleaning up baseball.

The expulsion of the four Louisville players was reviewed by the National League at their annual meeting in December, and at the insistence of Hulbert the league's board of directors unanimously voted to expel these players from playing professional baseball again. A message had finally been sent to crooked players, gamblers, and the clubs alike—game throwing would not be tolerated in the National League. The repercussions of the scandal served to put two teams out of business: the Louisville Grays franchise, as well as the St. Louis Browns franchise, which had signed Devlin and Hall for the 1878 season at the time they were expelled.

The ensuing story is a sad one. Craver, Hall, and Devlin tried to win reinstatement to no avail. Hulbert remained firm on making their expulsion permanent. Devlin was a particularly sad case. An uneducated and semiliterate man, Devlin encountered great difficulties in making ends meet. Al Spalding described the following scene, when Devlin, who had been friendly with Hulbert, appealed for mercy:

> One player came to Chicago, appeared in Mr. Hulbert's office with tears in his eyes, down on his knees in prayer, and begged him not to expel; that his family was starving. Those were pathetic times. I remember Mr. Hulbert going into his pocket and giving the man $50.00. He said, "Devlin, that's what I think of you personally; but, damn you, you have sold a game; you are dishonest and this National League will not stand for it. We are going to expel you."[13]

Devlin continued his efforts to be reinstated every year. The following letter was sent in 1879:

> Philadelphia, January 27, 1879—Dear Sir: In presenting this petition for reinstatement in the International Base Ball Association, I am actuated by a desire to retrieve the errors of the past and put myself in a position for which, by my past record, I feel myself qualified. That I have suffered tenfold for the errors into which I permitted myself to be drawn is fully attested by the present condition of myself and family, who for several months past have, at very frequent intervals, gone without the common necessities of life; and I have endeavored by every means in my power to alter my condition, even at a rate of remuneration that would barely furnish bread. You will perceive by this that my punishment has not only reached me, but has overtaken those nearer and dearer to me than life itself. Since I have become convinced that an honorable, straightforward course brings with it the reward of the honest man, I sincerely and firmly pledge myself to sustain an honest and industrious course under all circumstances, and further assert that, should I be reinstated, my professional ability will eclipse my former merit. Rather than plead any excuse for my former conduct, at cost of the really guilty party, I prefer to acknowledge the wrong I committed and beg your cooperation in my efforts to regain that which I have lost. Should you do this, I shall not again during my life shame your favor by any act of mine. I have gone through the fire of affliction and feel myself all the better and purer for the

ordeal. Should you give me any hope of my petition being favorably received, I will get to Utica if I have to walk. Yours respectfully, James Devlin.[14]

When appeals fell on deaf ears, some of the players looked for other ways to continue in their chosen profession. For example, the Utica club in the minor league International Association signed Devlin and Hall for 1878, and the Association's judiciary committee voted to admit Craver to play also. Heavy pressure from Hulbert, Henry Chadwick, and the National League forced the reversal of this action.

Devlin eventually obtained employment with the Philadelphia Police Force, but his years of poverty took a toll on his health, and he died in Philadelphia on October 10, 1883, of consumption. Unfortunately for his family, Devlin left few worldly possessions.

George Hall moved back to Brooklyn after his expulsion, and there were some rumors that he continued to play under assumed names in New Jersey. Hall eventually found employment as an engraver, and later as a clerk in an art museum. He died on June 11, 1923, in Brooklyn.

Despite his highly checkered career, Craver was the most successful of the players in his life after baseball. Craver joined the police force in his native Troy, New York, and served with distinction. He died on June 17, 1901, in Troy and was generally mourned by the city. In fact, Superintendent of Police Coughlin issued a glowing statement about Craver, which read in part:

> William H. Craver was a faithful officer, careful and conscientious in the performance of his duties. I wish to thus publicly express the esteem and respect with which he was held by his superior officers.
> As a mark of honor to this faithful officer I order that the members of the police force display the customary badge of mourning for a period of 30 days.[16]

Nichols proved the most persistent in attempting to continue his baseball career. Getting nowhere with his applications for reinstatement, Nichols tried to find employment with independent and semipro clubs. In 1887 it was reported that Nichols was playing with the semipro Bergen Point club under the name of Williams. In 1890 the *Sporting Life* uncovered Nichols playing third base for the semipro Senators of Long Island City under the name of Al Williams. According to the *Sporting Life*,

> Last week he lost a game for the Senators by such apparent and willful errors that a suspicion was raised that he was at his old tricks. As a consequence, he was discharged by the manager of the Senators. The Senators have a big following in Long Island City and a great deal of money is bet on all their games. Whether Nichols was crooked or not, he is not now playing ball and is not likely to do so again, not with the Senators at any rate.[16]

Nothing was heard of Nichols after 1890. He faded into obscurity and his death is as yet unrecorded.

In the aftermath of the Louisville scandal, a new era dawned for professional baseball. Because of the actions taken by the Louisville management, and the strong support of National League President William Hulbert, confidence in the game's integrity was restored. While the exposure gave baseball a black eye, the players' expulsion and Hulbert's unrelenting attitude to their pleas for reinstatement established a strong code for the National League, which held during the rest of the century—no gambling or game fixing would be tolerated. This allowed the game to grow and prosper and truly become the national pastime.

Chapter 4

The Game Grows Up

Baseball after the Louisville scandal and until the turn of the century was filled with strife. Franchises came and went, leagues came and went, and clashes between labor and management culminated in the formation of the Players' League in the 1890 season. In addition, the game continued to refine its rules, including the advent of widespread use of gloves and a gradual increase in the distance from the pitcher's mound to the plate, so that by the turn of the century the game of baseball was very similar to that which is played today.

Perhaps the most important change in baseball after 1877, however, was the lack of gambling scandals and the improvement in the confidence of fans in the integrity of the game. This confidence that the outcome of games had not been predetermined by gamblers and crooked ball players led to the increasing popularity of professional baseball.

The firm action taken by William Hulbert of the National League against the Louisville players in 1877 paid immediate dividends. In a review of the 1878 season, Henry Chadwick wrote the following:

> During 1878, honest play in the professional arena was the rule and not the exception. There was no just cause for any action expelling crooked players from the league nines, as there was in 1877.[1]

A few years later, in 1881, Chadwick wrote that "the league has been death to crooked play, and has made crookedness so costly to players prone to indulge in it that what used to be a general thing in professional baseball has become quite a rare exception."

How destructive the lack of honesty in professional baseball had become is hard to underestimate. Perhaps it is best stated by quoting from an article by Henry Chadwick, written in 1882:

> The baseball public of the great cities — such as New York and Philadelphia — have never, even for a single season, lost their admiration of the game itself; but years ago, in both cities, they became disgusted with the apparent rottenness of the professional fraternity at large, and they determined to put a stop to it by keeping away from the public ball grounds, and this they did until professional

52

Honest John Clapp. Honest John earned his nickname by reporting it to the police when Chicago gamblers tried to bribe him in 1881. *Courtesy of Transcendental Graphics.*

playing reached its lowest ebb, and almost died of the cancer of "crookedness." Then came an era of quietness, during which the effect of driving out the "crooks" of the profession and presenting a successful opposition to pool gambling was felt, and baseball began to work a reformation. There was a desire all over the country to see the old ball game revived again, but under honest auspices.[2]

In spite of this cleanup, however, the general view by baseball historians that the Louisville incident was the last baseball scandal in the nineteenth century is simply not true. Baseball still felt the influence of the gambling element, and scandals popped up periodically throughout the last two decades of the century.

One such incident occurred in 1879, less than two years after the Louisville scandal. Early in the season, the Cincinnati Reds' president, J. Wayne Neff, wrote a letter accusing his players of crookedness, although there was no evidence to support his claim. Neff sent this letter to manager Deacon White, one of the nineteenth century's great baseball players, demanding it be read aloud in the clubhouse. White, quite justifiably, felt there was absolutely no substance behind these charges and refused to read the letter, resigning as manager instead. The Reds, 9-9 at the time of Neff's charges, ended the season in fifth place at 43-37, and no more was heard about Neff's charges.

The next incident took place in May 1881, when Chicago bookmakers attempted to bribe Cleveland catcher John Clapp. According to Clapp, Chicago gambler James S. Woodruff offered him $5,000 to "allow one or two pass-balls where one or two men happen to be on base." Clapp rejected the offer and reported the incident to the Chicago police, which resulted in the apprehension of Woodruff.

Because of his forthrightness in promptly reporting the incident to the police, Clapp earned the nickname "Honest John," which stuck throughout his career. After his professional career ended in 1884, Clapp joined the police force in his hometown of Ithaca, New York, and died of a heart attack while on the job in 1904.

The next charges of scandal were aimed at one of the game's most respected players, Lipman E. Pike. Pike, who is believed to be the first Jewish professional baseball player, began his career in 1866 with the Philadelphia Athletics. He then moved to the New York Mutuals, but left the club, disgusted with the corruption of Boss Tweed.

Pike was a batting star throughout his National Association days with Troy, Baltimore, Hartford, and St. Louis, and continued as a productive player in the National League with St. Louis, Cincinnati, and Providence through the end of the 1878 season.

Pike moved to the minor league National Association in 1879, continuing in that organization until he joined the Worcester club of the National League toward the end of the 1881 season.

On September 3, 1881, Pike played in center field with the Worcester team. Going into the ninth inning, Worcester led Boston by a score of 2–1, but things quickly unraveled. Pike made three errors in the ninth inning, leading to two Boston runs and a 3–2 victory over Worcester. Some of the Worcester players accused Pike of throwing the game, and he was immediately suspended.

On September 29, a meeting of the National League was held. A number of players were expelled from the game, according to the 1882 *Spalding Baseball Guide*, for "confirmed dissipation and general insubordination." Included among these players was Lip Pike.

At 36, Pike was pretty much at the end of the baseball trail anyway, so he announced his retirement and entered the clothing business in Brooklyn. Although he was reinstated by the National League a year later, Pike stayed in retirement until 1887, when O. P. Caylor, manager of the American Association's New York Metropolitans, and one of the key men in the founding of the major league American Association, induced Pike to return to the game. Pike played only one game, going hitless. Pike once again retired, this time staying away from the game.

No evidence was ever presented that Pike actually threw the game in Boston. Furthermore, Pike was well respected by his contemporaries both as a player and a person. Shortly after his death in October 1893, the *Sporting News* wrote:

> Those who knew Pike best appreciated him the most. He was one of the baseball players of those days who were always gentlemanly on and off the field – a species which is becoming rarer as the game grows older. Such men as Pike, Barnes, Spalding, Reach, Jim White, George Wright, and Morrill, creditable to the game personally and professionally, are becoming scarcer every year.[3]

Baseball's next scandal, which occurred in 1882, involved a man who was the antithesis of Lip Pike. While Lip Pike was well respected as a man of integrity, the 1882 scandal involved Richard Higham, probably the most corrupt figure in nineteenth century baseball.

Dick Higham was the central figure in many of the baseball scandals of the National Association outlined in Chapter 2. After the demise of the National Association, Higham continued his career in the National League with Hartford in 1876 and Providence in 1878. A good hitter, Higham batted over .320 each of these years and led the National League in doubles in both the 1876 and 1878 seasons. Higham also had the distinction of hitting into the National League's first triple play while a member of the Hartford team in a game against New York on May 13, 1876. Higham closed his playing career by playing one game with Troy of the National League in 1880.

For reasons that are hard to fathom, Higham was hired by the National League as an umpire in 1881, despite his reputation for shady dealing. The only possible explanation was that Higham had occasionally umpired games during his days in the National Association.

Suspicion focused on Higham early in the 1881 season. During the season's first series, a Providence fan wrote:

> Last year, Boston claimed the umpires lost them games, so this year they are starting under the kindly protection of umpire Richard Higham, who has already

presented them with two pure gift games. Even Boston papers say his work is bad, and the Providence club the sufferer.[4]

Higham's downfall, however, came in 1882. In order to save money, umpires in those days often stayed with a team for a period of weeks, and during the first part of the 1882 season, Higham umpired in 26 of the Detroit Wolverines' first 29 games. Every close play seemed to go against Detroit—so much so that William G. Thompson, the president of the Detroit team, grew suspicious.

Thompson hired detectives to follow up on his suspicions. Among other things, the detectives intercepted a letter from Higham to gambler James Todd. The letter reads as follows:

> Friend Todd: I just got word we leave for the East on the 3 P.M. train, so I will not have a chance to see you. If you don't hear from me, play the Providence Tuesday, and if I want you to play the Detroits Wednesday, I will telegraph you in this way, "Buy all the lumber you can." If you do not hear from me, don't play the Detroits but buy Providence sure, that is in the first game. I think this will do for the Eastern series. I will write you from Boston. You can write me at any time in care of the Detroit BB Club. When you send me any money, you can send a check to me in care of the Detroit BB Club, and it will be all right. You will see by the book I gave you the other day what city I will be in. Yours truly, Dick[5]

As it turned out, Higham had been working with Todd by telling him in advance the likely winners of certain games in which he umpired. Todd placed bets based on this information, resulting in nice profits for both Higham and Todd.

Armed with the letter to Todd, Thompson called for a special meeting of the Board of Directors of the National League, which was held on June 24 in Detroit. Higham vehemently denied any wrongdoing and also denied authorship of the incriminating letter. Anticipating such a move, Thompson had procured a number of innocent letters written by Higham, of which Higham acknowledged authorship. Thompson then introduced three of the top handwriting experts in Detroit, each of whom testified that all the letters were written by the same person.

Providence President Freeman Brown and manager Frank Bancroft also testified against Higham. Brown told the league board that Higham was seen associating with a well-known gambler in Worcester earlier in the year.

Based on this overwhelming evidence, the National League board found the charges against Higham to be fully sustained and resolved that "the said Richard Higham be forever disqualified from acting as umpire in any game of ball participated in by a league club."

An interesting irony is the fact that the manager of the Detroit team during the period that Higham's dishonesty was costing the club games was none other than Mike McGeary, second only to Higham in corruption during the National

Association days. McGeary was released by the Detroit club the day after Higham's expulsion, although in McGeary's case the move was related to the deterioration of his playing skills, not to any charges of dishonesty.

After his expulsion, Higham moved to Chicago and became a bookmaker. Based on his history, this would appear to have been a much more appropriate profession for him.

Higham died in Chicago on March 18, 1905. While totally forgotten today, during his baseball career Higham had the dubious distinction of being associated with crooked play as a major league player, as a minor league player, and as an umpire.

Richard Higham stands out as the only major league umpire associated with game fixing. Some histories also name Herman Doescher, a former umpire, as having been expelled for dishonesty, also during the 1882 season. However, Doescher's crime was being on the payrolls of both the Cleveland and Detroit clubs, and Doescher was never accused of throwing games or engaging in dishonest baseball.

The Higham case led some to look upon professional baseball with renewed scrutiny. In 1883 rumors arose that certain games were being thrown by western clubs. When asked about this, Harry Wright, baseball pioneer and manager of the Providence Grays of the National League, dismissed these charges saying, "I would wager any amount that there is not one man in the league who could be bought off; nor a club in the league that would throw a championship into another's way."[6]

Later during the same season, rumors began to circulate regarding the play of Sam Wise, shortstop for the Boston Red Stockings of the National League. Wise, who was involved in a landmark court case when he jumped his contract with Cincinnati of the newly formed American Association in 1882 to go to the Boston club, went through a period of poor fielding late in the season, leading to the rumors. However, no evidence was ever produced to support the charges — and in fact, an article in the *Boston Daily Globe* stated that

> The scandalous reports about Sam Wise, the shortstop of the Bostons, are utterly ridiculous. Everyone knows that no player on the team is a harder worker and more earnest fielder than he. Considering the chances he tries for and accepts, it is wonderful that his record is as good as it is.[6]

Neither of these 1883 rumors was ever substantiated, and they were soon forgotten.

Major league baseball was undergoing many changes in the early 1880s. In 1882, a rival major league, the American Association, was formed. The National League had turned off patrons in cities such as Cincinnati and St. Louis with its 50¢ admission price, a ban on selling alcohol at the games, and the refusal to play on Sundays. The American Association filled this void, charging a 25¢ admission fee, playing Sunday ball where it was legal, and selling beer in the ball parks. In fact, a number of the owners of the association clubs had made their living through the sale of alcohol, leading National League partisans to refer to the American Association as "the beer and whiskey circuit."

After raiding each other's ranks throughout the 1882 season, the National League and the American Association reached a peace settlement in 1883. These major leagues existed peacefully, side by side, until 1891, when renewed warfare led to the demise of the American Association after that season.

A third major league came into being for the 1884 season. This league, the Union Association, was spearheaded by Henry Lucas, a wealthy resident of St. Louis. Lucas felt that baseball's labor practices, including the reserve clause, were unethical and immoral, and he formed the Union Association to eliminate these abuses. Unfortunately, the Union Association was unsuccessful, lasting only one year. Lucas built a tremendous club in St. Louis, the Maroons, which ran away with the pennant, leading to a lack of interest on the part of the fans in other cities.

While Lucas's team was of top quality both on the field and off the field, some of the clubs in the league lacked discipline. Preeminent baseball historian Lee Allen described Dan O'Leary, manager of the Cincinnati Union Association club, as "one of those picturesque characters of early baseball who eschewed discipline, drank beer with his players, and gambled heavily on his team's games."[8] While there is no evidence that O'Leary ever bet against his club, having a manager place bets on baseball games was clearly not a practice to be encouraged, and O'Leary faded away from the game after the 1884 season.

The 1884 season produced perhaps the greatest pitching performance in the history of baseball. Pitching for Providence in the National League, Charles "Old Hoss" Radbourn won a record total of 60 games*, pitching the Grays to the pennant. He then won all three games in the postseason series against the American Association champions, the New York Metropolitans. Early in the season, however, Radbourn was suspended and accused of throwing a game.

The circumstances leading up to the game fixing charge are as follows: The Grays began the season with two outstanding pitchers, Radbourn and Charlie Sweeney (we will learn more about Sweeney when reviewing minor league scandals). Both were talented and egotistical, and each resented the other's presence. The situation reached a boiling point on June 17, when Radbourn's "careless" pitching cost Providence a game, and he was suspended. While Radbourn was never tied in any way to gamblers or other game fixers, his jealousy of Sweeney and his conviction that he was underpaid led to his not putting forth his best efforts. Less than a week later, Sweeney quit the team and jumped to St. Louis of the Union Association. Radbourn was reinstated and took on the pitching burden. The result was a great season, a pennant, and a spot in the Hall of Fame.

*Recent research shows that Radbourn should have been credited with 59 wins.

The 1885 season resulted in one scandal—and this one had nothing to do with the gambling element. On June 17, Brooklyn pitcher John Francis "Phenomenal" Smith was shelled by St. Louis, losing by a score of 18–5 in his debut with the Brooklyn club. Smith's poor showing was largely attributable to 14 Brooklyn errors behind him. As it turned out, Smith's teammates admitted playing lackadaisically behind him because they disliked his personality. Smith, who gave himself the name "Phenomenal," was an early-day Dizzy Dean without the talent. Upon joining the club, he bragged that he was so good that he did not need his teammates to win, creating a great deal of resentment. The guilty players were fined, and Smith was dropped by the team in the name of harmony.

Smith, whose career had started with the Union Association in 1884, bounced from club to club until 1891. His lifetime record was an unphenomenal 57-78 with a 3.87 earned-run average. His best season was in 1887 with the third-place Baltimore team in the American Association, wherein he compiled a record of 25-30 and was among the league leaders in complete games, games pitched, and strikeouts.

With the exception of the Higham affair, the major scandal of this era occurred in 1886 and involved Tony Mullane, star pitcher with the Cincinnati Reds of the American Association. On June 18 of that year, the *Cincinnati Enquirer* created a sensation by charging five Cincinnati players, including Mullane, with crooked work. The following is the *Associated Press* dispatch of this story:

Cincinnati, June 18.—The *Enquirer* this morning devotes two columns of its first page to an article charging five players of the Cincinnati Base Ball Club with "throwing" games. The only player against whom direct evidence is offered is "Tony" Mullane, one of the pitchers of the team. In support of the charges two affidavits are printed, the first from P. J. McMahon, of Indianapolis. Mr. McMahon declares that he has known Mullane for the past six months, and says that on June 3, 1886, he received a letter postmarked New York, advising him to bet all the money he could on the Brooklyn Club to win after the fourth, fifth and sixth innings of the game played in Brooklyn June 4. The score in this game at the end of the seventh inning was seven to nothing in favor of Cincinnati. In the eighth inning, Brooklyn made eight runs and in the ninth four runs, winning the game. Ten of these twelve runs were earned. Mullane pitched. This affidavit does not state who signed the letter advising the recipient to bet on the Brooklyns.

George Clayton, of Indianapolis, makes the second affidavit. He swears that he is acquainted with Mullane and that on the 23rd day of May, 1886, he received a letter signed by Mullane and postmarked Baltimore, advising him to bet all the money and buy all the pools he could on the Athletics to win in the game played between the Athletics and Cincinnati on the 24th of May at Philadelphia. McKeon pitched in this game, and the Cincinnatis were defeated by a score of 10 to 4. The *Enquirer* calls attention to the fact that of the seven errors made by the Cincinnatis, four were made by Fennelly and two by Jones. The other four men hinted at in this article as implicated with Mullane in selling games are not mentioned, but are understood to be McKeon, pitcher; Keenan, catcher; Fennelly, shortstop; and Jones, left field.[7]

Mullane was no stranger to controversy—indeed, notoriety followed Mullane throughout his career. Known as the "Apollo of the box" due to his good looks, Mullane broke into the major leagues with the Detroit Wolverines in the National League in 1881. He then bounced around, moving to the Louisville Colonels of the American Association in 1882 and the St. Louis Browns of the American Association in 1883. In November 1883, Mullane turned down St. Louis's contract offer of $1,900 and jumped to the St. Louis Maroons of the Union Association for a reported salary of $2,500. Under threat of being blacklisted by the established major leagues, Mullane then jumped back to the American Association, this time signing with the Toledo club for the same $2,500 figure he had reportedly been offered by the St. Louis Unions. The move to Toledo, a second-division team, was engineered by the American Association's leaders as a way of getting Mullane back into the fold.

The St. Louis club of the Union Association then sued Mullane and succeeded in obtaining a court order restraining Mullane from playing in St. Louis with any club other than the Union Association club. The case was appealed to the United States Circuit Court, where the injunction was dissolved.

With Toledo, Mullane's battery mate was Fleetwood Walker, the first African American to play major league baseball. Pitching for an eighth-place team (in a 12-club league), Mullane won a career-high 37 games against 26 losses. He also led the league with eight shutouts. It marked the third straight season that Mullane had won 30 games.

The Toledo club disbanded after the 1884 season, making Mullane a free agent. A number of clubs desired Mullane's services, and after some discussions with the Louisville club he promised to accept their offer of $3,000 per year. After agreeing to accept Louisville's terms, Mullane spoke to Chris Von der Ahe, owner of the St. Louis club, who offered Mullane $3,500, which Mullane also agreed to accept. Since Mullane was still technically under contract with Toledo, he could not sign either deal, which left him free to continue negotiations.

After agreeing to sign with both St. Louis and Louisville, Mullane was approached by the management of the Cincinnati club of the American Association. The president of the club, Aaron Stern, and manager O. P. Caylor huddled with Mullane on the eve of his contract expiration and made him an offer of $4,000. To dramatize the offer, Stern laid $2,000 in twenty-dollar bills on the table—cash in advance for 50 percent of Mullane's $4,000 contract. Mullane accepted the offer and signed the contract.

Unfortunately, neither the management of St. Louis nor the management of Louisville was prepared to accept the situation. They demanded action from the American Association. Mullane was declared to be the property of Cincinnati

Tony Mullane. Mullane was known for his good looks, his stellar pitching, and his penchant for controversy. *Courtesy of Transcendental Graphics.*

but was suspended for the entire 1885 season and forbidden to play baseball in any professional capacity during that season. Mullane was forced to return half of the $2,000 he had been advanced as part of the settlement.

After sitting out the 1885 season, Mullane joined Cincinnati in 1886. Mullane was off to a good start and was en route to a 33-win season when the *Enquirer* charges were leveled.

Mullane immediately denied the charges, calling them "a malicious libel." Furthermore, he said he had never met George Clayton and declared that there were no pool rooms in Indianapolis where two parties could have possibly bet against the Cincinnati club. Mullane then published a letter, which reads as follows:

Cincinnati, June 18, 1886 – To the Base Ball Patrons, Managers and Players
of the United States: The article which is published in to-day's *Cincinnati Enquirer* is an unmitigated lie, a mean, vile and malicious attempt to injure myself
and other members of the team and the management of the Cincinnati Base Ball
Club for reasons well-known to the public of Cincinnati. I would respectfully request that judgement be withheld until the matter has been fully investigated.
Yours respectfully, Tony J. Mullane, Member of the Cincinnati Base Ball Club.[8]

The reasons Mullane refers to in his letter are quite revealing and shed a
great deal of light on the newspaper business of the 1880s. The *Enquirer* was
owned by a man named McLean, who had been a stockholder in the Cincinnati
club but had been forced out. For revenge, McLean had been constantly involved in moves to injure the club, including bankrolling the Cincinnati club
of the Union Association. McLean was joined by his managing editor, Allen
Meyers, who had once been expelled from the Cincinnati grounds for "drunken
and disorderly conduct." An investigation by the *Sporting Life* revealed that the
"flimsiest part of the story is that relating to Indianapolis. As Mullane points
out, there are no pool rooms in Indianapolis, at least none of any account, as
there is no considerable gambling fraternity to support them. Baseball is com-
paratively dead there, and there is probably little betting done upon any sporting events."[11]

A special meeting of the board of the American Association was held in
Cincinnati on June 30, 1886, to fully investigate the charges. Representatives
of the *Cincinnati Enquirer* refused to appear before the board. In advance of
this meeting, the Association had sent a committee to Indianapolis to interview
the witnesses, where they found that "said witnesses were men of criminal
character who had been suborned to make a case against Mullane."[12]

The result of the investigation was that Mullane was totally cleared of any
wrongdoing. In addition, the Association resolved that

> *Resolved.* That it is the sense of this Association that said charges appearing
> from the evidence to be false, it is the plain duty of said Mullane and the Cincin-
> nati Base Ball Club to institute proceedings at law and thus compel the *Cincinnati
> Enquirer* to produce any evidence it may have, to substantiate said charges, or
> pay the penalty of its failure to do so.[9]

After he was exonerated, Mullane launched a libel suit, oddly against the
Cincinnati *Times Star* rather than the *Enquirer*. Later that year, Mullane dropped
the suit under pressure from the Cincinnati management, which was fearful of
creating bad relations with the local press.

The next controversy for Mullane occurred in May 1887. A crisis arose
when Mullane informed Cincinnati manager Gus Schmelz that he refused to
pitch a game against Brooklyn. Mullane's refusal was based on the perception
that he was being overworked and underpaid, and he declared "I don't intend
to do any more work than the rest of the pitchers."

Manager Schmelz fined Mullane $100 and suspended him indefinitely. Mullane left the park, and when a meeting with Cincinnati President Aaron Stern on June 3 failed to alleviate the situation, Mullane left for Rutland, Vermont, where he agreed to pitch for a local club for $200 per month.

Initially it looked as if this would be the end of Mullane's career in the major leagues, but cooler heads prevailed and Mullane was back with Cincinnati before the month of June ended.

Mullane continued his career with Cincinnati, moving to the National League when the Cincinnati franchise moved from the American Association to the National League in 1890. He again became the center of controversy in 1892 when, with the dissolving of the American Association, the National League owners moved to reduce expenses by cutting salaries. In the middle of 1892 Mullane's salary was cut by $700, after which he left to join an outlaw club in Butte, Montana. He reconsidered in 1893 and agreed to join the Cincinnati club at a reduced salary, but during the season he was traded to Baltimore.

Mullane's last year in the major leagues was 1894, a season he split between Baltimore and Cleveland. He then played in the minor leagues until 1899, reappearing in the minors in 1902.

In addition to being a controversial figure, Mullane was a great pitcher. He won 30 games five times and had a lifetime record of 285 wins and 220 losses, with an earned-run average of 3.05. Mullane was also a good hitter for a pitcher, compiling a lifetime batting average of .243.

In addition to his success on the diamond, Mullane had the unique advantage of being ambidextrous. During his career, on more than one occasion Mullane, a right-hander, switched to his left hand to face a tough left-handed batter or simply to confuse the opposition.

Mullane set two major records during his career, both of which have since been broken. The first occurred in 1882, when Mullane, as a member of the Louisville team, pitched a no-hit game against the Cincinnati Reds on September 11. He followed up this performance the next day by not allowing a hit until the seventh inning. This record of 15 consecutive hitless innings stood until the twentieth century. Mullane's other record occurred early in his career, when he threw a ball 416 feet on the fly.

A great pitcher and a controversial character, Mullane has been all but forgotten in the twentieth century. Arguably the greatest pitcher in the history of the American Association, Mullane would appear to deserve serious consideration for the Baseball Hall of Fame.

Shortly after the Mullane incident, the first scandal in World Series history occurred. Long before the founding of the American League, the National League and the American Association played a postseason series for baseball supremacy. The 1886 series featured the National League champion Chicago Colts (now known as the Cubs) playing against the American Association's St. Louis Browns, arguably two of the greatest teams of the nineteenth century.

Chicago was led by manager and first baseman Cap Anson. On Anson's team were John Clarkson, one of the greatest pitchers of all time, and catcher-outfielder King Kelly, one of the most colorful players in the history of baseball. Other stars on the team included outfielder George Gore, pitcher Jim McCormick, second baseman Fred Pfeffer, outfielder Jimmy Ryan, and shortstop Ned Williamson, who in 1884 had set a single-season record of 27 home runs that stood until Babe Ruth broke it in 1919.

The Browns were also a formidable group, led by Charles Comiskey, who managed the club and played first base. Comiskey was to play a prominent role in baseball's greatest scandal, the 1919 Black Sox scandal. Among the stars on Comiskey's team were pitchers Bob Caruthers and Dave Foutz, outfielder Tip O'Neill, outfielder Curt Welch, and catcher Doc Bushong.

Chicago and St. Louis had met the year before for the championship, and the outcome was unsatisfactory to all parties. After a tie in the first game, the second game was marred by horrible umpiring and eventually forfeited to Chicago. The Browns then won three out of the next five games, so the series officially ended in a tie.

In 1886 the stakes were increased. It was agreed that the clubs would play a seven-game series on a "winner-take-all" basis—in other words, the team that won the series would get all of the receipts from the games. As it turned out, this agreement sparked tremendous controversy.

Led by the five-hit pitching of John Clarkson, Chicago won the first game by an easy 6–0 score. Chicago was extremely confident, and now the Colts were heavy favorites to win the series. In game two, however, the Browns came back, crushing Chicago by a score of 12–0. Rumors immediately began to circulate that Chicago had thrown the game in order to prolong the series, which would increase the gate receipts and their winnings. Chicago came back to win game three by a score of 11–4, again behind Clarkson. The teams then traveled to St. Louis for the last four games of the series.

Further suspicion was aroused when Chicago elected to leave Jim McCormick, the team's number two pitcher and a 31-game winner, in Chicago. Asked why McCormick did not accompany the team, Chicago manager Anson replied, "He's got the rheumatism and stayed at home." Apparently the trouble was with his feet, and it kept him out of action for the remainder of the series.

In game four, Chicago jumped out to an early 3–0 lead, but St. Louis prevailed by a score of 8–5. In his fine chronicle of the nineteenth-century World Series Jerry Lansche reports the scene after the game as follows:

> At the Lindell Hotel that evening, the White Stockings, with the exception of Cap Anson, seemed strangely undisturbed by their loss. The team stood around smoking big black cigars, toasting each other with champagne, and joking with reporters. Clarkson, although the losing pitcher, was in especially good humor. Shortstop Ned Williamson smiled enigmatically and said, "yes sir, they beat us today on the level," and King Kelly told funny stories to a group of friends. Not

surprisingly, the team's unusual behavior caused a resurrection of the charges of hippodroming.[10]

Of course, the charges were heartily denied by the players and management from both sides. However, events in the fifth game rekindled the debate. With McCormick out, Chicago chose Mark Baldwin to pitch game five. Unfortunately, Baldwin, who had signed with Chicago for the 1887 season, had not been with the club in 1886, and therefore was not eligible for the series. Rather than replacing Baldwin with his other pitcher, John Flynn, Anson chose to use shortstop Ned Williamson on the mound. After surrendering two runs in the first inning, Williamson was replaced by right-fielder Jimmy Ryan, who finished out the game, a 10–3 loss to the Browns.

Game six was by far the most dramatic contest of the series. The game was tied going into the tenth inning when Clarkson uncorked a wild pitch, allowing Browns center fielder Welch to score the winning run. Although he scored easily, Welch, a colorful player, chose to slide into home, an event that became known as "Curt Welch's $15,000 slide," in honor of the $15,000 (actually $14,000) purse in the winner-take-all series.

Rumors had persisted throughout the series that the Chicago team, overly confident, had thrown games to increase the purse. The main evidence was Anson's refusal to use Flynn to pitch in game five. It was claimed that Flynn was injured, but some experts, including Jerry Lansche, claim that this was the forerunner of the Black Sox scandal. Regardless, the rumors soon quieted, and the matter was forgotten.

The next scandal also occurred during the World Series, this time in 1888. The 1888 series matched the Association champions, the St. Louis Browns, against the National League champions, the New York Giants. The St. Louis Browns had just captured their fourth and final pennant in 1888. This was a much weaker team than the 1886 version. Gone were Welch, Caruthers, Foutz, and Bushong. Prominent replacements included pitcher Charles "Silver" King and right fielder Tommy McCarthy, a future Hall of Famer.

Matched against them were the New York Giants, winners of their first National League pennant. The Giants had a tremendous group of stars, including Roger Connor, Buck Ewing, Tim Keefe, Jim O'Rourke, Monte Ward, and Mickey Welch, along with stars such as George Gore and Mike Tiernan. After six games, the Giants led the Browns, five victories to one. The players, officials, and umpires then boarded a train en route to St. Louis. When the train stopped at Pittsburgh, everyone got off to stretch his legs.

In addition to the usual group of writers, waiting to meet the train was Curt Welch, formerly of the St. Louis Browns. Welch confronted umpire "Honest John" Kelly at the station platform and accused him of having bet on the Giants. Welch had been drinking, and Kelly refused to dignify his charges with a response.

Curt Welch. After his retirement from the Browns, the drunken star accosted an umpire and accused him of favoring Chicago during the 1888 World Series. *Courtesy of Transcendental Graphics.*

The incident might have ended there if not for the intervention of Chris Von der Ahe, the owner of the St. Louis Browns. Von der Ahe was one of the most flamboyant owners in baseball history. German born, he knew little about baseball, but he founded the St. Louis team in the American Association during its maiden year of 1882 because he felt that a baseball team would be good for his saloon business, conveniently located near the ball park. A great showman, Von der Ahe was one of the first owners to use promotions to help draw crowds and always felt that the main objective of the game was to provide entertainment for the fans. What started as a way to build saloon traffic turned into a thriving business for Von der Ahe. The Browns won the American Association pennant in 1885, then repeated in 1886, 1887, and 1888. This winning streak thrust Von der Ahe even more into the public spotlight, and always the showman, Von der Ahe never shied away from controversy.

Unfortunately, the character traits that made Von der Ahe colorful also made him a problem during the 1888 World Series. Unhappy about being down five to one in a best-of-11 series, Von der Ahe told writers that he agreed with Welch, and that umpires Kelly and Gaffney had bet on the Giants and favored them in close decisions.

As can be imagined, these allegations created quite a storm. By the time the train arrived in St. Louis, Welch and Von der Ahe's charges had erupted into a full-blown scandal. Umpire John Gaffney angrily responded, "I don't mind anyone finding fault with my judgement, and I don't care about anyone's opinion of my work. But I do object to being called crooked, and I will quit the business before taking any more of that." "Honest John" Kelly added, "If Gaffney will not umpire any more games, I won't either."

At that point, the series appeared to be in jeopardy. Backed into a corner, Von der Ahe then claimed that he had been misquoted and had never charged the umpires with dishonesty. While Von der Ahe's statement that he had been misquoted was an obvious falsehood, it gave him a somewhat graceful way out of this mess.

More important, no proof was ever uncovered that there was any dishonesty in the series, and the incident was soon forgotten. In the end, New York won the series, six games to four.

Not long after that, Von der Ahe's temper resulted in another baseball scandal. In May of 1889, St. Louis second baseman Louis "Yank" Robinson was suspended and fined after a heated argument with Von der Ahe. By this time, tired of Von der Ahe's antics, his teammates threatened to strike, refusing to go to Kansas City for the St. Louis club's next series. A strike was averted, but St. Louis dropped three poorly played games in a row to Kansas City, which brought on charges that the club was intentionally losing to get back at Von der Ahe. There was no way to prove this, and the matter went no further.

The rest of the nineteenth century was relatively free of scandal. However, rumors or charges did occasionally surface. In late 1891, Chicago partisans charged some of the eastern teams with throwing games to help Boston win the pennant, and in 1892 Boston was accused of throwing games in the second half of the split season to necessitate an extra payday from a postseason playoff. However, no evidence was ever offered to substantiate either of these rumors. While gamblers remained active—for example, Chicago manager Cap Anson was once offered $10,000 by a gambler to keep star pitcher Clark Griffith out of an important game (Anson used Griffith in relief to save the game)—no evidence was ever uncovered of any game throwing.

The end of the nineteenth century brought new turbulence to baseball. After the American Association folded in 1891, the National League expanded to 12 teams, taking on four clubs from the Association. A 12-team pennant race proved unwieldy, and after the 1899 season the National League streamlined itself by dropping four clubs. At the same time, the minor league Western League, headed by Ban Johnson, changed its name to the American League and by 1901 claimed major league status, setting off a new baseball war.

As baseball prepared to face these new challenges of the twentieth century, one thing was clear: The game had overcome its early legacy of dishonest play, and baseball had grown to the point where it had truly become America's national game.

Chapter 5

The Calm
Before the Storm

As the twentieth century dawned, organized baseball again faced a period of uncertainty. On the one hand, the National League's move after the 1899 season to cut the league from 12 teams to eight eliminated weaker franchises and created a much stronger entity. At the same time, this move helped create an opening for Ban Johnson's Western League, renamed the American League in 1900, to claim major league status in 1901. Johnson's bold move touched off a three-year "baseball war," which proved to be extremely expensive for the baseball industry.

Baseball had faced "wars" before—the American Association war in 1882, which led to a ten-year run by that organization as a major league; the Union Association war in 1884, which proved unsuccessful; and the one-year Players' League war in 1890. In Ban Johnson, however, the National League found a worthy opponent, and one who soon brought the older league to its knees. The American League signed Larry Lajoie, Rube Waddell, Sam Crawford, Jack Chesbro, Ed Delahanty, and many of the older league's other leading stars, forcing the National League to sue for peace. In 1903 the rival leagues agreed to a treaty, which led to the formalization of the modern two-league system of organized ball. Most baseball historians consider the National League–American League peace treaty to be the beginning of modern baseball.

The coming of the American League proved to be a great boon to organized baseball. The American League lured many great stars and soon developed many more of their own, men such as Ty Cobb, Walter Johnson, Chief Bender, Eddie Plank, Eddie Collins, Tris Speaker, and Joe Wood, and the game rose to new heights in popularity.

In the early years of the twentieth century, baseball scandals appeared to be a thing of the past. Charles Ebbets, president of the Brooklyn Dodgers, summed up the feelings of most baseball executives by saying that "those who have followed baseball apparently had their confidence in its promoters established for all time by the summary action taken with players back in the 1870's

69

who were in league with gamblers and tried to hippodrome the professional games of that period."[1]

The new American League claimed equal vigilance in making sure that baseball would be free of gambling. On August 17, 1903, Ban Johnson ordered that all betting at baseball parks be banned. Baseball executives felt they were in control of the game and that the game was beyond corruption.

Unfortunately, there were warning signs that the picture was not as rosy as some baseball executives would have liked it to be. In writing about the 1903 World Series, Fred Lieb reported that "bettors with fistfuls of folding money camped in the lobby of the Vendome Hotel in Boston prior to the first game." The 1903 series marked the first World Series in modern baseball, and the betting activity was an eerie foreshadowing of the events of 1919, which produced baseball's greatest scandal.

In fact, the 1903 World Series should have opened the eyes of many baseball executives. Shortly before the series, gamblers approached Boston Red Sox catcher Lou Criger, offering to bribe him and star pitcher Cy Young to ensure a Pittsburgh victory. Criger refused the bribe and reported the attempt to Ban Johnson, exposing the plot. Criger was well rewarded for this action, as reported by Lee Allen:

> Because of his honest action, Criger for years was given a pension out of American League funds, long before the philosophy that all faithful employees should be pensioned became general. Suffering from tuberculosis in Arizona, he put the money to good use.[2]

The first real scandal of the twentieth century happened a short time later. The scandal did not involve a regular season game, but the City Series between the Chicago Cubs and the Chicago White Sox. In cities such as Chicago, Philadelphia, St. Louis, and Boston that housed teams in both the American League and the National League, a postseason City Series was quite popular in the early days of the century.

This scandal revolved around Jack Taylor, the Cubs' star pitcher. Long forgotten today, Taylor's career was noteworthy in many respects. Born in 1874 in New Straightsville, Ohio, Taylor first reached the major leagues with Chicago at the tail end of the 1898 season. He posted losing records the next three years with weak Chicago clubs, but in 1902 the fortunes of both Taylor and the Cubs improved. During that year, Taylor had a record of 23 wins and 11 losses, and a league-leading earned-run average of 1.33.

The preceding season, in 1901, Taylor had begun one of the most remarkable "ironman" pitching feats of the twentieth century. For a five-year period, from June 20, 1901, to August 9, 1906, Taylor completed all 187 games he started, including one 19-inning game and one 18-inning game. He also appeared in relief in 15 games. During the 1904 season, Taylor pitched 39 complete games—a modern major league record that may never be broken.

Jack O'Connor. A hard-living manager, O'Connor gave orders that led to the 1910-batting title scandal. *Photograph by Patrice Kelly.*

Taylor continued to enjoy success in 1903, finishing with a record of 21 wins and 14 losses and an impressive 2.45 ERA. The City Series between the White Sox and Cubs was played between October 1 and October 15, 1903. Coming off an outstanding season, Taylor was naturally the choice to start the first game of the series, and he handily mastered the seventh-place White Sox by a score of 11–0. However, Taylor lost his other three starts by scores of 10–2, 9–3, and 4–2.

Cubs President Jim Hart was suspicious of Taylor's work during the series. In December, Hart traded Taylor and rookie catcher Larry McLean to the St. Louis Cardinals for pitcher Mike O'Neill and young Mordecai "Three-Finger" Brown. Brown developed into one of the great pitchers of all time and was a linchpin in the great Chicago Cubs teams during the next decade.

In early 1904, Taylor visited Chicago with his new team, the Cardinals. Responding to jeers from the people in the stands over his poor performance in the City Series, Taylor stated, "Why should I have won? I got $100.00 from Hart for winning and I got $500.00 for losing."[3]

Hart then went public with his charges of dishonesty on the part of Taylor. No action was taken against Taylor, however.

The next episode in the Taylor scandal took place in July 1904, when Taylor was accused of throwing a game against the Pittsburgh Pirates. This time Gary Herrmann, president of the Cincinnati Reds and chairman of the National Commission, baseball's ruling council, declared that Taylor was "not an honest

ball player." Taylor was
allowed to continue playing,
but after the season an investigation was held. Herrmann focused strongly on
Taylor's connection to
"Slim" Dinneen, a Pitts-
burgh gambler.

During the hearing,
Taylor testified that he and
teammate Jake Beckley, a
former Pirate and future
Hall of Famer, had been on
a drinking and gambling
spree the night before the
game. He credited his poor
performance in the game to
wildness rather than dis-
honesty. Regarding his connection to "Slim," Taylor
stated:

"Slim," the fellow Herr-
mann referred to, was
introduced to me that
night and went down-
town with us. We had a
couple of hours sleep
and foolishly renewed
drinking when we woke
up. We stopped in a
saloon on the way to the
hotel and Slim said,
"Taylor, I'll bet $10.00

Jack Taylor, who was accused of throwing games
in the Chicago City Series in 1903. *Photograph
by Patrice Kelly.*

if you pitch today." I told him I was not in any shape to pitch for any man's money
and hoped Nichols would not work me. Jake was as unfitted to play as I was. Both
of us were ordered in the game and we lost, 5–2. They made seven hits off me,
but I was wild, giving five bases on balls and hitting a couple of basemen.

Many roasts were handed to me from the stands and I heard that fellow "Slim"
yell to me, "no wonder you are wild, you slob, you were drunk last night!" All
the players knew the condition we were in and Nichols must have been on, but
he gave no reproof to me.

I am not a saint. I have generally kept myself in shape during the playing
season, but at times have dissipated. I have shot craps, and have played poker.
But that doesn't show that I am a baseball crook and I challenge anyone to prove
that I ever made a dishonest dollar on the diamond.[4]

On February 15, the National League Board of Directors handed down its verdict: Taylor was acquitted of the charge of throwing games, but he was found guilty of bad conduct and fined $300. Taylor angrily refused to pay the $300 fine, saying, "they had no case against me for crookedness over in Pittsburgh."[5] Taylor hired former baseball star and future Hall of Famer John Montgomery Ward as his attorney, instructing him to "fight the case to the last ditch."[6]

Shortly after the verdict was reached, W. H. Locke, the Pittsburgh Pirates club secretary, sent a letter to Gary Herrmann discussing the case. The letter stated, in part:

> Believing that Taylor was guilty, he [club president Barney Dreyfuss] thinks it was unfortunate that we could not make out a stronger case. This is the popular opinion here, but the newspapers are willing to drop the case and allow the people to forget it as they surely will if the baseball men refuse to talk about it. Of course they cannot refuse to print any news that develops and the case will be kept before the public as long as Taylor continues to talk. What Mr. Dreyfuss fears most, is that the St. Louis club may consent to pay the $300.00 fine. He believes this would be a very serious mistake.
>
> Taylor would promise not to talk about it, but he could not be depended upon to keep his word and it would put the league in a bad light to have it known that the alleged punishment of Taylor was merely a bluff. Mr. Dreyfuss says that Nichols showed by his testimony before the board that he is willing to take a desperate chance to keep the player and may enter into some deal with him.[7]

Locke went on to say that Dreyfuss thought it would be a good thing for the league if St. Louis could get rid of Taylor and Beckley, preferably sending them to the American League. In a prophetic statement, Locke concluded the letter by saying, "if Taylor escapes punishment the crusade will be a difficult one, as gamblers will be convinced that the league is only bluffing."

The next month Taylor was called before the National Commission for a hearing on the charges from the 1903 Chicago City Series. The National Commission consisted of Chairman Gary Herrmann, along with American League President Ban Johnson and National League President Harry Pulliam.

At the hearing, Chicago President James Hart submitted three affidavits from people who overheard Taylor's statement about being paid $500 to lose the games. Hart also stated that he could provide many more affidavits along the same lines. Despite this, the commission ruled that "the evidence submitted, alleging that the player made certain remarks relative to the post season games of 1903, is insufficient to find him guilty of conduct detrimental to the welfare and good repute of the game."[8]

After being acquitted, Taylor resumed his pitching career for the Cardinals. Taylor was again accused of throwing games during the 1905 City Series between the St. Louis Browns and the St. Louis Cardinals, won by the Browns five games to two. No action was taken on these charges, and Taylor was back with St. Louis in 1906. On July 1, 1906, Taylor was traded to the Cubs, of all teams, for catcher Pete Noonan, pitcher Fred Beebe, and cash. Taylor finished the 1906 season with a record of 20-12. Taylor's career went downhill quickly after that. In 1907 he compiled a record of 7-5 with the Cubs and then drifted to the minor leagues. Taylor died in 1938 at the age of 64 in Columbus, Ohio.

The Taylor scandal was soon forgotten after 1905. Unfortunately, as Pittsburgh's W. H. Locke had predicted, Taylor's whitewashing sent a message to gamblers and players that baseball's days of vigilance against corruption were over.

The next scandal involved Rube Waddell of the Philadelphia Athletics and the 1905 World Series. Waddell, one of the greatest pitchers of all time and a member of the Baseball Hall of Fame, was also an eccentric whose devotion to drinking and hard living was responsible for shortening his major league career and sending him to an early grave. But while Waddell was in top form, he was fabulous. His lifetime earned-run average was 2.16, and in 1904 he set a modern major league record with 349 strikeouts, a record that stood for many years.

In 1905 Waddell's career reached its zenith. He led the American League in wins with 27 against 10 losses and also led the league in winning percentage (.730), strikeouts (287), and earned-run average (1.48). He was, without a doubt, the dominant pitcher in the American League in 1905.

On September 1 of that year, however, Rube injured his shoulder during some friendly horseplay with teammate Andy Coakley. The injury limited his effectiveness the rest of the season and led Philadelphia A's manager Connie Mack to keep him out of that fall's World Series with the New York Giants.

With Waddell out, the Giants won the series four games to one. The series is considered one of the all-time classics, as all five games were won by shutouts. The immortal Christy Mathewson pitched three shutouts for the Giants and Joe McGinnity added another. Chief Bender won Philadelphia's lone game.

Rumors surfaced that Waddell's injury in September was actually deliberate. It was claimed that he was being paid by gamblers to stay out of the series. However, no real proof was ever forthcoming, and given Waddell's reputation and life-style, the injury from horseplay is much more likely than the game fixing charge.

The 1908 season was a classic in baseball history. In both leagues the pennant races went down to the wire. In the American League, the Detroit Tigers won their second straight pennant, edging Cleveland by only one-half game. Chicago finished one and one-half games back, and the fourth-place St. Louis Browns were only six and one-half games out of first.

In the National League, the New York Giants and the Chicago Cubs finished in a dead heat. This was the year of the famous Merkle incident, in which young Giant Fred Merkle was called out at second base in a late-season game against Chicago for failing to touch second, thus invalidating the winning run. The

game was called a draw, and a decision was made that it would be replayed
if it affected the pennant race. When Chicago and New York finished the
season tied for first place, the game was replayed, and the Chicago Cubs won
to take the pennant. The Giants finished tied for second with Pittsburgh, one
game behind.

The 1908 season produced many events that are still remembered today,
including the Merkle incident and one of the greatest pitching duels of all time,
when Cleveland's ace Addie Joss threw a perfect game to defeat Chicago's Ed
Walsh, a 40-game winner that year, by a score of 1–0.

In addition to these classic games, the 1908 National League race produced two cases of attempted bribery. One case received great publicity soon
after it happened, and the other one did not come out until the aftermath of
the Black Sox scandal.

One of the incidents involved the season-ending replay of the Merkle game,
the game that won the pennant for the Chicago Cubs. After the game, rumors
began to circulate that "an employee of the Giants" unsuccessfully attempted
to bribe Bill Klem, who was umpiring the game behind home plate. Klem, considered by most the greatest umpire in the history of baseball and a tower of
integrity, angrily refused the bribe, and as stated earlier, the Cubs prevailed
that day.

The story of the incident came out during the off-season. The attempted
briber was identified as Dr. Joseph M. Creamer, the Giants' team physician and
a man well known in professional sports circles. Creamer was a close friend
of Giants' manager John McGraw, and as it turned out had been hired without
the knowledge of Giants President John T. Brush.

Klem stated that shortly before he took the field, Creamer approached him
under the stands with a large wad of bills and said, "Here's $2,500. It's yours
if you'll give all the close decisions to the Giants and see that they win sure.
You know who is behind me and you needn't be afraid of anything. You will
have a good job for the rest of your life."[9]

Creamer angrily denied the charges, stating, "it's a job to ruin me. I never
saw Klem to speak to him on that day or any other day. I never tried to bribe
anyone in my life. I have not decided what I should do yet, but I have been
advised to seek legal redress."[10]

The National League Board of Directors voted to expel Creamer from every
park in organized baseball for life. The threatened lawsuit against Klem and
the National League never materialized.

While the league took action against Creamer, it never investigated who
was really behind the bribery offer. In commenting on baseball's lack of vigor
in prosecuting the case, Harold Seymour wrote:

> The Commission cited lack of evidence as its reason for doing so little. New
> information shows that it took this course on advice from Brush. After consulting

an attorney, he advised Herrmann: "While the individual mentioned is unques-
tionably an S.O.B. it would be hazardous for any one financially responsible . . .
to publicly charge him with having committed the offense." Brush sought to turn
the case to his advantage by using it to show the public "how next to impossible
it is to corrupt the game, even if anyone was disposed to do so." If as little as
possible was said, the press and the public would turn their attention to the coming pennant race, he added.[11]

The second incident involved Horace Fogel, former president of the
Phillies (and a man whom we will discuss further in this chapter), catcher
Charles "Red" Doonin, and first baseman Kitty Bransfield. New York gamblers
had tried to bribe them to throw games to the New York Giants in 1908, thereby
helping to assure the Giants of winning the pennant.

Doonin, Bransfield, Mike Doolan, Otto Knabe, Sherry Magee, and other
Phillies players were offered tens of thousands of dollars to throw the games,
but they indignantly refused. In fact, Doonin reported that Bransfield, a solid
5'11" and 207 pounds, threw one of the gamblers down a staircase after refusing the bribe. None of this was publicly known at the time, but players came
forward in investigations after the 1919 Black Sox scandal. Said Doonin, "I've
never said anything about this before because the other players and myself
believed it would be in the best interest of baseball not to say anything as none
of us accepted any of the bribes." Doonin also reported that he was actually
kidnapped during the final series against the Giants and locked in a room in
the Bowery district of New York, but he escaped and played in the series.

The bribery offers apparently made the Phillies more determined than ever
to beat the Giants. Behind the pitching of Harry "Giant Killer" Coveleskie, the
Phillies won some key games against the Giants down the stretch, helping to
force a tie at the end of the season and ultimately depriving the Giants of the
pennant.

The next major scandal was, in many ways, one of the most sordid ones
in the history of baseball, because the motive was not personal gain for the corrupt individuals, but spite against a fellow player. This scandal involved the
1910 batting title and the attempts of two members of the St. Louis Browns to
deprive the great Ty Cobb of this honor.

The root of the trouble occurred in March 1910, when the Chalmers Motor
Company announced that it would present a new automobile to the winner of
the batting title in each league. Chalmers made a highly desirable product, particularly in those days before the widespread ownership of automobiles.

The background to the incident, however, goes back even further. Ty
Cobb, arguably the greatest baseball player of all time, broke into the major
leagues in 1905 with the Detroit Tigers. Already a fierce competitor, Cobb was
deeply affected by his father's violent death just two weeks before he was sold
to the Detroit club. Years later, when asked why he fought so hard, Cobb
replied:

> I did it for my father, who was an exalted man. They killed him when he was
> still young. They blew his head off the same week I became a major leaguer. He
> never got to see me play. But I knew he was watching me and I never let him
> down.[12]

To compound Cobb's misery, he was viciously hazed by Detroit Tiger
veterans. Tough treatment of rookies by veterans was fairly common in those
days of baseball, but rather than playing along until things subsided, Cobb
reacted, which led to increased harassment of him and permanent ill will with
many of his teammates.

Cobb's popularity as a player never really improved. He was all business on the diamond, which enabled him to set numerous batting records, including a lifetime average of .367, perhaps the one record that will never be
broken.

While Cobb was widely disliked by his fellow players, Cleveland's Napoleon "Larry" Lajoie was one of the most popular players of his day. One of the
great second basemen of all time, Lajoie began his career with Philadelphia
in the National League in 1896 and later was a fixture with Cleveland in the
American League. Lajoie was so popular that the club was nicknamed after
him, commonly referred to as the Cleveland Naps. The club's current nickname, the Indians, was adopted after Lajoie's retirement.

Lajoie's career had been in a downward mode coming into the 1910 season. In 1910, however, Lajoie had a great year, battling Cobb down to the wire
for the batting title. Nevertheless, at the end of the season Cobb was com-
fortably ahead in the race and sat out the last two games with an eye ail-
ment.

Cleveland played its final two games of the season in a doubleheader in
St. Louis against the Browns. In his first at-bat, Lajoie hit a triple over the center
fielder's head. He went to the plate eight more times that day with the following
results:

- Six bunt singles down the third base line. St. Louis rookie third baseman
  John "Red" Corriden played on the line well behind third base and
  had no chance to get Lajoie on any of these occasions.
- A bunt down the third base line to advance a runner. This time he was
  credited with a sacrifice.
- Grounded to shortstop. Future Hall of Famer Bobby Wallace fielded the
  ball but threw wildly.

Lajoie was credited with one sacrifice, one triple, and seven singles (including Wallace's wild throw). For the game he had turned in an eight-for-eight performance which, according to the papers, meant that he had edged out Cobb
for the batting title.

An uproar was immediately raised. An article in the *Detroit Free Press*
summed up one sportswriter's opinions of the incident:

ST. LOUIS TEAM "LAYS DOWN" TO LET LAJOIE WIN
Gets Eight Hits in Race with Cobb When Opponents Refuse to Field "Gift" Bunts

ST. LOUIS, Oct. 9—A palpable case of "lay down" on the part of members of the St. Louis club occurred here today, enabling Nap Lajoie to make eight hits and either come very close or go ahead of Ty Cobb in the race for the Chalmers 30 automobile and batting championship.

After today's farce—a hippodrome which should be investigated by the highest authorities—the winner probably will not be known until the official averages are made public weeks from now.

Lajoie got one hit even halfway legitimate today—a fly to center his first time up. It went for a triple, although any kind of fielding by Northen of St. Louis could have converted it into an easy out.

The hate-Ty-Cobb-campaign never was so miserably evident as today.

The other seven hits by Lajoie were the product of bunts laid down toward third base and shortstop and which the St. Louis men allowed to roll, without any sort of fielding effort. Six of them went to Red Corriden, playing third, and one to Wallace, at short. In each instance, while the ball was fielded perfectly, it was not thrown to first.

According to local figures, Lajoie had to make eight hits out of as many times at bat to catch and go ahead of Cobb. Lajoie seldom uses the bunt. Today he did—through connivance that has made a mockery of American baseball.[13]

An investigation was immediately launched by Ban Johnson, president of the American League. He started by questioning St. Louis third baseman Red Corriden. Corriden told Johnson that "my orders were to play Lajoie back on the edge of the grass." In answer to Johnson's probing, Corriden told him that St. Louis manager Jack "Peach Pie" O'Connor had given him those orders. Johnson also learned that Browns pitcher-coach Harry Howell had authored an anonymous note to the St. Louis official scorer, promising him a suit of clothes if he gave Lajoie the benefit of the doubt on all close plays. Howell also visited the press box several times during the game to inquire how Lajoie's bunts were being scored.

O'Connor had a long history of sordid dealings. Born in St. Louis in 1869, O'Connor broke into major league baseball with Cincinnati in the old American Association in 1887. Primarily a catcher, O'Connor's playing career continued until the 1910 season, when as manager of the Browns he appeared in one game. A lifetime .263 hitter in the major leagues, his best year was 1890 with Columbus in the American Association, when he hit .324.

Throughout his career O'Connor was known as a hard drinking, hard living player. The 1892 *Spalding Guide* reported:

> On July 3, President Kramer of the American Association expelled John O'Connor of the Columbus club from the Association, for habitual drunkenness, disorderly conduct and insubordination. He was suspended by the club the day before without pay, for disgraceful conduct.[14]

Harry Howell. "Handsome Harry" helped tip the scales for the 1910 batting title. *Photograph by Patrice Kelly.*

O'Connor resurfaced with Cleveland in the National League the next year after the demise of the American Association.

On a later occasion, while with the Browns, O'Connor got into a heated argument with umpire Jack McNulty and broke McNulty's jaw. O'Connor was forced to pay $1,250 in damages for this act.

By contrast, the 1910 scandal was the first of its kind for Harry Howell. Nicknamed Handsome Harry, Howell broke into the major leagues with Brooklyn of the National League in 1898. He jumped to the Baltimore Orioles during the American League–National League war in 1901 and moved over to the Browns in 1904. Pitching with weak teams, Howell finished with a record of 131 wins and 146 losses, but with a very respectable 2.74 earned-run average.

When Johnson questioned O'Connor and Howell, they denied any wrongdoing. O'Connor feigned amazement, claiming that "Lajoie outguessed us."

After the October 9 doubleheader, the unofficial figures showed Lajoie edging out Cobb for the batting title. However, when the official figures came out, Cobb was declared the winner of the batting title, with an average of .385 compared to Lajoie's .384. The Chalmers Motor 'Company presented both Cobb and Lajoie with new automobiles as a gesture of goodwill.

The results of Johnson's investigation were that Corriden and Lajoie were absolved of all blame. O'Connor and Howell were also officially "cleared," but both were immediately dropped by the St. Louis club and found the doors of the American League closed to them. Ban Johnson's reason for publicly clearing

O'Connor and Howell is generally believed to be the wish to avoid exposure of the scandal, but some historians feel that O'Connor's role in helping to recruit players for Johnson during the American League's early days was a factor in Johnson's decision.

O'Connor, who was in the middle of a two-year contract, later sued the St. Louis club and won $5,000. While he never appeared in organized baseball again, he did wind up returning to professional baseball, playing a role in the founding of the outlaw United States League in 1912 and managing the St. Louis club when that league became the Federal League in 1913. By the time the Federal League claimed major league status in 1914, O'Connor was out of the picture. He became a saloon keeper in St. Louis and lived until 1937.

After being thrown out of the American League, Howell later resurfaced as a minor league umpire. He lived until 1956, passing away in Spokane, Washington.

Corriden, who by all accounts was blameless in the affair, bounced around the major leagues until 1915, when he moved to the minors for a long career as a player and a manager. In 1931 he became a coach with the Cubs under Rogers Hornsby, continuing in that job until 1941, when he became a coach for Brooklyn. He moved over to the Yankees in 1947, to San Diego in 1948, and to the White Sox in 1950. He became manager of the White Sox on May 27, 1950, and managed the club through the end of the season. He joined the Dodgers' scouting staff in 1951 and retired in 1958. He died in 1959 in Indianapolis.

The controversy over the 1910 batting title resurfaced in 1981 when Paul MacFarlane, associate editor of the *Sporting News*, uncovered evidence to show that errors had been made in calculating both Cobb's and Lajoie's averages. According to MacFarlane, one of Cobb's games was counted twice, and the correct averages for the year should show Lajoie edging out Cobb, .383 to .382. Given Lajoie's seven gift hits on the last day of the season, however, it is difficult to argue that Cobb did not deserve to be considered the batting champion.

At least two other batting titles in baseball history created controversy. In the Pacific Coast League in 1934, Joe DiMaggio was in a close batting race with minor league star Ox Eckhardt. On the last day of the season, DiMaggio had four hits in the first game of the twin bill, three on bunts toward a pulled-back third baseman (shades of Red Corriden), and the fourth on an easy fly to center that was allowed to drop for a double. To DiMaggio's credit, he argued with the scorer between games, convincing him to change the double to an error. DiMaggio said, "I don't want to lead the league if I don't deserve to." Eckhardt ended up beating DiMaggio for the batting title with a .399 mark to DiMaggio's .398.

The other controversial batting title occurred in 1976, when George Brett edged Hal McRae by one point for the American League batting title. Brett clinched the title when a short fly ball dropped in front of Twins outfielder Steve

Brye and skipped over his head for an inside-the-park home run. McRae believed the misplay was deliberate and charged the Twins with racism. However, no evidence was forthcoming to substantiate the charges.

While not a complete whitewash, such as the Taylor affair was, baseball's exoneration of Howell and O'Connor, and the fact that Howell was later allowed back into organized baseball as an umpire, showed that baseball had forgotten the lessons learned in the 1870s. A warning from the past came from baseball great Al Spalding, who had lived through those corrupt times as a player, manager, and club executive. Spalding warned that the publicity being given to betting on the World Series was a danger to baseball.

The next scandal occurred during the 1912 season and centered on charges brought by Horace Fogel, the president of the Philadelphia Phillies. Fogel, a sportswriter by trade, had carried on a close association with baseball for a number of years and had managed the Indianapolis club in the American Association for part of the 1887 season and the New York Giants for part of the 1902 season.

In November 1909, it was announced that the Philadelphia Phillies had been sold for $350,000 to a group headed by Fogel, who was named club president. As it turned out, two-thirds of the stock in the club was really owned by Charles P. Taft and Charles W. Murphy, both of whom were also involved in the ownership of the Chicago club, against league rules.

A controversial character often held up to ridicule, Fogel vociferously complained about the conduct of the National League umpires, claiming that they showed favoritism toward other clubs. These charges did not do much for Fogel's popularity in baseball's executive councils, and Fogel and National League President Tom Lynch became bitter enemies.

In 1912 Fogel published an article in the *Chicago Post* in which he claimed that Roger Bresnahan, manager of the St. Louis Cardinals and former catcher for the Giants, had helped his former team win by having the Cardinals "take it easy" against them. He also accused league president Lynch and the umpires of conspiring to help the Giants win the pennant.

Lynch furiously demanded Fogel's expulsion, and on October 17, 1912, Fogel was tried by the National League directors on seven counts of violating baseball's rules. He was found guilty on five counts and barred from the National League forever. It is interesting to note that shortly after that, St. Louis manager Roger Bresnahan was released by the club with four years remaining on his contract.

At the time, the perception of Fogel was that of a buffoon creating spurious charges. Few believed Fogel, and the scandal did not have lingering consequences. However, in light of the widespread corruption in baseball that was revealed at the time of the Black Sox scandal, looking back one wonders whether Fogel was indeed a clown, or a crusader trying to clean up the game.

After leaving baseball, Fogel returned to the newspaper business. He resurfaced briefly in an attempt to become involved with the Federal League. His name again came up in baseball circles in 1920 when he corroborated Red Doonin's story about the attempt to fix the 1908 pennant race.

At this point in baseball history, corruption was growing rapidly. A central figure in this activity was Hal Chase, a notoriously corrupt player who was to haunt baseball for a number of years. Chase's exploits were occurring throughout this period, but rather than deal with them in chronological sequence, we will save discussion of the scandals involving Chase for the next chapter.

A scandal very similar to the Fogel affair occurred in late 1916. Again, the National League had a close pennant race, and again the New York Giants were involved.

Going into the final two games of the season, the Brooklyn Dodgers were locked in a close race with the Philadelphia Phillies. The Dodgers were managed by Wilbert Robinson, one of the great characters in baseball history. Robinson, now in the Baseball Hall of Fame, had been a coach for the Giants and McGraw's closest friend until the two had a falling out, which led to Robinson's taking over the reins of the Dodgers.

The Giants went into Brooklyn on October 2 to play the last two games against the Dodgers. Brooklyn needed to win both games to clinch the pennant over the Phillies. Brooklyn won the first game, and on October 3 they were leading the Giants, seemingly on their way to a pennant. At that point, McGraw stormed off the field, calling his players quitters. Brooklyn won the game and the pennant, and the newspapers interpreted McGraw's outburst as a charge that his team had let Brooklyn win to help them capture the pennant.

There is definitely some logic behind this charge—Robinson was friendly with many of the Giants, and on his team were former Giants Rube Marquard and Chief Meyers. There was also some bad blood between the Phillies and the Giants, emanating from the Phillies' ruining the Giants' chances during the 1908 season.

When confronted by reporters, McGraw denied charging that his players would try to lose the game. However, he did say that his players had refused to obey orders and had disregarded his signals. Such behavior was totally out of character for a team piloted by McGraw, who was aptly nicknamed "The Little Napoleon."

The controversy raged for a short time, and it looked as if an investigation would be undertaken. Baseball, however, was not eager to expose its dirty linen, and the furor soon died away.

A similar incident, this time pitting a club owner against his players, occurred on September 8, 1917. St. Louis Browns owner Phil Ball publicly accused two of his players, shortstop Doc Lavan and second baseman Del Pratt, of "laying down" during that day's loss to the Chicago White Sox. Lavan and Pratt demanded an apology, and when none was forthcoming, they sued for slander.

No action was taken to investigate whether Ball's charges were true. Indeed, the concentration of baseball executives was on convincing Pratt and Lavan to drop their lawsuits. After a fact-finding mission to St. Louis, Ban Johnson "passed the St. Louis trouble over lightly," saying that the lawsuits were ridiculous and would only serve to cause the players trouble. He blamed "outside influencers" and said that the players would come to see they were being badly advised.

Johnson's view was generally supported by the press. The *Sporting News* called for the players to drop their suits, while at the same time ridiculing the scandal, which they said was becoming a yearly event. "If the Browns quit on their manager, they have quit on every team in the league, for they haven't won a series from any team in the league."[15]

For a while it appeared that the libel suits, with each player claiming $50,000 in damages, would continue. However, both players desperately wanted to get away from the St. Louis Browns, and Phil Ball told them that no deal would be made until they agreed to drop the lawsuits.

With additional pressure from executives, Lavan agreed to drop his suit and was promptly traded to Washington. Pratt vowed to continue his suit, and in fact, his trade to the Yankees was held up for a number of weeks pending final disposition. The trade finally went through, and after a great deal of posturing, Pratt finally agreed to settle.

Other rumors of game fixing surfaced periodically, including some vague rumors about the 1914 and 1918 World Series. While there does not seem to be any evidence in either case, such talk presaged the events of 1919.

Corruption was growing in baseball by leaps and bounds, and rather than attacking the problem, baseball was doing its best to cover it up. The situation was reminiscent of the 1870s, and during the next few years baseball's laissez-faire attitude would lead to the Black Sox scandal, which put the game's very survival in doubt. The atmosphere in baseball at the time, however, can best be summed up by repeating a conversation that Washington catcher Eddie Ainsmith had with prominent sports memorabilia collector Joel Platt shortly before Ainsmith's death. Ainsmith told of John McGraw offering opposing players money for tipping pitches to his batters. Referring to the Black Sox players, Ainsmith called them "poor s.o.b.'s—everybody was doing it in those days."[16]

Emboldened by baseball's lack of zeal in prosecuting the scandals of the early 1900s, gamblers and corrupt players continued their activities. Leading the way was first baseman "Prince Hal" Chase.

Chapter 6

Hal Chase

While baseball managed to reduce severely the corruption in its ranks after the Louisville scandal in 1877, it was never able to eliminate the cause of the problem – gambling. While not the dominant, all-pervasive force that they were during the National Association days, gamblers continued to play a part in the baseball scene in the late nineteenth and early twentieth centuries. Fans made friendly wagers with each other on the outcome of a game or a pennant race; baseball pools were started in various eastern cities, attracting laborers, casual fans, and even youths; and wealthy individuals – "sportsmen" such as George M. Cohan, Harry Sinclair, and Harry Payne Whitney – would bet huge amounts of money on individual games or the World Series "just to keep things interesting."

While baseball gambling rose steadily during the first two decades of the twentieth century, it positively surged during World War I. The Wilson administration's "work or fight" order served to push able-bodied males into "essential" industries (particularly the manufacturing of war-related products), or into the service. Baseball shortened its season during 1918, and many minor leagues suspended play. Much harder hit, however, were the race tracks, which for the most part were closed for the duration of the war.

The race tracks had served as a congregating point for the heavy gamblers, and the races served as an outlet for their betting impulses. Shut off from this venue, gamblers flocked to major league baseball parks, and their gambling activity focused on baseball rather than the horses. Along with the dramatic increase in the amount of money bet on baseball games came the temptation for gamblers to create a "sure thing" – that is, to fix the outcome of games. This created an extremely dangerous situation for major league baseball.

Unfortunately, the leadership of professional baseball was unable or unwilling to deal with this challenge. While bemoaning and denouncing the increase in gambling in public, baseball owners and executives took little concrete action to stem the tide of baseball gambling. There were a number of reasons for this failure to act: Executives believed that most ball players were essentially honest and would not succumb to temptation; many baseball owners, such as Charles Stoneham and Harry Frazee, traveled in the same social

84

Hal Chase. "Prince Hal" was at the center of many of the game's scandals during the early twentieth century. *Photograph by Patrice Kelly.*

set as gamblers such as Harry Sinclair and gambling boss Arnold Rothstein; and, most important, there was a general perception among owners that a certain amount of gambling was good for business, since it created more interest in the games. As a result, despite an occasional raid on nickel-and-dime gamblers at ball parks, the high-stakes gambling element was able to move their operations from the race track to the ball park relatively unmolested.

The worst city of all for baseball gambling was Boston. Boston gamblers essentially "took over" the Boston American and National League parks as their bases of operations. Commenting on the prominence of gambling in Boston, sportswriter Jim Crusinberry wrote, "Although gambling may take place more or less in all big league parks, there is no other city where it is allowed to flourish so openly."

Boston gamblers even went so far as to interfere with the playing of games if the results of the game were threatening the outcome of their wagers. For example, on June 16, 1917, the Chicago White Sox were visiting the Boston Red Sox for an important series between these two main contenders for the American League championship. With the home club trailing by a score of 2–0 in the top of the fifth inning, rain began to fall, an event which gamblers knew could lead to cancellation of the game, saving them from paying off their bets. In order to help events along, a large crowd of gamblers stormed onto the field to create a delay, which they hoped would give the rain time to intensify, making the cancellation of the game inevitable. As it turned out, the game was continued, and the White Sox won by a score of 7–2.

The rise in gambling led to the greatest increase in baseball corruption since the National Association days. The central figure in much of the corruption was the legendary Harold "Prince Hal" Chase.

Hal Chase was born on February 13, 1883, at Los Gatos, California. He began his baseball career while attending Santa Clara University, playing on the college team in 1902, 1903, and 1904. He supplemented his college experience by playing semipro ball during the summers. During a game in 1904, Chase's play caught the attention of Jim Morley, president and owner of the Los Angeles club in the Pacific Coast League. Later that month, Chase left Santa Clara to sign a contract with the Los Angeles club.

Chase's PCL debut occurred on March 27, 1904, and he immediately made a strong impression. By March 30, the *Los Angeles Times* wrote, "Chase has a future before him that any ball player might look forward to. He plays first base as well as anyone would care to see." Chase had a good year in Los Angeles, hitting .279 in 173 games. Much more impressive than his hitting, however, was his fielding. While first base was traditionally a haven for weak fielders, Chase turned the position into an art form. He stood further away from the bag than his predecessors, allowing him to make fielding plays that were impossible for others. His agility and quickness were legendary, allowing him to cover a tremendous amount of territory and still get back to the bag to record a putout. Players, sports writers, and fans were impressed with Chase's tremendous skills.

After the 1904 season, Chase was drafted by the New York American League club. At that time the club was called the Highlanders, in reference to their playing field, which was on some of the highest ground in Manhattan. During Chase's era, the club's nickname was changed to the Yankees.

Chase's connection with controversy began almost immediately. After Chase had been drafted, Los Angeles owner Morley claimed that Chase's selection had been illegal, and it was said that Chase had again signed with Los Angeles. New York manager Clark Griffith dispatched a representative to bring Chase to New York's spring training camp, and on March 28 Hal Chase joined the club.

Before the end of his rookie season in New York, Chase was being hailed as a superstar. His defensive play was magnificent, and he revolutionized the way first base was played. He developed the now-common tactics of charging bunts and moving into the outfield to retrieve cutoff throws. A master of the spectacular play, Chase quickly became a crowd favorite.

After a disappointing batting performance in 1906, his first year, when he hit only .249, Chase finished third in the American League batting race in 1906 with a .323 average. This solidified his position as a star, and on January 26, 1907, the *Sporting Life* called Chase "perhaps the biggest drawing card in baseball."

Chase was offered a contract for $3,500 for the 1907 season, which he rejected. He became coach of the St. Mary's College baseball team, which included future Hall of Famer Harry Hooper, and led St. Mary's to an undefeated season. He then began playing with San Jose in the outlaw California State League (outlaw leagues were those not affiliated with organized baseball and not recognizing major league baseball's reserve clause) before agreeing to join the Yankees for $4,000. Chase had played winter ball in the California State League after the 1905 and 1906 seasons, and he would continue to play post-season ball with California State League teams until baseball's ruling body, the National Commission, barred players in organized baseball from playing in outlaw leagues.

Chase enjoyed another good season in 1907, hitting .287. Controversy followed him that year when his common-law wife, Nellie Heffernan, was arrested for helping the wife of Highlander trainer Mike Martin dispose of the body of Mrs. Martin's dead infant. Mrs. Chase, who did not actually marry Hal until 1908, was later absolved of any charges.

Chase again became embroiled in controversy in 1908, when he jumped the New York club in a pique on September 3 and signed with Stockton in the outlaw California State League. Much of Chase's dissatisfaction was due to the fact that veteran Kid Elberfeld had replaced Clark Griffith as manager for the 1908 season—a post that Chase himself had coveted. Chase sulked, and during the 1908 season there were rumors that he was "laying down"—that is, not playing up to the best of his ability.

Chase finished the 1908 season with Stockton and then applied for reinstatement to organized baseball. After paying a $200 fine, he signed with the Yankees again for the 1909 season. Despite being stricken with smallpox, which kept him out until May 3, Chase had another good season in 1909, hitting .283, a 26-point improvement over his 1908 performance.

For the 1909 season, Kid Elberfeld was replaced as manager by George Stallings. Stallings, later to be the manager of the 1914 "Miracle Braves," was a brilliant manager, but a strict disciplinarian. He and Chase did not get along well from the start, a situation exacerbated by the fact that Chase wanted the manager's job for himself.

By 1910 the Chase-Stallings feud had developed into open warfare. Although the club thrived under Stallings's leadership, improving from last place in 1908 to second in 1910, Chase launched an all-out campaign to have Stallings replaced. Among his tactics was throwing games—not putting forth his best effort in an attempt to hurt the team's record. Chase's methods of throwing games were very subtle; in fact, he often made his own misplays look like the result of a bad throw from one of his teammates. Stallings, however, was not fooled, and in late September 1910 Stallings publicly charged Chase with throwing games.

Club president Frank Farrell, an unsavory character in his own right, summoned Stallings to New York to explain his charges, and the two met on

September 22. Farrell exonerated Chase, and on September 23 American
League President Ban Johnson backed up Farrell, saying that "Stallings has
utterly failed in his accusations against Chase. He tried to besmirch the
character of a sterling player. Anybody who knows Hal Chase knows he is not
guilty of the accusations made against him." A few days later, despite his success on the field, Stallings was fired as manager of New York and Chase was
appointed to replace him. Chase got off to a good start as manager, winning
10 of the season's final 14 games in 1910. In 1911, however, the Yankees
slumped to sixth place, and Chase was succeeded by Harry Wolverton.

By 1911, Chase had already developed a reputation for dishonesty and corruption. In his excellent book *Baseball as I Have Known It*, longtime sportswriter Fred Lieb relates the following story which took place that year:

> Jim Price, my sports editor at the Press, gave me this summary of Chase soon
> after I reported for duty. "He is a remarkable fielder. I don't think anyone ever
> played first base as well as Hal Chase can play it — if he wants to play it. But he
> has a corkscrew brain."
>
> I was a little surprised and asked, "What do you mean, 'a corkscrew brain'?"
>
> "Well," Price said, "I don't want to tell you all I know. I'll just say he can be
> the greatest player in the world if he wishes. Some days he doesn't want to be.
> He isn't a man I would trust."
>
> Price's comment made an impression on me. I looked up Chase's fielding
> averages and discovered that for about six years in succession, Chase, supposedly
> the peerless first baseman, wound up with something like nineteen to twenty-one
> errors. Now that, I knew, was pretty unusual for a first baseman, who normally
> has far fewer errors than the other infielders. In fact Stuffy McInnis, while with
> the Red Sox, once went through a season with only one error. I made a mental
> note of Chase's suspicious error totals.[1]

By this time Chase had moved from sulking to gambling. Having found it
very easy to throw games, and having gotten away with it, Chase began turning
his histrionic talent into a profitable venture. Rumors continued that Chase was
"not playing up to his abilities" during the 1912 season and into 1913, when
future Hall of Famer and legendary manager Frank Chance replaced Wolverton as manager of the Yankees.

The situation finally came to a head in 1913, when Chance went public with
his suspicions. In a conversation with reporters Heywood Broun and Fred
Lieb, Chance stated, "I want to tell you fellows what's going on. Did you notice
some of the balls that got away from Chase today? They weren't wild throws;
they were only made to look that way. He has been doing that right along. He
is throwing games on me!"[2]

While fear of libel suits prevented publication of these remarks, Broun did
publish carefully worded accusations against Chase. Two days later, on May
13, 1913, Chase was traded to the Chicago White Sox for infielder Rollie Zieder
and first baseman Babe Borton. Zieder was well known for having bunions,

leading to a famous headline in the New York papers saying that Chase was traded "for a bunion and an onion," Zieder being the bunion, and Borton being the onion, another word for a "lemon." An interesting side note is that Borton was later the leading figure in a scandal in the Pacific Coast League, which will be covered in detail later in this book.

In writing about the Chase trade many years later, Fred Lieb had this to say:

> What struck me then and has remained with me since was that the American League must have known the Chase record and the suspicions underlying what Chance told Broun and me. But instead of disciplining Chase or calling for an investigation, they let Farrell trade him to a club that was much higher in the standings. The other thought I got out of it was that other players saw Chase get away with it and surely thought, "why don't we give it a try?"[3]

The White Sox were initially elated with the trade. Chicago owner Charles Comiskey was quoted as saying "it means the pennant," but the general consensus was that the Yankees were well rid of Chase. Despite his acknowledged greatness as a player, Chase had firmly established his reputation as a bad influence on the team, and worse yet, a dishonest player.

Before the 1914 baseball season, the outlaw Federal League declared itself a major league and began raiding the rosters of organized baseball for players. Veteran stars such as Joe Tinker, Mordecai Brown, and Frank La Porte, along with up-and-coming stars such as Benny Kauff, Russell Ford, and Claude Hendrix, found they could dramatically increase their salaries by forsaking organized baseball for the Federal League. Chase initially resisted the approaches of the outlaws, but on June 20, 1914, he gave the White Sox ten days' notice on his contract and jumped to Buffalo of the Federal League. Although he was under contract with Chicago, the contract contained a clause that allowed the club to cancel the contract with ten days' notice. Chase reversed the intent of the clause and gave ten days' notice to the club.

Comiskey did not take the defection of Chase lying down. On June 22 he went to court and received an injunction, but the injunction could not be served because Chase had fled to Canada. On June 25 Chase returned to the lineup in Buffalo and was presented with the injunction prohibiting him from playing.

Chase fought back, bringing suit in Buffalo on July 1 to overturn the injunction. On July 21 Judge Herbert Bissell upheld Chase, ruling that Chase's contract with the White Sox was unfair and lacked "mutuality." Chase then rejoined the Buffalo club, hitting .347 during the remainder of the year and .291 with the club in 1915. He also belted a league-leading 17 home runs in 1915.

The Federal League disbanded after the 1915 season, and when the White Sox expressed no interest in him, Chase was declared a free agent. Despite his talents, no major league club bid for his services. Detroit manager Hughie Jennings summed up the feeling of most baseball executives in early 1916 when he stated, "For all his ability, I would not have him [Chase] on my club, and I do not believe any other major league manager will take a chance on him."

Despite this, the San Francisco club of the Pacific Coast League expressed interest in Chase. Finally, on April 6, Chase signed a three-year contract for $25,000 to play for the Cincinnati Reds of the National League.

In 1916 Chase enjoyed his finest season, leading the National League in hits with 184 and in batting average, hitting .329. However, rumors continued to circulate about Chase's playing, and Reds manager Christy Mathewson reportedly harbored suspicions that Chase was not always playing on the level. As gamblers flocked to baseball in increasing numbers in 1917, Chase's temptations increased until finally, on August 9, 1918, he was suspended by Mathewson for "indifferent playing." Indifferent playing, or course, was a euphemism for throwing games.

Commenting on the suspension and the events leading up to it, Lee Allen stated the following in his book *The Cincinnati Reds*:

> Sometime during the summer Christy Mathewson came to the conclusion that Hal Chase was acting in a most peculiar manner. Though he was still one of the greatest players in the game, his work at times was so bizarre that Matty could only conclude he was not playing to win. That was a serious charge, and because it was so grave a thing, the manager remained quiet and just watched. Chase and Lee Magee were great friends off the field, and were often observed in hushed conversations. That seemed meaningless, though Chase was not one to inspire close friendship.
>
> The play that Chase consistently made that aroused his boss' suspicion was when he retrieved a ground ball and made the toss to the pitcher covering first base. Matty had been a pitcher all his life, and he had engaged in this play so often he knew exactly how it should be executed. And Chase, being a wizard at all phases of first-base work, knew the mechanics of the play to perfection. But Matty noticed that Chase would often make his throw to the pitcher just erratic enough so the play would miss, and the batter would be safe. To all appearances, when this play went wrong, the fault was with the pitcher. But Matty knew better.
>
> Finally, in a series at Boston, Chase's work became so erratic that Matty, knowing full well what was implied when he took action, conferred with Garry Herrmann. A statement was issued in which it was said that Chase was suspended without pay. Hal left the club, and Sherry Magee was brought in from the outfield to take over first base.[4]

Given Chase's track record and reputation, his actions in his defense and the prosecution of him were strange from the start. Immediately after the suspension, Chase announced that "he must have a settlement with the club by which he receives his pay in full or he will take the case into court and not only sue for salary, but for damages to his character." Gary Herrmann, owner of the Cincinnati club and head of baseball's ruling body, the National Commission, stated, "I hope and feel that Hal will be able to clear himself." Leading sportswriters such as William Phelon defended Chase, saying "there is unquestioned evidence that, during the Cleveland/Reds series last fall, Hal put up a flock of coin on Eller to beat Cleveland twice, and won each time—betting honestly on his own team."

Chase was formally charged by the National League on August 26, 1918. Hearings began before National League President John Heydler in January 1919. Chase's chief accusers were Reds manager Christy Mathewson, Giants pitcher William "Pol" Perritt, and Reds pitcher Jimmy Ring. Also testifying against Chase were Giants manager John McGraw and Reds players "Greasy" Neale and Mike Regan. The hearing was held behind closed doors and lasted for five hours.

The main evidence against Chase came from Ring and Perritt. Ring testified that in 1917, shortly after he entered a game, Chase walked over to him and said, "I've got some money bet on this game and there is something in it for you if you lose." Ring sent Chase away and put forth his best effort but eventually lost the game by one run.

The next morning Ring was sitting in the lobby of the Majestic Hotel in Philadelphia. Chase walked over to him, dropped a fifty-dollar bill in his lap, and walked out onto the street. Ring then went to Mathewson with the story, but no action was taken.

Perritt testified that Chase had asked him which game in the day's double-header he was going to pitch. When Perritt responded he did not know, Chase said, "I wish you'd tip me off, because if I know which game you'll pitch, and connect with a certain party, you'll have nothing to fear." Perritt reported this to McGraw, who confirmed that he had seen the two of them together.

Mathewson by that time was in France in the armed forces, but he provided an affidavit. Mathewson claimed that he was convinced that Chase was "laying down" after watching him carefully the whole season.

Before the hearing, McGraw boldly stated that if Chase was found not guilty he would like to have him play for the Giants. Given Chase's track record, one certainly would question the wisdom of anyone who wanted Chase on his team. This relaxed attitude toward corruption served to do nothing but encourage more of it.

On February 5 Heydler announced his decision, which was as follows:

> In substance the player was charged with making wagers against his club on games in which he participated. In justice to Chase, I feel bound to state that both the evidence and the records of the games to which reference was made, fully refute this accusation. In one game in which it was intimated that Chase bet against his club, the records show that in the sixth inning, with two men on bases and the score two to nothing against his team, Chase hit a home run, putting Cincinnati one run ahead.
>
> All available evidence has been carefully taken and considered. If the charge

were proved, it would follow as matter of course that the player would forever be disqualified from participating in National League games. Under such circumstances I would not hesitate to so decide, as the interests of the public and of the game of baseball are far more important than the fate of any individual. These interests it is my clear duty to protect, no matter what the effect may be on players or clubs.

Any player who during my term as President of the National League is shown to have any interest in a wager on any game played in the League, whether he bets on his club or against it, or whether he takes part in the game or not, will be promptly expelled from the National League. Betting by players will not be tolerated.

My conclusion and finding, after full consideration of the evidence, is that it is nowhere established that the accused was interested in any pool or wager that caused any game of ball to result otherwise than on its merits, and that player Hal H. Chase is not guilty of the charges brought against him.[5]

After handing down this decision, Heydler added, "At the same time I feel strongly that the Cincinnati club was justified in filing the charges on the ground that rumors were flying about with a mingling of gossip and some facts in a way that made Chase's actions demand an investigation." In other words, the club was right in filing the charges, Chase was innocent, and the case was closed.

The Hal Chase trial was without a doubt the greatest whitewash in the history of baseball. No one familiar with Chase's career could doubt that the charges against him were true, particularly when they were supported by direct evidence from Ring, Perritt, and Mathewson. In fact, National League President Heydler confided to Fred Lieb that he knew Chase was guilty but let him off because he did not have any proof that would stand up in a court of law.

This whitewashing did immense harm to baseball. Not only did Chase get away without punishment, but shortly thereafter he signed with the New York Giants and thus was encouraged to continue his corrupt ways. Other players, seeing Chase get away with flagrantly throwing games, were encouraged to do the same. It is not surprising that, just a few months after the decision, baseball's greatest scandal occurred, when the Chicago White Sox threw the 1919 World Series.

After the Black Sox scandal was made public, Heydler was widely criticized for acquitting Chase. Heydler agreed to be interviewed by *Baseball Magazine*, and a very revealing article called "A Defense of the Hal Chase Affair" appeared in that publication in its December 1920 issue. In the interview, Heydler defended his actions, citing a fear of libel laws, lack of evidence, and the fact that Chase was the "first player" accused of throwing games. He went on to add:

Were I called upon to handle a similar case today, I should doubtless do differently. But conditions are greatly changed. At that time the gambling evil seemed a remote peril and baseball as a whole was above suspicion. Now the gambling evil is a very present danger and the integrity of the game itself has been called in question. Were I confronted with a similar dilemma today I should undoubtedly immediately banish such a player from the National League and cheerfully await any libel against us.[6]

Had Heydler taken this approach earlier, baseball would have been spared a lot of anguish.

However, it is unfair to put all the blame on Heydler. After the decision was announced, sportswriters generally applauded it, and Heydler was supported by the owners. McGraw eagerly welcomed Chase to the Giants, and as far as official baseball was concerned, the case was then forgotten. Ironically, on the same day that Chase signed his contract for 1919, Christy Mathewson, Chase's main accuser, joined the team as assistant manager and coach.

The 1919 season turned out to be the last year Chase played major league baseball. He played regularly with the Giants through early September and then was out of the lineup with a sprained wrist. He seldom played after that, occasionally pinch-hitting. At the end of the season it was announced that Chase and Giants third baseman Heinie Zimmerman had retired from baseball. It was later learned that they, along with Chicago infielder Lee Magee, another Chase compatriot, were quietly pushed out of the game for crooked play.

Lee Magee's real name was Leopold Christopher Hoernschemeyer. Born in Cincinnati in 1889, Magee broke into the major leagues with the St. Louis Cardinals in 1911. During the next nine years he compiled a .276 batting average. His best year was 1915, when he batted .323 as the playing manager of the Brooklyn Federal League team.

The other player in the scandal, Henry "Heinie" Zimmerman, by contrast, had quite a distinguished career. Born in 1887 in New York, Zimmerman began his big-league career in 1907 with the Chicago Cubs and became a regular in 1911. In 1912 Zimmerman had his greatest year, winning the National League's Triple Crown with an average of .372. He went on to compile a lifetime batting average of .295. A colorful player known for his temper, Zimmerman's name still comes up in many humorous baseball stories. Zimmerman is most remembered not for his triple crown or for his involvement with Hal Chase, but as the supposed "goat" in the 1917 World Series, which pitted Zimmerman's Giants against the Chicago White Sox. In the sixth and final game of that series, White Sox outfielder Happy Felsch hit a big bouncer back to the mound. Giants pitcher Rube Benton, seeing Eddie Collins halfway between third and home, threw to Zimmerman at third, hoping to trap Collins off base. Unfortunately, catcher Bill Rariden had already moved up the line to start the rundown. Neither Benton nor first baseman Walter Holke covered the plate for Rariden, so the slow Zimmerman was left in a foot race, trying to catch the speedy Collins from behind. Collins scored easily, and the Sox won the series.

Zimmerman was roundly criticized by the press for his play, but he was

Left: **Heinie Zimmerman. Zimmerman was another of Chase's confederates in 1919.** *Photograph by Patrice Kelly.* ***Right:*** **Lee Magee. Magee was an indifferent player who assisted Chase in his schemes.** *Photograph by Patrice Kelly.*

completely innocent. As Zimmerman said at the time, "Who the hell was I supposed to throw the ball to, (Umpire Bill) Klem?"

The atmosphere in official baseball in the early 1920s was one of fear. There was little doubt in the minds of most insiders that the 1919 World Series had not been played on its merits. However, official baseball was more concerned with keeping the story out of the public limelight than with exposing the truth, a story to be explored in depth in the next chapter.

All the same, it appears that baseball had determined that it was time to begin a low-key cleanup campaign. The dropping of Chase, Zimmerman, and Magee was the first step in the campaign. Slowly and quietly, the doors of organized baseball were being closed on corrupt players and game fixers.

The public exposure of Chase's guilt began on March 23 when Lee Magee issued the following statement:

On Saturday I shall make public the charges on which the National League bases its action in barring me from its circuit. I'll show documents both in my favor and against me and let the public judge if I have been fairly treated. I'll add to this; I'm going to burn my bridges behind me and then jump off the ruins. If I'm barred, I'll take quite a few noted people with me. I'll show up some people for tricks turned ever since 1906. And there will be merry music in the baseball world.[7]

We could assume that Magee's threat was meant to bring baseball to its knees by forcing it to rush to settle his lawsuit rather than face public exposure, but this time, baseball decided that enough was enough. Ban Johnson and John Heydler, presidents of the American and National leagues, agreed that "the suit of Lee Magee against the Chicago Nationals is a matter in which both major leagues are concerned, and there will be a joint defense of the case." Baseball was prepared to go to trial.

The Lee Magee trial began on June 7, 1920, and ended two days later. It was revealed that in February 1920 Magee had confessed to throwing games, also implicating Hal Chase, to Chicago President William Veeck, Sr., and John Heydler. Testimony by Veeck, Heydler, Christy Mathewson, and gambler John Costello led to an overwhelming body of evidence against Magee. Capping the evidence was the fact that Magee had placed a bet with Costello totaling $500 for his club to lose and had had the audacity to make the payment by check, leaving a very clear trail of evidence. The result was that Magee lost his lawsuit.

The *Sporting News* reported on the suit as follows:

Magee and his defense charged that Hal Chase had double-crossed him. He said he went with Chase to Costello to place bets on Cincinnati, not against that team, and that Chase had secretly bet the money the other way. When he found that Chase had done that, he stopped payment on the check. . . .

Magee's impression on the jury was so bad that the defense did not think it necessary to bring out other evidence it had prepared. Magee, some weeks back, declared he would disclose the names of other ball players who were as guilty as he was at throwing games, or trying to. He has not yet made public the statement he had promised.

Hal Chase, now playing independent ball in California . . . called attention to the fact that he had been exonerated of charges brought by Christy Mathewson against him at the end of the 1918 season after a hearing before President Heydler.[8]

The details on Zimmerman's release by the Giants came out later that year. According to the *Sporting News:*

Zimmerman was dropped when McGraw learned he had attempted to bribe Benny Kauff to throw games. McGraw said he believed Kauff was innocent. Kauff himself also stated that Zimmerman's bribe offers had been spurned. Kauff, according to McGraw, was released to Toronto for reasons entirely apart from the

allegations concerning throwing games. McGraw also testified that Fred Toney
had told of Zimmerman trying to bribe him to throw games.[9]

Zimmerman's name surfaced again in 1921, when he publicly accused
Kauff, Fred Toney, and Rube Benton of throwing games. No evidence was
forthcoming to support Zimmerman's case, which appeared to be an attempt
at vengeance against Toney and Kauff for reporting Zimmerman's bribe offer
to Giants management. No action was taken against these players.

Zimmerman and Magee soon faded into obscurity. Zimmerman played
semipro ball, later becoming a partner of the infamous Dutch Schultz in a
speakeasy between 1929 and 1930. He later became a steam fitter and died
in New York in 1969. Magee died in Columbus, Ohio, in 1966.

By this time, there was no doubt that Chase had been guilty of throwing
games on many occasions over the years. While never officially expelled, Chase
found he was not welcomed in organized baseball, and he returned to his home
in California. In August 1920 he was banned from Pacific Coast League parks
for his part in attempting to bribe a Salt Lake City player. Chase was subsequently banned by the Mission League and the outlaw San Joaquin Valley
League, in which he was playing. The Pacific Coast League scandal will be
covered in detail later in this book.

The Black Sox scandal broke wide open in September 1920, and once
again Chase was right in the middle of things. Rube Benton revealed that he
had had advance knowledge of the World Series fix and testified that his knowledge came from Chase. According to Benton, Chase won over forty thousand
dollars betting on the World Series.

Chase's later life was a sad affair. After leaving the Giants, Chase purchased a one-third interest in the San Jose club of the outlaw Mission League and
announced he would play Sunday and holiday ball with the club. After being
banned by the Mission League, he joined Madera in the outlaw San Joaquin
Valley League, but he was soon expelled from that league also as his past actions became more and more public.

In the early twenties Chase was still doing well. In 1920 he was offered a
job with the Sperry Flower Company. The position would have paid him $300
a month and given him the opportunity to work in the business world. Chase
turned the job down, electing instead to continue playing baseball. He then
drifted to Arizona, playing in various outlaw leagues and drinking heavily.

In 1925 Chase moved down to Douglas, Arizona, where he managed the
Douglas team in the outlaw Copper League. Douglas was a wide-open town,
filled with hard-working and heavy-drinking copper miners. Chase brought
Black Sox Buck Weaver and Chick Gandil to town. Other players in the league
included Lefty Williams of the Black Sox and Jimmy O'Connell and Tom
Seaton, both of whom had been expelled from organized baseball for charges
related to game fixing. Their chronicles will be told later in this book.

In March 1925 it was reported that Chase had been invited by the Mexican government to form a national baseball league in Mexico. Chase was to be commissioner of the league. In commenting on the move, Chase stated: "I feel I would have an opportunity here in Mexico of placing baseball on a sound and honest foundation and demonstrate to baseball fans of the United States that I was the Dreyfuss, and not the Benedict Arnold, of organized baseball."[10] Chase's dream of being commissioner did not materialize. In 1926 he seriously injured his knee in an auto accident. He left the Douglas club after that season, and the Copper League disbanded after the 1927 season.

Chase went downhill quickly after that. He worked for a while in the copper mines and continued to drink heavily. He then sold cars in Douglas and later ran a chicken ranch for his brother-in-law. When the depression came on, Chase moved to Oakland, California, and then took to the California wilderness with a mining prospector, panning for gold. He also played Sunday baseball in Reno, California.

In 1931 Chase wrote to Commissioner Landis about his status. In the letter he talked about his past mistakes and how he had learned from them. Landis responded that officially Chase was still a member in good standing of organized baseball but asked to know more about the mistakes. On the advice of his lawyer, Chase destroyed Landis's letter and never responded.

In 1932 Chase moved to Williams, Arizona, and found a job in a pool hall. He remained at Williams for two years, earning a living by occasionally playing baseball and handling odd jobs. He then moved to Tucson, making a living in the same way. By 1934 he was doing odd jobs for government relief programs and washing cars for fifty cents per car.

Chase then moved back to Oakland and in 1937 worked part-time on a Works Progress Administration (WPA) program, assisting plumbers and carpenters. His health ruined by years of drinking and neglect, he contracted beriberi and later had kidney problems. He quit drinking in 1940 and spent the rest of his life in ill health.

Shortly before his death in 1947, Chase was interviewed from his hospital bed. He admitted that he knew about the 1919 World Series fix but denied any involvement. About his career and life, Chase commented:

> I was foolish and all the stuff I thought was so smart only robbed me of the kind of life I should be living today.
>
> I'd give anything if I could start all over again. What a change there would be in the life of Hal Chase. I was all wrong, at least in most things, and my best proof is that I am flat on my back, without a dime.
>
> I could have made a million dollars out of baseball on bets and gambling. I used to bet on games. My limit was $100 per game and I never bet against my own team. That was easy money. Certainly, I bet, and later on I drank too much. It's an old story now, but it's a sad one for a man whose name, I am told, is often linked with the greatest players.

I wasn't satisfied with what the club owners paid me. Like others, I had to have a bet on the side and we used to bet with the other team and the gamblers who sat in the boxes. It was easy to get a bet. Sometimes collections were hard to make. Players would pass out IOUs and often be in debt for their entire salaries. That wasn't a healthy condition. Once the evil started there was no stopping it and the club owners were not strong enough to cope with the evil. That's why Commissioner Chandler has to be the strong man today.

You note that I am not in the Hall of Fame. Some of the old-timers said I was one of the greatest fielding first basemen of all time. When I die, movie magnates will make no picture like *Pride of the Yankees* which honored that great player, Lou Gehrig. I guess that's the answer, isn't it? Gehrig had a good name; one of the best a man could have. I am an outcast, and I haven't a good name. I'm the loser, just like all gamblers are.

I lived to make great plays. What did I gain? Nothing. Everything was lost because I raised hell after hours.

Had Judge Landis been in power before 1919, there wouldn't have been any Series scandal. Betting on games and gambling on the side would have been out. I wouldn't have been in baseball at all had Landis been Commissioner. If I had, I'd have been going straight. Landis saved baseball, and Chandler has to be baseball's G-man.[11]

Chase's words provide a good deal of food for thought. Perhaps most interesting is Chase's comment that had there been a strong baseball commissioner, the Black Sox scandal never would have happened, and he would have gone straight. Chase recognized the mistake baseball made by allowing players to get away with corrupt practices until it mushroomed into a disease that almost killed organized baseball.

A few weeks after the interview appeared in the *Sporting News*, Hal Chase was dead. Chase's death was major news, and he was eulogized as a great ballplayer who squandered it all for ill-gotten gains.

The most difficult thing in looking at Hal Chase's career and life is to put him in perspective. Chase is generally considered the most corrupt individual in the history of baseball, although one can make an argument that Richard Higham is also a worthy candidate for that title. There is no question, however, that Chase was a game thrower, a game fixer, and a deadly influence on organized baseball. He, along with the baseball structure that winked at his activities, caused tremendous damage to the game and to the integrity of everyone connected with organized baseball. At the same time, Chase was undoubtedly a great player. In 15 years in the major leagues he compiled a lifetime batting average of .291—but statistics do not begin to tell the story of Hal Chase. Chase was instantly recognized as a superstar, and despite his antisocial behavior, he appeared to have a regal magnetism that drew people to him. His nickname was Prince Hal, and perhaps no baseball player has ever had a more appropriate nickname.

How great was Chase? He is generally acknowledged to be the greatest fielding first baseman of all time and one of the best overall first basemen of all time. Clyde Milan, star outfielder of the Washington Senators and a contemporary of Chase's, said, "You could hardly believe that Hal Chase was making those great fielding plays of his, even when you actually saw him make them." Jimmy Austin, a teammate of Chase's in New York, and a man who personally loathed Chase, said that Chase and George Sisler were "the two greatest fielding first-basemen who ever lived, and that's in anybody's book. Of the two, I guess I would have to say that Chase was the better fielder. In a way I hate to say that, but you have to give the devil his due."[12]

Chase was considered the greatest first baseman of all time by many of his contemporaries, including the great Ty Cobb. In fact, Cobb had so much respect for Chase's ability that it was said that he would avoid hitting the ball to the right side of the infield when batting against the Yankees.

Longtime baseball writer Arthur Daley wrote that "Chase could move faster and think faster than anyone else. The reason he didn't pull even more of his dazzling plays was only because his less nimble-minded teammates wouldn't have known what to do with the ball that he unexpectedly delivered to them."[13] In writing about Chase shortly after his death, sportswriter Joe Williams called Chase "the most talented baseball player California ever produced."[14] This is strong praise indeed, considering that at the time the article was written, Joe DiMaggio and Ted Williams, both California natives, were in the prime of their careers.

Perhaps one statistic sums up Chase's talent better than any other. In 1936 the first election was held for the Baseball Hall of Fame. Led by Ty Cobb, baseball's charter class in the Hall of Fame also included Babe Ruth, Honus Wagner, Christy Mathewson, and Walter Johnson. Despite the fact that he had left baseball in disgrace, Hal Chase finished among the top 25 vote-getters for that Hall of Fame election.

Perhaps the most fitting epitaph for Chase was provided by the *Sporting News* in an editorial after his death.

> Let us try to forget about Hal's absence from Cooperstown and remember that he was a king in his time, and, in the bright annals of diamond technique, still is a monarch sans reproach.[15]

Chapter 7

The Black Sox

The whitewashing of Hal Chase by organized baseball in the winter of 1919 set the stage for the greatest scandal in the history of sports: the 1919 Black Sox scandal.

More than 75 years have gone by since this incident took place, and the Black Sox scandal is still one of the most talked-about events in baseball history. Numerous books have been written about the Black Sox scandal, two major motion pictures have been made drawing heavily on the scandal, and millions of words have been written in newspapers, magazines, and journals analyzing the events and how they affected baseball and America. In spite of all this attention, the story of the Black Sox scandal is still unclear today. Exactly how was the scandal organized? Which players truly took part in it?

Perhaps the answers will never be known. What is known are a few basic facts. The Chicago White Sox won the 1919 American League pennant by three and one-half games over the Cleveland Indians and were according to most experts heavy favorites to beat the Cincinnati Reds, the National League champions, who won the National League pennant that year by a nine-game margin. The World Series that year was a best-of-nine affair, and the Sox lost to the Reds five games to three. Ugly rumors floated both during and after the series, and almost a year later the story broke that gamblers had paid off the White Sox to lose the World Series. In the aftermath, eight Chicago players, along with two other players with guilty knowledge, were permanently expelled from baseball for their roles in the scandal.

The full story, however, is a complex one, full of contradictions. To attempt to totally recount the scandal and its aftermath in one chapter would be a futile exercise. This chapter will, instead, present an overview of the scandal, provide a brief look at the lives of the players who were implicated, and discuss their roles in the scandal.

As this book has suggested many times, the stage for the Black Sox scandal was set by the way baseball handled the Hal Chase case and other instances of corruption. Baseball owners ignored the growing corruption because they felt that negative publicity would damage their industry. This laissez-faire attitude, of course, merely encouraged more corruption. If some players could routinely get away with fixing games, it should have come as no surprise that some enterprising players would take on a bigger goal—the fixing of a World Series.

Another factor that contributed heavily in fostering the scandal was the way in which the Chicago White Sox franchise was run. The owner of the franchise was Charles Comiskey. Comiskey was a former star player and one of the leading figures in professional baseball during the last two decades of the nineteenth century and the first two decades of the twentieth century.

Comiskey was born in Chicago in 1859 and began his professional career in Dubuque, Iowa, in 1878. The first baseman joined the St. Louis Browns of the American Association during that major league's first season in 1882. Although he was not a great hitter, Comiskey immediately won the admiration of the St. Louis fans and management for his innovations in fielding. Rather than playing on the bag as other first basemen did, Comiskey moved back and away from the foul line, enabling him to get balls that other first basemen would miss. In time his approach was copied by other first sackers, and it is still the way the position is fielded today.

Comiskey's intelligent play led the St. Louis owner, Chris von Der Ahe, to appoint Comiskey interim manager for parts of the 1883 and 1884 seasons, and in 1885 Comiskey assumed the role of full-time manager of the club. He led the St. Louis Browns to the pennant each of the next four seasons and a second-place finish in 1889. In 1890 Comiskey, along with most stars of the day, joined the Players' League, which was formed to protest the high-handed conduct of baseball owners. Comiskey managed the Chicago Players League Club, bringing them home to a fourth-place finish. He then rejoined the Browns for one last season, leading them to a second-place finish.

By that time Comiskey's playing career was beginning to wind down. He continued managing, moving to the National League with the Cincinnati Reds for the 1892, 1893, and 1894 seasons. He ended his playing career in 1894, retiring with a lifetime batting average of .264.

While managing the Cincinnati club, Comiskey became friendly with a local sportswriter named Ban Johnson. Due to Comiskey's influence, Johnson was named president of the failing Western League. In 1895 Comiskey joined Johnson in the Western League, buying the Sioux City franchise and transferring it to St. Paul, Minnesota. Under the guidance of Johnson, with strong assistance from Comiskey, the Western League flourished and grew strong. In 1900 the league changed its name to the American League and Comiskey moved the St. Paul franchise to Chicago.

By 1901 the American League was ready to claim major league status. Johnson hoped for a peaceful coexistence with the National League, but when that became impossible, a bitter and costly baseball war ensued. Many of the great stars of the game—such as Ed Delahanty, Nap Lajoie, Sam Crawford, Jack Chesbro, Clark Griffith, and Jimmy Collins—jumped to the American

League, and by 1903 the National League was ready to make peace. One of the immediate results of this peace was the first modern World Series, in which the 1903 American League champions, the Boston Pilgrims, defeated the National League's Pittsburgh Pirates. Although no World Series was played in 1904, the World Series was reinstated in 1905 and remained uninterrupted until 1994, when a baseball strike in August resulted in cancellation of the final six weeks of the regular season and all postseason play.

Comiskey's team won the American League title during the American League's inaugural major league season in 1901. The club again captured the pennant in 1906 and upset the heavily favored Chicago Cubs, one of the greatest teams in baseball history, in the World Series.

During the next ten seasons the White Sox continued to play well, usually finishing in the first division. Not content with this, Comiskey spent large sums of money to acquire stars such as second baseman Eddie Collins and outfielder Joe Jackson. The result was the American League pennant in 1917, when the White Sox outdistanced Boston by nine games. The Sox then captured the World Series from John McGraw's New York Giants, four games to two.

While Comiskey was quick to spend money to obtain ball players, he was not eager to pay it out in salaries. Stars such as Jackson, pitcher Eddie Cicotte, and third baseman Buck Weaver were paid much less than their counterparts on lesser teams. Only Eddie Collins, who had joined the Sox with a large multiyear contract still in force, received wages in line with his performance. Comiskey also infuriated the entire team by promising a bonus if the club won the pennant in 1917, but instead of a cash bonus, the players received a case of champagne for their victory celebration.

The 1918 season was one of grave uncertainty for major league baseball. The United States was in the midst of World War I, and the country's energy was focused on winning the conflict. During that summer, the government issued a "work or fight" order and initiated a military draft. Eligible adult males were expected either to join the service or to have employment in what was classified as "essential industry," primarily shipyards and other manufacturing endeavors related to the war effort. Major league baseball received permission to continue its season until September 2 and to follow the season with the World Series. As the summer wore on, more and more players left their clubs to join the service. A number of other players chose to go into war-related industrial work. Among the players choosing the latter option were Chicago stars Joe Jackson and Lefty Williams.

With many of the leading players unavailable, the White Sox slumped from first place in 1917 to sixth place in 1918, finishing with an unenviable record of 57 wins and 67 losses. Attendance in 1918 was low, since most fans were in the service or working long hours to aid the war effort. Many observers

Opposite: **The 1919 Chicago White Sox.** *Courtesy of Transcendental Graphics.*

were highly critical of those players who chose war-related industrial employment rather than the armed forces, calling these players "slackers." One of the most outspoken critics was Charles Comiskey.

On November 11, 1918, the armistice was signed, ending World War I. Over the next few months the players returned from the armed forces, and it appeared that baseball in 1919 would be business as usual. However, many of the owners were worried by the financial disaster of 1918. As a precautionary measure, the season was shortened from 152 games to 140 games, and salaries were held in line or reduced. For the already underpaid White Sox, this created additional bitterness.

The 1919 off-season was also notable for the continuing controversy over the members of the White Sox that Comiskey referred to as slackers. During the 1918 season Comiskey was quoted as saying "there is no room on my club for players who wish to evade the army by entering the employ of ship builders." Comiskey was particularly vocal about Joe Jackson.

Once the war ended, Comiskey changed his tune. In late December, he announced that he would welcome all his players back into the fold. Yet some hard feelings still remained.

As the 1919 season approached, Comiskey was having a difficult time getting his players signed for the less-than-generous wages that he offered them. One rumor that surfaced in–mid February was that Joe Jackson and shortstop Swede Risberg would be traded to the Detroit Tigers for outfield star Bobby Veach and shortstop Donnie Bush. As it turned out, this trade never came to pass—with tragic consequences for Jackson and Risberg.

The White Sox played well throughout the 1919 season and went into the 1919 World Series favored by most experts to beat the Cincinnati Reds. A few sportswriters, such as Chicago's Hughie Fullerton, called the White Sox the greatest team of all time.

The notion of the White Sox being a great and unbeatable team has continued to the present day. On closer examination there seems to be little basis in fact for putting the White Sox in that class. The Sox won the 1919 American League pennant by a margin of only three and one-half games. While they were a solid team, only Jackson and Cicotte were dominant during the 1919 season. More important, the fact that the team was able to win two pennants in three years hardly would classify the White Sox as a dynasty—other contemporary clubs had compiled far superior records. For example, the Philadelphia Athletics captured four American League pennants during the five-year period between 1910 and 1914, and the Boston Red Sox claimed four American League pennants and four world championships between 1912 and 1918.

In truth, the aura of invincibility that surrounds the 1919 Chicago White Sox is more legend than fact. While they were favored to win the 1919 World Series, the sentiment was by no means unanimous. In reality, the fact that the Sox were favorites probably had less to do with their playing abilities than the fact that the American League was perceived as being far superior to the National League during that period, since the American League had won the World Series eight of the nine previous years.

While history may have overrated the White Sox team, there is no denying that they were a talented group. The team led the league in batting in 1919 and was strong from top to bottom. Without a doubt, the star batter on the team was left fielder "Shoeless Joe" Jackson.

Jackson was born in Branden Mills, South Carolina, on July 16, 1888. He began his professional baseball career with his hometown team in Greenville, South Carolina, leading the Carolina Association in hitting with a .346 average. He was then acquired by Connie Mack of the Philadelphia Athletics but appeared in only five games before getting homesick and fleeing back to his native South. Mack farmed him out to Savannah in the South Atlantic League in 1909, where he again won a batting title, this time hitting .358. He moved to New Orleans in 1910 and again won a batting championship, leading the Southern League with a .354 average.

By that time, Connie Mack had begun to despair that Jackson might never be comfortable playing in the big northern cities. In addition, Mack's team was dominating baseball at the time, and it was difficult for a young player to break into the lineup. Therefore, Mack traded Jackson to the Cleveland Indians during the 1910 season, and by the end of the year Jackson was back in the big leagues.

Joe Jackson appeared in 20 games at the tail end of the 1910 season and batted an outstanding .387. Returning in 1911, Jackson turned in the greatest rookie performance in baseball history: In 147 games he had 233 hits, scored 126 runs, batted in 83 runs, and hit an amazing .408. Unfortunately, the timing of his finest season was bad, as Jackson lost the batting title to the immortal Ty Cobb, who recorded a .420 average that year. Jackson continued to excel with Cleveland, turning in averages of .395 in 1912, .373 in 1913, and .338 in 1914. After getting off to a slow start in 1915 due to injuries suffered in an automobile accident, Jackson was sold to the Chicago White Sox and ended up with a .308 average that season.

Jackson continued to flourish with Chicago, consistently hitting over .300 and winning a reputation as one of the game's best players. While he was never able to win a batting title—Ty Cobb won every batting championship in the American League between 1907 and 1919 with the exception of the 1916 season, when Tris Speaker edged him out—Jackson was usually among the batting leaders and became a great star. In 1919 he had one of his finest years, hitting .351 to finish fourth in the league in batting. Jackson also was among the league leaders in a number of offensive categories, finishing third in RBIs, third in hits, fifth in slugging percentage, and fourth in total bases.

Playing next to Jackson in center field was Oscar "Happy" Felsch. Born on August 27, 1891, in Milwaukee, Wisconsin, Felsch was poorly educated,

Joe Jackson. The role of "Shoeless Joe" in the Black Sox scandal is still the subject of great controversy. *Courtesy of National Baseball Library and Archive, Coopers- town, New York.*

making it only to the sixth grade. After playing ball with local factory teams and having a brief tryout with the Eau Claire team in the Minnesota-Wisconsin League, Felsch began his professional baseball career with Fond du Lac in the Wisconsin-Illinois League in 1913, batting .319 in 92 games. He was then acquired late in the season by Milwaukee in the American Association, where he finished the season by hitting .183 in 26 games. In 1914, however, he batted .304 and led the American Association in home runs with 19. After the season, Comiskey purchased his contract for the White Sox.

After a somewhat disappointing rookie season, in which he batted only .248, Felsch began to hit his stride in 1916, when he batted .300 in 146 games. He increased that to .308 in the Sox championship year of 1917 before falling to .252 when the war interrupted the 1918 season. In 1919 Felsch had another strong season, batting .275. He was considered an outstanding fielder, and in 1919 he set a record that still stands today by participating in 19 double plays from the outfield.

In right field was the platoon of Harry "Nemo" Leibold and John "Shano" Collins. Leibold had been acquired from Cleveland in 1915 and had the best season of his career in 1919, batting .302 in 122 games. Collins, who had been with the team since 1910, hit .279 in 63 games in 1919.

The Sox also boasted a strong infield. At first base was Arnold "Chick" Gandil, a strong hitter and a reliable fielder. Gandil, a native of St. Paul, ran away from home at the age of 17 to Amarillo to play semipro ball. He also played ball in Mexico near the Arizona border and supplemented his income with boxing matches, fighting in the heavyweight class for $150 per bout. When he was not playing ball or fighting, he worked part-time in the Arizona copper mines as a boilermaker. This rugged lifestyle exposed the young Gandil to the rough side of life—his associates were tough characters, hard drinkers and gamblers—and it taught him a way to succeed in the world. Gandil then turned his efforts to professional baseball, hitting .269 with Shreveport in the Texas League in 1908. After that season he was drafted by the St. Louis Browns, but he refused to report either to St. Louis or back to Shreveport. He was then moved to Sacramento in the Pacific Coast League, where he hit .282 in 1909.

Gandil joined the White Sox in 1910 but had a disappointing season, hitting .193 in 77 games. After more seasoning at Montreal in the Eastern League, where he hit .304 in 1911 and .309 during the club's first 29 games in 1912, he was sold to the Washington Senators, where he finished the 1912 season with a .305 average. Gandil remained a consistently good player with Washington, and after the 1915 season he moved on to the Cleveland Indians. He was acquired by the White Sox in 1917, and he provided the team with strong hitting and outstanding defense.

The second baseman on the White Sox was future Hall of Famer Eddie Collins. Collins, who broke in with the Philadelphia Athletics, was a star in Connie Mack's famous "$100,000 infield" during the period between 1909 and

1914. When Mack dismantled his championship team after the 1914 season, Collins was sold to the Chicago White Sox. Collins was an outstanding hitter, batting over .300 every year between 1909 and 1916. He was also consistently among the league leaders in stolen bases and runs scored and was considered by many to be the greatest defensive second baseman of all time. Collins had another fine year in 1919, hitting .319 with 80 RBIs. In addition, he led the league in stolen bases with 33 and led all second basemen in putouts and in double plays.

At shortstop for the Sox was Charles "Swede" Risberg. Born in 1894 in San Francisco, Risberg joined the Sox in 1917. While hitting only .203, Risberg proved himself a strong defensive player. In 1919 Risberg hit .296 in 119 games and stole 19 bases. His fielding average of .963 was second by only four points to Boston's Everet Scott.

At third base for the Sox was George "Buck" Weaver, one of the rising stars of the American League. Born in 1890 in Pottstown, Pennsylvania, he was discovered by a team of barnstorming major leaguers in 1910 and began his professional career in North Hampton, Massachusetts, in 1911. Weaver was quickly released by North Hampton, but he was able to catch on with a club in York, Pennsylvania. At the end of the season he was sold to the White Sox for $750 and was farmed out to San Francisco, where he spent the 1911 season.

In 1912 Weaver joined the White Sox, but he was not an instant success. He batted a disappointing .224, and at shortstop he committed many errors, leading to the nickname "Error-a-Day" Weaver. Weaver refused to give up, working harder and harder to improve both his hitting and defense. Sox coach Kid Gleason, a former major league infielder, would hit balls to Weaver by the dozen, and gradually Weaver began to improve his fielding. In 1916 the Sox began to play Weaver more and more at third base, and he developed into an outstanding fielder during the next few years. In 1917 Weaver split his time between third base and shortstop, and he batted .284. After hitting .300 in 1918, Weaver batted .296 in 1919, again splitting time between third base and shortstop. He was considered the premier defensive third baseman in the league and was the only third baseman that Ty Cobb refused to bunt against.

Sharing time with Weaver at third base was Fred McMullin. Born in 1891 in Scammon, Kansas, McMullin broke into the majors in 1914 with Detroit, failing to get a hit in his only at-bat. He reached the big leagues to stay in 1916 with the White Sox, compiling a .257 average in 68 games. During the next few years McMullin continued to play sparingly, primarily backing up Weaver at third base. In 1919 he had his finest season, hitting .294 in 60 games.

The catcher for the White Sox was future Hall of Famer Ray Schalk. A native of Harvey, Illinois, Schalk broke in with the White Sox in 1912, and by 1913 he was the team's regular catcher. While not a strong hitter, Schalk was an outstanding defensive catcher and a fiery leader. He was also surprisingly fast for a catcher, stealing as many as 30 bases in one season. In 1919 Schalk had one of his finest years, batting .282 and leading all catchers with 551 putouts. He was also among the league leaders in assists, double plays, and fielding average.

In addition to their strong hitting, the Sox featured a trio of outstanding pitchers. Leading the way was right-hander Eddie Cicotte. Cicotte, whose pitching repertoire featured a knuckle ball and a pitch called a "shine ball," was born in Detroit in 1884. After a brief tryout with his hometown team in 1905, he moved to the minor leagues, playing in cities such as Augusta, Georgia; Indianapolis; Des Moines; and Lincoln, Nebraska. Cicotte made it back to the big leagues in 1908, winning a job as a starting pitcher on the Boston Red Sox. Cicotte remained with Boston until early in the 1912 season, earning the reputation as a good but not outstanding pitcher. Probably his best season with Boston was 1909, when he had a record of 11-5 with a 1.97 earned-run average.

In 1912 Cicotte was traded by Boston to the Chicago White Sox. After finishing with only 10 wins in 1912, Cicotte began to come into his own in 1913, winning 19 games against 12 losses with an outstanding 1.58 earned-run average. After mediocre years in 1914 and 1915, Cicotte won 15 games in 1916 with a fine 1.78 earned-run average. In 1917 Eddie Cicotte developed a shine ball, rubbing paraffin or talcum powder on the ball to make it break more, and became one of the star pitchers in the American League. He led the league with 28 victories and lost only 12 games in 1917. He pitched a no-hit game against the St. Louis Browns that year and turned in a league-leading 1.53 earned-run average. After a poor year in the war-ravaged 1918 season, Cicotte returned to stardom in 1919, again leading the American League in wins with 29. Cicotte also led the league in winning percentage, complete games, and innings pitched. He was without a doubt the outstanding pitcher in baseball in 1919.

Joining Cicotte on the White Sox staff was left-handed Claude "Lefty" Williams. Williams was born in Aurora, Missouri, in 1893, and had brief trials with Detroit in 1913 and 1914 before reaching the big leagues to stay with the White Sox in 1916. Williams, noted for his outstanding control and great curve ball, had his finest season in 1919 with a record of 23-11 and a 2.64 earned-run average. Williams finished among the league leaders in wins, winning percentage, strikeouts, complete games, and games started.

The third outstanding pitcher on the Sox roster was future Hall of Famer Urban "Red" Faber, who began his career with the White Sox in 1914. Ironically, Faber had one of his worst seasons in 1919, compiling a record of only 11-9 during an injury-plagued season. Because of his injuries, Faber was unavailable to pitch in the 1919 World Series.

Chicago's fourth starter was rookie Dickie Kerr. Born in 1893 in St. Louis, the small (5'7") left-hander had a record of 13-7 with a strong 2.88 earned-run average in his inaugural season.

The manager of the White Sox was William "Kid" Gleason. A longtime

White Sox coach, Gleason was in his first season as manager of the club. A native of Camden, New Jersey, Gleason broke into organized baseball in 1887 as a pitcher with Williamsport in the Pennsylvania State League. In 1888 he joined the Philadelphia Phillies of the National League and over the next eight years compiled a record 138 wins and 131 losses with an earned-run average of 3.79. Arm problems in 1894 finished Gleason's career as a pitcher, but his major league days were far from over. Moving to the infield, Gleason continued to play regularly with a variety of teams in both the National and American leagues until 1906. Primarily a second baseman, Gleason's best year was in 1897, when he hit .319 with the New York Giants. He played a reserve role for the Philadelphia Phillies in 1907 and was released early in the 1908 season. During the next few years Gleason continued to play, appearing with minor league teams such as Jersey City, Harrisburg, and Utica. In early 1912 he joined the White Sox as a coach. Gleason was extremely popular with his players and empathized with them in their problems with Comiskey. He knew Comiskey's methods quite well; in 1918 he sat out the entire season because of a salary dispute with the White Sox owner.

While the White Sox were outstanding, the Cincinnati Reds were also a good team. Cincinnati featured a future Hall of Famer of its own in the outfield, center fielder Edd Roush. Roush, one of the premier players in the National League, led the senior circuit with a .321 average in 1919.

In right field was Alfred "Greasy" Neale, who batted .242. Neale went on to achieve greater fame in football and is a member of the Professional Football Hall of Fame. Neale is the only man to have played in the World Series, coached a football team in the Rose Bowl, and won a National Football League title.

Left field was patrolled by Raymond "Rube" Bressler and veteran Sherry Magee. Bressler, who had achieved some success as a pitcher before he hurt his arm, was in his first year as an outfielder and batted .206 in 61 games. Magee, a veteran who had led the National League in hitting in 1910, was winding down his career, hitting .215 in 56 games.

At first base for the Reds was the veteran Jake Daubert, who batted .276 in 1919. Daubert, who began his major league career with the Brooklyn Dodgers in 1910, was considered one of the game's stronger performers, having won National League batting titles in 1913 and 1914. Daubert was also a strong defensive player and is often mentioned as a Hall of Fame candidate.

The second baseman for the Reds was journeyman Morrie Rath. Rath had one of his better years in 1919, hitting .264.

At shortstop for the Reds was the veteran Larry Kopf. Kopf enjoyed his finest season in 1919, hitting a strong .270.

The Cincinnati third baseman was Henry "Heinie" Groh. Groh, who broke into the major leagues with the New York Giants in 1912, was considered by most to be the best third baseman in baseball. In 1919 he had another outstanding season, hitting .310 with 21 stolen bases.

The catching duties were split between two veterans, Bill Rariden and Ivy Wingo. Wingo received the largest share of the duty, hitting a strong .273 while Rariden, who was winding down his career, hit only .216.

The real strength of the Reds, and the one key advantage that they had over the White Sox, was their pitching. While lacking any single pitcher who could compare to Cicotte that year, the Reds mound staff was deep and talented. The Reds also led the National League in fielding average; they won games with pitching and defense.

The Reds were managed by Pat "Whiskey Face" Moran. After playing 12 full seasons and parts of two others as a backup catcher, Moran took over the managerial reins of the Philadelphia Phillies in 1915, bringing the Phillies their first pennant in the history of the franchise. He led the Phillies to second-place finishes in 1916 and 1917, but after they dropped to sixth place in 1918, Moran was relieved of his duties and moved over to join the Reds. He was well respected as a smart strategist and tough leader.

The 1919 World Series was awaited with great anticipation by fans across the country. It was expected that a hard-fought battle would be waged for the championship, an exciting confrontation between two good teams.

By all accounts the mastermind of the plot to throw the series was Chicago first baseman Chick Gandil. The idea of fixing the series occurred to Gandil relatively early in the 1919 season, as the players grew more and more discontented with Comiskey's miserly ways. With attendance booming, the players on the team decided to demand raises and asked manager Gleason to take their demands to Comiskey. When Comiskey refused to discuss the subject with Gleason, the players' anger boiled over—and Gandil saw an opening.

Analyzing the possibilities of the fix, Gandil saw that he would need a number of players. Most important, he would need pitchers. His number-one target, of course, was Cicotte.

During the month of August and into early September, Gandil pursued Cicotte, expounding on the reasons the fix made sense. Given the fact that Cicotte made under $6,000, the possibility of a payoff from gamblers had to be very appealing to him. Besides, Cicotte was winding down his career and had recently purchased a farm in Michigan for his family with a $4,000 mortgage. In debt and near the end of his playing days, and with an uncertain future ahead, logic demanded that Cicotte listen to Gandil's proposal. At first Cicotte rebuffed Gandil's approaches but Gandil was a persuasive salesman. Finally, Cicotte relented, on condition that he receive $10,000, in cash, *before* the start of the series.

Gandil's next target was Swede Risberg. The two of them had already been discussing the fix, and Risberg was all for it. Unfortunately, Risberg's friend Fred McMullin had overheard one of their conversations. Since McMullin knew about the plans, Gandil reluctantly agreed to make him part of the plot.

Gandil's next target was Lefty Williams. While first basemen and short-

Bill Burns. After his playing days were over, Burns turned into a game fixer. *Courtesy of National Baseball Library and Archive, Cooperstown, New York.*

stops could assist in throwing games, no one could control a game like the pitcher. With Cicotte and Williams, Gandil would be able to ensure that the plan was feasible. Like Cicotte, Williams initially resisted Gandil's overtures, but when Gandil told him that the plan would go ahead with or without him, and that Cicotte was part of it, Williams reconsidered and joined in.

The White Sox that year were a team riddled with dissension. Gandil and Risberg were not even on speaking terms with Eddie Collins or Ray Schalk, and the club was divided into cliques. It was easy for Gandil to select his other targets for the fix—he merely went to the other players that he was on friendly terms with: Buck Weaver, Joe Jackson, and Happy Felsch.

In mid–September, Gandil approached Boston gambler Joseph "Sport" Sullivan, with whom he had been friendly for some time. Sullivan made a living as a bookmaker and gambler and had a reputation as an expert in baseball. Gandil explained to Sullivan that he could guarantee that the White Sox would throw the World Series in return for $80,000 to be split among the players. The money was to be delivered before the series began. Sullivan was interested, but $80,000 was more than he could raise on such short notice. He then went to work to see what he could do.

As often tends to happen when too many people know about a secret plan, the plan did not remain secret for very long. Rumors about a possible fix soon began to circulate. Among those who heard the rumors was "Sleepy Bill" Burns, a former major league pitcher who was now in the oil business. As a pitcher, Burns had been mediocre at best. In five seasons he had compiled a record of 30 wins and 52 losses, with a 2.72 ERA. Burns achieved a degree of notoriety when, on May 21 and July 31, 1909, he had no-hitters broken up with two outs in the ninth inning. This feat of having two no-hitters spoiled in one season was unmatched in the history of major league baseball until Dave Stieb met the same fate in 1988.

Burns, however, had achieved much greater success as an oilman than as a pitcher. During the boom days in the Texas oil business, Burns had been able to acquire oil leases that by 1919 had a value well over $100,000.

After hearing about the possible World Series fix, Burns approached his old friend Eddie Cicotte to find out if the rumors were true. Cicotte denied the rumors at first but finally admitted that there had been some discussion among the players, although nothing had been finalized. Burns was excited by the project and volunteered his services to come up with the money to make the fix possible. The fact that two gamblers were working to fix the series was not at all disturbing to Gandil. Multiple bidders for the players' services meant an increased payoff, since there was no reason that the players could not deal with both sets of gamblers.

In order to pull off the fix, Burns decided he needed a partner that he could trust. He decided to approach an old friend of his, a former professional boxer named Billy Maharg. Maharg, who was working in an automobile plant in Phila-

delphia, had also played some professional baseball. He appeared in one game
in 1912 as a substitute when the Detroit Tigers went on strike to protest the
suspension of Ty Cobb, and in another game with the Phillies in 1916. Some,
in fact, believed that Maharg was really George "Peaches" Graham (Maharg
spelled backward), a catcher who appeared in the big leagues between 1902
and 1912. As it turned out, Maharg and Graham were two separate people, and
the reverse spelling was merely a coincidence.

Burns then went to Montreal, where he had some oil-related business, and
approached a number of gamblers there looking to finance the fix. Maharg went
to Philadelphia with the same goal. Both came up empty-handed, but the advice they received was unanimous: The man they needed to see was New York
gambling king Arnold Rothstein, known as "The Big Bankroll."

By 1919 Arnold Rothstein was one of New York's best-known citizens.
While his father had been a self-made man in New York's garment trade, Arnold Rothstein was a self-made man in the gambling business. Generally a poor
student but a whiz with arithmetic, Rothstein took up gambling at an early age
and soon developed a reputation. He was taken under the wing of Big Tim
Sullivan, one of the most powerful figures in New York's Tammany Hall, and
Rothstein used his political ties to prosper. In addition to illegal bookmaking,
Rothstein had interests in gambling clubs, racetracks, and "bucket shops," that
is, fraudulent stock-selling operations.

Burns and Maharg approached Rothstein at his box at the Saratoga racetrack. Rothstein said he was busy and asked the two gamblers to wait in the
club for him. Rather than meet with Burns and Maharg in person, Rothstein
decided to send one of his associates, Abe Attell.

Abe Attell was quite a character in his own right. Born Albert Knoehr, Attell was the former featherweight boxing champion of the world. During his
boxing career he fought 365 professional bouts and lost only six times. At that
time the fight game was heavily infested with gamblers, and it was rumored that
some of the "Little Champ's" losses were of a suspicious nature.

Attell met with Burns and Maharg to hear their proposition. The gamblers
told Attell that eight Chicago players were willing to throw the World Series for
$100,000 in up-front cash. Attell listened to the plan and told them he would
talk to Rothstein.

That evening Attell relayed the proposal to Rothstein. The Big Bankroll was
extremely skeptical of both the feasibility of the operation and the chances of
keeping it secret. In addition, he had never heard of Burns or Maharg—and
Rothstein did not like to deal with small-time figures. Attell related the news
to the disappointed gamblers.

The plan for a fix was nevertheless still very much alive. Rumors soon
reached the ears of the infamous Hal Chase, who was profiled in the preceding
chapter of this book. Chase felt the plan had great merit and urged Burns to
continue to pursue it.

Arnold Rothstein. Rothstein's role in the Black Sox scandal was central, despite his lukewarm response to the idea. *Courtesy of Transcendental Graphics.*

Soon after turning down Burns and Maharg, Rothstein was approached by Sport Sullivan. While suspicious of Burns and Maharg, Rothstein knew Sullivan's reputation well and trusted him. After talking with Sullivan, Rothstein apparently reconsidered and agreed to finance the fix for $80,000. He gave $40,000 to Sullivan as a down payment for the players, with the other $40,000 to be delivered to the players once the series had been lost.

At that point, a web of deceit and double crosses began that was to turn the series and its aftermath into a nightmare. After Burns and Maharg had almost given up hope, they received a call from Attell saying that Rothstein had changed his mind and would go ahead with the fix. There was one stipulation: Rothstein was not to be mentioned, and all contact was to be through Attell.

Unknown to Burns and Maharg, Rothstein had not agreed to cooperate with them in the fix—Attell was merely using Rothstein's name to get in on a good thing. Attell did not have anything close to $100,000, and he had no intention of paying this type of money to the players.

As the opening of the series approached, Gandil continued to assure everyone that things were under control. Gandil, however, had only the word of Burns and Sullivan to show for his efforts—no money had been forthcoming. Cicotte remained adamant; he would not go along with the fix unless he received his $10,000 in advance. In addition, other members of the fix were becoming restless and disillusioned with the whole idea.

According to Eliot Asinof, whose book *Eight Men Out* is the definitive chronicle of the Black Sox scandal, a key event in cementing the fix occurred on September 29, the day before the players were to leave for Cincinnati. Sullivan and Nat Evans, one of Rothstein's partners, who would use the alias of "Brown" during the World Series, contacted Gandil and arranged a meeting with the players. While this meeting was inconclusive, it was enough to convince Evans that the plan was real. Shortly after the meeting, Evans presented Sullivan with $40,000 for the players' first installment.

By this time Arnold Rothstein had begun placing bets on the Reds to win the series. As the rumors of the fix began to reach other gamblers, the betting odds began to shift dramatically. While the White Sox started out as 8–5 favorites, by the time the series started the odds were down to even money. The "smart money" was going on the Reds.

Sullivan took the $40,000 from Burns and used $29,000 as an interest-free loan in order to place bets. He then went to Gandil and presented him with $10,000 for the players.

Gandil was furious at what he perceived to be a double cross. He had asked for $80,000 up front, and now all he was getting was $10,000. Gandil knew that every cent would have to go to Cicotte and that none of the other players would receive a cent before the series started. How was Gandil supposed to convince the other players to go along with the fix? Sullivan assured Gandil that the players would get their full $80,000, and Gandil reluctantly agreed to go ahead with the deal. There was certainly no profit in calling things off now—he would have to trust Sullivan. According to Asinof:

Opposite: **Abe Attell. Attell (holding World Boxing Association banner) was an underling of Rothstein's who tried to play both ends against the middle.** *Courtesy of Transcendental Graphics.*

Cicotte found the $10,000 in his room, carefully hidden under his pillow. He immediately sewed the bills into the lining of his jacket.[1]

In Cincinnati Burns and Maharg met with Attell to pick up the $100,000 for the players. Attell was evasive—he said that Rothstein was reluctant to hand over the money until the players had done their part. However, Attell agreed to meet with the players, and the evening before the first game Burns and Attell went to Cicotte's room to meet with Gandil, Cicotte, Risberg, Williams, McMullin, Felsch, and Weaver.

At this meeting, Attell faced an angry group of players. They wanted their money and they wanted it now—but Attell had a counterproposal. He would give them $20,000 after each loss, for a total of $100,000.

The talk then turned to the mechanics of the fix. Cicotte and Williams were pitching the first two games, and it was agreed that the Sox would throw these games. They also decided to throw the third game, since Dickie Kerr, who was disliked intensely by the players, would be pitching. The Sox would then win games four and five for Cicotte and Williams, and the rest of the series would be planned out at that point.

During this time the rumors continued to multiply. Even some of the participants in the fix were betting on the Reds, although most were doing it through third parties. For example, Swede Risberg wired his friend, St. Louis Browns second baseman Joe Gedeon, to advise Gedeon of the fix and to ask him to place bets on the Reds for the two of them.

In addition to the gamblers, rumors of the fix reached the ears of sportswriters. While some writers shrugged it off as a ploy by gamblers to get better odds, Hugh Fullerton, a leading sportswriter for the *Chicago Herald and Examiner*, took the rumors seriously. Fullerton warned fans not to bet on the series because of "ugly rumors afloat." Fullerton discussed the possibility of a fix with his friend, former pitching star Christy Mathewson, a man who was Hal Chase's manager and had seen firsthand how games could be fixed. Mathewson and Fullerton agreed to sit together, keeping separate scorecards and circling plays that seemed to be suspicious in nature.

The series opened on October 1 with great excitement. It was a beautiful day in Cincinnati—a great day for a ballgame. However, one player who did not feel great was Joe Jackson. Jackson's role (or lack thereof) in the fix is a subject of great controversy and will be addressed later in this chapter. Be that as it may, on what should have been one of the most exciting days in Jackson's life, he went to Kid Gleason and said he did not feel well and did not want to play in the series. Gleason refused the request, and the White Sox star took the field.

After the White Sox failed to score in the top of the first inning, the Reds came to bat. According to most accounts of the scandal, it was agreed that Cicotte would hit Reds leadoff batter Morrie Rath with a pitch to signal to the gamblers that the fix was on. Cicotte's first pitch to Rath was a high fastball, which Rath took for a strike. Cicotte's next pitch was inside, hitting Rath in the back.

The Reds scored a run in their half of the first, but Chicago tied the game in the top of the second when Chick Gandil scored. The game looked like a pitchers' duel until the bottom of the fourth inning, when the Sox fell apart. The *Spalding Official Baseball Guide* described what happened next.

> Felsch raced to deep left center and pulled down Roush's long drive on the first ball pitched. Duncan hit to right center for a clean single. Cicotte made a dazzling stop of Kopf's torrid smash in time to throw to Risberg for a forceout of Duncan at second. Risberg's slow throw to Gandil failed to double up Kopf. The latter raced to second when Neale sent a floater back of short which Risberg knocked down but could not field. On the first ball pitched Wingo hit to right center for a long single. Kopf beating John Collins's throw to the plate, Neale taking third and Wingo second. Ruether hit over short into the crowd in left center for three bases, sending Neale and Wingo home. Rath kept up with a single over Weaver's head, scoring Ruether. When Daubert followed Rath's single with a hot smash to right center, scoring Rath from second, Gleason jumped up, beckoned Cicotte in from the box and waved for Wilkinson to go to the rescue. Cicotte slowly walked off the field, the more sportsmanly of the fans expressing their sympathy by cheers and hand claps. The ripple of applause was drowned out in the general roar of exultation. The exulting roar still boomed across the field as Groh, first to face Wilkinson, lifted to Felsch and ended the inning.[2]

The result for the Reds was five runs on six hits and a 6–1 lead. The Reds added two more runs in the seventh and one in the eighth for a 9–1 victory. Chicago baseball fans were shocked by this game. Not only did the Sox lose, they were totally outclassed. Chicago looked terrible at bat, on the mound, and in the field.

Lefty Williams started the second game and was brilliant for the first three innings, not allowing a single hit. In the bottom of the fourth the Reds scored three runs, primarily due to walks by Williams, who was known as one of the best control pitchers in the league. The *Spalding Official Baseball Guide* described the inning as follows:

> Rath was given a base on balls. Daubert's first attempt to sacrifice resulted in a foul. His second was better, and Rath went down to second base, Williams to Gandil. Groh walked. Roush came through with the first Cincinnati hit, a beautiful line single to center which scored Rath. Roush was held at first base and Groh at third. With the count two and two, Schalk called for another waist ball, and Roush tried to steal. Here the Sox got a break on a very spectacular play. E. Collins ran in to take the short throw, but the ball went through his glove and it looked as if Groh would get home. Risberg, however, was just behind Collins, and the ball slipped into his hands. Roush had pulled up in the expectation that he might draw a play that might enable Groh to score, and thus he was caught flat footed, when Risberg tagged him. Duncan then drew a fourth ball. Kopf

hammered the first ball for a clean three-bagger to left center, scoring Groh and Duncan. Eddie Collins threw out Neale.[3]

The Reds scored again in the bottom of the sixth, partially aided by Williams's fifth walk. The White Sox scored twice in the seventh inning on hits by Risberg and Schalk and a throwing error, but they were unable to do any further damage to Reds pitcher Slim Sallee. The final score was 4–2 in favor of Cincinnati.

At this point, the fix seemed to be proceeding on schedule. There was one big problem: The players still had not received any money other than the initial $10,000 payment to Cicotte. Sport Sullivan was nowhere to be found, and Burns and Maharg were having no luck with Abe Attell. When they approached Attell after the first game, he and his partner Curly Bennett (whose identity was later revealed to be David Zelser, a St. Louis gambler) told the two fixers that the money was "out on bets." Burns and Maharg found this a little difficult to believe, since the room was littered with stacks of bills.

After the second game, Burns and Maharg went to Attell's room, this time expecting to receive $40,000. The gambler again refused but after much arguing finally relented and gave Burns $10,000 for the players. Burns knew this meant trouble, but this was all he could squeeze out of Attell. Attell had the gall to suggest to Burns that the ball players should win the third game, which would increase the odds.

Gandil was furious when he received the $10,000 payment. While Burns assured Gandil that this was only a delay, Gandil refused to commit himself any further. He told Burns that he would think about the gambler's suggestion that the players win the next game to increase the odds.

The morning before game three, Gandil told Burns that the third game would go just like the first two—the Sox would lose. Burns relayed this information to Attell, and Burns and Maharg proceeded to take their winnings so far ($12,000), and bet them on game three of the series. Attell claimed that he would do the same, but it was later found out that the Little Champ was suspicious and hedged his bets. While Rothstein and Sullivan bet primarily on the series rather than individual games, Burns, Maharg, and Attell primarily bet game to game. These men lacked the financial resources of Rothstein, and rather than go for the big killing on the safer series bet they were forced to pyramid their resources by making bets on the individual games.

Pitching for the Sox in game three was Dickie Kerr. Kerr was not in on the fix; he pitched the game of his life, shutting out the Reds by a score of 3–0 on three hits. Chicago won the game in the second inning on a single by Jackson, an error by Fisher, and a two-run single by Gandil. After Risberg was hit by a pitch, Schalk laid down a beautiful bunt, but, according to the *Spalding Guide*, "Gandil loafed on the play and was forced at third by a step on Fisher's late toss to Groh." The Reds escaped further damage, although the Sox added another run in the fourth on a triple by Risberg and a bunt single by Schalk.

Burns and Maharg were wiped out by the Reds' victory. Every cent they had made on games one and two was lost, and it looked as though the entire fix was in jeopardy. When Burns approached Attell, the ex-boxer pleaded poverty, claiming that he had lost heavily on the third game. When Burns told Attell that he would need at least $20,000 to put the fix back on track again, Attell agreed to the payment—if the players lost the next game. Burns would have to face the players without a cent.

Burns met with the players and apprised them of the situation. By this time the players were sick of being lied to and stalled. Seeing that Attell's promise of $20,000 would not be enough, Burns told the players that he was ready to just drop the whole matter, and asked for a share of the $10,000 he had gotten for the players. Gandil refused, telling Burns, "Sorry, Bill, it is all out on bets." After losing $12,000, Burns was in no mood for wisecracks, and he threatened to blow the whistle on the fix unless he was given his share of the money. As it turned out, Burns was earnest with his threats, and refusing to pay him was a mistake that the players would live to regret.

At that point, the fix was over. The players were obviously being double-crossed, receiving only $20,000 of the promised $80,000. The Sox were down only two games to one—it was by no means too late for them to get back into the series.

Furthermore, Gandil's control over the players was slipping away. The fix had never been well organized—it was often unclear which players were trying to win and which players were trying to lose. Weaver and Jackson, both supposedly in on the fix, were playing extremely well, while Eddie Collins, the team's captain, who was above suspicion, was off to a horrible start. And even Gandil, the ringleader of the plot, had gotten some big hits. The whole plot, which had not been well thought out from the start, was now a hopeless web of confusion.

If the players had indeed dropped the fix at that point, it is unlikely that the Black Sox scandal would be the infamous event that it is today. Even if the Sox had lost the series, their defeats in the first two games could easily have been explained by asserting that some key players had had bad games. If they had gone on to win the series, the talk of game fixing would have been ridiculed. If Burns and Maharg had made their involvement public after a Sox world championship, it would have seemed the word of two shady characters against that of an honest ball team.

As luck would have it, at that point Sport Sullivan reentered the picture. When Sullivan called Gandil the morning before the fourth game, the first baseman informed him that the players had decided that they could not trust the gamblers anymore and they had decided to drop the whole business. This news put Sullivan into a panic. If the White Sox won, Sullivan stood to lose much more than money—after all, he was the one who had promised Arnold Rothstein that he could take care of the details. People who crossed a man in Rothstein's position often did not live to tell about it. Sullivan promised an immediate $20,000 payment and another $20,000 before the fifth game. Gandil agreed to these terms and the fix was back on.

Game four was the closest and most exciting game of the series. Cicotte took the mound, and Jimmy Ring was the pitcher for Cincinnati. Both pitched brilliantly, and through four innings the game was a scoreless tie. The fifth inning proved to be Cicotte's undoing. The Reds scored two runs on two hits and two Cicotte errors. The *Spalding Guide* described the inning as follows:

> Roush was out, Schalk to Gandil. Duncan smashed a hot one to Cicotte, who recovered the ball but threw wild, and reached second on the error. Kopf followed with a single to left and Duncan ran to third. Jackson made a throw in the direction of the plate and Cicotte deflected the ball out of Schalk's reach, so that Duncan scored and Kopf reached second. Neale hit a curve ball and whipped it over Jackson's head for two bases, scoring Kopf. Eddie Collins threw out Wingo on a sharp grounder and Neale raced to third. Ring smashed hotly to Eddie Collins, who threw him out.[4]

Neither team scored again that day, and the Reds had a 2–0 victory and a 3–1 lead in the World Series.

With Sullivan's $20,000 payment, Gandil had the fuel to keep the fix alive. To date, he and Cicotte had each gotten $10,000, and the additional $20,000 was to be divided among Risberg, Felsch, Williams, and Jackson. Whether Jackson actually received the money or had any involvement in the fix will be discussed later in this chapter. Weaver received nothing—there was no doubt in Gandil's mind that, despite the fact that Weaver had been present in meetings and had agreed to go along with the fix, Buck Weaver was playing to win.

Lefty Williams again took the mound in the sixth game, facing Hod Eller. Both pitchers were brilliant for the first five innings, Eller giving up two hits and Williams giving up one. In the sixth, however, Cincinnati put together another big inning, scoring four runs on only three hits. The *Spalding Guide* chronicled the inning as follows:

> Eller hit into a fast one, sending it to left center, and neither Jackson nor Felsch could get it. Felsch's throw to Risberg was too high and when the Chicago shortstop only partly stopped the force of it the ball rolled away far enough for Eller to reach third. The Sox infield moved in, but after Williams had made it two and two on Rath the Cincinnati lead off man drove a clean single between Collins and Gandil, scoring Eller. Daubert sacrificed, Weaver to Gandil. Groh walked on four straight balls. Felsch played Roush's fly badly and finally muffed it, but the scorers were liberal and called it a three base hit, Rath and Groh both scoring on this break, the latter sliding in and beating a close play at the plate. To many it appeared that Schalk had tagged his man before he reached the plate on a

head-long slide, and Schalk was so incensed at Umpire Rigler's decision that he leaped over Groh's prostrate form and made a lunge at the umpire. For this he was ejected from the game and Lynn took his place behind the bat. Rigler also chased Jimmie Smith to the bench for misbehavior on the third base coaching line. Duncan's sacrifice fly to Jackson put Roush over with the fourth run. Jackson made a good throw to the plate, which might have beaten Roush, but it took a bound and it was then fumbled by Lynn. Kopf flied to Felsch and ended the agony.[5]

The Reds added another run in the ninth to finish the 5–0 shutout, giving the Reds a 4–1 lead in the World Series. Chicago had managed to score only five runs in the series, and two of those were on errors. Chicago looked overmatched against the strong Cincinnati pitching.

Despite the promises of Sport Sullivan, no additional payment of $20,000 was made after the fourth game. When the same held true after the fifth game, the players decided that the fix was over, or as Asinof wrote, "if there was no cash, there would be no corpse."

In game six, the Reds jumped out to an early lead against Dickie Kerr, scoring twice in the third and twice in the fourth. Given the way the Sox were hitting, a 4–0 Cincinnati lead looked insurmountable. In the fifth inning, however, the Sox began their comeback, scoring a run on two walks, a hit, and a sacrifice fly by Eddie Collins. The Sox then tied the game in the sixth inning on hits by Weaver, Felsch, and Schalk.

The game remained tied until the tenth inning, when the Sox struck again. Weaver led off with a cheap double, and Jackson moved him to third with a bunt. After Felsch struck out, Gandil singled to drive in Weaver. Cincinnati was not able to score in their half of the tenth, giving the Sox a 5–4 victory.

A new mood permeated the White Sox locker room as game seven approached. Cicotte, one of the leaders of the fix, was ready to win; he went to Kid Gleason, telling him he wanted to pitch and assuring him that he would win. This prediction proved to be prophetic, as the Sox beat the Reds by a score of 4–1.

At this point the Reds still had a critical 4–3 lead. Although Chicago had won two straight games, the Sox would need two more victories to take the championship. Even though the momentum was on the side of the Sox, the Reds still had to be considered strong favorites to win the championship.

Arnold Rothstein, however, was taking no such chances. He called Sullivan and arranged for a meeting. According to Eliot Asinof, the discussion between Arnold Rothstein and Sullivan went as follows:

> The meeting took place in the foyer of Rothstein's Riverside Drive apartment. It was simple enough. Rothstein was polite. There was no show of anger. Certainly none of fear. His coolness lent a businesslike tone to his message. He merely suggested that Sullivan see to it that the Series end tomorrow. He did not think it was wise that it be allowed to go to the ninth game. He did not even think it

wise that the outcome of the eighth game be held in suspense, for the purpose of public show, for the ballplayers' pride, or for any other reason. In short, he hoped to see the Series end quickly, in the first inning, if such a thing were possible.[6]

Sullivan knew that despite his friendly manner, Rothstein meant business. Sullivan also knew that money was not the answer—it was too late. Sullivan put a call in to a man he knew in Chicago who was an expert at persuasion. This man agreed to make contact with Lefty Williams to ensure that the next game would be lost. Sullivan also informed his contact that although Williams had no children, he did have a wife.

No one knows exactly what transpired next. What is clear is that Sullivan's contact went to Williams and explained the situation. If Williams wanted to stay healthy and keep his wife healthy, he would lose the eighth game—and lose it in the first inning.

As sportswriter Hugh Fullerton entered the ball park for game eight, he was approached by a gambler with whom he was acquainted. The gambler advised him to bet on Cincinnati, explaining "it will be the biggest first inning you ever saw!"

The first batter of the eighth game was Morrie Rath, who flew out to Risberg. Chicago's elation was short-lived, however, as Daubert and Groh singled and Roush doubled Daubert home. After Duncan singled in Groh and Roush, Gleason removed Williams and put in Bill James. The Reds scored another run before the inning was over.

From the beginning of the game it was apparent that something was wrong with the pitching of Lefty Williams. A curve ball specialist, Williams threw nothing but fast balls in game eight, regardless of what Schalk called for. Williams kept throwing fast balls, and the Reds hit them hard.

The Reds added to their lead with a run in the second. After the Sox scored a run in the third, the Reds added a run in the fifth, three in the sixth, and one in the eighth. The Sox rallied for four runs in the bottom of the eighth, but it was too little too late—the Reds won the game, and the series, by a score of 10–5.

Looking at the series, it is apparent that Chicago lost primarily for lack of hitting. The Reds outhit the White Sox, .255 to .224, and outscored them, 35–20. The Sox received particularly weak performances from conspirators Felsch, Risberg, Cicotte, and Williams, along with non-conspirators Leibold, James, Lowdermilk, and Eddie Collins. The composite statistics for both teams, as published in *Total Baseball*, are shown on pages 126–129.[7]

One more important detail remained: the payment of the remaining $40,000 to the players. According to Asinof, Gandil gave $15,000 to Risberg, of which $5,000 was to go to McMullin, and kept $25,000 for himself.

The World Series was over, but the scandal was just beginning. A key part of this scandal was the coverup effort of Charles Comiskey.

Comiskey and other baseball officials had been aware of the fix rumors from the start of the series. Both Gleason and Comiskey received verbal and telegraphic warnings from around the country, and after the night of the first game Gleason confided his suspicions to the Chicago owner. This put Comiskey in a very difficult situation. As the owner of the team, and as the person who built the team, he did not want to believe the rumors. Furthermore, if the rumors were true, he did not want to do anything that would jeopardize his investment in the team.

Further complicating matters was the fact that baseball's National Commission, the game's ruling body, was chaired by Garry Herrmann, the owner of the Cincinnati Reds. The other two members were American League President Ban Johnson and National League President John Heydler. Normally Comiskey would have confided his suspicions to Ban Johnson, but Johnson and Comiskey were engaged in a bitter feud.

After mulling over the situation, Comiskey decided that the problem was too big to keep to himself. Late on the night after the first game, he approached Heydler and relayed his suspicions to the National League president. Heydler initially dismissed Comiskey's fears, but seeing how concerned the Chicago owner was, he agreed to intervene and speak with Ban Johnson. According to Asinof, the scene that took place was as follows:

> It was close to 3 A.M. when they got to Johnson's room. He, too, had to be awakened. When Heydler told him what was on Comiskey's mind, Ban Johnson roared his contempt in a classically vindictive exhalation: "That is the whelp of a beaten cur!"
>
> The phrase was well turned. Johnson must have felt pleased with himself as he shut them out of his room. It wasn't often that he got a good crack at Comiskey. Any thought that the humiliated Old Roman might have some better cause than being a bad loser was quickly dismissed. Ban Johnson had a rigorous mind, but his ego filled it with blind spots. His hatred of Comiskey would critically plague the development of the Series scandal and alter its history.
>
> Comiskey nodded his appreciation to John Heydler and swallowed his shattered pride. He was through for the night.[8]

By the time the series had ended, Comiskey had more than suspicions—he had information from enough sources to confirm his worst fears. Comiskey loyalists like sportswriter Hughie Fullerton conveyed their suspicions to Comiskey, confident that the Chicago owner would do what was best for baseball. In this regard, however, they were doomed to disappointment.

Shortly after the end of the series, Comiskey retained his close friend Alfred Austrian, who was one of Chicago's most prominent attorneys. Austrian had strong baseball connections, also serving as the attorney for the Chicago Cubs. Austrian's advice was that it was critical for Comiskey to protect his business investment. Whether or not the players were guilty, Comiskey had a lot of money invested in them, and losing these players could ruin his business.

CIN (N)

PLAYER/POS	AVG	G	AB	R	H
Jake Daubert, 1b	.241	8	29	4	7
Pat Duncan, of	.269	8	26	3	7
Hod Eller, p	.286	2	7	2	2
Ray Fisher, p	.500	2	2	0	1
Heinie Groh, 3b	.172	8	29	6	5
Larry Kopf, ss	.222	8	27	3	6
Dolf Luque, p	.000	2	1	0	0
Sherry Magee, ph	.500	2	2	0	1
Greasy Neale, of	.357	8	28	3	10
Bill Rariden, c	.211	5	19	0	4
Morrie Rath, 2b	.226	8	31	5	7
Jimmy Ring, p	.000	2	5	0	0
Edd Roush, of	.214	8	28	6	6
Dutch Ruether, p-2	.667	3	6	2	4
Slim Sallee, p	.000	2	4	0	0
Jimmy Smith, pr	.000	1	0	0	0
Ivey Wingo, c	.571	3	7	1	4
TOTAL	.255		251	35	64

PITCHER	W	L	ERA	G	GS
Hod Eller	2	0	2.00	2	2
Ray Fisher	0	1	2.35	2	1
Dolf Luque	0	0	0.00	2	0
Jimmy Ring	1	1	0.64	2	1
Dutch Ruether	1	0	2.57	2	2
Slim Sallee	1	1	1.35	2	2
TOTAL	5	3	1.63	12	8

Composite box score of the 1919 World Series—Cincinnati Reds. Source: Reprinted from John Thorn and Pete Palmer, eds., *Total Baseball* (New York: Warner, 1989), p. 129. Reprinted by permission of Warner Books. Copyright ©1989 by Professional Ink, Inc.

CIN (N) (cont.)

2B	3B	HR	RB	BB	SO	SB	
0	1	0	1	1	2	1	
2	0	0	8	2	2	0	
1	0	0	0	0	2	0	
0	0	0	0	0	0	0	
2	0	0	2	6	4	0	
0	2	0	3	3	2	0	
0	0	0	0	0	1	0	
0	0	0	0	0	0	0	
1	1	0	4	2	5	1	
0	0	0	2	0	0	1	
1	0	0	2	4	1	2	
0	0	0	0	0	2	0	
2	1	0	7	3	0	2	
1	2	0	4	1	0	0	
0	0	0	0	0	0	0	
0	0	0	0	0	0	0	
0	0	0	1	3	1	0	
10	7	0	34	25	22	7	

CG	SV	SHO	IP	H	ER	BB	SO
2	0	1	18.0	13	4	2	15
0	0	0	7.2	7	2	2	2
0	0	0	5.0	1	0	0	6
1	0	1	14.0	7	1	6	4
1	0	0	14.0	12	4	4	1
1	0	0	13.1	19	2	1	2
5	0	2	72.0	59	13	15	30

CHI (A)

PLAYER/POS	AVG	G	AB	R	H
Eddie Cicotte, p	.000	3	8	0	0
Eddie Collins, 2b	.226	8	31	2	7
Shano Collins, of	.250	4	16	2	4
Happy Felsch, of	.192	8	26	2	5
Chick Gandil, 1b	.233	8	30	1	7
Joe Jackson, of	.375	8	32	5	12
Bill James, p	.000	1	2	0	0
Dickie Kerr, p	.167	2	6	0	1
Nemo Leibold, of	.056	5	18	0	1
Grover Lowdermilk, p	.000	1	0	0	0
Byrd Lynn, c	.000	1	1	0	0
Erskine Mayer, p	.000	1	0	0	0
Fred McMullin, ph	.500	2	2	0	1
Eddie Murphy, ph	.000	3	2	0	0
Swede Risberg, ss	.080	8	25	3	2
Ray Schalk, c	.304	8	23	1	7
Buck Weaver, 3b	.324	8	34	4	11
Roy Wilkinson, p	.000	2	2	0	0
Lefty Williams, p	.200	3	5	0	1
TOTAL	.224		263	20	59

PITCHER	W	L	ERA	G	GS
Eddie Cicotte	1	2	2.91	3	3
Bill James	0	0	5.79	1	0
Dickie Kerr	2	0	1.42	2	2
Grover Lowdermilk	0	0	9.00	1	0
Erskine Mayer	0	0	0.00	1	0
Roy Wilkinson	0	0	1.23	2	0
Lefty Williams	0	3	6.61	3	3
TOTAL	3	5	3.42	13	8

Composite box score of the 1919 World Series—Chicago White Sox. Source: Reprinted from John Thorn and Pete Palmer, eds., *Total Baseball* (New York: Warner, 1989), p. 129. Reprinted by permission of Warner Books. Copyright ©1989 by Professional Ink, Inc.

CHI (A) (cont.)

2B	3B	HR	RB	BB	SO	SB
0	0	0	0	0	3	0
1	0	0	1	1	2	1
1	0	0	0	0	0	0
1	0	0	3	1	4	0
0	1	0	5	1	3	1
3	0	1	6	1	2	0
0	0	0	0	0	1	0
0	0	0	0	0	0	0
0	0	0	0	2	3	1
0	0	0	0	0	0	0
0	0	0	0	0	0	0
0	0	0	0	0	0	0
0	0	0	0	0	0	0
0	0	0	0	0	1	0
0	1	0	0	5	3	1
0	0	0	2	4	2	1
4	1	0	0	0	2	0
0	0	0	0	0	1	0
0	0	0	0	0	3	0
10	3	1	17	15	30	5

CG	SV	SHO	IP	H	ER	BB	SO
2	0	0	21.2	19	7	5	7
0	0	0	4.2	8	3	3	2
2	0	1	19.0	14	3	3	6
0	0	0	1.0	2	1	1	0
0	0	0	1.0	0	0	1	0
0	0	0	7.1	9	1	4	3
1	0	0	16.1	12	12	8	4
5	0	1	71.0	64	27	25	22

Furthermore, Austrian pointed out that in previous scandals, such as the Hal Chase matter, organized baseball had simply whitewashed the accused players. Did Comiskey wish to take unilateral action, only to see the players cleared, opening the way for lawsuits, and allowing the players in whom he had invested so much to go to other teams?

In response, Comiskey pointed out that the sellout rumors were hardly a secret. Comiskey argued that he had to protect his reputation at all costs. If indeed the series had been sold, could he merely sit by and let the players go unpunished?

The strategy that Comiskey and Austrian finally agreed upon addressed both these issues. Comiskey would launch a half-hearted investigation, the stated purpose of which was to get to the bottom of the series rumors. In reality, Comiskey would have no intention of pushing for exposure. If the details of the scandal became public, Comiskey would be able to point to his investigation and claim that he was actually a crusader for the good of baseball, all the while working closely to ensure the coverup.

As a first step, Comiskey went public, stating that the series had been played on its merits, and offered a $20,000 reward to anyone who could provide evidence to the contrary. Of course, the last thing that Comiskey really wanted was to uncover more proof of the fix. In fact, shortly after the series Joe Jackson had attempted to see Comiskey to tell him about the fix, but Jackson had been refused an audience. Furthermore, if the scandal had become public, Comiskey would be in no mood to pay someone $20,000 for the favor of ruining his club.

Not surprisingly, Comiskey found some takers for his offer of a reward. The first person to take Comiskey up on his offer was Joe Gedeon, second baseman with the St. Louis Browns. Born in 1893 in Sacramento, Gedeon broke into the big leagues with the Washington Senators in 1913. After bouncing around between the Senators and the New York Yankees, Gedeon moved to the Browns in 1918 and became their regular second baseman. By no means a star, Gedeon ended his major league career with a batting average of .244.

As the reader will recall, Gedeon had learned about the fix in a telegram from his close friend Swede Risberg, who had contacted Gedeon to place bets for him. Gedeon revealed this to Comiskey, along with information Gedeon had received from a number of St. Louis gamblers, including Ben Franklin, the Levi brothers, and Joe Pesch.

Comiskey listened to Gedeon politely and professed his disappointment. This was not the proof that Comiskey was looking for — and Gedeon left without his $20,000 reward.

Comiskey was also approached by St. Louis theater owner and gambler Harry Redmon. Redmon had been a confidant of Attell's and offered details of Attell's maneuvers. Again, no money changed hands.

Shortly after the World Series, Comiskey received a letter from Joe Jackson,

Joe Gedeon. Gedeon sought a reward for his guilty knowledge of the Black Sox scandal. *Photograph by Patrice Kelly.*

written by his wife Katie. In this letter Jackson offered to tell Comiskey what he knew. Unfortunately for both, Comiskey never replied.

As the weeks went on, Comiskey began to learn more and more details of the fix. Comiskey hired a private investigator, John Hunter, who investigated the scandal and the finances of the implicated players, and looked into other baseball scandals. For many years the details of Hunter's investigation were unknown. Fortunately, White Sox club secretary Harry Grabiner had recorded Hunter's reports in a small notebook, and years later White Sox owner Bill Veeck discovered the notebook in Comiskey Park.

It is apparent from Grabiner's notes that Hunter uncovered most of the details of the scandal. In addition, Hunter reported rumors that other players, including Hal Chase, Heinie Zimmerman, pitcher Claude Hendrix, catcher Bill Killefer, second baseman Johnny Rawlings, and even Hall of Famer Grover Cleveland Alexander had been involved in corruption. While Chase and Zimmerman were undoubtedly involved in game fixing, and Hendrix was later implicated in a scandal, no proof was ever forthcoming against Killefer, Rawlings, or Alexander.

Comiskey was not the only one who was investigating the series. Disappointed that Comiskey had taken no action, Hugh Fullerton continued to dig, and by December he was ready to publish his accusations. Unfortunately, the Chicago papers refused to publish his story out of their fear of libel laws. After much work, Fullerton finally found a buyer for his story, the *New York Evening World*, but even the *Evening World* demanded that Fullerton water down his work considerably, using innuendos rather than explicit charges.

On December 15, 1919, Fullerton's first article was published in the *New York Evening World*. The article was not able to state that the series had been fixed, but he did lash out at the corruption that had become pervasive in baseball.

Fullerton's charges were met with ridicule by the baseball powers. Comiskey reported that his investigation revealed "nothing to indicate that any member of my team double-crossed me or the public last fall." Other baseball officials dismissed Fullerton's charges, and leading baseball publications such as F. C. Lane's *Baseball Magazine* and J. G. Taylor Spink's *The Sporting News* ridiculed Fullerton, calling him a rumormonger.

The furor soon died down and things began to return to normal. Rumors about the series continued, but Comiskey still found Austrian's judgment to be sound: No one really wanted exposure, and no real action would be taken.

Comiskey then set about his mission of signing his players for the 1920 season. Despite his knowledge of the guilt of some players, Comiskey attempted to sign all key members of the team. In fact, Comiskey offered substantial raises to most of the players—which is ironic because had he done so before the 1919 season, it is possible that the scandal would never have taken place.

The players were less than impressed with the proposed raises. As one of baseball's best clubs, winners of two American League pennants in a span of three years, they wanted more money than Comiskey offered. All the same, by April the last holdout, Swede Risberg, had signed to complete Comiskey's 1920 team. Only one important player was missing—Chick Gandil had refused Comiskey's offer and retired from organized baseball. The main beneficiary of the fix, Gandil was smart enough to know that he was better off as far away from Chicago as possible, and he remained in California.

The White Sox got off to a strong start in 1920, and as the summer wore on they were engaged in a tight battle for first place with the Cleveland Indians and the New York Yankees. Jackson, Weaver, Cicotte, and Williams were having great years, and attendance was breaking all records. Then, as the season moved into August, the White Sox began to play poorly. When the Sox lost three in a row to a weak Boston team, talk of the World Series fix resurfaced. Many years later, Eddie Collins told the following story:

> It was in Boston the incident happened that cost us the 1920 pennant. Some gamblers got panicky that we'd win again and they must have gone to the players they had under the thumb and ordered the rest of the games thrown. We were leading by three games with seven to go. We knew something was wrong but we couldn't put the finger on it. The feeling between the players was very bad. Dickie Kerr was pitching for us and doing well. A Boston player hit a ball that fell between Jackson and Felsch. We thought it should have been caught. The next batter bunted and Kerr made a perfect throw to Weaver for a forceout. The ball pops out of Weaver's glove. When the inning was over Kerr scaled his glove across the diamond.

He looks at Weaver and Risberg who are standing together and says, "If you'd told me you wanted to lose this game, I could have done it a lot easier." There is almost a riot on the bench. Kid Gleason breaks up two fights. That was the end. We lose three or four more games the same way. Just before the season ended Gleason uncovered the whole mess. Charles Comiskey suspended the eight players, and even with infielders filling in the outfield and a jumble of subs, we finished second by winning the last game, 11–10, or something like that.[9]

Despite all the evidence against the White Sox, it is possible that news of the fix would never have broken had it not been for a new scandal that erupted on August 31, 1920, involving Chicago's other baseball team, the Cubs.

The August 31 game was a seemingly insignificant affair between the sixth-place Cubs and the last-place Philadelphia Phillies. However, before the game, Chicago Cubs President William Veeck, Sr., received six telegrams and two telephone calls, all with the same message: There was heavy betting on Philadelphia to win, and the game had been tampered with.

The scheduled pitcher for the Cubs that day was Claude Hendrix. Hendrix was born in 1889 in Olathe, Kansas. He attended both St. Mary's College in Kansas and Fremont College, and he began his professional career in Lincoln of the Nebraska State League in 1908. Hendrix moved on to the Salina club of the Central Kansas League and in 1911 joined the Pittsburgh Pirates. In 1912, his first full season in the major leagues, he had an outstanding year, compiling a record of 24-9 for a league-leading .727 winning percentage. Hendrix also struck out 176 men and had an outstanding 2.58 earned-run average.

After dropping to 14-15 in 1913, Hendrix jumped to the Chicago club of the outlaw Federal League. He had another outstanding season in 1914, leading the Federal League with 29 wins, 34 complete games, and a 1.69 earned-run average. When the Federal League folded after the 1915 season, Hendrix moved on to the Cubs. After two poor seasons, he helped lead the Cubs to a pennant in 1918 with a 20-7 record, again leading the league in winning percentage with a .741 mark. Continuing his history of up and down years, Hendrix fell to 10-14 in 1919 and was 9-12 as the 1920 season wore down.

Once the rumors of the fix reached Veeck, he ordered Cubs manager Mitchell to bench Hendrix and substitute pitching star Grover Cleveland Alexander. Alexander was fully apprised of the situation, and he was offered a $500 bonus if the Cubs won the game. Despite Alexander's best efforts, the Cubs lost by a score of 3–0.

Veeck released the text of the telegrams warning him of the fix and asked the Chicago chapter of the Baseball Writers Association to assist him in launching an investigation. The writers sensed that another coverup was in the offing. To avoid this result, Jim Crusenberry approached prominent Chicago businessman Fred Loomis to ask for his help. Loomis suggested that Crusenberry write a letter to be made public over Loomis's signature, and the resulting effort was published on the front page of the sports section of the *Chicago Tribune*. Crusenberry used this opportunity to push for an investigation of both the Cubs-Phillies scandal and the 1919 World Series. The letter read in part, "those who possess evidence of any gambling on the World Series must come forward so that justice will be done in this case where public confidence has been seen to have been so flagrantly violated."

The result of this letter was a flurry of publicity and anger. The citizens of Chicago demanded action, and they got it. Illinois State's Attorney Maclay Hoyne, who was up for reelection, conferred with Charles MacDonald of the Illinois Criminal Court, and on September 7, a grand jury of Cook County was convened with Judge MacDonald presiding.

The mission of the grand jury was to investigate the charges surrounding the Cubs-Phillies game of August 31, to investigate the broader charges of the corruption in baseball, and to look into the 1919 World Series. It was unlikely that either MacDonald or the members of the grand jury ever had an inkling of what they would uncover.

While the incident that sparked the grand jury was the Cubs-Phillies scandal, the investigation almost immediately began to reveal information about the 1919 World Series. Consequently the Cubs-Phillies scandal was ignored, and it still tends to be looked on as merely a footnote in history, an event that led to the exposure of the 1919 World Series fix. Since the mission of this book is to deal with all scandals, however, let us discuss the Cubs-Phillies affair before returning to the Black Sox scandal.

In addition to Hendrix, suspicion fell on three other Cubs, first baseman Fred Merkle, infielder Charles "Buck" Herzog, and pitcher Paul Carter. Both Merkle and Herzog were veteran major leaguers, each having attained his greatest fame with the New York Giants. While best remembered for failing to touch second base in a late-season game against the Chicago Cubs in 1908, an incident that played a major role in costing the Giants the pennant that year, Merkle had a long and distinguished career that spanned 16 major league seasons. Herzog, a fiery competitor who once challenged the great Ty Cobb to a fight during spring training (he lost), played a total of 13 years and won the admiration of his teammates as a man continuously striving to win. Carter was in his seventh season as a relief pitcher.

The only real evidence that was uncovered served to implicate Hendrix. It was claimed that on the day of the game, Hendrix sent a telegram to a Kansas City gambler named Frog Thompson, placing a bet against his own team, the Cubs. While no conclusive proof was uncovered against Hendrix, he was given his unconditional release by the Cubs after the season and found that the doors of baseball were closed to him. While never officially expelled, Claude Hendrix never again appeared in organized baseball. He died in 1944 in Allentown, Pennsylvania.

No evidence at all was ever uncovered against Carter, Herzog, or Merkle,

Claude Hendrix. An investigation of Hendrix in a 1920 scandal led to the exposure of the Black Sox scandal. *Photograph by Patrice Kelly.*

but Carter and Herzog were released by the Cubs after the 1920 season, and neither played major league baseball again. Merkle moved to the minor leagues after the 1920 season but later returned to the major leagues as a player-coach with the Yankees in 1925 and 1926.

The grand jury investigation soon shifted away from the Cubs-Phillies scandal and on to major areas of corruption. The first key witness was New York Giants pitcher Rube Benton, of whose exploits we will learn more in the next chapter of this book. Benton claimed that he had been offered $800 by Buck Herzog and Hal Chase to throw a game to the Cubs in September 1919. Benton also claimed that Giants manager John McGraw had been informed of the bribe offer but had taken no action. Benton stated that this was the only incident of corruption that he was aware of. Herzog furiously denied the accusation, attributing the story to a grudge held against him by Benton.

The investigation then began to focus on the 1919 World Series. Behind this shift was American League President Ban Johnson, still the most powerful man in baseball. Johnson was committed to cleaning up the game, but even

more committed to destroying his old enemy Charles Comiskey. It was Johnson
who urged Judge MacDonald to proceed with full force. Johnson also promised
to use the resources of the American League to help uncover corruption in
baseball.

One of the first witnesses to testify about the 1919 World Series was Charles
Weegham, former owner of the Chicago Cubs. Weegham claimed that his
friend Monte Tennes, a well-known Chicago gambler, told Weegham in August
1919 that seven Chicago White Sox players had agreed to throw the World
Series. Weegham claimed that he did not report this story because he did not
believe it.

Monte Tennes was called to testify next. He totally denied Weegham's
allegations and in fact claimed to have bet on the White Sox in 1919. He stated
that he saw no evidence of foul play in the World Series.

Frustrated with the lack of progress, Ban Johnson went to New York to visit
Arnold Rothstein. After the meeting, Johnson told the press that Rothstein was
innocent of the charges. Although Rothstein claimed that he had heard about
the fix, he told Johnson that he was not involved, and Johnson believed him.

The investigation took a dramatic turn on September 24, when Rube Benton was again called to testify. Confronted with affidavits from Boston Braves
third baseman Norm Boeckel and Braves catcher Art Wilson, Benton admitted
that Hal Chase had tipped him off that the 1919 World Series had been fixed.
Boeckel and Wilson also claimed that Benton had won $3,800 betting on the
Reds, which Benton denied. According to Benton, he was in a room with
pitcher Jean Dubuc when a telegram arrived from Bill Burns, telling Dubuc that
the series was fixed. Benton also claimed that Chase had received similar telegrams, and that "The Prince" had won over $40,000 betting on Cincinnati.
Benton went on to say that he met with a Cincinnati gambler named Hahn, who
told him that a number of White Sox players, including Gandil, Felsch, Williams, and Cicotte, had been paid $100,000 to fix the series. Benton recom-
mended that the grand jury call Cicotte to get the complete story.

On September 27 the story of the Black Sox scandal broke in the *Philadelphia North American*. Based on an interview conducted by sportswriter Jimmy
Isaminger with Bill Maharg, the article told the saga of Burns and Maharg and
their role in the fixing of the series. Maharg revealed that three of the games
in the series, the first, second, and eighth, were lost by the White Sox in return
for the promise of money. He named Abe Attell as the man behind the fix and
the man who double-crossed the players and the gamblers.

The story was quickly picked up by newspapers across the country, including those in Chicago. Complete exposure was near, and the players could
see the handwriting on the wall.

Perhaps more than on any other player, the fix had been weighing heavily
on Eddie Cicotte for the past year. Cicotte felt driven to the scandal by his
need for money and the miserliness of Comiskey. Although Cicotte was having

another fine year in 1920, compiling a record of 21-10 with a 3.27 ERA, he was ready to crack.

On September 29, Eddie Cicotte testified in front of the grand jury. Before testifying, assistant district attorney Harvey Replogle and Alfred Austrian gave Cicotte a waiver-of-immunity form and told him to sign it. Cicotte signed the form without reading it.

In the courtroom, the details of the fix were revealed. Cicotte told that Risberg, McMullin, and Gandil hounded him until he finally agreed to go along with the fix. Cicotte named a price of $10,000 — cash in advance. Gandil tried to convince him to take some of the money in installments as the series went along, but Cicotte held his ground and demanded the money up front. The night before the White Sox left for Cincinnati, he found the money under his pillow and sewed it into his jacket.

Cicotte named eight players as being part of the fix: Gandil, McMullin, Felsch, Williams, Jackson, Weaver, Risberg, and Cicotte himself. Cicotte also named gamblers Hahn, Attell, Burns, and Maharg.

One key portion of the testimony, as reported in *Eight Men Out*, was as follows:

> It's easy. Just a slight hesitation on the player's part will let a man get to base or make a run. I did it by not putting a thing on the ball. You could have read the trade mark on it the way I lobbed it over the plate. A baby could have hit 'em. Schalk was wise the moment I started pitching. Then, in one of the games, the first I think, there was a man on first and the Reds' batter hit a slow grounder to me. I could have made a double play out of it without any trouble at all. But I was slow — slow enough to prevent the double play. It did not necessarily look crooked on my part. It is hard to tell when a game is on the square and when it is not. A player can make a crooked error that will look on the square as easy as he can make a square one. Sometimes the square ones look crooked.
>
> Then, in the fourth game, which I also lost, on a tap to the box I deliberately threw badly to first, allowing a man to get on. At another time, I intercepted a throw from the outfield and deliberately bobbled it, allowing a run to score. All the runs scored against me were due to my own deliberate errors. In those two games, I did not try to win. . . .
>
> I've lived a thousand years in the last twelve months. I would not have done that thing for a million dollars. Now I've lost everything, job, reputation, everything. My friends all bet on the Sox. I knew it, but I couldn't tell them. I had to double-cross them.
>
> I'm through with baseball. I'm going to lose myself if I can and start life over again.[10]

Especially important in that passage are Cicotte's comments on game four. We will discuss these later when evaluating the guilt or innocence of Joe Jackson.

The news that Cicotte had confessed spread like wildfire. Joe Jackson had made a number of attempts to reveal what he knew of the fix during the previous 12 months, but his efforts had been rejected. As recently as the morning of September 29, Jackson had called Judge MacDonald to protest his innocence, which drew a heated response from the judge. Upon hearing the news about Cicotte, Jackson went down to the courthouse to tell his story.

Like Cicotte, Jackson was told to sign a waiver of immunity. While Cicotte chose not to read his document, Jackson had no choice, since he was totally illiterate, and knew only how to sign his name. Jackson signed the waiver because, as he later stated, "I would have signed my own death warrant if they had asked me to."[11] Jackson then went in front of the grand jury and gave his confession. We will discuss the particulars of Jackson's story later in this chapter.

The confessions of

Jean Dubuc. Dubuc's guilty knowledge of the Black Sox scandal led to his explusion from baseball. *Photograph by Patrice Kelly.*

Cicotte and Jackson left Comiskey with little choice but to take action. He sent the suspected players a telegram, which of course he made public, suspending them from the Chicago White Sox. Comiskey wrote that

> . . . Your suspension is brought about by information which has just come to me, directly involving you in a baseball scandal now being investigated by the Grand Jury, resulting from the World Series of 1919. If you are innocent of any wrongdoing, you and each of you will be reinstated; if you are guilty, you will be retired from organized baseball for the rest of your lives, if I can accomplish it.[12]

The telegram from Comiskey is an interesting piece of hypocrisy. His claim that the information had just been brought out is, of course, not true. The fact that Comiskey held out hope that the players would be reinstated if found innocent gave him a way out. If somehow this scandal blew over, Comiskey would be able to protect his investment and put his fine team back together.

The next day Lefty Williams went to the grand jury to confess. Like Cicotte and Jackson, Williams was not represented by an attorney. Williams also dutifully signed a waiver of immunity before going in front of the grand jury to tell them his side of the story. During his testimony, Williams talked about a key meeting at the Warner Hotel in which he was present with gamblers Sullivan and Brown and players Cicotte, Gandil, Weaver and Felsch.

The story that Williams told was a confusing one of an ill-conceived plot poorly handled. It is interesting that Williams did not mention the death threats made against him before the eighth game.

The final confession came not in front of the grand jury but to Harry Reutlinger, a reporter for the *Chicago American*. Reutlinger asked some of the sportswriters who the dumbest of the accused players was, and they all agreed it was Felsch. Reutlinger then approached Felsch and invited him to tell his story. With the confessions now public, Felsch had no reason not to talk to the reporter. Felsch admitted his involvement in the fix, and he admitted receiving $5,000, but he denied that he had actually played to lose, saying:

> I'm not saying that I doubled-crossed the gamblers, but I had nothing to do with the loss of the World Series. The breaks just came so that I was not given a chance to throw the game. The records show that I played a pretty good game. I know I missed one terrible fly ball, but you can believe me or not, I was trying to catch that ball. I lost it in the sun and made a long run for it, and looked foolish when it fell quite a bit away from where it ought to be.[13]

The confessions removed any hope the baseball establishment had that the scandal would fade away, as the reports created a tremendous outcry from the public. Baseball officials, the sporting press, and the public closed ranks, condemning the "eight evil men" who had tried to ruin the honest game of baseball.

The White Sox technically still had a chance to win the 1920 pennant—they trailed Cleveland by only one-half game. However, with the eight players suspended, the White Sox were forced to play with a makeshift lineup. The Sox finished in second place, two games behind the pennant-winning Indians.

During the course of the investigation, Chicago's Democratic Party had held its primary elections. In these elections, State's Attorney Maclay Hoyne was defeated and promptly went to New York for one last vacation on the public payroll. When the scandal broke, Hoyne was still in New York—a situation that was embarrassing for him, since his opponents lost little time exploiting it. To counter this, Hoyne claimed that he was in New York investigating charges that the 1920 World Series had also been tampered with, and that he had evidence that members of the National League champion Brooklyn Dodgers had agreed to throw the World Series.

Hoyne's revelation brought forth another tremendous public outcry. Brooklyn authorities immediately began an investigation and asked Hoyne to supply his evidence. Hoyne did not comply with this request because, in fact, there was no evidence. While initially some members of the press called for the cancellation of the World Series, cooler heads did prevail, and once it was ascertained that there was no plot afoot, the Series between the Brooklyn Dodgers and the Cleveland Indians proceeded on schedule. As it turned out, it was a very exciting World Series, in which the Indians defeated the Dodgers. Among the highlights were the first World Series grand slam, hit by Cleveland outfielder Elmer Smith, and the only unassisted triple play in World Series history, which was turned in by Cleveland second baseman Bill Wambsganss.

The Black Sox scandal brought about increased scrutiny into baseball's past, and new information was revealed about previously undisclosed scandals. Prominent among the newly revealed scandals was the attempt to bribe the Phillies to lose to the Giants in 1908, the details of which were covered in the previous chapter of this book.

After the confessions, the eight accused players awaited their fate. Would they be indicted? Would the case come to trial? None of them knew how to proceed.

If the players were unsure about what to do, the gamblers were not. The names of Attell and Sullivan came up repeatedly in everyone's testimony, and they seemed to have little hope of escaping the long arm of the grand jury. Given this situation, Arnold Rothstein and his attorney, the famous criminal lawyer William J. Fallon, organized a meeting with Attell and Sullivan. It was agreed that each of them would take a little trip—Attell to Canada, Sullivan to Mexico, and Rothstein and his wife to Europe. Of course, these little vacations would be financed by Rothstein.

While Attell and Sullivan did leave the country, Rothstein did not. Instead of boarding a ship to Europe, Rothstein boarded a train to Chicago to voluntarily appear before the grand jury. Before proceeding to the grand jury, however, Fallon arranged a meeting with Comiskey's attorney, Alfred Austrian. Although no one knows for sure what transpired during this meeting, Asinof's theory is that the result was an agreement to join forces to protect the interests of Comiskey and Rothstein by taking measures to assure that neither was damaged by the scandal. Specifically, the primary task was to make sure that all evidence that could incriminate Rothstein, along with the signed confessions, would be removed from the files. With Maclay Hoyne and his administration on the way out, Fallon conjectured that such a thing would not be difficult to arrange.

Rothstein's testimony before the grand jury was well staged by Fallon. Rothstein implicated Abe Attell as the fixer and claimed that he had turned down the opportunity to be involved in the series fix. Rothstein further stated that once he found out that the series would not be played on the level, he did not place any more bets on the series. Rothstein's testimony was extremely successful from the gambler's point of view. The prevailing sentiment was summed up best by Alfred Austrian, who stated that "Rothstein in his testimony today proved himself to be guiltless."[14]

On October 22 the grand jury handed down its indictments. Those indicted included the eight ball players, along with Abe Attell, Bill Burns, Sport Sullivan, Rachael Brown (Nat Evans), and Hal Chase. Since fixing baseball games was not a crime, the defendants were charged with conspiracy to defraud.

As these events were taking place, baseball was going through a major restructuring. The general explanation from baseball was that the reason for the scandal was that baseball's governing structure, the National Commission, had collapsed. Without strong central leadership, baseball had floundered, providing an opening to evil gamblers and crooked ball players. Their solution was a strong central leader, an outsider whose integrity was above question, who would clean up the game and nurse baseball back to health. A number of candidates were considered, all with strong credentials. In the end, baseball selected federal judge Kenesaw Mountain Landis as commissioner of baseball.

A man of humble beginnings, Landis had risen to a place of prominence in America. As a federal judge, he had presided over the antitrust suit against the Standard Oil Company. Landis fined Standard Oil over $29 million—and while the fine did not stand up to appeal, Landis had made a name for himself.

During World War I Landis was often in the public eye. Intensely patriotic, Landis railed at anyone who he perceived was not being fully behind America's war effort. Chief among his targets were labor leaders such as Big Bill Haywood, secretary of the International Workers of the World (IWW). Haywood and 93 other union leaders were brought into Landis's court on charges of obstructing the nation's war program. Landis found them guilty and sentenced them to heavy penalties in the federal penitentiary. Landis also handed out stiff penalties to many socialists, including Wisconsin congressman Victor Berger. However, many of Landis's penalties were reversed in appellate courts. According to journalist Jack Lait:

> Landis was an irascible, short-tempered, tyrannical despot. His manner of handling witnesses, lawyers and reporters was more arbitrary than the behavior of any jurist I have ever seen before or since. He resented what we wrote; he resented what we did, and probably what we wore. He regarded his courtroom as his personal private preserve and even extended his autocracy to the corridors beyond.[15]

From baseball's standpoint, however, Landis's most significant legal duties had come in 1915, when he served as the presiding justice in a suit against organized baseball by the Federal League. The Federal League was a rival to the American and National leagues, an outlaw league that did not respect baseball's reserve clause or the legitimacy of baseball's contracts. Landis's handling of the suit no doubt won him the gratitude and admiration of organized baseball. Despite Landis's reputation as a "trust buster," he was a baseball fan, and he believed that baseball held a special place in society. During the hearing Landis once stated that "both sides must understand that any blows at the thing called baseball would be regarded by this court as a blow to a national institution."[16]

Most observers expected a quick decision by Landis in the Federal League case, but Landis made no judgment at the end of the hearings. As the 1915 season wore on, Landis still refused to hand down a decision. In retrospect, there is little doubt that Landis believed that the Federal League suit was valid from a legal standpoint, but as a lover of baseball he did not want to do anything to harm the game. Therefore, he refused to rule in the hope that the situation would work itself out. When the Federal League folded at the end of 1915, Landis's refusal to hand down a decision was vindicated.

The hiring of Landis was a strong public relations move for baseball. And with the upcoming trials of the eight players, organized baseball would need all the good public relations it could get.

The arraignment in the Black Sox case was held on February 14, 1921. The original indictments were poorly worded and key evidence was missing. Because of this, the court granted Robert Crowe, the new state's attorney, time to reformulate the case. The grand jury was reconvened, and new indictments were handed down against St. Louis gamblers Ben Franklin, David Zelser, the Levi brothers, and Des Moines gambler Carl Zork. By late April the prosecution was ready to go to trial.

The leaders of the fix would never stand trial. Rothstein was never indicted. No one knew who Brown was; Sport Sullivan and Bill Burns were in Mexico; Hal Chase was arrested in California, but his extradition was refused because of a technicality.

The most amusing story of all was that of Abe Attell. The gambler was arrested in New York, but Fallon came up with a unique defense. While acknowledging Attell's identity, Fallon claimed that he was not the same Attell who was indicted in Chicago. This Attell knew nothing about the scandal and was completely innocent. To counter Fallon's maneuver, the prosecution sent an eyewitness to New York to identify Attell. According to Asinof, money changed hands, and when confronted with Attell the witness claimed that this was not the same man he had had dealings with in Chicago. As a result, Attell went free.

The prosecution was extremely concerned about its case. Without the confessions, most of the evidence was weak. There seemed little chance of convicting any of the defendants, and in fact the whole trial could prove to be a waste of time and money.

A white knight for the prosecution appeared in the form of Ban Johnson. Johnson tracked down Bill Burns in Mexico and convinced him to testify as a witness for the prosecution in return for immunity. With Burns and Maharg as witnesses, the prosecution was ready to go to trial.

The preliminary motions and jury selection process began on June 27,

1921. Representing the players was a battery of high-powered attorneys. The players found this puzzling, since they had been asked to make only token payments. Who was paying for their defense? The obvious answer in their minds was Comiskey, who was hoping for their acquittal and the chance to bring them back to his team.

The defendants were actually charged with five counts: (1) conspiracy to defraud the public; (2) conspiracy to defraud Ray Schalk; (3) conspiracy to commit a confidence game; (4) conspiracy to injure the business of the American League; and (5) conspiracy to injure the business of Charles A. Comiskey.

The trial began on July 18, 1921. On July 19, Bill Burns, the key witness for the prosecution, began his testimony. Burns laid out the conspiracy in detail, shocking the court with the revelation that he was approached by the players rather than vice versa. He indicated that he had been double-crossed, and that when the players had refused to pay him a commission on the $10,000 he got for them, he vowed revenge. When asked whether he had gotten even, Burns replied, "I am liable to be before I leave here."

The complete story of the trial would make a book in itself. It is sufficient to say that Burns's testimony, along with the collaboration of Maharg, was extremely damaging. In one key piece of testimony, Burns testified that he had attended a meeting to discuss details of the fix in Cincinnati shortly before the first game. When asked who was at the meeting, Burns replied, "there was Gandil, McMullin, Risberg, Williams, Cicotte, Felsch, and Buck Weaver." When asked whether Joe Jackson was there, Burns replied, "I did not see him there." This testimony was partially rebutted by defense attorney Thomas Nash, who forced Burns to admit that he may have been mistaken on the exact time of the meeting. However, Burns stuck to his story that the meeting had taken place.

The most sensational moment during the trial came when the prosecution advised the court that the original signed copies of the confessions of Cicotte, Jackson, and Williams had disappeared, along with their waivers of immunity. This was obviously a major blow to the case, and it was theorized by some reporters that this disappearance was a result of the Comiskey-Rothstein cooperation. The prosecution asked permission to use unsigned copies of the confessions as evidence, to which, of course, the defense strongly objected. After taking the matter under advisement, Judge Friend agreed that the confessions could be used—but only as evidence against the confessors, and not against their fellow conspirators. While this was good news for the gamblers and five of the players, it was bad news for Cicotte, Williams, and Jackson.

At this point in the trial, Judge Friend stated that there was so little evidence against Buck Weaver, Happy Felsch, and Carl Zork that "I doubt if I would allow a guilty verdict to stand." For Weaver, who had asked for and was denied a separate trial, this was a point of vindication.

The proceedings finally came to an end on August 2, 1921. At that point the judge issued the following instructions to the jury:

> The State must prove that it was the intent of the ball players that have been
> charged with conspiracy through the throwing of the World Series to defraud the
> public and others, not merely to throw ball games.[17]

For the players and gamblers this was great news—the prosecution had the
burden of not only proving that the games had been thrown, but that they had
been thrown with the intent to defraud the various parties named in the indictment. From a historical standpoint, this means that the verdict reached in the
trial is of little use in trying to determine the guilt or innocence of the players
involved in the fix—they were being tried for conspiracy to defraud, not for
fixing games. In this book we are interested only in whether they were involved
in the Black Sox scandal.

Not surprisingly, given the judge's instructions, the verdict came back
quickly—all the players and all the gamblers were found not guilty. When the
verdict was read, the courtroom broke out in self-congratulations. Chick Gandil, the only player who had retired before the scandal hit, issued the classic
line, "I guess that'll learn Ban Johnson that he can't frame an honest bunch of
ball players."[18] The players and jurors then adjourned to a local Italian restaurant for a celebration.

The gamblers were home free, but for the players the celebration was
short-lived. Shortly after the verdict was reached, Commissioner Landis issued
the following statement:

> Regardless of the verdict of juries no player who throws a ball game, no player
> who undertakes or promises to throw a ball game, no player who sits in a con-
> ference with a bunch of crooked players and gamblers, where the ways and
> means of throwing a ball game are planned and discussed and does not promptly
> tell his club about it, will ever play professional baseball.
>
> Of course, I do not know that any of these men will apply for reinstatement
> but if they do, those are at least a few of the rules that would be enforced.
>
> Just keep in mind that, regardless of the verdict of juries, baseball is entirely
> competent to protect itself against crooks, both inside and outside of the game.[19]

In addition to the eight players, Joe Gedeon and Jean Dubuc were placed
on baseball's ineligible list, "being that they also had guilty knowledge." Surprisingly, not on the ineligible list were Hal Chase, whose exploits were discussed in the previous chapter, and Rube Benton, whose case will be discussed
in detail in the next chapter.

From organized baseball's perspective, this was the end of the Black Sox
scandal. Although the players had escaped punishment by the law, baseball
had proved to be capable of policing itself. The "evil" men were punished, the
game was clean, and everything was back to normal.

In reality, of course, the book on the scandal was far from closed. An event
such as the throwing of a World Series does not simply fade away. Historians
are still not sure what actually happened in the 1919 World Series, and fans,

researchers, and historians still debate the guilt or innocence of individual players.

The complete story of the scandal will never be known. All the principal characters have passed away, and even during their lifetimes a veil of secrecy shrouded the scandal. The secrecy was kept not only by the players implicated, but by members of the White Sox and Reds who had no involvement in the fixing of the World Series.

An interesting piece of information about the scandal came out many years later, when author Larry Ritter was interviewing Edd Roush for his outstanding book *The Glory of Their Times.* During the interview, Roush revealed that gamblers had also approached members of the Cincinnati Reds in an attempt to fix the series for Chicago to win. Roush told of being approached by a man after the second game of the series:

> "Roush," he says, "I want to tell you something. Did you hear about the squabble the White Sox got into after the game this afternoon?" And he told me some story about Ray Schalk accusing Lefty Williams of throwing the game, and something about some of the White Sox beating up a gambler for not giving them the money he'd promised them. "They didn't get the payoff," he said, "so from here on they're going to try to win."
>
> I didn't know whether this guy made it all up or not. But it did start me thinking. Later on in the Series the same guy came over to me again.
>
> "Roush," he says, "you remember what I told you about gamblers getting to the White Sox? Well, now they've also got to some of the players on your own ball club."[20]

Roush, one of the fiercest competitors in the history of baseball, wasted no time taking this information to Cincinnati manager Pat Moran. As it turned out, Hod Eller admitted having been offered $5,000 to throw the game, to which he replied, "I said if he didn't get far away from me real soon, he wouldn't know what hit him, and the same went if I ever saw him again."[21]

Eller proved himself completely innocent by pitching a fine game, one of his two victories in the series. Nevertheless, when Roush was interviewed by Paul Green for his book *Forgotten Fields,* he recounted the following:

> GREEN: But you honestly felt something was going on with players on your team, too?
> ROUSH: Yeah, well, I always thought there was something going on. I saw some damn funny pitching out there myself.
> GREEN: On your team?
> ROUSH: Yeah.[22]

Roush would never give specifics, so we will never know the full story.

Evaluating the ten players who were expelled from baseball, the eight White Sox plus Gedeon and Dubuc, we can conclude that each one of these men had some degree of guilt in the scandal. At the same time, however, each was in many ways a victim. Corruption was becoming more and more widespread by 1919, and baseball's whitewashing of the infamous Hal Chase gave a green light to players to consort with gamblers and fix games. So, despite baseball's official version that the scandal was a result of action taken by greedy and evil players and gamblers, baseball itself had set the stage for the Black Sox scandal.

At the same time, all ten of the expelled players were aware of the fix. At least in theory they could have come forth and made their knowledge public and averted the entire tragedy. In today's world, players with guilty knowledge would deserve whatever punishment was handed out. With rising corruption and Hal Chase's whitewash as a backdrop, however, it is easy to see how players were reluctant to inform on their friends and teammates, especially since informing would probably result in no action from baseball and subject them to ridicule from the other players.

Let us look at the expelled players individually, starting with Chick Gandil. Gandil was the acknowledged ringleader of the fix, and definitely the controlling influence. In 1956, Gandil went public, telling his story to Melvin Durslang of *Sports Illustrated*. Gandil told of the miserly Comiskey and how baseball's rules made it impossible for the players to escape from Comiskey's clutches, leaving them susceptible to corruption. According to Gandil, the idea of the fix came from Sport Sullivan. Gandil claimed he and Cicotte were approached by Sullivan and offered $80,000 to throw the Series. Gandil and Cicotte then arranged a meeting with the other six players, all of whom were interested and agreed to go along if the money was paid up front. According to Gandil, Weaver suggested "if things got too hot, we could double-cross the gamblers."[23]

Gandil also told of being approached by Bill Burns with a similar offer. However, according to Gandil, the deal had already been made with Sullivan and Arnold Rothstein, who met with the players personally.

Gandil claimed that only $10,000 changed hands in payment for throwing the series, and that once the word of a possible fix leaked, the players decided not to go through with the conspiracy. Gandil told Durslang:

> Our losing to Cincinnati was an upset all right, but no more than Cleveland's losing to the New York Giants by four straight in 1954. Mind you, I offer no defense for the thing we conspired to do. It was inexcusable. But I maintain that our actual losing of the Series was pure baseball fortune.[24]

There are certainly many elements of truth in Gandil's story. When all is said and done, however, the preponderance of evidence points to the fact that there was indeed a fix, and that Gandil was the ringleader, despite the fact that his actual performance in the Series was better than those of many players not involved in the fix. There is also little doubt that Risberg acted as Gandil's henchman in organizing the fix. Cicotte's testimony clearly established the fact that Risberg was actively involved in recruiting him into the scandal. Also, Risberg's performance in the series was abysmal.

One of the primary reasons the White Sox lost the series was the performances of Lefty Williams and Eddie Cicotte. While both pitched well at times, Williams showed uncharacteristic wildness, and Cicotte's flagrant errors in game four were highly suspicious. In addition, in the fateful eighth game, Williams refused to obey Schalk's signals. Finally, both Cicotte and Williams confessed their involvement in the fix.

It is virtually impossible to evaluate the role of Fred McMullin in the Black Sox scandal. According to Cicotte, McMullin was instrumental in recruiting players, including Cicotte himself. In addition, Asinof defined McMullin's role as a combination of errand boy and bag man—relaying messages and delivering money from Gandil to other players involved in the fix.

Certainly it would be difficult to prove that McMullin was actually involved in attempting to lose games. McMullin came to bat twice as a pinch hitter, delivering one hit. Yet McMullin was certainly aware of the fix, and it appears likely that he played some role in managing the process.

Happy Felsch was the most open about his knowledge of the fix and his involvement in it. Felsch clearly admitted to being a conspirator (in fact, he was a primary source for Asinof) but denied that he actually played to lose. While Felsch played poorly at times, he also made some spectacular plays. We can conclude that Felsch was certainly a conspirator in the fix, but not one of its more active participants.

The question of Buck Weaver is a much more difficult one. Burns, Cicotte, and Gandil all placed Weaver at key meetings where details of the fix were planned. On the other hand, at least one person who should know—Abe Attell—claimed that Weaver had never been a party to the fix. *Minneapolis Tribune* writer George Barton gave the following account of his discussion with Attell about the 1919 fix:

> Abe declared Weaver refused to be a party of the fix but was sworn to secrecy by Gandil and Risberg, who threatened him with physical violence if he tipped off the deal to Charley Comiskey, owner of the White Sox, or Ban Johnson, then president of the American League.
>
> "I'm the guy who swung the deal with Gandil and Risberg who handled other players in on the fix," Attell told us. "They assured me they had fixed Cicotte, Williams, Jackson, Felsch and McMullin, but couldn't reach Weaver. Chick and Swede guaranteed they would make Buck keep his mouth shut.
>
> "I was the payoff man and you gentlemen may rest assured Buck did not accept a penny of the loot."[25]

Virtually all contemporary observers accepted the idea that Weaver played to the best of his ability throughout the series. It is also generally acknowledged that Weaver did not receive any money from the gamblers and played no part in throwing the World Series.

Weaver was the most persistent of the Sox in attempting to gain reinstatement from baseball. His first attempt was made in 1922, and Landis gave his answer on December 12 of that year. Landis denied Weaver's reinstatement based on the fact that Bill Burns, Joe Jackson, and Lefty Williams all testified that Weaver had knowledge of the fix and was present in at least one key meeting. Landis's response to another Weaver bid was reported by Fred Lieb in the *Sporting News*. According to Lieb, Landis told the press:

> Gentlemen, I had Weaver in this office. I asked him, "Buck, did you ever sit in on any meetings to throw the 1919 Series?" He replied, "Yes, Judge, I attended two such meetings but I took no money and played the best ball I could."
> So I told him, anyone who sat in on such a meeting and did not report it was as guilty as any of the others. "Buck, you can't play ball with us again." That, too, is my answer to you gentlemen.[26]

Weaver publicly appealed for reinstatement in 1927 while appearing as a witness in the hearings into Swede Risberg's charges that the White Sox bribed the Detroit Tigers to throw games in 1917. Landis asked Weaver to put his request in the form of a letter, which he did. Landis denied the application for reinstatement, saying in part:

> All three, Cicotte, Jackson and Williams testified that you were implicated in this. Indictments were returned against all the players named by them, including you, but on trial of these indictments you made common cause with these three players, who, you knew, had implicated you, and one of whom you say had twice solicited you to join in game throwing. At the trial, you were confronted with a witness who testified that he acted as an agent between the gamblers and the crooked players, arranging the fixing of the Series, and he also named you as one of the participants. Thus there is on record the sworn testimony of four admitted participants in the "fixing" that you were implicated.
> It is true that the jury verdict was "not guilty" and that the idea apparently prevails to some extent that this exonerated you and the other defendants of the charge of game throwing. However, this same jury returned the same verdict as to the three other players who admitted accepting bribe money to throw the Series.[27]

Weaver continued to bid for reinstatement throughout his life without success. He also sought financial compensation for what he viewed as a miscarriage of justice. Weaver had signed a three-year contract before the 1920 season and sued Comiskey for the remaining two years of pay. The case was initially dismissed by the courts, but eventually Weaver won an out-of-court settlement from Comiskey. Weaver always viewed this as exoneration and additional proof of his innocence.

The role of Joe Gedeon and Jean Dubuc in the fix is clear—they were neither participants nor conspirators. In both cases the players had guilty knowledge, and along with others such as Hal Chase and Rube Benton, they profited by betting on the Reds. These players can be faulted only for failing to blow the whistle on the fix. As discussed earlier, this was not the automatic course of action in 1919 that it would be today.

Perhaps the most interesting case of all is that of Joe Jackson. Jackson was one of the three players who appeared before the Chicago grand jury to "confess" his involvement in the fix. Before the trial, however, Jackson, along with Williams and Cicotte, recanted his confession. While Jackson himself did not bother to apply for reinstatement, his friends and supporters did so for him, and Jackson went to his grave insisting on his complete innocence.

The character of "Shoeless Joe" Jackson has taken on almost mythical proportions in today's society. The illiterate mill worker, great natural hitter, and disgraced baseball star has an avid following even now. The popular movie *Field of Dreams* helped build his legend, making Joe Jackson almost a household name.

This increasing interest in Joe Jackson has led to renewed bids for his reinstatement. Initially many of these bids were based on the fact that Jackson was found innocent in a court of law—but as was discussed earlier, Jackson and the other players were on trial for conspiracy to defraud, and the verdict had nothing to do with their guilt or innocence of throwing baseball games.

Another argument traditionally made was that, as an illiterate, Jackson should be excused for his involvement in the fix since he was too stupid to know what else to do. While Jackson was illiterate, all evidence points to the fact that he was by no means mentally deficient, which would invalidate mental weakness as an excuse for being involved in the fix.

Over the years, the key reason for dismissing the claims of Jackson and his supporters was the fact that Jackson did indeed confess. Despite the fact that he was one of the star performers in the series, Jackson did confess to the grand jury, and therefore it was assumed he was guilty. Recently, however, a startling development occurred—a copy of Jackson's confession was uncovered in the files of Alfred Austrian's old law firm.

Jackson's confession makes for fascinating reading. On the one hand, Jackson admits being part of the fix, but at the same time he also denies any wrongdoing and professes ignorance in regard to many of the details of the fix. One of the most damaging excerpts of Jackson's testimony is as follows:

Q: Did anybody pay you any money to help throw that series in favor of Cincinnati?
A: They did.
Q: How much did they pay?
A: They promised me $20,000, and paid me $5,000.
Q: Who promised you the $20,000?
A: "Chick" Gandil.
Q: Who is Chick Gandil?
A: He was their first baseman on the White Sox Club.

> Q: Who paid you the $5,000?
>
> A: Lefty Williams brought it in my room and threw it down.

Later in his testimony, Jackson provided more details about the incriminating $5,000 payment, while at the same time revealing that he had offered to come forward to Comiskey with information about the fix.

> Q: After the fourth game you went to Cincinnati and you had the $5,000, is that right?
>
> A: Yes, sir.
>
> Q: Where did you put the $5,000, did you put it in the bank or keep in on your person?
>
> A: I put it in my pocket.
>
> Q: What denominations, in silver or bills?
>
> A: In bills.
>
> Q: How big were some of the bills?
>
> A: Some hundreds, mostly fifties.
>
> Q: What did Mrs. Jackson say about it after she found it out again?
>
> A: She felt awful bad about it, cried about it a while.
>
> Q: Did it ever occur to you to tell about this before this?
>
> A: Yes, where I offered to come here last fall in the investigation, I would have told it last fall if they would have brought me in.

While supposedly "confessing," however, Jackson also tells how he refused to become involved in the scandal.

> Q: Weren't you in on the inner circle?
>
> A: No, I never was with them, no sir. It was mentioned to me in Boston. As I told you before, they asked me what would I consider, $10,000? and I said no, then they offered me $20,000.
>
> Q: Who mentioned it first to you?
>
> A: Gandil.
>
> Q: Who was with you?
>
> A: We were all alone.
>
> Q: What did he say?
>
> A: He asked me would I consider $10,000 to frame up something and I asked him frame what? And he told me and I said no.
>
> Q: What did he say?
>
> A: Just walked away from me, and when I returned here to Chicago he told me that he would give me $20,000 and I said no again, and on the bridge where you go into the club house he told me I could either take it or let it alone, they were going through.
>
> Q: What did they say?
>
> A: They said, "You might as well say yes or no and play ball or anything you want." I told them I would take their word.

Jackson also showed a great deal of confusion about the plot and ignorance about its plans. Let us look at Jackson's testimony in a conversation he had with Bill Burns during the series:

Q: Then what happened?
A: He (Bill Burns) told me about this stuff and I didn't know so much, I hadn't been around and I didn't know so much. He said, "Where is Chick?" I said, "I don't know." He walked away from me. I didn't know enough to talk to him about what they were going to plan or what they had planned, I wouldn't know it if I had seen him, I only knew what I had been told, that's all I knew.

One thing Jackson was consistent about in his testimony was that he always played to win. At no time did he ever say that he threw a game or participated in the fixing of any game. Below is one example of Jackson's statements:

Q: Did you make any intentional errors yourself that day?
A: No, sir, not during the whole series.
Q: Did you bat to win?
A: Yes.
Q: And run the bases to win?
A: Yes, sir.
Q: And field the balls at the outfield to win?
A: I did.

Analyzing the confession, we can conclude that Jackson played to win at all times during the World Series and at least initially rejected all advances of the conspirators. On the negative side, it appears that Jackson was aware of the plot and received money for his proposed participation.

A number of Jackson supporters have done extensive research into the scandal and Jackson's role in it. Among the leaders to clear Jackson's name are Donald Gropman, whose revised version of the book *Say It Ain't So, Joe!* is an extremely well researched and compelling argument for Jackson's complete innocence, and Ray Allen, an Atlantic City school teacher who heads the Shoeless Joe Jackson Society. These men, along with other Jackson supporters, have developed a model that they believe demonstrates the innocence of Joe Jackson.

The first part of the model deals with Jackson's performance on the playing field, which was outstanding. Jackson hit .375, had the only home run in the series, and tied a World Series record with 12 hits. He also fielded flawlessly and by every standard distinguished himself.

Detractors of Jackson point out that averages can be misleading—the key is what he did in the clutch. Others claim that Jackson's play improved toward the end of the series, once he realized that he would not get his full $20,000.

The evidence, however, does not support Jackson's detractors. One of the most compelling arguments against Jackson's involvement was supplied by Eddie Cicotte himself in game four. As mentioned earlier, the game had been a scoreless tie going into the fifth inning, when two errors by Cicotte allowed the only two Cincinnati runs of the game. The most damaging error was when

Cicotte cut off Jackson's throw to the plate and let the ball roll off his glove for an error. Ray Allen analyzes the incident as follows:

> According to the newspapers, "Jackson charges the ball, fields it on a hop, and unleashes a heave to the plate. It has the runner out by several feet, but for some unknown reason Cicotte cuts off the ball and kicks it into the dugout." Well, today we know that reason. That reason is that Cicotte is in on the fix, but that single event shows Cicotte's view of Jackson's involvement in the scandal. If they are all in collusion as it is commonly assumed, Cicotte knows he has nothing to worry about, that somehow the ball's going to be wide or short or high. But, Cicotte chose to cut the ball off because he did not believe that Jackson was in on the fix.[29]

Another powerful piece of evidence in Jackson's defense was supplied by Bellcore statistician Jay Bennett in 1992. Bennett evaluated Jackson's performance in the series using a statistical formula called Player Game Percentage (PGP), which factors in hitting, fielding, and game situations to come up with a total performance level. From his analysis, Bennett concludes the following:

> Almost every statistical view of the game data supports the contention that Joe Jackson played to his full potential in the 1919 World Series. Not only did Jackson have higher batting statistics than he did during the regular season, but his batting PGP was also higher than expected from those statistics. . . . This conclusion is also supported by the following analysis results:
> • Jackson was the third most valuable player in the Series for his team and the seventh most valuable overall.
> • As a batter, Jackson made a greater contribution to his team's chances for victory than any other batter in the Series.
> • Jackson made a positive overall contribution toward White Sox victory in the Series while all other Black Sox had negative impacts.
> • Jackson had high traditional batting statistics in most clutch situations (especially leading off and in late inning pressure).[30]

Looking at all this evidence, we must conclude that Joe Jackson did give his best effort in the World Series. To assume that Jackson could perform at this level while not giving his best lacks credibility. While Jackson was a great baseball player, he was not the preeminent star of the day, certainly not capable of performing at extremely high levels without putting forth strong effort.

So what was Jackson's role in the scandal? Guilty knowledge as his confession indicates? Everyone agrees that Jackson did receive $5,000 — what was the $5,000 for? Did he agree to be part of the fix and then change his mind or double-cross the gamblers by playing his best?

Understanding the answers to these questions is much more difficult than analyzing Jackson's play in the series. Indeed, we will never know the whole truth. What can be done, however, is to present both sides of the argument and let the reader draw his or her own conclusion.

The case against Jackson has been fairly well documented. In his confession he admits knowing about the fix and accepting money after game four. He was named as part of the fix in the confessions of Cicotte, Williams, and Felsch, and while Attell indicated that Buck Weaver was innocent, he clearly believed that Jackson was part of the Black Sox scandal. Finally, in the opinion of leading baseball historians such as Bill James, Harold Seymour, and, most importantly, Eliot Asinof, Jackson was guilty. Readers are encouraged to read Asinof's book *Eight Men Out* for his view of Jackson's role, as well as an outstanding history of the fix as a whole.

The case in defense of Jackson as made by Donald Gropman, Ray Allen, and others is less well known. Central points of their argument are as follows:

- While Jackson admittedly had guilty knowledge, he made numerous attempts to report this knowledge to Comiskey.
- The confession was actually scripted by Alfred Austrian as part of a coverup effort to protect Charles Comiskey.
- Jackson never agreed to be part of the fix. His name was used by the conspirators without his permission.
- Jackson actually received the $5,000 payment after the World Series, not during the World Series, and he kept the money only because he was instructed to do so by White Sox management.

Let us look at the guilty knowledge claim first. Ray Allen has documented five times that Jackson tried to come forward to baseball management with what he knew but was met with rejection on each occasion. The first time was the day of the opening of the World Series, when Jackson asked White Sox manager Kid Gleason to remove him from the series. The fact that Jackson had asked to be removed from the series is documented not only by Jackson's testimony, but also by the testimony of Happy Felsch. According to Allen, the reason for Jackson's request was that he was aware of the talk of a crooked series and did not want any part of it.

The second instance in which Jackson attempted to come forward was the day after the final game of the series. Jackson visited Comiskey's office trying to get an appointment with the White Sox club owner. According to Jackson, Harry Grabiner told him that "the old man is not feeling well," and he would not be able to see Jackson. Jackson then claimed that he showed the $5,000 to Grabiner, told him how he came by it, and asked what to do. According to Jackson, Grabiner told him to "take the money and go to my home in Savannah. He told me that if anything further was to be done here, Comiskey would write about it."

Jackson's third attempt to tell what he knew came when he sent a letter to Comiskey dated November 15, 1919. Jackson had written to Comiskey (the letter was actually written by his wife, Katie), to ask why he had not received his World Series check. Comiskey responded that his check was being held up based on rumors that the 1919 World Series had been fixed. Jackson replied as follows:

> I sure am surprised to hear that my name has been connected with any scandal
> in the recent World Series, as I think my playing proved that I did all I could
> to win, and I wrote Mr. Gleason yesterday and as soon as I hear from him I will
> be only too glad to come to Chicago or any place you may say and clear my name
> and whoever started this will have to prove his statements.[31]

Jackson's fourth attempt to tell what he knew came in February 1920, when
White Sox club secretary Harry Grabiner came to Jackson's home in Savannah
to sign Jackson to a new contract for the 1920 season. According to Jackson,
he questioned Grabiner about why no one wanted to hear what he knew about
the scandal and asked him what to do with the $5,000. Grabiner told him to
keep the money, but then used the fact that Jackson had the money to pressure
the player into signing a three-year contract for $8,000 per year, which was
$2,000 less per year than what Jackson had been asking for, and far less than
other stars were receiving.

Jackson's fifth attempt to tell about the scandal ties into his defenders' second claim, that Jackson's testimony was in fact scripted by Alfred Austrian in
an attempt to cover up for Charles Comiskey. A coverup was necessary because
Comiskey knew most of the details of the fix soon after the World Series had
ended but still denied this knowledge and went on to sign seven guilty players
for the 1920 season. Jackson had attempted to reveal what he knew about the
scandal on many occasions, and once Cicotte confessed, the last thing that
Comiskey and Austrian wanted was for Jackson to discuss the number of times
that he had tried to reveal what he knew to Comiskey. Therefore, when Jackson
came to Comiskey's office after Cicotte had confessed, it was Austrian's job to
manipulate Jackson to assure that his testimony would not be damaging to Comiskey, Austrian's client.

In the interview with Austrian, Jackson professed his innocence. However,
according to Jackson's supporters, Austrian listened to Jackson's story and told
the player that it would not be believed. Jackson had already been named by
Cicotte in his confession and Maharg in his newspaper interview. Supporting
Austrian's contention was the fact that when Jackson telephoned Judge Mac-
Donald earlier in the day to protest his innocence, the judge angrily told Jackson that he did not believe him and hung up on the player.

In *Say It Ain't So, Joe!* Gropman describes what happened next:

> Austrian hammered away. He repeated that Jackson's story, true or not, was
> not believable. The judge didn't believe it. If the case went to trial, a jury wouldn't
> believe it either. Whether he had done it or not, the best way out, the only way
> out, was to admit it and say he was sorry. If he did that, the club would stand
> behind him.
>   Then Austrian reminded Joe of the gamblers who, unlike the fans, would not
> forgive. If Joe told the truth, that is, that he had refused the offer and had played
> to win, the gamblers would think he had double-crossed them, for they believed
> he had accepted the offer. And they knew he had taken their $5,000. In light

of the death threat made against Lefty Williams, Joe saw it could be dangerous for him if the gamblers thought he had deceived them.

The meeting in Austrian's office lasted for several hours. Sometime toward the end, still under the mistaken assumption that Austrian was acting in his behalf, Jackson agreed to follow Austrian's advice. They went over the details of the story Jackson would tell to the Grand Jury. He would say he was guilty, repeat Cicotte's version of the fix, and blame everything on Gandil, who had retired from baseball right after the Series. Austrian must have thought it best to underline the fact that Gandil had been the instigator. (In his testimony Jackson did call Gandil the "instigator," probably the only time in his life he ever used that word.) Jackson would say that Gandil had talked him into it and then double-crossed him over the money—he promised $20,000 and only paid $5,000. Joe would present himself as the ignorant yokel who'd been taken by the sharpers. Poor old Shoeless Joe.[32]

There is some definite logic behind the third claim of Jackson's defenders, that Jackson's name was used by the conspirators without his permission, and that in reality Jackson had no involvement in the fix. Looking at things from the gamblers' perspective, in order to truly believe that the fix was well organized and feasible, they would want to make sure that the team's star player—in this case Jackson—was in on the plot. Even with Cicotte and Williams, it might have been difficult for Gandil to convince the gamblers that the plot would succeed without Jackson's involvement.

Proving that Jackson did not have knowledge of the fix, however, is much harder. The bulk of the evidence for this claim comes from Jackson's testimony during a 1924 trial when the player sued Comiskey to recover the balance owed to him on his contract. There are two interesting items to note about this later trial. One is that Jackson's 1920 confession to the Chicago grand jury somehow mysteriously reappeared in the possession of Comiskey's lawyer during the trial. The second is the fact that the jury ruled that Jackson was entitled to his full salary for 1921 and 1922. The primary reason for this ruling was that the jury believed that Jackson was not involved in the 1919 World Series fix. Unfortunately for Jackson, the judge overruled the jury and threw out the verdict, claiming that the decision was based on Jackson's testimony at the trial, which was contradicted by his testimony before the grand jury. The case was eventually settled out of court. In addition to Jackson's own testimony, Gropman cites portions of other testimony from the 1921 and 1924 trials. For example, during the 1921 trial, when describing his meeting with the conspirators, Bill Burns stated, "They were all there except for Jackson, and Williams was kind of representing Jackson." Gropman then presents the following excerpt from Lefty Williams' testimony in the 1924 trial:

Q: Did you yourself have any talk with Joe Jackson before or during the World Series with reference to the throwing of the Series to the Cincinnati team?
A: No, sir.

Q: Did Joe Jackson tell you at any time prior to or during the World Series that
  you could use his name in dealing with the gamblers?
A: No, sir.
Q: In reference to throwing the games?
A: No, sir.
Q: Did you have any talk with him in that connection at all?
A: No, sir.
Q: At any time?
A: No, sir.
Q: To your knowledge did Joe Jackson know his name was being used by
  anybody for the purpose of dealing with the gamblers?
A: No, sir.
Q: In throwing the 1919 World Series?
A: Not to my recollection, his name was never mentioned.[33]

The final claim of Jackson's supporters—that Jackson had received $5,000
after the World Series and not during it, and only kept it when instructed to
do so by White Sox officials—is the most difficult one to prove. In his own
testimony before the 1920 grand jury, Jackson stated that he received $5,000
after the fourth game in Chicago. Even if we accept the fact that Jackson's
testimony was scripted by Austrian, it is hard to understand why it was in Comiskey's interest for Jackson to lie about this particular detail.

Supporters of Jackson point to two pieces of evidence in Jackson's favor.
One is that Jackson's grand jury testimony contained some factual errors.
Jackson claimed that after the fourth game the team was going back to Cincinnati for game five, although in reality game five was also in Chicago. Also, when
asked who won the fourth game, Jackson mistakenly replied "Dick Kerr,"
which Jackson supporters believe shows that Jackson was tending to follow a
script rather than actually telling his side of the events.

The second piece of evidence is that in Jackson's 1924 trial, he very clearly
states that he did not receive the $5,000 until after the series.

Q: Did you have a talk with "Lefty" Williams one or two days after the World's
  Series was over?
A: I had a talk with Mr. Williams the night after the World Series was over, that
  day.
Q: In Chicago?
A: Yes, sir.
Q: Where?
A: I think it was in the Warner Hotel.
Q: What talk did you have with Williams at that time?
A: Mr. Williams came in my room and held out a couple of envelopes and said,
  "Here, do you want one of these?" I said, "No, what is it?" He pushed it
  over to me again. I said, "Go on, what is it that you got?" He told me,
  "Why," he says "it is money." I says, "I don't want your money." He said
  it was part of what he got in a frame-up with some eastern gamblers and
  they had used my name.

Q: Who had used your name?

A: Cicotte and Gandil.

Q: And Williams?

A: And Williams.

Q: Did you give him permission to use your name?

A: No, sir.

Q: At any time?

A: No, sir.

Q: Did you know before that time that your name had been used by Williams with the gamblers?

A: Not up to that time, no sir.

Q: Or by Cicotte or Gandil?

A: Or by Cicotte or Gandil.

Q: What did you say to Williams then?

A: I told him they had a lot of nerve. I don't know just the word I used, but "Big bums" or something, to be out pulling that kind of stuff on me, knowing that it was the only way I had of making a livelihood.

Q: What else?

A: We had a few hot words there, and he was drinking, and I walked out of the room. As I was going I told him I was going down to see Comiskey about this in the morning. So the next morning I went down to Comiskey's office to see him and tell him all about it.[34]

After evaluating the evidence, it can be said with a high degree of certainty that Jackson played to the best of his ability in the 1919 World Series and had no involvement in the fixing of the games. We also know that while Jackson had guilty knowledge, he made numerous attempts to report this knowledge, and to fault him for his actions would be totally unfair.

On the other side, there is very strong evidence that although he was not an active participant in the fix, Jackson was at least aware of it and was compensated for going along with the plot. While we have presented evidence of Jackson's innocence in this regard, the evidence is less than conclusive.

The worst case against Joe Jackson is that he grudgingly agreed to go along with the 1919 World Series fix for $20,000. When it came time to throw games, however, Jackson could not go along with it, and he attempted to expose the fix to Comiskey but was rebuffed at every turn. The best case for Jackson is that he was an innocent man, a victim of the World Series fix. He had heard about the fix but refused to go along with it and may have doubted that the scandal would ever take place. When he began to believe that the fix would actually happen he attempted to disassociate himself from the series and tell what he knew but was unable to do so. In the end, Joe Jackson was thrown out of baseball, not because he participated in the fix, but because he could prove Charles Comiskey was involved in a massive coverup.

Which of these scenarios is true? We will leave the reader to decide. It should be noted that all that Jackson's supporters are asking for is a fair hearing on the subject, but they have been consistently denied this by baseball officials from 1921 until the present day. The final chapter of this book will discuss what action baseball should take regarding Jackson and others who were implicated in various scandals throughout history.

The aftermath for most of those involved in the Black Sox scandal makes for a very sad story. On the positive side, "Clean Sox" Ray Schalk and Eddie Collins had long careers in baseball after their playing days were over, and both reside today in the Baseball Hall of Fame. Few of the other central characters were as fortunate.

Kid Gleason continued to manage the White Sox through the 1923 season and later coached for Connie Mack's Philadelphia Athletics. He died in 1933 in Philadelphia.

Charles Comiskey, who was probably the primary cause of the scandal, officially escaped all responsibility for the fix and today is enshrined in the Baseball Hall of Fame. On the other hand, Comiskey's reputation was forever soiled, and his once-great club was in ruins. The White Sox would not win another American League pennant until 1959, 28 years after Comiskey's death.

Arnold Rothstein was shot the evening of November 4, 1928, and died the next day. His murderer was believed to have been gambler George McManus, who was pursuing Rothstein to collect unpaid gambling debts from a high-stakes poker game. Rothstein outlived Bill Fallon by one year.

The expelled players on the periphery of the scandal, Jean Dubuc and Joe Gedeon, were soon forgotten. Gedeon briefly played outlaw ball in his native California and finally settled down in San Francisco, passing away on May 19, 1941. Dubuc settled in Fort Myers, Florida, where he died on August 28, 1958.

Dickie Kerr, the star of the series for the White Sox, continued to perform heroically, winning 19 games for a seventh-place Chicago team in 1921. Not willing to accept Comiskey's miserly salaries, however, Kerr refused to sign with the Sox in 1922 and played outlaw ball. He was then placed on organized baseball's blacklist for competing against some of his former teammates while out of organized baseball. Kerr was reinstated by Landis in 1925 and appeared with the White Sox during that season. Kerr closed out his pitching career in the Texas League in 1927.

After leaving baseball, Kerr went into the cotton business but later came back to baseball as a minor league manager in the St. Louis Cardinals system. In addition to his performance in the 1919 World Series, he will always be remembered for the fact that while managing the St. Louis Cardinals Class D Daytona Beach club, he converted a young player named Stan Musial from a pitcher to an outfielder. Musial became one of the greatest players in baseball history and is now in the Baseball Hall of Fame. Kerr left the game for good in 1955 and became an office manager for an electrical company in Houston. He died in Houston on May 4, 1963, at the age of 69.

For the Black Sox, life after baseball was filled with tragedy. Part of this tragedy was their unfulfilled destiny: These men were among the best baseball players in the world and suddenly, in the prime of their careers, the doors of organized baseball were closed to them. All eight men tried to keep playing baseball in other leagues and on semipro teams across the nation, but they soon found this activity a poor substitute for their major league careers.

The other part of the tragedy was that these eight men were considered national villains, the Benedict Arnolds of baseball. Unlike criminals who serve their sentences and are soon forgotten, these eight players spent the rest of their lives in disgrace. While their teammates enjoyed public admiration as former big league players, most of the Black Sox did not volunteer their identities and lived reclusive lives.

Joe Jackson spent the summer of 1922 in the New York–New Jersey area playing on a number of semipro teams. While he initially played under an assumed name, New York sportswriter Eddie Phelon built a team around Jackson and announced a petition drive to demand Jackson's reinstatement into organized baseball. The petition, with several thousand signatures, was sent to Commissioner Landis but received no action. By the end of the season, Jackson's team had disbanded.

Jackson then returned to his native territory and spent the rest of his life in the South. In 1923 Jackson signed to play for the Americus Club of the South Georgia League. The South Georgia League was an outlaw league and was outside the boundaries of organized baseball. He later played, along with Cicotte and Risberg, in an outlaw league in Louisiana and managed a semipro team. Jackson also owned a successful dry-cleaning business in Savannah, Georgia.

In 1929 Jackson returned to his old hometown, Greenville, South Carolina. Jackson opened a liquor store and continued to make a fairly prosperous living. While his national reputation was one of villainy, he was loved and respected in Greenville and considered one of the town's leading citizens. Jackson continued to play semipro ball on occasion for many years. When he finally stopped playing, he was appointed chairman of the Protest Board of the Western Carolina Semi-Pro League, which made Jackson extremely proud.

As he grew older, Jackson's health began to fail. In 1949, he decided to tell his version of the story in a *Sport Magazine* article by Furman Bisher. Jackson maintained his innocence, saying, "I can say that my conscience is clear and I will stand on my record in that World Series."[35]

In 1951 a major effort began to clear Jackson's name. The South Carolina legislature passed a resolution asking Commissioner Chandler to reinstate Jackson to baseball. No action was ever taken on this resolution, and Chandler later claimed that he never even saw it. The efforts to clear Jackson's name culminated in an invitation to appear on the "Ed Sullivan Show" on December 16, 1951. Although Jackson initially declined the invitation, his family convinced him to change his mind, and he accepted. Unfortunately, Jackson died of a heart attack on December 5, 1951.

Fred McMullin disappeared from the public eye soon after the scandal. He moved to Southern California, where he got a job working in the office of the U.S. marshal in Los Angeles. McMullin died in Los Angeles on November 21, 1952.

Buck Weaver devoted much of his energy after his expulsion to clearing his name. Weaver made numerous appeals to Landis for his reinstatement, but all were denied. Despite the assistance of many leading figures in baseball, in addition to the help provided by Judge Hugo Friend, who had presided over the 1919 trial, Weaver was doomed to the bitter disappointment of never having his name cleared.

After his career in organized baseball, Weaver remained in Chicago. He continued to play semipro baseball until 1931. Weaver also briefly played with the Douglas club and the outlaw Frontier League in 1925.

Weaver then went into the drugstore business with his brother-in-law, William Scanlin. The business went sour with the onset of the Great Depression, and when Scanlin died, Weaver and his wife took his sister-in-law and her two children into their home. Weaver was extremely close with the children and served as their surrogate father. Weaver and his wife Helen then opened a sandwich shop called "Buck Weaver's," which also failed. Weaver later drifted to a job as a painter for the city of Chicago for $10 per day. He then became interested in horse racing and soon developed strong connections at Chicago's Sportsman's Park. Weaver got a job as a pari-mutuel clerk and continued this occupation for the rest of his life.

Weaver was well liked in Chicago and his bids for reinstatement received a great deal of public support. In 1954 leading author and longtime White Sox fan James Farrell interviewed Buck Weaver at his home in Chicago. Talking about his expulsion from baseball, Weaver stated, "a murderer even serves his sentence and is let out. I got life."[36] On January 3, 1956, Buck Weaver suffered a heart attack on West 71st Street on the South Side of Chicago. Within a few hours, he was dead.

After the trial, Lefty Williams operated a pool hall in Chicago, which he bought from Joe Jackson. He also continued to play baseball, pitching for the Bayard team in the Frontier League against former teammates Buck Weaver and Chick Gandil and the infamous Hal Chase. Williams later moved to Springfield, Missouri, where he pitched in a semipro softball league. Like Fred McMullin, Williams ended up on the West Coast, settling in the San Fernando Valley. He moved to Laguna Beach in 1954 and operated a garden nursery business there. Williams died in Laguna Beach on November 4, 1959.

Happy Felsch continued to play baseball on semipro teams in the Wisconsin State League, later playing for a club in Havre, Montana. After his playing days were over, Felsch became a crane operator in his native Milwaukee. He later ran a tavern and a grocery store in his hometown.

Of all the players, Felsch was by far the most willing to talk about the scandal.

He was a principal source of Eliot Asinof's research for *Eight Men Out.* On August 17, 1964, Happy Felsch died in Milwaukee. He was 73 years old.

Eddie Cicotte returned to Detroit and got a job as a paymaster with Ford Motor Company. He occasionally talked with sportswriters such as Joe Falls and Lee Allen about the scandal but never really told his side of the story. Falls quoted Cicotte as follows:

> I admit I did wrong, but I've paid for it. I've paid for it for the past 46 years.
> Sure, they asked me about being a crooked ballplayer. But, I've become calloused to it. I figure if I was crooked in baseball, they were crooked in something else.
> I don't know of anyone who ever went through life without making a mistake. Everybody who has ever lived has committed sins of his own.
> I've tried to make up for it by living as clean a life as I could. I'm proud of the way I've lived, and I think my family is, too.
> That's all I think about, my family. I think they're proud of me—I know they are. I know they look up to me. And my friends, they feel the same way.[37]

After his retirement, Cicotte raised strawberries on a small farm behind his house. He died in Detroit on May 5, 1969.

Chick Gandil continued to play baseball for some time after his banishment. Among the teams he played for were the Douglas Blues in the outlaw Frontier League. Gandil also played ball in Shreveport, Louisiana, and then became a plumber, working first in Los Angeles and later in Oakland, California. Gandil and his wife retired to Calistoga, in the heart of the California wine country. He lived a quiet life there, and few of his neighbors knew of his involvement in the 1919 Black Sox scandal.

Throughout his life, Gandil continued to protest his innocence. While admitting his involvement in the plot to throw the series, he maintained that he and his teammates had not gone through with the plot. He wrote to Landis on three occasions and asked for reinstatement, but he never received a reply. In a 1969 interview with Dwight Chapin of the *Sporting News,* Gandil stated, "I will tell you this. I am going to my grave with a clear conscience." Gandil died on December 13, 1970, in a convalescent home in Calistoga.[38]

Like most of the rest of the banished players, Swede Risberg continued to play baseball for a short time after his expulsion. He later operated a dairy farm near Rochester, Minnesota. Risberg again came into the public eye in 1927 when he publicly claimed that the Detroit Tigers threw games to the White Sox in 1917. This incident will be discussed in a later chapter.

Late in his life Risberg left Minnesota for northern California. Historians made many attempts to get Risberg to discuss the Black Sox scandal, but the player never told his side of the story. Only 26 years old at the time of his expulsion, Risberg was the last surviving member of the eight Black Sox. He died in Red Bluff, California, on October 13, 1975.

The Black Sox scandal was both the greatest scandal and the greatest tragedy in American sports history. The expelled players suffered tremendously for the rest of their lives.

Why did it happen? An interesting perspective is provided by Fred Lieb, one of the greatest of all sportswriters. Lieb cited five factors which led to the scandal.[39]

- The greed and avarice that is inherent in so much of the human race.
- The presence of polarized groups of players on the Chicago team, and the bad effect that the ringleaders of the fix had on the other members of their group.
- The free-spending atmosphere that followed World War I and the rising affluence of underworld characters.
- The fact that the players knew that Hal Chase and others were "getting away with it."
- Penurious salaries paid by Comiskey to the members of the 1919 Chicago team.

As time goes on, the events that led up to the scandal will continue to fade into the background. The memory of the Black Sox scandal, however, will live forever.

Chapter 8

Days of Scandal

The revelation of the Black Sox scandal totally changed organized baseball's posture toward corruption in its ranks. As has been documented in previous chapters, in the years leading up to 1920 organized baseball's reaction to any threat of scandal was to sweep it under the rug—to cover up any hint of scandal for fear of injuring the game and the business of baseball. The rulers of baseball took the view that if they paid no attention to corruption it would eventually go away. The truth was that by not dealing with the problem they allowed it to fester until the corruption threatened the game's survival.

As a result of the Black Sox scandal, baseball discovered that the key to survival was constant vigilance against corruption. Any suspicious action was investigated, any scandal was pursued, and any dishonest players were expelled from baseball.

Leading this anticorruption frenzy was Commissioner Kenesaw Mountain Landis, a zealous crusader for the cause of clean baseball. His actions in the aftermath of the Black Sox scandal—while not necessarily appropriate from the standpoint of players such as Buck Weaver, Joe Jackson, and Joe Gedeon—were exactly what the public was looking for from the new commissioner.

For baseball, the challenge was not just to clean up the game, but to convince the public that the reorganization of baseball would prevent a recurrence of the corruption that led to the Black Sox scandal. Aggressive and uncompromising action was needed, and Judge Landis filled the bill. Landis even *looked* stern and unrelenting, with a scowling face and mop of gray hair. Baseball needed good publicity, and Landis craved publicity. "His career typifies the heights to which dramatic talent may carry a man in America, if he only has the foresight not to go on the stage," was the way Heywood Broun, sportswriter and dramatic critic for the *New York Herald-Tribune*, summed up Landis.

Baseball's state of corruption and Landis's zeal to clean up the game led to a rash of public scandals between 1921 and 1924. As we will see, in some cases Landis played the avenging angel, but in at least one case he was more concerned with the players' well-being than with his crusade for justice. Baseball insiders came to know that the one constant about Landis was his inconsistency.

The first of these post–Black Sox scandals broke in March 1921. The player involved was Eugene Paulette, first baseman for the Philadelphia Phillies.

Gene Paulette was born in 1891 in Centralia, Illinois. He first reached the big leagues in 1911, appearing in ten games with the New York Giants. He resurfaced again with the St. Louis Browns in 1916 and was traded to the St. Louis Cardinals early in the 1917 season. While not a great hitter (his lifetime major league average was .269 with two home runs and 165 RBIs in 1,780 at-bats), Paulette was extremely versatile, playing all nine positions during his years in the majors.

After hitting .273 in 1918, Paulette was traded during the 1919 season to the Philadelphia Phillies. He enjoyed his best year in 1920 with the Phillies, hitting .288, primarily as a first baseman.

Paulette's problems stemmed from his actions early in the 1919 season, before he was traded from the Cardinals to the Phillies. Paulette was accused of being in cahoots with, and receiving gifts from, St. Louis gamblers Elmer Farrar and Carl Zork. This is the same Carl Zork who was later indicted for his connection with the Black Sox scandal. While there was no evidence that Paulette had actually thrown a game, a letter to the gamblers came into Landis's hands in which Paulette offered to throw games and claimed he could get two other St. Louis players to go along with him.

Paulette was summoned by Commissioner Landis to appear before him in Chicago on March 7 to explain the situation. Paulette refused to go before the commissioner, and later that month Landis expelled Paulette from baseball for life. Landis's decision was as follows:

> Player Eugene A. Paulette admitted that he received money from Elmer Farrar of St. Louis, as a loan, which is not repaid; this money was given to him by Farrar sometime after an interview with Farrar and another St. Louis man named Carl Zork, in which interview Farrar and Zork urged Paulette to co-operate with them in crooked gambling on ball games to be thrown by this player.
>
> Subsequently, Paulette wrote to Farrar asking for more money, which he did not obtain. In this letter Paulette mentions the names of two other ball players who he claims he could get to co-operate with him. In his statement to the Commissioner, Paulette denied absolutely that he had any basis whatever for using the names of these players and asserted that so far as he knew they were honest men.
>
> Paulette denies that he had ever thrown a ball game and asserts that during the last playing season he held himself aloof from corrupting associations; but the fact remains that he offered to betray his team and that he put himself in the vicious power of Farrar and Zork. He will go on the ineligible list.[1]

Landis further stated that "my only regret is that the real culprits, the gamblers, cannot be reached by this office."

Hot on the heels of the Paulette case was Landis's expulsion of Cincinnati pitcher Ray Fisher. We will not dwell on this case in depth, since no gambling

Judge Kenesaw Mountain Landis. Landis was chosen as the first commissioner of baseball for his incorruptible reputation. *Courtesy of Transcendental Graphics.*

or game fixing was involved, but it is worth touching on since the injustice done to Fisher shows the arbitrary nature of some of Landis's actions.

Fisher was born in 1887 in Middlebury, Vermont. A right-handed pitcher, Fisher's best year was with the Yankees in 1915, when he won 18 games against 11 losses. Fisher continued with the Yankees through the 1917 season, and after a year out for a tour of duty in the army he moved to the Cincinnati Reds in 1919. As a member of the Reds, Fisher appeared twice in the infamous 1919 World Series, losing game number three to Dickie Kerr by a score of 3–0.

After he slipped to a 10-11 record in 1920, the Reds sent Fisher a contract calling for a salary cut of $1,000 to $4,500 for 1921. Fisher signed the contract

166 The Fix Is In

under a great deal of protest. Shortly after this, Fisher was offered the job as the baseball coach of the University of Michigan, which he gladly accepted. He was then placed on the ineligible list for violating his contract. Fisher was surprised that he was placed on the ineligible list as opposed to the voluntarily retired list.

The next year Fisher decided to rejoin the Reds and applied for reinstatement. Fisher expected his reinstatement to be a routine matter, but he was in for quite a shock. As Lee Allen wrote, "when the appeal for reinstatement reached the Commissioner's office, Judge Landis made one of his few inexplicable decisions. He made Fisher's ineligibility permanent."[2]

Fisher went on to enjoy a long, successful career with the University of Michigan, living until the ripe old age of 95.

Another of Landis's inexplicable decisions came in the Benny Kauff case, also in 1921. Again, this case did not involve gambling, but it is worth studying since it helps demonstrate baseball's zeal for ridding the game of any scandal in the post–Black Sox era.

Benny Kauff was born in 1890 in Pomeroy, Ohio. He started his professional career with Parkersburg in the Virginia Valley League in 1910, moving to Bridgeport in the Connecticut League, Rochester in the Eastern League, Brockton in the New England League, and Hartford in the Connecticut League over the next few years, with a brief five-game tour with the New York Yankees mixed in. After the 1913 season, Kauff was sold to the Indianapolis club of the American Association, but by that time the outlaw Federal League had declared major league status and was raiding the rosters of organized baseball. Kauff took the opportunity to jump to the Indianapolis Hoosiers of the Federal League.

Kauff was an instant sensation in the Federal League, hitting .370 to win the batting title in 1914. He also led the league in runs, hits, doubles, stolen bases, and on-base percentage. He became known as the "Ty Cobb of the Federal League."

The Federal League was struggling, so Kauff, as one of the league's big drawing cards, was shifted to the Brooklyn Tip-Tops in 1915. Despite the fact that he was under a Federal League contract, Kauff decided that he was too great a player to stay in the Federal League and jumped to the New York Giants. National League President John Tenner refused to approve his move to the Giants, and Kauff returned to the Federal League.

Kauff put together another outstanding season in 1915, again winning the batting title, with a .342 average. He also led the league in slugging percentage, stolen bases, and on-base percentage.

After 1915 the Federal League folded, and Kauff was sold to the New York Giants for the sum of $30,000. Kauff held out for a share of the proceeds and eventually received a $10,000 bonus.

By that time Kauff had come to believe his "Ty Cobb of the Federal

Gene Paulette. Paulette was the first player to learn of Landis's determination the hard way. *Courtesy of National Baseball Library and Archive, Cooperstown, New York.*

League" press clippings. When he reported to the Giants' spring training camp, he was decked out in extremely expensive clothes and adorned with a huge diamond stickpin, a large diamond ring, and a gold watch encrusted with diamonds. It took four trunks to carry his silk shirts and other clothing.

Kauff never quite lived up to his Federal League reputation with the Giants, although he was a useful player. His best full season was in 1917, when he hit .308. He also hit two home runs in the 1917 World Series.

In 1920 Kauff was a witness in front of the Chicago grand jury, testifying in regard to the gambling activities of his former Giant teammates Hal Chase and Heinie Zimmerman. Zimmerman countercharged that Kauff and other players were involved in game fixing, but the story was given little credence. Kauff was considered an honest player, if a somewhat wild character. In 1919 Kauff had run into some problems with the law, and in December of that year he was arrested in New York and charged with being involved in a stolen car ring. He was indicted in February 1920 on charges of stealing an automobile and receiving a stolen automobile. Kauff's play suffered, and he split the 1920 season between the Giants and the Toronto team of the International League.

In April 1921 Landis placed Kauff on the ineligible list. Although Kauff's case was still going through the legal system, Landis claimed that "the mere presence of such a player in the line-up would be so unjust to the other players, so deeply offensive to baseball, the baseball public, and so strongly suggestive of a lack of appreciation of elemental morality on the part of those charged with protecting the good repute of the game, that it is an obvious impossibility." The next month Kauff was found not guilty in court, but his application for reinstatement by Landis was denied. Landis had reviewed the court testimony and claimed that "I read every line of the testimony, and the acquittal smells to high heaven. That acquittal was one of the worst miscarriages of justice that ever came under my observation."

Kauff then went to court and received a temporary injunction restraining Landis and National League President John Heydler from preventing him from playing in the National League. Kauff expected to be playing in 1922, but his joy was short-lived, for the injunction against Landis and Heydler was dismissed by an appellate court on January 17, 1922. Despite the fact that he was an honest player, that he had come forward with information about crooked players, and that he had been acquitted of the auto theft charges, Kauff never played in organized baseball again. He left with a career average of .311.

The next major scandal was one that did not come into the public light for many years. This scandal involved pitcher Carl Mays, one of the most controversial players in baseball history.

Mays was born in 1891 in Liberty, Kentucky. He broke into the major leagues as a pitcher with Boston, teaming with Babe Ruth, Ernie Shore, and Dutch Leonard to form one of the best staffs in the American League. The Red Sox won the American League pennant (and the World Series) in 1915, 1916,

Bennie Kauff. Kauff, the "Ty Cobb of the Federal League," was expelled by Landis on charges of auto theft—despite the fact that a court of law found him innocent. *Photograph by Patrice Kelly.*

and 1918. Mays played a big part in the club's success between 1916 and 1918, averaging more than 20 wins per year during that stretch. His best year was in 1917, when he turned in a record of 22 wins and seven losses with a 1.74 earned-run average. In 1918 he led the American League in complete games with 30 and also recorded a league-high eight shutouts.

Mays had a strange personality and was never a popular player. He was very demanding with his teammates, and errors and misplays behind him led to fits of rage.

His first major flap occurred in 1919. He got off to a poor start with the Red Sox that year, coming into July with a record of 5-11. Mays publicly blamed the poor fielding of his teammates for his substandard start.

In a game in Chicago on July 13, 1919, Mays lost all patience with his teammates and stormed off the field after two innings. He told his manager, future Hall of Famer Ed Barrow, "I'm through with this ball club; I'll never pitch another game for the Red Sox." At first it was assumed that Mays would soon be back in the fold, but this did not come to pass. He was then suspended by American League President Ban Johnson.

While Mays was under suspension, Red Sox owner Harry Frazee, the man who would later that year sell Babe Ruth to the Yankees for $125,000, dealt Mays to the New York club for $40,000. American League President Johnson refused to approve the trade, and the Yankees went to court to seek an injunction. The Yankees' legal fight was successful, and Mays was allowed to join the club on August 2. The battle between Johnson and the Yankees and Red Sox

Carl Mays. Mays was suspected by Fred Lieb of throwing a game in the 1921 World Series. *Courtesy of Transcendental Graphics.*

over Carl Mays was the beginning of Johnson's demise as the absolute ruler of the American League and helped lead to the establishment of the office of the commissioner of baseball and the coming of Judge Landis.

In 1920 Mays was on his way to a fine season with the Yankees when tragedy struck. On August 16, 1920, the Cleveland Indians were visiting New York in a battle between the clubs for first place. The 1920 pennant race was to go down to the wire, with the Indians edging out the Yankees and the Chicago White Sox, who were devastated at the tail end of the season by the suspension of eight of their players.

One of the keys to the success that Carl Mays enjoyed was his unique "submarine" motion, in which his hand sometimes scraped the ground as he pitched the ball. He was also known not to be averse to pitching inside, and he led the American League in hit batsmen in both 1917 and 1918.

In that August 16 game, Cleveland shortstop Ray Chapman led off the fifth inning. Chapman, one of the most popular players in the game, was a fine hitter and fielder. Recently married, he had originally planned on retiring after the 1919 season to go into his father-in-law's business, but the club talked him into returning for one more year. He planned to leave the game at the conclusion of the season to be with his wife and the child they were expecting.

Chapman had a habit of crowding the plate and laying down bunts for base hits. As Mays delivered his first pitch, Chapman leaned in and stood motionless as the ball came toward him. The pitch struck him on the head, and Chapman collapsed.

Chapman was able to get to his feet and was helped off the field, but he later collapsed in the clubhouse. He was immediately taken to a New York hospital, where he died that night. Chapman was the first and only player to be killed in a major league baseball game. (Three former major leaguers have been killed in minor league games.)

The tragedy created a storm of controversy around Mays, one that he would have to contend with for the rest of his life. Many players in the league demanded that Mays be expelled from baseball. Mays retreated to the sanctuary of his apartment, refusing to talk to reporters or answer questions. Cleveland player-manager Tris Speaker later publicly absolved Mays of any blame, and Mays returned to the game. He went on to win 26 games that season, and in 1921 he led the American League with 27 wins against only nine losses.

While the Chapman tragedy was certainly the greatest controversy in the career of Carl Mays, the incident of most relevance to this book occurred in the 1921 World Series between the New York Yankees and the New York Giants. Coming off his tremendous year, Mays pitched the World Series opener, throwing a five-hit shutout to win 3–0. The Yankees also won the second game by a 3–0 score, which gave them a 2–0 lead in the World Series. (From 1919 to 1921, the World Series was the best five out of nine rather than the more usual seven-game format.)

The Giants came back in the third game with a 13–5 win. Mays again took the mound for the Yankees in game four, facing Phil Douglas, about whom we will hear more later in this chapter. The Yankees led 1–0 going into the eighth inning, but Mays then fell apart, giving up three runs on four hits in the eighth inning and another run in the ninth inning to hand the Giants a 4–2 victory. The key hit during the eighth inning was a triple by Giants star Emil "Irish" Meusial, which occurred when Mays ignored Yankee manager Miller Huggins's signal for a fastball and instead threw a slow-breaking curve.

The evening after the game an actor, whose name was never revealed, approached sportswriter Fred Lieb with a startling story. Lieb related the story as follows:

> The actor's tale went something like this: At the start of the eighth inning, Mrs. Mays, sitting in the grandstand, flashed a signal to Carl by wiping her face with a white handkerchief. Some persons, he said, who regarded a Giants victory in the Series as absolutely necessary for their welfare, had offered Carl a rather substantial sum of cash if in close games he would serve up enough hitable pitches to lose the game. Mrs. Mays was to be the one who, by the prearranged handkerchief signal, would advise her husband that the money had been handed over.[3]

Lieb brought the story to the attention of Yankee co-owner Colonel Till-inghast Huston and then to Judge Landis. Landis immediately called in a detective agency and had Mays tailed throughout the rest of the series. Landis asked Lieb not to put the story in the papers until Landis had had time to investigate the matter.

Mays was followed throughout the rest of the series, but no evidence was uncovered to incriminate him. Since it was not unusual for a pitcher to lose his effectiveness in the late innings, it appeared at that point that the story was simply idle gossip.

A couple of years later, however, Lieb was on vacation with a number of baseball figures, including Huston and Dodger manager Wilbert Robinson. Lieb tells the story as follows:

> Some time in the evening, after Huston had imbibed more than a little, he turned to me and said, "Freddy, I am going to tell you the damnedest story a baseball owner has ever told a reporter." Every time he repeated this remark, Uncle Robby would sh-sh-sh him and say, "No, no Colonel! Don't tell him!" But Huston would return to the subject. As the rum and Coca-Cola had its effect, some of the people in the room gradually disappeared and Robby fell asleep. Only Huston, Grayson and I were left. Grayson, still consuming Coca-Cola and rum, tried to stay awake to hear the story that Huston apparently intended to tell me, but finally he too fell asleep. So I said to Huston, "Now that we're alone, what is this story you're holding back on me?"
>
> "I wanted to tell you that some of our pitchers threw World Series games on us in both 1921 and 1922," he mumbled.
>
> "You mean that Mays matter of the 1921 World Series?" I asked. He said, "Yes, but there were others—other times, other pitchers." By now he was almost in a stupor and stumbled off to bed.
>
> I suppose as a good reporter I should have stuck around the next morning and pressed Huston for specifics—names, dates, and all that. But I didn't. Huston hadn't appeared before Traband and I were scheduled to leave to play golf at Sea Island, Georgia. After our game we continued north. When I next spoke with Huston alone a year or two later, he would say only that he stood by what he had told me at Dover Hall.[4]

The final piece of information from Lieb came in a discussion he had with Miller Huggins, the Hall of Fame Yankee manager. Discussing indigent former ball players in need of a helping hand, Huggins stated that he would always help any of his players if they needed it with two exceptions: Carl Mays and Joe Bush. In the case of Mays, Lieb was fairly certain that Huggins's animosity stemmed from the 1921 World Series.

Mays fell into disfavor with the club after 1921, and by 1923 he was a seldom-used backup pitcher. He was then waived out of the league and picked up by the Cincinnati Reds, with whom he rebounded to win 20 games in 1924. He stayed with Cincinnati until the end of 1928 and finished his career with the Giants in 1929.

After his retirement, Mays stayed in the game as a scout for the Indians and the Braves. He lived to the age of 79, passing away in El Cajon, California, on April 4, 1971.

The career totals for Carl Mays are quite impressive. He won 207 games against 126 losses and had an earned-run average for his career of 2.92. These would seem to be Hall of Fame–quality statistics, but Carl Mays is not in the Hall of Fame. Mays was haunted throughout his life by the Chapman incident, despite the fact that all evidence showed that Chapman's beaning was purely an accident. Mays himself stated, "It's not on my conscience, it wasn't my fault," but his name was always associated with the incident.

Mays went to his grave believing that the Chapman beaning kept him out of the Hall of Fame. Lieb, however, was a member of the Hall of Fame's Veterans Committee, the body in charge of selecting old-time players for the Hall of Fame, and he claimed that when the name of Carl Mays came up for discussion, it was the 1921 World Series rather than the Chapman beaning that kept Mays from being elected.

It will never be known whether Carl Mays was guilty of corruption in the 1921 World Series. If he was innocent, there is little doubt that he belongs in the Hall of Fame. In a survey conducted by the Society for American Baseball Research in the early 1970s to determine which players not in the Hall of Fame were most deserving of enshrinement, Mays placed eleventh—and all ten of those finishing above him are now in the Hall of Fame.

The next scandal in the early 1920s was perhaps the most tragic of all. It involved pitcher Phil Douglas, nicknamed "Shufflin' Phil."

Phil Douglas was born in 1890 in Cedartown, in the back hills of Georgia. His family moved across the border to Tennessee when Douglas was young, and except for the time he spent in the big leagues, he lived all his life in this region. During Douglas's lifetime, the Tennessee hills were filled with poverty, illiteracy, and moonshine. The residents of the hills were poorly schooled but strong-willed and independent, living life in their own way. Phil Douglas was an apt representative of this culture.

Douglas began his baseball career in 1910 with the Rome, Georgia, club of the Southeastern League. He then moved to the Macon club in the South Atlantic League, and after an excellent year in 1911, his contract was purchased by the Chicago White Sox. The White Sox farmed him out to Des Moines in 1912, and he was called up to the major league club at the tail end of the 1912 season, appearing in three games. In 1913 Douglas began the season with San Francisco in the Pacific Coast League and then moved to Spokane in the Northwestern League. In 1914 he was sold to the Cincinnati Reds.

Douglas immediately showed that he had major league talent with the last-place Reds. In 1914 he won 11 games (against 18 losses) and finished the season with an earned-run average of 2.56. He also struck out 121 batters.

Despite his good pitching, Douglas was a problem for the club. He was

**Phil Douglas. Douglas's rash letter of spite against John McGraw got Douglas ex-
pelled from baseball for corruption.** *Courtesy of National Baseball Library and
Archive, Cooperstown, New York.*

beginning to drink heavily and frequently broke training rules. The independent streak in Douglas was coming out, and he resisted the authority of his
manager, Buck Herzog.

After beginning the 1915 season with the Cincinnati Reds, he was traded
to the Brooklyn Dodgers. As disciplinary problems grew worse during his time
with the Dodgers, he often disappeared for several games between his pitching
turns. Douglas's comment was, "a guy needs a little vacation now and then,"
but Dodgers manager Wilbert Robinson did not agree, and Douglas was sold
to the Cubs in September of that year.

In 1916, Douglas returned to the minor leagues, pitching for St. Paul. In
1917 he was back in the major leagues to stay, finishing the season with a 14-20
record and a 2.55 ERA with a weak Chicago Cubs team, but his discipline
problems continued. In 1918 Douglas turned in a 10-9 record with a fine 2.12
earned-run average, but he was often missing in action. The Cubs won the National League pennant in that abbreviated 1918 season (the regular season
ended September 2 because of World War I), and Douglas was extremely upset
that he pitched only one inning in the Cubs' World Series loss to the Boston
Red Sox. Douglas returned to the Cubs for the 1919 season, but his drinking
and discipline problems had become intolerable. On July 23, 1919, Douglas
was traded to the New York Giants.

The manager of the New York Giants was John J. McGraw. McGraw was a strict disciplinarian and was known to take a chance on difficult characters, often successfully turning them around. McGraw viewed Douglas as a tremendous bargain, a player who could really solidify his team. When he was warned by friends that Douglas's alcohol and discipline problems would make him useless, McGraw said, "He can win the pennant for me."

Douglas's initial performance for McGraw was not good. Soon after joining the club, he took off on one of his drinking "vacations" and missed a turn on the mound. He then disappeared for most of the month of September, and when he returned McGraw told him he was through for the year. McGraw had constantly badgered Douglas and fined him, but none of these actions was able to turn Phil around.

In the beginning of 1920, McGraw took more determined action. McGraw decided that the key to Douglas was to keep him under constant observation, assigning private detectives and others (fans and club employees) to shadow Douglas and report on his activities. One of these keepers was a private detective named Jim O'Brien, who developed a close friendship with Douglas. One night they got separated, and Douglas waited outside the hotel until O'Brien could return, telling friends, "I didn't want the hackshaw to get in trouble with McGraw for losing me."

Despite his frequent absences and the aggravation he caused, Douglas turned into a solid pitcher under McGraw. He had a 14-10 record in 1920 and a 15-10 record in 1921. His 1921 pitching helped the Giants to the pennant, leading to New York's first "subway series," matching the Giants against the crosstown New York Yankees.

Douglas lost the first game of the 1921 World Series to Carl Mays by a 3–0 score and then bested Mays in the controversial fourth game, which was the game that cast suspicion on the character of Carl Mays. Douglas then came back in the seventh game, beating the Yankees 2–1 and giving the Giants a 4–3 lead. (The Giants also won game eight to win the world championship.)

By this time the relationship between McGraw and Douglas was an irritant to both. Douglas resented and hated McGraw for his constant interference in his life, as well as his verbal abuse—by all accounts, McGraw had the most caustic tongue in the history of baseball. McGraw had no personal love for Douglas either, but after the 1921 World Series he was convinced that the pitcher had great talent and could be a key to the Giants' continued success if he could be straightened out.

Douglas got off to a great start in 1922. He was winning consistently, and it looked like another pennant year for the Giants. In late June of that year, an event occurred that was to have a profound effect on Douglas's life. McGraw learned about the friendship between O'Brien and Douglas and fired O'Brien. He fined and lectured Douglas, threatening to "put him through the cure" if he did not stop his drinking.

To replace O'Brien, McGraw assigned 52-year-old Giants coach Jesse Burkett to be Douglas's "keeper." Burkett had been a great outfielder at the end of the nineteenth century and was later to be enshrined in the Hall of Fame. He turned in three seasons in which he hit .400, putting him in elite company with Rogers Hornsby and Ty Cobb. Although a great hitter, Burkett was never known for his personality—he had the well deserved nickname "The Crab." Being in the constant company of the grim Burkett did nothing to improve Douglas's attitude—in fact, if anything, the ever-watchful eye of Burkett made Douglas even more unhappy and rebellious.

Off to an 11-1 start in mid–July, Douglas's pitching, as well as his morale, started to suffer. After Douglas lost his second game, McGraw gave him a verbal tongue-lashing, which sent Douglas into a deeper state of gloom. He decided that his only hope was to make McGraw trade him, preferably to the St. Louis Cardinals, where he could be closer to his Tennessee home.

The next day, Douglas chatted with two of his friends on the Cardinals, future Hall of Famer Rogers Hornsby and outfielder Leslie Mann, a former teammate of Douglas's. He discussed his desire to go to the Cardinals, and the players were friendly and sympathetic.

Douglas continued to slump, losing his next two games. On July 30, after his fourth loss of the season, McGraw lit into Douglas once again, abusing him in front of his teammates. Douglas responded by demanding to be traded to St. Louis, to which McGraw responded, "You'll play for me or you'll play for nobody." Douglas then told the manager, "What you are doing is getting to be more than a man can stand."[5] McGraw stormed away without a word.

That afternoon, Douglas left the clubhouse with Burkett at his side. After dinner, Douglas told Burkett he wanted to walk over to Times Square, and Burkett accompanied him. In the crowd, however, Douglas managed to elude Burkett and sought solace in the bottle.

After an evening of drinking, Douglas returned to his home but left early the next morning before Burkett came to find him. Douglas disappeared the whole next day, and when he did not return that evening Douglas's wife phoned the club's offices. The next morning Douglas was arrested in the Upper West Side apartment of a friend and drinking companion and was taken down to the local station house, charged with a "noise complaint."

Still drunk, he was turned over to his keeper, Jesse Burkett. In his excellent book *One Last Round for the Shuffler*, Tom Clark described what happened next.

> It was clear on first sight to "The Crab" that he was going to have trouble handling Phil in his present condition, so he phoned the club treasurer, Judge Francis X. McQuade, for instructions. McQuade was a powerful figure in the magistrates' courts and possessed political clout. At his request, the police assisted Burkett in transporting Phil by taxi to a sanitarium on Central Park West, where for the next five days he was forcibly confined. The Giants' management had decided

that Phil was going to be "put through the cure." Whether the order to kidnap and abduct the big pitcher and administer "medical treatment" to him against his will originated from club treasurer McQuade, owner Charles Stoneham, or manager (and part owner) McGraw, is unknown. It is also largely academic.

The fact is that Phil was held against his will from early Tuesday until Saturday at the West End Sanitarium and put through what was known as "The Keely Cure," an alcohol-detoxification program. The exact details of Phil's treatment were never disclosed, but the type of "cure" he received was regarded with dread by the other ballplayers, who have described it as "sheer torture." "Boiling out," i.e. hot baths, stomach-pumping, and massive sedation have been mentioned to me as some of the milder components of this "cure." "I don't know what kind of a thing it is," George Kelly told me, "but they put him through hell."

Phil was not allowed to make any phone calls from the sanitarium, so his wife did not know where he was until Wednesday afternoon, when she received first a call from Burkett, telling her not to worry, and then a call from McGraw, telling her Phil's whereabouts. She visited her husband in the sanitarium on Thursday. On Friday, Phil expected to be released; instead, as he later told a reporter, "they give me something that knocks me out again." When Phil awoke from a drug-induced coma on Saturday, he was informed that he was free to go. Burkett put him in a taxi and saw him home to Washington Heights. Phil's legs were wobbly. He had trouble making it into his house from the taxi.[6]

On August 7, Douglas rejoined his club at the Polo Grounds, still in a daze. According to teammate George Kelly, "You could see in his eyes that he didn't know what the hell was going on, with the kind of torture they put him through. Whatever it was, the kind of treatment they were giving him, the man wasn't himself. He wasn't right." It was later learned that Douglas had been drinking heavily all weekend, which on top of the drugs from his "cure" had totally fogged his mind.

On arriving at the ball park, he was handed a bill for his sanitarium and taxi charges totaling over $200. When Douglas asked McGraw the meaning of the bill, McGraw told him that he was also being fined $100 plus five days' pay. McGraw then followed Douglas into the clubhouse and heaped abuse on the depressed and confused player.

The game that day was rained out, and most of the players left to go home. Douglas, however, stayed in the clubhouse and wrote the following letter to his friend Leslie Mann of the Cardinals:

> I want to leave here. I don't want to see this guy (McGraw) win the pennant. You know I can pitch, and I am afraid that if I stay I will win the pennant for him.
> Talk this over with the boys and if it is all right send the goods to my house at night and I will go to fishing camp. Let me know if you will do this and I will go home on the next train.[7]

In Leslie Mann, Douglas could not have picked a worse person to make this type of offer to. Mann was, in the words of Harold Seymour, "a tee-totaling YMCA enthusiast." While a few years before Mann probably would have simply thrown the letter away, the advent of Landis and the expulsions of Jean Dubuc and Joe Gedeon in the aftermath of the Black Sox scandal had put the fear of God into all players, and Mann turned the letter over to Cardinals president Branch Rickey. Douglas later claimed that he called Mann that night urging him to destroy the letter, but Mann denied that he had ever received the call.

Upon receiving the letter, Rickey did the only thing he could do, which was to turn the letter over to Commissioner Kenesaw Landis.

On August 15, the Giants arrived in Pittsburgh for a series with the Pirates. Landis also came to Pittsburgh and immediately summoned McGraw to discuss the Douglas case. Later that day, Douglas was summoned to face the judge. At the time, he had no idea what the meeting was for.

When Douglas entered the room, Landis showed him the letter and asked him if he had indeed written it, which Douglas acknowledged. Landis asked Douglas why he had written it, but Douglas declined to tell his side of the story. Finally fed up, Landis proclaimed, "Douglas, you are through with organized baseball." The hearing was then over.

Before returning to New York, Douglas met Landis in the lobby of the hotel. They engaged in the following exchange:

> "Is this all true, Judge," he said, "that I am through with baseball?" "Yes, Douglas, it is," said the Judge. "Do you mean that I never can play baseball again?" said Douglas. "Yes, Phil, I am afraid that is just what it means."[8]

The expulsion of Douglas was a huge story throughout the country. In the aftermath, McGraw was quoted as saying that Douglas was "the dirtiest ball-player I've ever seen," more than a bit of a stretch given the fact that McGraw had managed such players as Hal Chase and Heinie Zimmerman. The press was skeptical, assuming that there was more to the scandal than had been told. Most journalists seemed to feel that for the scandal to be taken seriously, something more must be involved. Regardless, Landis was generally praised for his tough action.

A few days later Douglas demanded a new hearing with Landis, but he was denied. He threatened to sue, but he eventually returned to the hills of Tennessee from where he had come. Douglas was trained to do one thing, play baseball. After organized baseball threw him out, Douglas was never able to pick up the pieces and put his life back together.

During the remainder of the 1920s Douglas played semipro ball back in Tennessee and worked off and on in various jobs. He continued to drink heavily, and his health deteriorated. When the Great Depression hit, Douglas was swept up in the sea of poverty and never really recovered. He died in Sequatchie Valley, Tennessee, on August 1, 1952.

Over the years, attempts were made to clear Douglas's name, or at least to secure a new hearing. The most recent of these was in 1990, when Commissioner Fay Vincent refused to hear the case. Organized baseball has consistently

refused to reexamine past scandals. Given Douglas's personality and the ex-
tenuating circumstances, there is little doubt in the author's mind that Douglas
had no intention of ever throwing games, and probably had little intention of
doing anything but forcing McGraw to trade him to St. Louis. Nonetheless, Phil
Douglas remains on baseball's blacklist to this day.

As we have seen, Landis's attitude toward ball players involved in scandals
was usually stern and unforgiving. Even Ray Fisher and Benny Kauff, who
were never suspected of dishonest play, were permanently expelled from the
game. In 1923 Landis showed a different side of his personality when he handled the Rube Benton case.

John "Rube" Benton was born in Clinton, North Carolina, in 1887. He began his professional baseball career with Macon in 1910 and appeared in 12
games with the Cincinnati Reds toward the end of that season. After spending
most of 1911 in the minor leagues, Benton was recalled by Cincinnati, and this
time he stuck. In 1912 Benton pitched in a league-leading 50 games, winning
18 and losing 20. Benton continued to struggle somewhat with mediocre Cincinnati teams, his best year being in 1914 when he won 16 games against 18
losses with a 2.96 earned-run average. The next year, he was traded in midseason to the New York Giants.

One of the reasons Benton was sent to the Giants was that he had become
a "problem player." Like Douglas, Benton was not averse to taking more than
a few drinks. Benton also liked the fast life and late hours and developed a bad
reputation.

Under John McGraw, Benton's record improved dramatically. He was 16-8
in 1916 and 15-9 in 1917. Still somewhat of a troublemaker, Benton enlisted
in the army in 1918 and quickly rose to the rank of sergeant. Benton did well
in the army, stating, "the army has made a man out of me, and given me some
sense." He entered the 1919 season with a new maturity and a determination
to succeed.

Benton enjoyed probably his finest season as a major league player in
1919, winning 17 games while losing 11 and turning in a 2.63 earned-run
average. That fall, however, he learned from teammate Hal Chase that the 1919
World Series would be fixed, and Benton reportedly won $3,200 betting on
Cincinnati. This information was uncovered during the Black Sox investigation,
but for some reason no action was taken against Benton at the time.

Benton also accused Buck Herzog of attempting to bribe him to throw
games. Benton claimed the offer had been made in a Chicago saloon (this was
during Prohibition), but Benton could not remember which saloon. National
League President John Heydler brought Benton to Chicago and toured every
possible speakeasy with him, but nowhere could Benton recognize the place
nor find a bartender who might help him support his story. No other evidence
was ever uncovered that Herzog was involved in crooked work.

Early in the 1921 season, Benton was released by the Giants as an "undesirable player." Benton then signed with St. Paul in the American Association, and in 1922 he had a fine year, winning 22 games. St. Paul then attempted to sell or trade Benton to the major leagues.

The New York Yankees first attempted to purchase Benton, but American League President Ban Johnson refused to approve the deal. Johnson stated that "Benton was barred from the American League for his prior knowledge of the Black Sox scandal." St. Paul then sent Benton to the Cincinnati Reds for pitcher Cliff Markle and cash.

Like Ban Johnson, National League President John Heydler refused to approve the trade. Cincinnati President Garry Herrmann fought the decision, arguing that if it was acceptable for Benton to pitch in the minor leagues, it should be acceptable for him to pitch in the major leagues. The National League owners supported Heydler, who then turned the case over to Judge Landis, confident of his support.

In March 1923 the baseball world was shocked when Landis ruled that Benton was indeed eligible and approved the trade to Cincinnati. Landis based his decision on the fact that no action had been taken against Benton at the time his illicit activities had been revealed, and that it was wrong for the league to "deprive a man of his chief means of livelihood" at its own discretion.

Normally a strong Landis ally, National League President John Heydler was outraged at the decision. On vacation in California, Heydler immediately wired Cincinnati that he could "not approve" of Benton playing in the National League. He stated that this was not an order, but an indication that he would put the matter up to the entire league for a vote. Landis's response was that his decision was final.

On his way back from vacation, Heydler stopped in Chicago to discuss the Benton case with Judge Landis. While no one knows exactly what was said at that session, Heydler emerged from the meeting to state, "Commissioner Landis has decided that the Cincinnati club is at liberty to sign and play Benton, and as far as I am concerned that ends the incident." Benton was free to join Cincinnati.

Benton played three more years with the Reds, winning 30 games and losing 29 during that time. He then drifted to the minor leagues and died in an automobile accident in Dothan, Alabama, in 1937.

A few months after the Benton affair, New York Giants owner Charles Stoneham was indicted for perjury by a federal grand jury. He was later to be indicted for mail fraud. Both indictments were related to Stoneham's activities in the Fuller-McGee "bucketshop case," a fraudulent stock brokerage operation that bilked investors out of millions of dollars.

Stoneham was also indicted for actions involving E. P. Dire and Company, in which Stoneham was one of the partners. Also a bucketshop operation, Dire and Company defrauded investors for $4 million. Compounding these charges was the fact that one of Stoneham's partners and close associates in the deals

Rube Benton. Benton's expulsion for guilty knowledge of the fixing of the 1919 World Series was overturned by Landis. *Courtesy of Transcendental Graphics.*

was the notorious Arnold Rothstein, the man responsible for fixing the 1919 World Series.

In the days before the stock market crash and the advent of the Securities and Exchange Commission, there were a number of brokerage firms engaged in the practice of selling fraudulent stocks — that is, hyping stocks of nonexistent companies or companies with no assets. These operations were known as bucketshops, and they were responsible for swindling thousands of investors out of their hard-earned savings. In his investigation of the bucketshop operations, Nat Ferber, a highly respected investigative reporter for the *New York*

American, stated that "the largest bucketeers in the country seem to stem from the Chicago and New York offices of Stoneham and Company."[9]

Stoneham was also closely associated with Rothstein in gambling activities. Stoneham was a heavy gambler and reportedly lost $70,000 to Rothstein in a single evening. He and Rothstein were also partners for a short time in a racetrack venture.

The trial against Stoneham and the other defendant in the bucketeering cases ended on February 27, 1925, when Stoneham was acquitted by a jury. The verdict was quite controversial, with repeated charges of jury tampering.

No action was ever taken against Charles Stoneham by baseball for his association with Rothstein or his bucketeering actions. Speculating on the situation in early 1924, the *Sporting News* stated that "Stoneham's indictment doesn't mean guilt unless convicted, Landis is said to have held." The same standard, however, did not apply to players such as Bennie Kauff. Stoneham continued to own the Giants throughout his lifetime, and he passed the club on to his son, Horace.

The final scandal to be dealt with in this chapter involved two players on the Cincinnati Reds, Sammy Bohne and Pat Duncan. Sammy Bohne, whose real last name was Cohen, was born in 1896 in San Francisco, California. He first reached the major leagues in 1916 with the St. Louis Cardinals and reached the majors to stay in 1921 with the Cincinnati Reds. Primarily a second baseman, Bohne was not a great hitter but was extremely versatile, playing every infield position, which made him very valuable to his club.

Pat Duncan was born in 1893 in Colton, Ohio. After playing three games with Pittsburgh in 1915, Duncan reached the majors to stay late in the 1919 season. An outfielder, Duncan holds the distinction of being the first player ever to hit a ball out of Crosley Field in Cincinnati, called Redland Field at the time. He is perhaps better remembered for a ball he hit back to Eddie Cicotte in the fourth game of the 1919 World Series. Cicotte deliberately mishandled the ball, beginning a rally that won the game for Cincinnati.

The Bohne-Duncan scandal developed when *Collyer's Eye*, a Chicago sports weekly dealing largely with racing, ran a story claiming that Duncan and Bohne were approached by gamblers and offered $15,000 each to throw games. The paper, known as a "scandal sheet," claimed that a large ring of gamblers was active in baseball and pointed to the Bohne-Duncan story as just one example of the gamblers' machinations. Just before the accusations came out, the Giants had beaten the Reds five straight times in Cincinnati, and these were the games that the paper claimed were fixed for the Giants to win.

Baseball immediately launched an investigation into the matter. The players denied that they had ever been approached by gamblers and testified that they had always played to the best of their abilities. Cincinnati sportswriters Jack Ryder, Tom Swope, Bill Phelon, and Bob Newhall all testified that they had seen nothing suspicious about either player's performance during the series (Duncan hit .350 and Bohne .286). National League President John Heydler handled the investigation in close communication with Judge Landis. There was absolutely no evidence against the players, and they were both cleared. At the same time, the players were urged by baseball to sue for slander, which they did. They sued *Collyer's Eye* for $50,000.

Burt Collyer, publisher of the paper, responded that he did not charge Bohne and Duncan with throwing games, but merely stated that they had been "approached by gamblers." He then sent a telegram to Landis, which was released to the public, claiming groups of gamblers still were operating in baseball circles and offered his cooperation in helping to solve this problem. Landis ignored the telegram.

With damages looming, Collyer agreed to admit his error and settled the case out of court for $100 and court costs. After the settlement was announced, Landis stated, "both the game and the players, Bohne and Duncan, have been vindicated before the American public."

Duncan continued in the major leagues through 1924, ending his career with a lifetime batting average of .307. Bohne lasted in the majors until 1926, ending with a lifetime batting average of .261.

In 1923 no players were expelled from baseball, and this was the first year since Landis took office that no permanent expulsions occurred. It was beginning to appear, and it was certainly hoped by Landis, that the days of scandal were coming to an end. Unfortunately, this was not to be the case.

Chapter 9

The O'Connell-Dolan Affair

As the 1924 season drew to a close, it looked as if Judge Landis could breathe a sigh of relief. The 1924 season had been the first to be free of scandals during his first four years in office. Other than the ongoing bad publicity from the Charles Stoneham trial, there seemed to be little cause for worry.

At the same time, 1924 was shaping up to be an exciting year for baseball. The New York Giants were attempting to win an unprecedented fourth straight National League pennant and were locked in a tight race with the Brooklyn Dodgers and the Pittsburgh Pirates. In the American League, the Yankees were also looking for their fourth straight pennant but were receiving stiff competition from Detroit and the Washington Senators. The Senators, who led going into the final week of the season, were the sentimental favorites since a Washington pennant would be the first in that city's history and it would give the immortal Walter Johnson, perhaps the greatest pitcher of all time, an opportunity to appear in a World Series.

Going into the season's final series, Washington was beginning to take control of the American League race, eventually winning the pennant over the Yankees by two games. The Giants seemed about to do the same in the National League as they prepared for their season-ending series at home against the seventh-place Philadelphia Phillies, while the second-place Dodgers faced the last-place Boston Braves in their final two games. With a one-and-a-half-game lead, the Giants' "magic number" was down to two.

The Giants that year had an extremely strong ballclub. Managed by future Hall of Famer John McGraw, arguably the greatest manager of all time, the team also featured seven future Hall of Famer players. Leading the way were star outfielder Ross "Pep" Youngs, who hit .355 that year, second baseman Frank "The Fordham Flash" Frisch, who hit .328, and first baseman George Kelly, who hit .324. Rounding out the Hall of Fame septet were shortstop Travis Jackson, who hit .302 in his first year as a regular, first baseman Bill Terry in his first full season, outfielder Lewis "Hack" Wilson, also in his first full season, and rookie infielder Fred Lindstrom. The team also included stars "Heinie" Groh, perhaps the top National League third baseman of the era, and a pitching staff led by 16-game winners Virgil Barnes and Jack Bentley. Two

Jimmy O'Connell. O'Connell was the butt of many practical jokes, and he may have been expelled in 1924 because he took one of Cozy Dolan's jokes seriously. *Courtesy of National Baseball Library and Archive, Cooperstown, New York.*

of the other members of the team were outfielder Jimmy O'Connell, who hit .317 in his second season, and Coach Albert "Cozy" Dolan. Dolan, a veteran of the game, was McGraw's righthand man. In addition to being a close friend and companion of McGraw's, Dolan was responsible for such undesirable duties as bed checks and monitoring the players' off-the-field behavior.

On September 27, the Giants and Phillies prepared for the opening game in their series. During batting practice, Jimmy O'Connell walked over to Phillies shortstop Heinie Sand, whom O'Connell knew well from their days together in the Pacific Coast League. According to O'Connell's later testimony, the conversation went something like this:

> "How do you feel about the game?" I asked him. "We don't feel," replied Heine—"We're going to beat you." Then I said to him: "I'll give you $500 if you don't bear down too hard." He just answered, "nothing doing." Then I walked back to the bench.[1]

The conversation left Sand in quite a quandary. His first inclination was to forget that the conversation ever took place, but like Leslie Mann in the Phil Douglas affair, he remembered the lifetime expulsions handed out by Landis to players such as Joe Gedeon. As Sand reported later, "after some thought, I resolved to tell the manager (Art Fletcher). I wanted to vindicate myself." Phillies manager Fletcher congratulated Sand on his forthrightness in telling him the story, saying, "go out and play your best, but I am glad you told me this. It puts you out in the clear and now I can protect you. I don't know what's behind this, but I mean to find out."

As it turned out, the pennant race ended that day. The Giants defeated the Phillies by a score of 5–1, while Brooklyn lost to Boston by a score of 3–2. The Giants had won their fourth straight championship and prepared for their World Series matchup against the Washington Senators.

The O'Connell-Dolan scandal, however, was just beginning. Fletcher telephoned National League President Heydler at Heydler's home the night of the game, saying, "I've got something important to tell you, but I do not wish to discuss it on the telephone. Where can I meet you?"

The two met for breakfast in New York the next morning. Fletcher brought along Sand and had him repeat the story for the National League president. Realizing that he was sitting on a powder keg, Heydler immediately telephoned Judge Landis at his office in Chicago. Landis was preparing to leave Chicago for Washington for the opening of the World Series, but instead he immediately got on a train and headed for New York.

After arriving in New York and meeting with Heydler, Landis summoned Sand to his room. After hearing Sand's story, Landis began to probe for something deeper, asking Sand if any other players were approached, but Sand had no knowledge of this. After informing Giants owner Charles Stoneham and manager John McGraw of the state of affairs, Landis summoned Jimmy O'Connell.

Born in Sacramento, California, on February 11, 1901, O'Connell appeared to have a bright future ahead of him in baseball. He was discovered in 1919 by George Putnam, secretary of the San Francisco Seals of the Pacific Coast League, when O'Connell was playing shortstop on the Santa Clara University team. Putnam immediately saw an incredible raw talent and signed O'Connell for the San Francisco club.

In 1920 O'Connell hit only .262 and fielded poorly. His natural ability and grace were apparent despite his statistics, and with hard work he improved to a .337 mark in 1921. After that season, John McGraw won a bidding war with a number of other clubs, purchasing O'Connell's contract for what was then an impressive sum of $75,000.

O'Connell was already drawing rave reviews before even appearing in a major league game. The immortal Ty Cobb stated, "O'Connell has perfect form, and it cannot be improved upon." Future Hall of Famer George Sisler said, "He sure is class at the plate," and Harry Heilmann, another future member of the Hall, remarked, "Doesn't he look wonderful with a bat in his hand?" From Rogers Hornsby, one of the greatest hitters of all time, came perhaps the most telling comment when he said that O'Connell was a "natural hitter."

An article in the *Sporting News* on January 12, 1922 — shortly after O'Connell was sold to the Giants — described the player as "still a boy, with his cherished youthful ideals." The story talked about O'Connell's kindness, such as arranging for the San Francisco club to pay for the team's 17-year-old mascot to go on a road trip and taking care of the mascot during the trip. The story also told of O'Connell's gullibility, as illustrated by the fact that after his college manager had told him "you don't show enough fight," O'Connell went out and offered to fight every member of the opposing team.

The Giants elected to leave O'Connell in San Francisco for more seasoning in 1922, and O'Connell responded with an excellent year. He hit .335 and stole 39 bases. In 1923 O'Connell joined the Giants, hitting a somewhat disappointing .250 in 87 games. Then he improved both as a fielder and a hitter in 1924 and looked like he was about to live up to his initial promise.

This great promise ended when O'Connell walked in the room to meet with Landis. The stenographer that Landis had hired was late, so O'Connell's original testimony was not recorded. O'Connell, however, was more than willing to talk to the press after the hearing and tell his side of the story. O'Connell readily admitted making the bribe offer to Sand. He claimed that he was merely following orders. According to O'Connell:

> They picked me because they knew I had sort of a friendship with Sand. It is true that I had known Sand since we were in the bushes together, but I never would have approached him with such a proposition had I not been told to do so.

> Cozy Dolan made the proposition to me. That was on Saturday morning before
> the game. He said the whole team would chip in to make up the $500. Frankie
> Frisch, Pep Youngs and George Kelly all knew about it. When I told Pep what
> Dolan had said about the money, Youngs said: "go to it." Then I told Frisch, and
> Frank told me to give him (Sand) anything he wants.
>
> I asked Kelly what he thought of it too, and he seemed to know what was com-
> ing off. He knew about it, for I could tell he had been let in on it by Dolan by
> the way he talked.[2]

O'Connell's revelations were startling, to say the least. As mentioned
earlier, Dolan was a close associate of Giants manager John McGraw, and
Youngs, Frisch, and Kelly were three of the brightest stars in the game. What
started off as an offhand remark to Heinie Sand was beginning to look like the
reincarnation of the Black Sox scandal.

Landis next summoned Cozy Dolan. Cozy, whose real name was James
Alberts, was born in Chicago in 1889. An infielder, he took the name Cozy
Dolan from Patrick Henry Dolan, an outfielder who played around the turn of
the century.

Dolan began his baseball career in 1905 in Oshkosh, Wisconsin. In 1908
he moved to Rockford and joined the Cincinnati Reds late in the 1909 season.
During the next few years, he bounced between the Yankees, Phillies, and
Pirates, ending his big-league career in 1915 with the St. Louis Cardinals. In
1914 Dolan had his best year, hitting .280 in 111 games. In 1916 he drifted to
the minor leagues, playing with Indianapolis through 1917 and then joining
Milwaukee. He took over as manager of the St. Joseph team in 1919, winning
a pennant in his first and only year as manager. In 1920 he was hired by the
Chicago Cubs as a coach.

Dolan had been extremely popular in his playing days, earning the reputation as quite an amusing character. His appointment to coach the Cubs was
greeted with great joy by the players and writers. In fact, the following notice
appeared in the *Sporting News* after Dolan was hired by the Cubs:

> Al (Cozy) Dolan is to return to the National League after a brief sojourn in the
> minors. Good ol' Coz, champion pie eater of baseball, comes back as a member
> of the Chicago Cubs. Fred Mitchell figured Dolan would put life into his
> somewhat dead team, so he signed him for coaching duties. As Coz puts it
> himself, he will play the role of goat. If a base-runner gets caught off base, they
> will blame Coz. If the runner by some accident advances, the runner will get the
> glory, but it's all the same to Coz. In whatever position he is put he will add to
> the gaiety of nations, and share in the joy of the fans. There is only one Dolan,
> though there are many other counterfeits.[3]

After a year with the Cubs, he joined the Giants as a coach and John
McGraw's righthand man. Dolan proved less popular with players on the
Giants, although it was a reflection more of his function than of his personality.
McGraw tended to use Dolan as his eyes and ears—or, in the words of his

players, a spy. It was Dolan who often did bed checks and was asked to report on players' activities off the field. While this would seem unusual today, monitoring players' off-the-field activities to make sure they stayed "in training" was considered fairly normal for baseball in those days.

Dolan proved to be a very exasperating witness for Landis. Landis was a very forthright man and liked people to come to the point. This was not Dolan's style, to say the least. The following are a few excerpts from the transcript of Dolan's interview with Landis:

> LANDIS: O'Connell says you asked him if he knew Sand. This was last Saturday that you asked him that, and that he told you he did, and that you told O'Connell to go to Sand and asked him not to bear down hard on us, meaning the Giants team, and for O'Connell to tell Sand, that is, you told O'Connell to offer Sand $500 if he would not bear down too hard.
>
> DOLAN: I don't remember it, Judge.
>
> LANDIS: You don't remember it?
>
> DOLAN: No sir.
>
> LANDIS: And that is the best answer that you can give, just that you don't remember?
>
> DOLAN: I don't remember.
>
> LANDIS: Before this conversation that Mr. O'Connell has told about, and which I have repeated to you, in which you have heard from him in part at least, did you have any talk with anybody about the general subject?
>
> DOLAN: Not that I can remember about.
>
> LANDIS: After O'Connnell came back to the bench, did you have a talk with anybody about this?
>
> DOLAN: Just what are you referring to?
>
> LANDIS: To the subject of talking with Sand.
>
> DOLAN: No sir.
>
> LANDIS: Did you have any talk with any member of the team?
>
> DOLAN: Not that I can remember.
>
> LANDIS: Have you any idea in your mind why O'Connell would tell me this if it had not happened?
>
> DOLAN: I don't know. I cannot recall any conversation like that.
>
> LANDIS: I wish you would think it over pretty carefully, Cozy, and see if you could recall any conversation with anybody else or any member of the New York team about this. This was only last Saturday and this is Tuesday. The subject of this conversation is one that would not escape your mind in three days time.
>
> DOLAN: I cannot remember any conversation of that kind.
>
> LANDIS: Is your memory pretty good?
>
> DOLAN: I guess so.
>
> LANDIS: Do you think that you might have had a conversation about the subject and forget it in three days?
>
> DOLAN: I don't think so. I don't remember. There was so much stuff going around the clubhouse.[4]

O'Connell was present during the interview with Dolan and repeated his story charging Dolan with spearheading the attempted fix. O'Connell was also present during Landis's interview with Ross Youngs, Frankie Frisch, and George Kelly. The following are excerpts from the testimony:

> LANDIS: I wish you would tell me that again, Mr. O'Connell, just what your talk with Mr. Youngs was?
> O'CONNELL: He asked me what Cozy said.
> LANDIS: What did you tell him?
> O'CONNELL: I told him he wanted me to see Sand and offer him $500 not to bear down against us.
> LANDIS: What did Youngs say to you?
> O'CONNELL: As far as I can recall he said, "go ahead."
> LANDIS: What do you say about that, Youngs?
> YOUNGS: No sir, I did not say anything to anybody about fixing anything or anything like that.
> LANDIS: Did you have any talk with O'Connell last Saturday?
> YOUNGS: I did not have any talk at all, no sir.
> LANDIS: Is this the first you ever heard of any such thing?
> YOUNGS: I've heard talking around and such things mentioned, but I don't remember who by.
> LANDIS: Do you hear fellas talking around that boys are offering money and something like that.
> YOUNGS: I've never heard anything like this, offering money here. This is the first I've heard of it.[5]

The following are excerpts of Landis's conversation with Frankie Frisch:

> LANDIS: Do you remember having a talk with O'Connell last Saturday at the Polo Grounds before the ballgame about any Philadelphia player?
> FRISCH: No sir.
> LANDIS ASKING O'CONNELL: Just what was the talk between you and Frisch?
> O'CONNELL: I told him what Dolan told me.
> LANDIS TO O'CONNELL: Did he ask you what Dolan said to you or did you just tell him?
> O'CONNELL: I just told him. I told him Dolan wants me to talk to Sand and offer him $500 not to bear down on us.
> FRISCH: I think he must've been kidding.
> LANDIS TO O'CONNELL: What did Frisch say to you after you told him what Dolan said to you?
> O'CONNELL: Give him anything he wants.
> FRISCH: I never said that. On a pennant contender you always hear a lot of stuff like that, a lot of kidding and some other things. That is all I ever hear.[6]

Because O'Connell admitted making the bribe offer, he was placed on baseball's permanently ineligible list, ending his baseball career. Given his extremely evasive answers, as well as the fact that he was implicated by O'Connell as the leader in the plot, Dolan was also placed on the ineligible list. Because

Frisch, Youngs, and Kelly strongly denied O'Connell's charges, it became a case of O'Connell's word versus theirs, and Landis exonerated them from all blame, giving the three stars a clean bill of health.

On October 1, Landis announced the expulsions of O'Connell and Dolan. He released the basic details of the scandal to the press, but not the transcripts of the testimony. According to Landis, the case was closed.

The press and the public were far from satisfied. It seemed totally fantastic and unbelievable that Giants coach Dolan and substitute O'Connell had hatched this plot and were offering $500 of their own money to fix the game. Who was really behind it all? Was a ring of gamblers responsible—or did the involvement go deeper in the Giant organization? Were Youngs, Frisch, and Kelly really guilty? What about John McGraw? Or Charles Stoneham—after all, this would not be the first illegal action that the Giants owner was involved in.

Coming on the eve of the World Series, the story created a sensation. American League President Ban Johnson, a strong political enemy of Landis's, suggested that because of the attempted bribe, Brooklyn should replace the Giants in the World Series against Washington. "And if Brooklyn isn't permitted to, there should be no World Series at all." Johnson also called for a federal investigation of the case.

Pittsburgh owner Barney Dreyfuss joined with Johnson in calling for a cancellation of the 1924 World Series. The Pirates finished only three games out of first, and Dreyfuss pointed out that if the Sand offer were just the tip of the iceberg, it might well be that his club had been denied the pennant by illicit activity. Dreyfuss's statements infuriated Landis, who publicly stated that Dreyfuss should "keep his shirt on."

The World Series was an exciting one, with Washington taking the crown in a hotly contested seven-game series. While the public was enjoying the series, the scandal refused to go away. Once the series was over, speculation about what was behind the O'Connell-Dolan scandal heated up again.

At that point, many rumors began to fly. A letter published in a New York newspaper claimed that a group of gamblers had wagered $100,000 on New York to win the National League pennant and that $5,000 had been paid to a Giants player who agreed to use the money to bribe opponents to let the Giants win. Late-season injuries to stars Frisch and Groh supposedly worried the gamblers, who were looking to protect their investment. In another published story, Pittsburgh Pirates pitcher Emil Yde claimed that players other than Heinie Sand had been approached in an effort to throw games. Yde later denied the story, claiming that he was misquoted. Pat Ragan, a coach with the Phillies, claimed that the whole incident was a joke, saying

> O'Connell is just a kid and was sort of butt for all the jokes of the Giants and they shot plenty at him. He took everything seriously. Sand of the Phillies is much the same kind of a fellow. He has no sense of humor.

> The Giants were joking in their clubhouse before that game of September 27, and someone suggested that it would be awful to get eliminated from the series by a team so lowly as the Phillies. "Why not buy 'em off?" someone chirped up. "It wouldn't cost much. They hadn't ought to be as expensive as the White Sox were in 1919. Why you ought to be able to buy the whole team for $500."
>
> "Cozy" Dolan thought it was a good joke. So did the rest — all except O'Connell, who took the whole thing seriously. Then Dolan suggested that O'Connell approach Sand because he had played in the Pacific Coast League.
>
> The incident was closed as far as Frisch, Kelly and the others were concerned. They had forgotten it. Little did they suspect that O'Connell would go to Sand, but he did.
>
> The next thing they knew, O'Connell and Dolan were summoned, and then everybody got frightened, fearful the practical joke would be misunderstood.[4]

Everyone involved denied Ragan's claim that the matter was a joke. As Frankie Frisch pointed out, the incident was anything but a joke. In the meantime, O'Connell continued to insist that he was merely acting on orders from his teammates. "They're making a goat out of me. I've been a damn fool," said O'Connell.

Dolan's memory suddenly improved, and he proclaimed his innocence to all who would listen. Dolan stated, "when I replied to the judge's questions, I don't remember, I really meant to say no. I always use that expression." Dolan then went on the offensive, hiring the famous criminal lawyer William J. Fallon to represent him. Fallon, of course, was Arnold Rothstein's personal attorney and had been a key figure in the aftermath of the Black Sox scandal.

Dolan then announced that he was suing Landis for $100,000 for libel. Also named in the suit were John Heydler and Ban Johnson. The suit also sought Dolan's restoration to good standing in baseball and demanded his share of the World Series money from the Giants' appearance against the Senators.

The announcement of the lawsuit brought forth fresh speculation. Who was paying Dolan's legal bills? And why was Dolan hooking up with Fallon, a shady character in his own right, who had just been acquitted in a controversial jury fixing trial.

During the next few months the controversy continued to rage. Baseball writers insisted that Landis release the full transcripts of his hearing, which the judge refused to do. While O'Connell returned to California and began to fade into the background, Dolan remained in the limelight, pursuing his lawsuit against Landis. Meanwhile, the public insisted on knowing who was behind the scandal and how far-reaching it was.

One detail that came out in early 1925 was that it was John McGraw who had introduced Dolan to William J. Fallon, and apparently the Giants were footing the legal bills for Dolan's defense. McGraw tried to justify this action on the basis that Dolan had been a longtime loyal employee, but Landis would have none of it. After some stern warnings from Landis, the Giants withdrew their support, and the lawsuit died away.

In January 1925 Landis released the transcripts of his hearing. As stated before, no transcript existed of O'Connell's original testimony, but the rest of the hearing was available for public consumption. While the release of the testimony and the dropping of the lawsuit satisfied some observers, others remained skeptical. The following is an excerpt from an editorial in the *Sporting News*:

> Having chloroformed the Dolan/O'Connell stench, at least for the time being, the Magnates are trying to arouse new interest in our much abused national game by giving out alleged news. But the fans still are waiting to hear something definite from Commissioner Landis concerning the futile attempt to bribe Heinie Sand of the Phillies to throw a certain game to the Giants last September.
>
> Dolan has sealed his lips and will not sue for damages. Stories have been published that he will receive $5,000 a year as long as he lives. Cozy, I believe, has denied making this assertion, but his continued silence in the face of his banishment and humiliation is significant, to say the least. Dolan's threat to resort to legal proceedings evidently frightened somebody or other. If innocent, he could have made the Moguls pay handsomely for the temporary blackening of his name and reputation. But is Dolan's silence to be taken to mean that he knew what O'Connell was doing when he approached the Philadelphia shortstop?
>
> Who is behind Dolan? If the high Commissioner doesn't know, why not say so in so many words? Surely there are smart detectives who might run the story to earth if properly paid.
>
> Publicity, not secrecy, is the only way to learn the identity of the rascals who are believed to be baseball fixers. If a wide open investigation should be instituted by the Commissioner, perhaps certain enemies of certain "sure thing" gamblers would be glad to furnish valuable tips. But so long as the impression prevails that the Magnates prefer to let the Dolan/O'Connell case die a natural death and graphic testimony is withheld, the real framers of the bribery scandal do not fear exposure.[8]

Unfortunately, it is unlikely that we will ever know the whole truth about the O'Connell-Dolan scandal. Looking back on the scandal, historians have advanced a number of theories, but perhaps the best analysis was provided shortly after the scandal by F. C. Lane, editor of *Baseball Magazine.*[9] Lane analyzed four theories: (1) the whole situation was an aborted joke, a fact that all the participants denied once the investigation started for fear that they would be thrown out of baseball; (2) Cozy Dolan was in league with gamblers and coerced O'Connell into being the tool for his dirty work; (3) O'Connell's story was essentially correct, that many Giants players were in it, and in fact, Giants management (Stoneham and McGraw) may well have been involved; and (4) this whole plot was an idea of Dolan's, and that he alone was responsible for recruiting O'Connell for the attempted fix.

One of the difficulties with the case is the lack of reason for the whole incident. Lane called it "a piece of sheer imbecility." Why make the bribe, when the Giants were almost assured of the pennant? And why pick out only Sand, the shortstop? While the shortstop is certainly a key player in the game, it is unlikely that he could fix a game on his own if he wanted to.

John McGraw echoed similar sentiments. When asked after the incident for his feelings, he stated, "I cannot understand why these two men did what they did, when the chances were 100 to 1 that New York would win the pennant. The only explanation I can give is that they are a couple of saps. If you search the country over, you probably couldn't find two bigger ones."

Of the explanations offered by Lane, only two seem to make any sense: Either the whole affair was a misinterpreted joke, or indeed there was a deeper plot by the Giants club. Both theories have holes. If it was a joke, why would no one, especially Dolan, admit it? And while the New York Giants were no strangers to corruption, why attempt to bribe Sand when the pennant was all but clinched anyway? It is unlikely that McGraw and Stoneham would have been party to such a nonsensical fix, although it is possible that a group of players (Youngs, Frisch, and Kelly) panicked because of late-season injuries and conspired with Dolan to make sure that there was no question about the Giants winning the pennant. All in all, this seems like the most likely explanation.

While the exact truth about the scandal will never be known, what is known is that it brought tragedy for the major participants. Hardest hit of all was O'Connell, the young man of such great promise. During the winter of 1925, he played professional basketball in California. Unfortunately, among his teammates in the basketball league were former Giants teammate George Kelly and Cincinnati Reds player Sammy Bohne. The fact that these players, especially Kelly, were appearing on the same team as O'Connell created an uproar, and the team eventually cancelled O'Connell's contract.

O'Connell continued his baseball career for a while, playing for a Ft. Bayard, New Mexico, team in the outlaw Copper Frontier League. Among the other players in the league were Hal Chase, Chick Gandil, Swede Risberg, Lefty Williams, and Tom Seaton, all of whom had been expelled from baseball for game fixing. Life was tough on the frontier in those days, and O'Connell soon returned to California.

O'Connell fell upon hard times at that point and went to work as a longshoreman. Despite repeated appeals for his reinstatement by notables such as sportswriter Damon Runyon, O'Connell remained outside the game. He eventually settled down in a job for the Richfield Oil Company, working in Bakersfield, California. He died on November 11, 1976, in Bakersfield.

The colorful Dolan's name kept popping up in the news for a number of years. His first act after dropping the suit was to move to Florida, where he got involved in Sarasota real-estate business. Dolan and McGraw had acquired property in Sarasota during the early 1920s, and in those days of speculative

Florida real estate, Dolan looked to make a career of buying and selling property.

Dolan then turned up in Cincinnati in 1928, when he appeared as a second-line comedian. He then moved to Chicago, opening a Prohibition-era nightclub. On July 31, 1930, Dolan was arrested when federal agents raided his nightclub and confiscated large amounts of liquor and beer.

Dolan made a number of attempts to clear his name in baseball. He also tried to stay in touch with the game. For example, in 1925 he contacted Cincinnati President Garry Herrmann with information about two prospects he was recommending for Cincinnati. After conferring with Landis, Herrmann wrote a polite reply saying that the Reds were not interested. Dolan remained in Chicago and died there on December 10, 1958.

The other key principal in the case, Heinie Sand, also had his share of problems. He was ridiculed by many fans for being a "squealer." Sand remained with the Phillies until the end of the 1928 season, leaving the game with a .258 career batting average. He died in 1958 in his native San Francisco, just a month before Cozy Dolan passed away.

Two of the other three men mentioned in the scandal, Frankie Frisch and George Kelly, went on to enjoy long and successful careers and long lives. Ross Youngs, however, contracted Bright's disease in 1927 and died that year at the age of 30. All three of these men are now enshrined in the Baseball Hall of Fame.

Chapter 10

The Cobb-Speaker Affair

The year 1925 proved to be free from scandal, and as the 1926 season drew to a close, baseball and the public breathed a sigh of relief. Baseball's power structure certainly hoped that this represented the end of an era of scandal that began with the Hal Chase case in 1918. The big news was saddening, but scandal-free. On November 3, 1926, the great Ty Cobb announced his resignation as player-manager of the Detroit Tigers and his retirement from baseball. He was replaced by former Tiger George Moriarty.

Ty had made his debut with the Tigers in 1905, playing in 41 games and hitting an unimpressive .240. He improved to .313 in 1906, and from that point onward performed at a level of excellence never seen before or since in the game of baseball. Beginning in 1907, Cobb won nine straight American League batting titles, lost out to Tris Speaker in 1916, and then won three more. He hit over .400 three times in his career and retired holding most of baseball's major offensive records with the exception of home runs and slugging percentage (Cobb spent most of his career in the dead-ball era, when home runs were rare and not an important part of the game). His lifetime average of .367 is still a record today, and it is a record that barring major rule changes in the game, will probably never be equaled.

Cobb took over the managerial role of the Detroit club in 1921. Cobb originally had no interest in becoming a manager, but he was convinced by outgoing manager Hughie Jennings, Detroit management, and the Detroit players that he was the only one who could handle the role. While his success as manager has tended to be downplayed by historians, Cobb's managerial efforts for six years produced a record of 479 wins and 444 losses, for a .519 winning percentage. His Detroit team, woefully short of pitching, finished second in 1923 and third in 1922 and 1924. In 1926 the club finished in sixth place but still had a winning record with 79 wins and 75 losses.

Baseball fans were just beginning to recover from the shock of Cobb's resignation when Tris Speaker resigned as manager of the Cleveland Indians and announced his retirement from the game. While not quite the equal of Cobb or Babe Ruth, Speaker was without question one of the greatest stars in baseball. Tris broke in with the Boston Red Sox in 1907 and was one of the

Ty Cobb. Dutch Leonard accused Cobb, probably the greatest hitter of all time, of colluding to clinch third-place money. *Courtesy of Transcendental Graphics.*

key players in the Red Sox dynasty in the early part of the second decade of the twentieth century. After the 1915 season he was traded to the Cleveland Indians and proceeded to win his first and only batting title, hitting .386 to break Ty Cobb's streak. Speaker was considered by most experts to be the greatest defensive outfielder of his time, and many historians still consider him to be the greatest defensive outfielder in baseball history.

Speaker was also quite successful as a manager. He took over the reins of the Cleveland club in 1919 and retired with a record of 616 wins and 520 losses for a .542 winning percentage. He led Cleveland to the world championship in 1920, and during the 1926 season the team finished in second place behind the powerful New York Yankees.

While Cobb's retirement was a surprise, his resignation as manager of the Tigers was not a total shock, given that the club had finished in sixth place. Speaker, however, had led the Cleveland club to a second-place finish, and his resignation did not sit well with the baseball public.

Soon the rumor mill began to churn about why these two stars had left the game. Before the year was out, a shocking story was made public: Retired pitcher Hubert "Dutch" Leonard had charged the two great stars, along with former Cleveland outfielder and onetime Boston pitching star Joe Wood, with throwing a game between Detroit and Cleveland on September 25, 1919.

According to Leonard, the plot revolved around Detroit's desire to receive a share of the proceeds from the World Series. According to a plan instituted in 1918, the second- and third-place teams in each league received a share (albeit a small one) of the World Series money. The ill-fated White Sox had already clinched the pennant in 1919, and Cleveland had clinched second place. The Tigers were battling the New York Yankees for third place and a share of the World Series money. (Detroit ended up finishing in fourth place, one-half game behind the Yankees.)

Before going into full detail on the scandal and the events surrounding it, it is important to examine the personality and career of "Dutch" Leonard.

Born in 1892 in Birmingham, Ohio, Leonard broke into the American League as a teammate of Speaker's with the Red Sox in 1913. In 1914 Leonard had one of the most remarkable seasons a pitcher has ever had. He won 18 games against five losses for the second-place Red Sox and also recorded four saves. More important, his earned-run average was a microscopic 1.01, the lowest earned-run average in the history of baseball for a starter. While this record has been approached—most recently in 1968 when Bob Gibson compiled an earned-run average of 1.12—it has never been equaled and may well stand the test of time.

While Leonard never again approached the heights he reached in 1914, he continued to be an effective pitcher through the 1918 season, when he joined the service. He was traded to the Tigers after the 1918 season but was not particularly effective with the Tigers during the next three years, winning a total of 35 games while losing 43.

After the 1921 season, Leonard fled organized baseball and signed to pitch with the Fresno team of the San Joaquin Valley League in California. For this action he was placed on the ineligible list by Commissioner Landis. Leonard broke his association with the Fresno team on August 6, 1923, and a year later he was reinstated by the commissioner.

Tris Speaker. Dutch Leonard also implicated this great player in the conspiracy. *Courtesy of Transcendental Graphics.*

Hubert "Dutch" Leonard. Leonard had much cause to resent Ty Cobb. *Courtesy of Transcendental Graphics.*

Leonard's career with the Tigers was a rather strange one, particularly after 1920, when Ty Cobb was made manager of the team. Despite his great year in 1914 and his two no-hitters, Leonard had a reputation throughout the American League for being "gutless." He had a history of making excuses for every bad outing and claiming physical injury when it was time to face a tough opponent. Cobb had disliked Leonard during the pitcher's days with the Red Sox—in fact, Cobb later claimed that he only intentionally tried to spike two players in his career, Leonard being one of them. Years later, when writing his memoirs, Cobb wrote, "Leonard played dirty—he deserved getting hurt."

Problems began almost as soon as Leonard rejoined the club in 1924. The problems reached a head early in 1925, when manager Cobb was openly warring with his pitcher. In his excellent biography of Cobb, Charles Alexander described the circumstances as follows:

> In the first half of the 1925 season, Leonard later told Damon Runyon of Universal News Service, Cobb had worked him so much that his physician warned that he was in danger of injuring his arm permanently. When he protested to Cobb, the Tiger manager berated him in the clubhouse in front of the other players, shouting "don't you dare turn bolshevik on me. I'm the boss here." Leonard then took the mound at Detroit against Philadelphia and gave up twelve runs. Cobb refused to take him out and laughed when, as Leonard said he later

learned, Connie Mack protested to Cobb, "you're killing that boy." Put on waivers after refusing to pitch on the road trip that followed, Leonard fully expected at least Cleveland to claim him for the $7,500 waiver price. But Speaker, his teammate on the 1913–15 Red Sox and his presumed friend, passed over him along with the other major-league managers. Thus Speaker had cooperated in Cobb's scheme to get rid of him.[1]

Leonard's personality was such that he was not about to let this perceived insult go unpunished. In 1926 he got his revenge.

Early in the 1926 season, Leonard relayed his charges of the fix to American League President Ban Johnson, Detroit Tigers President Frank Navin, Detroit star Harry Heilmann, Washington Senators manager Bucky Harris, and Washington secretary Edwin Eynon. According to Leonard, the plot was hatched beneath the stands in Detroit after the Indians-Tigers game of September 24, 1925. Cobb, Speaker, Wood, and Leonard got into a discussion about the Tigers' desire to finish in third place, to which Speaker replied, "don't worry about tomorrow's game. We have second place clinched, and you will win tomorrow."

According to Leonard:

> And everybody then agreed that if it was going to be a set-up we might as well get some money out of it. Then we talked about getting the money down on the game, that is, how to get up the dough and how much we would put up, and Cobb said he would send Fred West (a Detroit club employee, who ran errands for the players) down to us. I (Leonard) was to put up $1,500 and, as I remember it, Cobb $2,000 and Wood and Speaker $1,000 each. I had pitched that day and was through for the season and so I gave my check for $1,500 to Wood at the ball park and went to the hotel, packed my things and left that night for Independence, Mo.
>
> Several days later, I received the Wood letter at Independence, with a check for $1,630. He wrote that West was only able to get up part of the money and that my share of the winnings was only $130.[2]

Had the charges been merely the word of Leonard, it is quite likely that the situation would have blown over and perhaps never been made public. However, Leonard was in possession of two letters, one from Wood and one from Cobb, both of which clearly implied that there was some gambling on the game in question. These letters, which were released to the press on December 21, 1926, read as follows:

Cleveland, O., Friday
Enclosed please find certified check for sixteen hundred and thirty dollars ($1,630).
Dear Friend Dutch:
   The only bet West could get up was $600 against $420 (10 to 7). Cobb did not get up a cent. He told us that and I believe him. Could have put some at 5 to 2 on Detroit, but did not, as that would make us put up $1,000 to win $400.

We won the $420. I gave West $30, leaving $390, or $130 for each of us. Would not have cashed your check at all, but West thought he could get it up to 10 to 7, and I was going to put it all up at those odds. We could have won $1,750 for the $2,500 if we could have placed it. If we ever have another chance like this we will know enough to try to get down early. Let me hear from you, Dutch. With all good wishes to yourself and Mrs. Leonard, I am, always,

Joe Wood

Augusta, Ga., Oct. 23, '19.

Dear Dutch:

Well, old boy, guess you are out in old California by this time and enjoying life. I arrived home and found Mrs. Cobb only fair, but the baby girl was fine, and at this time Mrs. Cobb is very well, but I have been very busy getting acquainted with my family and have not tried to do any correspondence, hence my delay.

Wood and myself are considerably disappointed in our business proposition, as we had $2,000 to put into it and the other side quoted us $1,400, and when we finally secured that much money it was about two o'clock and they had no time, so we completely fell down and of course we felt badly about it.

Everything was open to Wood and he still can tell you about it when we get together. It was quite a responsibility and I don't care for it again, I can assure you.

Well I hope you found everything in fine shape at home and all your troubles will be little ones. I made this year's winner's share of World Series on cotton since I came home, and expect to make more.

I thought the White Sox should have won, but am satisfied they were too confident. Well, old scout, drop me a line when you can.

We have had fine weather here, in fact, quite warm, and have had some dandy fishing since I arrived home.

With kindest regards to Mrs. Leonard, I remain, sincerely,

TY[3]

Confronted with Leonard's story and letters, American League President Ban Johnson panicked. He realized how damaging it would be to his league, and to all of baseball, to have these charges against two of the game's greatest stars made public. Therefore, Johnson arranged to purchase the letters from Leonard for $20,000, thereby buying Leonard's silence.

Initially, Johnson just let the matter sit. On September 9, 1926, however, he brought the matter up before the directors of the American League, who voted to turn the evidence over to Commissioner Landis. Johnson was none too pleased at this move, since he and Landis were bitter rivals who had been feuding constantly since Landis became commissioner.

Johnson then confronted both Cobb and Speaker. While both strongly maintained their innocence, Johnson told the players that whether guilty or not, they were through in the American League and urged them to retire to protect their reputations. After thinking over the consequences to themselves and their families if such a story were made public, Cobb and Speaker agreed to retire. In Johnson's eyes, the case was now closed.

Joe Wood. Leonard named this Cleveland outfielder as a fourth member of the conspiracy. *Courtesy of the author.*

Landis, however, had a different view. In addition to being a fanatic about corruption, Landis sensed an opportunity to humiliate, and finally destroy, his longtime enemy Johnson. Therefore, Landis launched his own investigation.

Landis first asked Leonard to come to Chicago to testify, but Leonard refused. Landis then went out to California to meet with Leonard at his grape farm in the California San Joaquin Valley on October 29.

Cobb and Speaker then demanded to Landis that Leonard be brought to Chicago to make his accusations to their faces. Wood, by then the baseball coach at Yale University, seconded this demand. When Leonard again refused to come to Chicago, Cobb and Speaker demanded a full investigation of the incident.

On December 20, Landis met with Cobb, Speaker, Wood, and Fred West, the Detroit clubhouse man mentioned in the letters. Cobb admitted writing the letter but claimed that he had only acted as an intermediary for Wood and Leonard to place bets. Cobb denied there was any game fixing whatsoever; according to him the supposed meeting between the four conspirators never happened.

Speaker totally supported Cobb's story. In fact, Speaker knew nothing about any betting until the charges came out.

Had the game truly been fixed for the Tigers to win, one would have expected strong performances by Tigers Cobb and Leonard, and weak performances by Indians Speaker and Wood. In reality, Cobb was only one for five in the game, while Speaker had three hits in five trips to the plate, including two triples, and he played errorless ball. Neither Leonard nor Wood even appeared in the game. (See page 205.)

Wood supported the stories of Cobb and Speaker. According to Wood, neither had placed any bets. While Wood acknowledged having bet on the game, he denied that the game was not played on its merits. West acknowledged having made the bets for Wood but claimed that he had no knowledge that Leonard was involved. He also denied that he had ever placed any bets for either Cobb or Speaker.

At the conclusion of the hearing, Cobb and Speaker demanded that the case be made public. While initially they were willing to fade away to preserve their reputations, the growing rumors about the scandal made them realize that public exposure was inevitable, and they decided to fight to prove their innocence.

The exposure and publication of the details of the scandal on December 21 rocked the nation. Not since the Black Sox scandal had stars of this magnitude been involved in a baseball gambling scandal. However, unlike the Black Sox case, the public rallied to the defense of the beleaguered stars.

Umpire Billy Evans, in a newspaper column, reflected on the incident by saying:

> Only a miserable thirst for vengeance actuated Leonard's attack on Cobb and Speaker. Balked in his efforts to stick in the big show, he decided to drag down with him those whom he believed had cast him aside. As a pitcher, he was gutless. He refused to face the tough teams and picked the soft spots. We umpires had no respect for Leonard, for he whined on every pitch called against him. It is a crime that men of the stature of Ty and Tris should be blackened by a man of this caliber with charges that every baseballer knows to be utterly false.[4]

TIGERS WIN BATTING ORGY.

Score 18 Hits to Cleveland's 13 and Take Closing Game, 9 to 5.

DETROIT, Sept. 25.—Detroit closed its home season by defeating Cleveland today, 9 to 5. Cold weather, unfavorable to good pitching, turned the game into a hitting orgy.

The score:

DETROIT. (A.)	Ab	R	H	Po	A	CLEVELAND. (A.)	Ab	R	H	Po	A
Bush,ss	5	2	3	2	1	Graney,lf	5	1	3	1	1
Young,2b	4	0	2	4	6	Lunte,ss	4	1	1	2	5
Cobb,cf	5	2	1	1	1	Speaker,1b	5	2	3	6	0
Veach,lf	4	1	3	4	0	Harris,1b	5	0	1	11	1
Heilmann,1b	4	0	1	9	2	Gardner,3b	3	0	0	0	3
Shorten,rf	4	1	3	3	0	Wamb'g's,2b	3	0	1	2	4
Jones,3b	4	0	1	1	2	Smith,rf	4	0	1	0	0
Ainsmith,c	3	2	3	1	1	O'Neill,c	3	1	2	2	4
Boland,p	2	1	1	2	2	Meyers,p	4	0	1	0	3
Total	35	9	18	27	15	Total	36	5	13	24	21

Errors—Lunte (2.) Harris.

Detroit .... 2 2 0 0 2 1 0 2 .—9
Cleveland .... 0 0 2 0 1 1 1 0 0—5

Two-base hits—Harris, Heilmann, Graney. Three-base hits—Speaker (2.) Boland. Stolen bases—Bush, Cobb (2.) Sacrifice hits—Young, Ainsworth, Lunte, Boland. Sacrifice flies—Boland, Gardner. Double play—Bush. Young and Heilmann. Left on bases—Cleveland, 8; Detroit, 6. Base on balls—Off Boland, 2. Struck out—By Myers, 1. Wild pitch—Boland.

The telltale box score of the "fixed" game cited by Leonard. The *New York Times*, September 26, 1919.

Cobb himself released the following statement to the public:

Is there any decency left on earth? I am beginning to doubt it. I know there is no gratitude. Here I am, after a lifetime in the game of hard, desperate and honest work forced to stand accused without ever having a chance to face my accuser. It is enough to try one's faith.

I am branded a gambler on a ball game in which my club took part. I have never in the 22 years I have been in baseball made a single bet on an American League game.[5]

Politicians, celebrities, and dignitaries across the country rushed to the defense of Cobb and Speaker. Will Rogers stated, "I want the world to know that I stand with Ty and Tris. If they had been selling out all these years, I would like to have seen them play when they weren't selling!"[6]

Even American League President Ban Johnson, the man who forced Cobb and Speaker to retire, expressed support for Cobb, saying "I know Ty Cobb's not a crooked ballplayer. We let him go because he had written a peculiar letter about a betting deal that he couldn't explain and because I felt that he violated a position of trust." Johnson did not express the same support for Speaker, claiming that he was "a different type of fellow, cute."

Johnson added that his primary motive had been to protect the names of both of these men, saying, "I personally regret to see this turn of events . . . but if the Commissioner insists on publicity for the whole affair, I welcome an open hearing on our actions in the case." Johnson added that, in his mind, the case was closed.

After the hearing, Landis told reporters, "these men being out of baseball, no decision will be made, unless changed conditions in the future require it." In California, Dutch Leonard told writer Damon Runyon, "I've had my revenge."

Landis's statement to the contrary, there could be little doubt that the commissioner knew that this matter would surely lead to some type of resolution. It appears that Landis's primary motive for not reaching a quick decision was to let the case build and therefore multiply the embarrassment to Ban Johnson about the way he handled the situation.

The case continued to be front-page news throughout January 1927. In late January, Jack Dunn, owner of the Baltimore club of the International League, offered Ty Cobb a $25,000 contract as a player. Dunn stated, "I'm convinced that Cobb would be worth that much money to my club as a player."[7] It was speculated that Dunn's primary motive was to force Landis's hand and make him rule on Cobb's status as a player.

Despite the damaging letters, the case against Cobb and Speaker was not a strong one. Examining accounts of the game, it is hard to find any evidence of a fix. Cleveland did make three errors, but all were by reserves—two by shortstop Harry Lunte and one by first baseman Joe Harris. Lunte ridiculed the charges, claiming, "it's all bunk."

In addition, one would have expected a fixed game to result in a big day for Cobb and a mediocre one for Speaker, but the results were just the opposite. Also, with Wood and Leonard as key conspirators, why were they not playing?

Even the letters are fairly ambiguous. In the January 6 edition of the *Sporting News*, columnist John Sheridan summed up the situation as follows:

> Cobb says he wrote this letter, enigmatical in terms, because he promised Leonard, who left Detroit before the game in question was played, that he would advise him about the outcome of the speculation. It appears that in his desire to keep his promise to Leonard, he wrote a very foolish letter—especially as of that time, October 23, 1919, when the rumors of a crooked World Series were ripe. Cobb's loyalty to his promise was more honorable than his judgement.
>
> Wood also wrote the letter stating that Cobb did not wager a cent. This appears to be the entire case against Cobb. Against Speaker, the case appears to be even weaker. Leonard shows no letter from Speaker, nor does Wood mention Speaker in his letter to Leonard. The only testimony against Speaker is the unsupported word of a creature—Leonard—who confesses his own guilt.
>
> I can't see a thing in the testimony so far to justify condemnation of Speaker. Cobb's culpability seems to be limited to writing a damnful letter to Leonard—a letter which does credit to his spirit of friendship, but no credit to his acumen. Wood seems to have exercised himself to place bets for himself and Leonard against his (Wood's) team. This is not to Wood's credit.
>
> If Cobb did try to bet, he tried to bet on his own team to win. I've known Cap Anson, who I regard as possessing the highest character I have ever seen within or without baseball, to wager $1,000 on his own team to win, conditioned upon one certain pitcher, pitching not less than 7 innings. To win his bet, Anson took a long chance of losing that game. Did anyone who understood the circumstances think any worse of Anson? I didn't.
>
> Anson would bet on baseball games. Was Anson crooked? There wasn't anything but an honest drop of blood in Anson's body. Never anything but honest breath in his lungs. Of course, that was in the old days. You probably remember that the alleged Cobb/Speaker affair also occurred in the old days, prior to the time that the White Sox scandal of 1919 made betting an anathema in baseball.[8]

Sheridan makes an extremely important point, that before the 1919 World Series scandal, betting on baseball games—as long as you bet on your team to win—was not considered a dishonest practice. While technically illegal, most players would occasionally bet on games such as the World Series or, occasionally, on their own team to win certain games. Remember the defense of Hal Chase in 1918, when it was claimed that he had "honestly bet on his own team to win."

Finally, on January 27, Landis made public his decision on Cobb and Speaker, ruling that both were innocent of the charges of fixing a game or wagering on the results of the game. Key excerpts of Landis's decision are printed below:

> Cobb, Speaker, and Wood were available, but Leonard, a retired player, residing in *California*, declined to attend a hearing. . . .
>
> Cobb and Speaker appeared on November 27 and were informed of Leonard's attitude, whereupon they canvassed the whole situation with the Commissioner and reached the conclusion that they would rather quit baseball than have a hearing with the accuser absent. . . .
>
> While they insisted they had no doubt of their ability to answer the charges, they were concerned about the possible effect upon themselves and others in whom they were deeply interested. . . .
>
> Shortly thereafter, gossip and rumor got busy. As usually transpires when these two kindly, sympathetic agencies are at work, they left in their wake a variety of progeny infinitely more harmful to the individuals' concern than truth could possibly be.
>
> Many press associations and scores of newspapers were persistently demanding the facts. Therefore, Cobb, Speaker and Wood . . . realized that untrue, distorted and garbled accounts were being innuendoed, and agreed that a hearing had become desirable, even if Leonard persisted in staying away. . . .
>
> These players have not been, nor are they now, found guilty of fixing a ball game. By no decent system of justice could such finding be made. Therefore, they were not placed on the ineligible list.
>
> As they desire to rescind their withdrawal from baseball, the releases which the Detroit and Cleveland clubs granted at their request in the circumstances detailed above are cancelled and the players' names have been restored at the reserve lists of the clubs.[9]

While Cobb was pleased with the decision, he was still not satisfied. He was convinced that the whole matter was a conspiracy against him by his enemies, including Detroit President Frank Navin and Leonard. He also charged that Johnson and Landis were in on this conspiracy. Rather than let the matter end, Cobb threatened a lawsuit.

The public was pleased with the decision and looked forward to the two stars' returning to the game. In order to further humiliate Johnson, Landis insisted that the players must sign with American League clubs. While Cobb and Speaker were still technically on the reserve list of Detroit and Cleveland, respectively, both teams made the players free agents, free to strike their own deals.

Shortly after this, Speaker signed to play for the Washington Senators. While a number of clubs bid for Cobb, he initially resisted their overtures. Finally, when Philadelphia owner and manager Connie Mack—one of the few men in baseball that Cobb truly admired and respected—offered Cobb an extremely lucrative contract to join the Athletics, Cobb relented and returned to the game.

Both Cobb and Speaker played through the 1928 season, Speaker joining Cobb at Philadelphia in 1928. While both were past their peak, Speaker hit .327 with the Senators in 1927, finishing his career with a .267 average in 64 games with Philadelphia in 1928. Cobb was more productive, hitting .357 in 1927 and closing out his illustrious career with a .323 mark in 1928.

In 1936, Ty Cobb received baseball's highest honor. He was the first man elected to the Baseball Hall of Fame. Speaker joined Cobb in the Hall of Fame the next year.

As for Wood, the incident was soon forgotten, and he enjoyed a long career at Yale and lived a long and happy life. Things also turned out fairly well for Leonard, who ended up owning one of the largest grape growing, packing, and shipping businesses in California. When he died in 1952, Leonard's estate was valued at more than $2 million. In the days before big salaries, this was one of the largest estates left by a ballplayer, although it was eclipsed by the $12 million estate that Cobb left in 1961. Even in death, Cobb easily outperformed Dutch Leonard.

Shortly after the Cobb-Speaker scandal became public, baseball was rocked by another charge of game fixing. This one came from a familiar source, Charles "Swede" Risberg, one of the leaders of the 1919 World Series fix. In 1926 Risberg was making a living on a small dairy farm near Rochester, Minnesota. After hearing of the Cobb-Speaker affair, he contacted the *Chicago Tribune* with a statement that he had information that "wasn't quite as silly as the whole thing Cobb and Speaker were accused of participating in." Risberg continued: "I can give baseball's bosses information that will implicate 20 big leaguers who never before had been mentioned in connection with crookedness. Landis would never ask me to tell him what I know. The facts are there, but they don't want to know them."[9] As one would suspect, however, Landis did indeed want to know. After agreeing to pay Risberg's expenses, Landis met with the former player in baseball's administrative offices in Chicago on January 1, 1927.

Risberg's story involved two doubleheaders played on Sunday, September 2, and Monday, September 3, 1917. At that time Chicago was fighting for its first pennant since 1906, while the Tigers were out of the race. The White Sox swept all four games, winning by scores of 7–2, 6–5, 7–5, and 14–8. Detroit did not field particularly well in the games, committing a total of 10 errors, compared with three miscues by Chicago.

According to Risberg, the entire Detroit team "sloughed off" in the series, allowing the White Sox to win. Risberg further revealed that almost every member of the Chicago team contributed $45 to a purse for the Detroit players as a reward for their sloughing off. Risberg claimed that the entire White Sox team knew about the deal, including then-manager Clarence "Pants" Rowland. According to Risberg, the money was collected by him and fellow Black Sox member Chick Gandil, and the pair carried it from New York to Philadelphia and presented it to Tiger pitcher Bill James later in the month with instructions to split it among the Detroit players.

Finally, Risberg claimed that the White Sox had thrown two games to Detroit in 1919 after the Sox had locked up the pennant. As we know from the Cobb-Speaker affair, Detroit was in a battle for third-place money with the Yankees. According to Risberg, "we paid Detroit by sloughing off two games to the Tigers. I know I played out of position, and Jackson, Gandil, and Felsch also played out of position." With all the alleged help the Tigers were receiving in 1919, it is interesting to note that the Tigers still ended up finishing half a game behind New York in fourth place.

The reaction from the other players on the White Sox was swift. Other than Gandil, all the players vehemently denied Risberg's story of game fixing.

Just as the letters from Cobb and Wood complicated the Cobb-Speaker affair, the fund taken up by the White Sox and paid to Detroit complicated this new scandal. In fact, everyone acknowledged that a fund had been taken up, but the Chicago and Detroit players claimed that the fund was a reward to the Detroit pitchers for beating Boston, Chicago's rivals for the pennant, three straight games on September 19 and 20, 1917.

In response to the charges and the outcry that followed, Landis conducted an open hearing in Chicago on January 5, 1917. Thirty-seven ballplayers were called as witnesses, with Chick Gandil supporting Risberg's story. The other 35 men—including future Hall of Famers Ty Cobb, Eddie Collins, Ray Schalk, Ed Walsh, and Harry Heilmann—all denied the game fixing charges and reiterated that the fund for the Detroit pitchers was a reward for beating Boston.[10]

Looking at the situation from today's perspective, a fund to reward the Detroit pitchers for beating Boston seems a bit unusual, to say the least. However, this was not an uncommon practice for the time. The idea was to reward players for bearing down extra hard during a crucial series, particularly late in the season when a team far out of the pennant race would benefit from the extra motivation offered by a financial reward. In other situations, players were offered suits of clothes or other inducements as rewards for outstanding performances.

The hearings went on for two days. The key issue, and the key point of contention, was the purpose of the pool. Was it a bribe for throwing games, or a reward for beating Boston?

Each player in turn denied the charges. Manager Rowland not only insisted that the games were honest, but denied any knowledge of any type of pool. Former White Sox captain Eddie Collins admitted contributing $45 to the pool but insisted that it was to reward the Detroit pitchers.

Tiger pitcher George Dauss admitted receiving $180, which had been given to him by Tiger pitcher Bill James. According to Dauss, "it was understood that any pitcher that beat Boston would get $200. I got that idea from Bill James. He said that Chick Gandil told him that any pitcher that beat Boston would get the $200. The catcher who caught the Boston series was to get the other $20. I got $180. I think Stanage (the Detroit catcher) got sixty dollars."[11]

An amusing note came during the testimony of Detroit catcher Oscar Stanage. Stanage was unable to stop the Sox on the basepaths, as Chicago stole a total of 20 bases. Landis remarked to Stanage, "that's quite a crop of stolen bases," to which Stanage replied, "it happened to me lots of times," which resulted in laughter from everyone in the room.[12] On a serious note, however, Stanage stated, "If there were Detroit players sloughing these games, I didn't see it or hear anything about it. Neither did I see anything about those two 1919 games that was out of the ordinary."[13] The most emotional witness was Detroit pitcher Bernie Boland. During a heated exchange with Risberg, Boland screamed "you're still a pig!"[14]

Another dramatic part of the testimony was when Buck Weaver was called. Weaver was out with a broken finger during the controversial series, and he denied all knowledge of any game fixing. He also related that he had refused to contribute his $45 to the Detroit pool. Upon leaving the witness stand, Weaver stated, "Judge, I don't feel that I owe baseball anything, but baseball does owe me something. I ask you now for reinstatement." Landis was taken aback and responded, "drop me a line about that, Buck, and I will take the matter up."[15] As was related in Chapter 7, however, Weaver was denied reinstatement.

One of the strongest pieces of evidence in defense of the players is the timing of their payment. The fund was raised on September 28, almost a month after the alleged fix took place, and two weeks after the last Chicago-Detroit series of the year. It is much more likely that the fund was a timely reward for Detroit's sweep of Boston on September 19 and 20.

While Landis was content to let the Cobb-Speaker matter drag on, he moved quickly on Risberg's charges. On January 12 Landis released his decision. Excerpts from the text of this decision are printed below:

> The Chicago players other than Risberg and Gandil admitted the raising of a fund by Gandil and Risberg from the Chicago players at New York about September 28, 1917, but stated that this money solicited by Gandil and Risberg and contributed by them (Chicago players) was to be paid to Detroit pitchers in appreciation of, or as reward for, their beating Boston three games on September 20 and 21, 1917, Boston being Chicago's closest contender in the American League pennant race of 1917.

If the Gandil/Risberg version is correct, it was an act of criminality. If the other version is to be true, it was an act of impropriety, reprehensible and censurable, but not corrupt. . . .

Coming now to the collection of the money and the reason for it, it is Gandil's testimony that when the Chicago team returned home from the St. Louis series of September 4 and 5, 1917, there was a discussion of the matter at a meeting of the players at which Rowland and Risberg, among others, were present. However, Risberg testified that, "nothing was said about money until we got to the Ansonia Hotel, in New York" (September 28, 1917), and Gandil himself subsequently testified that he first spoke to Rowland about it in New York. . . . [That] the raising of this fund was mentioned September 28 at New York is also the evidence of John Collins, Schalk, Faber, Leibold, Murphy and Benz. . . .

The purpose of this fund is the most important question of all — whether it was a bribe for "sloughing" the games to Chicago, September 2 and 3, 1917, or a gift to Detroit pitchers for their work against Boston. . . .

The Chicago players' salaries were paid August 31; they had funds, yet there was no discussion about raising money to pay Detroit for "sloughing" that Risberg claimed was "common talk" on the Chicago team. Again, on September 12, Chicago players received checks, and two days later they played Detroit 3 games, in Detroit. Although Gandil and Risberg and James and the other pitchers were all there, and that was the last time these teams would meet that year, still not a word (was said) about the "bribe" money, and no inquiry or promise as to when payments would be made.

If the Gandil story of the transaction were true that he and James entered into a corrupt bargain for throwing the games, certainly those who were to receive the bribe would have been demanding their money. On the other hand, Detroit had not yet played Boston, so the Chicago players did not know how many games Detroit would win from Boston, or that any fund would be necessary. Then when those games had been played, the Chicago players raised the fund, notwithstanding it was shortly before another pay day and several of them had no money and Gandil and Risberg traveled to Philadelphia to deliver it. These facts discredit the testimony of Risberg and Gandil that it was payment for "sloughing" the games on September 2 and 3, and corroborate the testimony of all the others that it was for Detroit's work against Boston.

In addition to the charge of "sloughing" the September 2 and 3, 1917 series, Risberg alleges that Chicago "sloughed" to Detroit 2 of the 3 games at the close of the 1919 season. His only specific allegations are that he played out of position, that he believes that Gandil (and two other players out of baseball since 1920) also played out of position. Gandil corroborates this, testifying that he played out of position (first saying "I think it was 2 out of the 3 ball games" and later saying "I probably played out of position in all 3 games"); that he noticed Risberg playing out of position, so he figured he would do it also, without even a word between him and Risberg, or with any other Chicago or Detroit player about it. Of course, this testimony by Gandil and Risberg is evidence to that extent against them, but there is no evidence whatsoever supporting the charges involving any other Chicago player.

It is the finding of the Commissioner that the fund raised by the Chicago players on or about September 28, 1917, was not collected or paid to Detroit players for "sloughing" to Chicago the games of September 2 and 3, 1917, but was paid because of Detroit beating Boston; there was no "sloughing" of the September 2 and 3, 1917, nor the September 26, 27, and 28, 1919, games, except possibly by Risberg and Gandil.[16]

The continuing charges of scandals dating back before 1920 exasperated Landis. To friends he commented "won't these god-damn things that happened before I came into baseball ever stop coming up?"

Landis then moved to set down a statute of limitations on past charges and a code of conduct for players in the future. The key points in Landis's statement, all of which today are part of baseball law, are as follows:

1. A statute of limitations with respect to alleged baseball offenses, as in our state and national statutes with regard to criminal offenses.
2. Ineligibility for one year for offering or giving any gift or reward by the players or management of one club to the players and management of another club for services rendered or supposed to be, or have been rendered, in defeating a competing club.
3. Ineligibility for one year for betting any sum whatsoever upon any ball game in connection with which the bettor had no duty to perform.
4. Permanent ineligibility for betting any sum whatsoever upon any ball game in connection with which the bettor has any duty to perform.[17]

In putting down a statute of limitations, Landis effectively closed the books on one of baseball's darkest eras. His other three points set forth the conduct for all future players, and we will be reviewing the fourth point in detail when discussing the Pete Rose case later in this book.

Chapter 11

The Era of Tranquility

With the closing of the Cobb-Speaker case, baseball put the scandal-ridden era of the late teens and early twenties behind it. Attendance was up, public confidence was restored, and the future looked bright indeed for America's national pastime.

This began a period of relative tranquility for baseball, which to some extent has lasted until today. While gambling scandals continued to erupt periodically, major league baseball has been free of any serious charges of game fixing since the late 1920s, although a number of such instances have occurred in the minor leagues. These minor league scandals will be detailed in later chapters.

With the game fixing problems behind him, Commissioner Landis began to focus on the root cause of the fixes—gambling. Landis abhorred gambling and correctly realized that all the scandals that had threatened the very survival of professional baseball had been related to gambling activity.

Landis's attitude toward gambling put him on a collision course with Rogers Hornsby, the great National League second baseman. Hornsby was a fiery competitor with few bad habits—he didn't drink or smoke and did not attend movies for fear that they would hurt his vision, which was so critical to his success as a hitter. Hornsby did have one vice, however: He loved horse racing and loved to gamble on horses. This affection put him permanently in Landis's doghouse and led to a number of confrontations.

Hornsby was born in 1896 in Winters, Texas. He began his career in the Texas-Oklahoma League in 1914 and moved to Denison of the Western Association in 1915. While playing shortstop for Denison, St. Louis Cardinals scout Bob Connery saw Hornsby and purchased his contract for $500. In his book *Cooperstown, Where Baseball Legends Live Forever* Lowell Reidenbaugh reported on the transaction as follows:

> Wiring news of the purchase of Rogers Hornsby to the home office, the Cardinals' scout said, "If the boy fails to make good, you could take the money out of my salary."
>
> Before he died more than fifty years later, Connery had the satisfaction of seeing his discovery develop into the greatest right hand hitter of all time.[1]

Hornsby joined the St. Louis club late in the 1915 season, batting .246 in limited play. The next year he batted .313, and he continued at around the .300 mark until 1920.

In 1920 the balance between pitching and hitting in baseball was changed dramatically by rule changes and adjustments to the manufacturing of baseballs, which led to a huge surge in hitting. Hornsby was one of the primary beneficiaries of these changes, raising his batting average in 1920 to .370. Hornsby also led his league in hits, doubles, RBIs, and slugging percentage.

Hornsby achieved new heights in 1921, hitting .397 and leading the National League in most major offensive categories. He continued his assault on National League pitching through 1925, hitting over .400 three times. In fact, from 1921 to 1925 Hornsby had an incredible average of .402, a five-year mark unmatched in the history of baseball. The high point during this stretch came in 1924, when he hit .424 to establish a modern major league record that has never been approached.

In 1925 Hornsby took over the managerial reins of the St. Louis club. The team was in last place when he took over, but he rallied them to a fourth-place finish. In 1926 the playing manager led his team to the National League pennant and a dramatic world championship over the heavily favored New York Yankees. Although his batting average fell off to .317 during the 1926 season, Hornsby was the toast of St. Louis.

Hornsby's relationship with the St. Louis Cardinals was soon to end. While Hornsby was without question a great player, he was outspoken to a fault, often blunt in his criticism of players and management, especially Cardinals owner Sam Breadon. When Hornsby demanded a three-year contract for $150,000 after the 1926 season, he was traded to the New York Giants for future Hall of Famer Frank Frisch and pitcher Jimmy Ring.

By 1927 Hornsby's betting habits had started to cause him difficulties. During that year he was sued by Cincinnati bookie Frank Moore for $92,000, which Moore claimed Hornsby owed him on horse racing bets. While Hornsby won the suit, Landis was incensed. Hornsby, however, insisted that he had the right to spend his free time as he chose and correctly pointed out that gambling on horse racing was perfectly legal.

The feud between Hornsby and Landis simmered until 1932. Hornsby started that season as manager of the Chicago Cubs, but on August 4, tired of Hornsby's constant feuding with his players, the Cubs' general manager replaced Hornsby with first baseman Charlie Grimm. While discontent among the players was the reason given for Hornsby's firing, it later came out that Commissioner Landis had been investigating Hornsby for gambling heavily on horse racing, along with borrowing money from his players and pressuring his players to share bets with him. On August 13, Landis cleared Hornsby of any violation of baseball rules in regard to his gambling relationships with his players, but the incident aggravated the ongoing feud, which was about to boil over.

After Grimm took over, the Cubs rallied to win the National League pennant, but they then lost to the New York Yankees in the World Series. Before the World Series, the Cubs players met to divvy up their shares of the World Series money. Surprisingly, the players voted to give Hornsby nothing, despite the fact that he was manager for most of the season. Normally someone who was with a team for part of the year would get at least a partial share of the World Series loot.

The decision sent Hornsby into a rage, and he appealed to Landis. Despite the fact that both precedent and public opinion were with Hornsby, Landis turned Hornsby down and upheld the players' right to divide the shares as they saw fit. While technically Landis's ruling was correct, there was little doubt that in reality Hornsby was being punished for his betting on horse races, and that if another manager had been in the same situation, Landis would have reacted differently.

Landis occasionally voiced public displeasure with Hornsby, one time stating, "his betting has gotten him into one scrape after another, cost him a fortune and several jobs, and still he hasn't enough sense to stop it." Hornsby defended himself, saying, "I can see no difference from betting a horse would win than a lot of the club owners playing the market and betting a stock would go up or down." This was a not so subtle dig at Landis, who had lost money for baseball in the 1929 stock market crash. (It should be noted, to Landis's credit, that he made up these losses out of his own pocket.)

Hornsby continued as a part-time player, first with the Cardinals and then with the St. Louis Browns until 1937, when he served as player-manager of the Browns. Despite his strong managerial record, Hornsby was unable to obtain another big league managing job during Landis's lifetime. Hornsby believed that this was a result of a campaign against him by Landis.

After Landis's death, Hornsby returned to the game to manage the St. Louis Browns in 1952 and the Cincinnati Reds in 1952 and 1953. He later became a scout, working with the New York Mets during their formative years. Rogers Hornsby died in 1963 in Chicago, a member of the Baseball Hall of Fame.

In addition to his battles with Hornsby, Landis feuded with Detroit owner Frank Navin, who owned a stable and gambled heavily on horse racing. While Landis never took any official action against Navin, their relationship was always strained because of Navin's gambling activity.

In 1934 it appeared that a new scandal was about to erupt. That year the St. Louis Cardinals captured the National League pennant and won the World Series over the favored Detroit Tigers. Nicknamed the "Gas House Gang," the team featured such colorful characters as Hall of Famer Dizzy Dean and the great third baseman "Pepper" Martin. The club typified the depression mentality—a hungry, scrapping team that struggled for its wins.

After the World Series, the public learned that National League President

John Heydler had instructed detectives to shadow the team during their last series of the season. While Heydler admitted his action, he claimed it was purely a precaution without any particular grounds for suspicion. The revelation led to animosity between Heydler and Cardinals owner Sam Breadon, and shortly after the incident Heydler resigned from his office.

As baseball marched on through the depression and toward the war years, all was quiet on the gambling front. In fact, major league baseball was free of any major scandals until 1943, when Philadelphia Phillies owner Bill Cox was barred from the game.

The Philadelphia National League franchise dated back to 1883, when the club entered the league under the direction of former National Association great Robert Ferguson. The next year Harry Wright took over the helm and kept the Phillies in contention, finishing in second place in 1887. The Phillies had their ups and downs from the end of the nineteenth century to 1915, when the club won the National League pennant behind the leadership of Pat Moran and the pitching of Grover Cleveland Alexander.

By 1919 the club had settled into last place again, and with the exception of a fourth-place finish in 1932, they remained in the second division until 1949. During that dim period, the Phillies featured some exciting players, most notably the future Hall of Fame outfielder Chuck Klein and the great hitter Lefty O'Doul, but the club's total lack of pitching talent meant they gave up runs faster than they could score them.

As the club's fortunes sagged, attendance continued to drop, and by the end of 1942 the Phillies were bankrupt. In order to save the club, the National League purchased the franchise for less than $50,000 and announced that they were looking for a buyer.

At that point the history of major league baseball could have changed. Bill Veeck, who was later to achieve enshrinement in the Hall of Fame for his promotional abilities as owner of the Cleveland Indians, the St. Louis Browns, and the Chicago White Sox, offered to buy the team. His plan was to stock the team primarily with black ball players, who at that time were barred from organized baseball through an unwritten rule.

In retrospect, Veeck's plan was brilliant. In addition to saving the franchise, it would have turned the Phillies into instant contenders, since Veeck would have had his pick of the best players from the Negro leagues, the professional leagues in which black ball players were competing. The instant integration process would have been far easier than what Jackie Robinson encountered a few years later, and it would have contributed in a very positive way to social justice in America.

Veeck, unfortunately, made a major tactical error. He went to Judge Landis and explained his plan. Landis advised Veeck that there was no official ruling against blacks in baseball, after which the National League began looking at other buyers, and the club was sold to Bill Cox on February 18, 1943.

Bill Cox. Landis expelled the Phillies owner for betting on his own team. *Photograph by Patrice Kelly.*

Bill Cox was born in 1909 in New York City. At the age of 15 he entered New York University, later transferring to Yale. Although he left college after his sophomore year, during his time there he was on both the baseball and track teams.

On October 29, 1929, Cox went to work as a stockbroker on Wall Street. As luck would have it, that was the day of the great stock market crash, which ended his brokerage career. Shortly thereafter, Cox began to make his fortune by purchasing the rights to the famous *New York Sun* editorial, "Yes, Virginia, there is a Santa Claus," and republishing the essay on a national basis.

Cox then got into the lumber business and quickly began to build his wealth. He also was heavily involved in stamp collecting, which also proved quite profitable for him. As an active sportsman, Cox was pleased to buy the Phillies for the bargain price of $80,000.

The first move that Cox made was to hire future Hall of Fame manager Bucky Harris away from the Washington Senators. The move created publicity, and Harris was quite popular with the players. Suddenly, near the end of July, with the club in sixth place (an improvement over the team's eighth-place finish the year before), Cox fired Harris and replaced him with Fred Fitzsimmons. The players were furious, and a strike was averted only by a personal appeal from the deposed manager.

As it turned out, it was the Harris firing that led to the downfall of Cox. Harris had become aware that Cox was routinely betting on games that the Phillies were involved in (although he always bet that the Phillies would win) and went to Landis with the information. Landis then launched a quiet investigation into the matter.

These charges came on top of other problems Cox was experiencing with Landis. The first skirmish occurred when the judge discovered that Cox owned a racehorse and ordered him to sell it, a request with which Cox complied. Cox was then offered the job of New York State Racing Commissioner by Tom Dewey. Landis informed Cox that his acceptance of such a job would end his connection with baseball, and Cox refused the appointment.

When Landis initially approached Cox about the betting charges, Cox denied the charges. He insisted that bets on the Phillies had been made, but they were made by his associates in the lumber industry in May 1943. When Cox had found out about the bets, he spoke with his associates and the bets were discontinued. Landis, regardless, continued to look into the matter.

Thanks largely to the testimony of Bucky Harris, Landis quickly ascertained that Cox had indeed placed bets on baseball. On November 15, Landis sent a strongly worded letter demanding that Cox appear at a hearing to be held in New York on December 4 to look into Cox's activities. The last paragraph of the letter read

> In view of the statements you have heretofore made to me respecting this matter, I am obliged to inform you that pending the hearing and decision, it would not be appropriate for you to participate in any baseball meeting or transaction.[2]

On November 18 Cox responded as follows:

> I have your letter of November 15, 1943. Before I became interested in the Philadelphia club this year, all of my time was devoted to a business essential to the war effort. My activities as president of the club have not permitted me to give such business the time I should have, and I have therefore decided again to devote all of my time to my war-essential business. I have today submitted to the chairman of the board of the club my resignation as president and director thereof. I have, as you know, what to me is a large investment in the club, and I shall dispose of that investment, in its entirety, as soon as I can find a satisfactory purchaser. In view of my resignation, and the full statements which I have heretofore made to you, I do not see that any useful purpose would be served by my attending any further hearing before you.[3]

Cox could see a permanent expulsion coming, and he sought to avoid the verdict by voluntarily resigning from the club and promising to sell his stock. Unfortunately for Cox, this was not enough for Landis, and on November 23 Landis announced that Cox had been permanently expelled from baseball. Landis released all relevant correspondence and revealed that on November 3 Cox had admitted that he had "placed through a bookmaker approximately

15 or 20 bets of from $25 to $100 per game on Philadelphia to win." On the eve of his dismissal, Cox took to the airwaves, broadcasting a message on radio station WOR. Cox said, in part,

> I made some small and sentimental bets before I learned of the rule against this. I leave it to the public and my friends to decide whether I was wrong.
> My friends know I worked night and day to build up the team and its financial condition. Most of the money put into the club I put in myself. I now find that because I admitted backing my team with a few bets I have been banned from the game I love for the rest of my life. Good luck and goodbye to everyone in baseball.[4]

Robert R. M. Carpenter, Jr., of Wilmington, Delaware, was elected president of the Philadelphia Phillies and subsequently bought the franchise. Carpenter, an heir to the DuPont fortune, became a highly respected member of baseball management.

Soon after this, however, Cox had a change of heart. He sought to retract his admissions that he had wagered on the Phillies. The rationale that Cox gave for his admissions of guilt was that he was "trying to test the loyalty of an employee." He called on Landis to hold the originally scheduled December 4 hearing and attended the hearing accompanied by his attorney.

The hearing was unusual in that it was open to the press and to the public. According to Cox, he admitted making some small bets as part of his plan to smoke out an associate whom he suspected of disloyalty. He admitted having made some friendly bets of hats, cigars, and dinners on the batting and pitching records of his players or the position of the Phils in the race, but not on the results of any game.

Appearing as witnesses for Cox were William D. Miller, a contractor, Elizabeth Massey, secretary to Cox, and Mary Easterbrook, switchboard operator with the Phillies. Miller claimed that sometime before the betting investigation had begun, he had received a letter from Cox outlining a plan to trap a disloyal employee by circulating a story that Cox had bet on the team. Both Massey and Easterbrook denied knowledge of any wagers by the Phillies president.

The main witness for the prosecution was Bucky Harris. Harris testified that once in Cox's office, he heard Ms. Massey get betting odds over the telephone, and she told Harris that she placed bets for Cox. According to Harris, he replied, "if Judge Landis ever hears about this, it will be the end of Cox."

Also testifying against Cox was Nathan Alexander, an assistant to Cox. Alexander, who owned a small amount of stock in the club, had been a lifelong friend of Cox's, but he revealed that at a directors' meeting on October 15, he had called on Cox to resign. While not commenting on the betting, Alexander testified to a number of charges of mismanagement by Cox, including taking a $25,000 salary when he had said that he would take only $5,000. He also claimed that Cox had called him and asked him to tell manager Fitzsimmons to avoid pitching Dick Barrett, because Barrett had been promised a bonus of $1,500 if he pitched 200 innings, and the player was getting close to that. Alexander stated that he ignored the request.

The key evidence against Cox was his previous admission of betting on the club, including the WOR address. Landis reaffirmed his original decision, stating

> There is no escape from the conclusion, with such intelligence as I am endowed with – or inflicted with – that there is nothing I can do for Mr. Cox. Baseball rules on betting or otherwise are obligatory on me, as well as on other baseball men, and the order will have to be that I do not put out a new order.[5]

The most dramatic moment of the meetings was when the lawyer for Cox, Louis Stryker, stated that "in the absence of proof, I ask you to clear this man of the charge that he gambled on the outcome of baseball games, unless you want to hear Cox's explanation of why he played private detective to test the loyalty of one of his men. I don't think that would be good for baseball." Furious at the implied threat, Landis retorted, "if you think it would be bad for baseball, then bring it in. We'll hear it." No such evidence was forthcoming.

Thus ended the baseball career of Bill Cox, but not his career in sports. He was involved later in promoting professional football and basketball, and for a time he was a part owner of the San Diego club in the International Soccer League.

The final gambling incident in the Landis era occurred on October 1, 1944. This incident did not come to light until many years later.

The year 1944 was a war year, and the quality of baseball was significantly diluted. With most of the stars in the service, baseball clubs were forced to make do with players classified as 4-F (those players with health problems), players too young for the draft, and old-timers who were too old for active duty. The mixed-up talent pool totally changed the balance of power in baseball.

Going into the season's final day, the Detroit Tigers led the St. Louis Browns by one-half game. The Tigers were at home against Washington, while the Browns had a doubleheader at home in St. Louis against the Yankees. A victory by the Tigers would assure them at least a tie for first place, while the pressure was on the Browns to win both games. The Detroit-Washington game matched 27-game winner Dizzy Trout, pitching on one day's rest, against Washington hurler Dutch Leonard. Leonard, not related to the Dutch Leonard involved in the Cobb-Speaker affair, responded brilliantly, winning by a score of 4–1. Leonard later revealed that before the game, he had received a phone call offering him $20,000 to lose the game. Because Leonard did not reveal this until many years later, no investigation was held, and thus the story ends. Meanwhile, the Browns swept the Yankees and claimed their first, and only, American League pennant.

On the morning of November 25, 1944, Kenesaw Mountain Landis died in Chicago. Thus ended a stormy era in baseball, one that began in scandal but ended with the game ready to emerge from World War II in the best shape of its long history.

On April 24, 1945, the club owners elected A. B. "Happy" Chandler, then a United States senator from Kentucky, as the new commissioner. Chandler was different from Landis in many ways—he was smooth and diplomatic while Landis was rough and opinionated. At the same time, Chandler carried on Landis's passion for ensuring that baseball was above suspicion.

The first and only chance that Chandler had to put his commitment to the test came in 1947 in the case of Brooklyn Dodgers manager Leo Durocher. Durocher, nicknamed "Leo the Lip," was born in 1905 in West Springfield, Massachusetts. He began his professional baseball career in 1925 with the Hartford club in the Eastern League. While not much of a hitter, Durocher immediately established himself as a star fielder, which led the New York Yankees to purchase his contract.

After appearing in two games in 1925, the Yankees sent Durocher to the minor leagues for more seasoning. He played for Atlanta in 1926 and St. Paul in 1927. He made the big club in 1928 and won a job filling in at second base and shortstop. Although he never developed much hitting skill (his lifetime average was .220), Durocher continued to field extremely well, winning the warm affection of Yankee manager Miller Huggins.

Durocher immediately established himself as a "colorful character," running up debts to buy fancy clothes and speaking his mind to the Yankee veterans. By 1929 manager Huggins was the only member of the Yankees who liked Durocher, and after Huggins's death in late 1929 Durocher was shipped to the Cincinnati Reds.

With the Reds Durocher established himself as an everyday shortstop. Although his hitting continued to be weak, he fielded well enough to keep a regular job. Then, early in the 1933 season, he was traded to the St. Louis Cardinals.

With the Cardinals, Durocher held the position of an important player on a rising team. In 1934 the Cardinals won the pennant and the World Series and became known as the "Gas House Gang." The team was known for their wacky stunts, and Durocher was one of the leaders in the antics.

After the 1937 season Durocher moved on to the Brooklyn Dodgers. In 1939 he was named manager of the Dodgers, bringing the club a pennant in 1941, the franchise's first pennant in 21 years. New York turned out to be the ideal place for the colorful Durocher, and both he and the club thrived.

During his first four years at the helm of Brooklyn, Durocher teamed with Dodgers President Larry MacPhail to form a controversial duo. MacPhail and Durocher constantly feuded, with MacPhail firing Durocher on more than one occasion, although the firings never stuck.

Branch Rickey at bat, with Leo Durocher umpiring. *Courtesy of Transcendental Graphics.*

After the 1942 season MacPhail left the Dodgers to go to the New York Yankees, and Branch Rickey took over the Dodgers. Rickey, the architect of baseball's farm system, had already built a dynasty in St. Louis and was looking to do the same in Brooklyn.

By the time Durocher came to Brooklyn, he had a long history of run-ins with baseball management. Durocher was a notorious umpire baiter and was frequently involved in heated controversies with the officials. On more than one occasion, Judge Landis had summoned Durocher to warn him to curb his tongue, but in reality Landis liked and admired the scrappy Durocher.

Durocher's real problems with baseball began as early as 1942. During that season, Durocher and the players had an ongoing poker game—for stakes Durocher described as "friendly." When Branch Rickey found out about this he called Durocher on the carpet and asked that the game be discontinued. To Durocher's credit, the instruction was carried out immediately.

Durocher's next difficulty, in 1944, was due not to his own actions, but to the actions of friends. One of Durocher's close friends was Hollywood actor George Raft, who had friends in the underworld. During the off-season Durocher often spent time at Raft's mansion in California, and Durocher allowed Raft to use his apartment when the actor visited New York. In March 1944, while Durocher was at Bear Mountain, New York, for wartime spring training, Raft hosted a party at the apartment in which a man was supposedly cheated out of $12,000 in a game with loaded dice. While Durocher was totally innocent of all wrongdoing, Landis advised Durocher to keep away from Raft.

Durocher's next major controversy came in 1946, when he met and fell in love with Hollywood actress Laraine Day. Ms. Day was married at the time to a man named Ray Hendricks, and the result was a rather messy and public divorce. While this type of intrigue was not unusual for Hollywood, it certainly was unusual for the staid and conservative organized baseball of 1946.

In the middle of this controversy, Chandler called Durocher and told him that he wanted to have a meeting with him. Chandler named the date and the place: the Clairmont Country Club in Berkeley, California. Despite Durocher's protest that neither the time nor the place was convenient, Chandler insisted. In the meeting, Chandler went through a list of Durocher's acquaintances, including Joe Adonis and Bugsy Siegel, two of the nation's leading mobsters. Chandler also mentioned Memphis Engelberg, a horse handicapper, and Connie Immermann, former manager of the famous New York Cotton Club. Chandler also brought up George Raft.

Chandler's reasons for concern are certainly understandable. First of all, a major point-shaving fix had just been uncovered in college basketball, and there was a great deal of public scrutiny into the honesty of sports. Also, World War II had just ended, and it must be remembered that the period just after World War I brought about some of baseball's biggest scandals. Finally, New York sportswriter Westbrook Pegler was insisting in print that Chandler clean up baseball, naming Durocher as the main villain. Chandler was a politician, and politicians are sensitive to the press.

The result of the meeting was a stern warning from Chandler not to associate with the men Chandler mentioned, or any others with ties to gambling or organized crime. Chandler's warning was of such a nature that Durocher felt that he was in trouble—and he was.

It later came out that Chandler's call to Durocher was at the urging of Dodger management, primarily Branch Rickey and Arthur Mann. They were concerned about Durocher's associations, coming on top of the divorce and the marriage to Laraine Day, and they felt that a stern call from the commissioner would throw the fear of God into Durocher. There was no question that the meeting had the desired effect.

Shortly after the meeting, Pegler blasted Durocher in print, linking him with Siegel and Adonis. To top it all off, the head of the Brooklyn chapter of the Catholic Youth Organization pulled his fifty thousand boys out of the Dodgers Knothole gang on the grounds that Durocher was "a powerful force for undermining the moral and spiritual training of our young boys."

The 1947 campaign began with the Dodgers' training in Havana. During his first days in Havana, Durocher managed to avoid conversations with Engelberg and Immermann and also avoided an introduction by a fan to notorious gangster Lucky Luciano.

Despite his caution, however, Durocher soon became embroiled in a major controversy with the Yankees. The controversy started when Larry MacPhail approached Durocher about managing the Yankees in 1947. Durocher refused, and MacPhail hired Bucky Harris, who led the club to the pennant. MacPhail then hired Charlie Dressen and Red Coriden, who had served under Durocher as Dodger coaches. (Coriden, readers may remember, had been an innocent victim in the 1910 Ty Cobb–Larry Lajoie batting title scandal. Coriden was the third baseman who played an extremely deep third base one day against Lajoie under orders from Browns manager Jack O'Connor.)

The hiring of Dressen and Coriden led to heated verbal jousting between MacPhail and Rickey, and MacPhail and Durocher. Fuel was added to the fire when, in his *Brooklyn Eagle* column (actually written by Dodger traveling secretary Harold Parrott), Durocher blasted MacPhail.

The controversy reached a breaking point a few days later when Branch Rickey saw Engelberg and Immermann, two of the men that Durocher had been warned to stay away from, sitting in boxes assigned to the Yankees right beside Larry MacPhail's box. Rickey was furious, saying:

> There they are as guests of the President of the Yankees, while my own manager can't even say hello to this actor, George What's-His-Name. He won't have anything to do with these gamblers or any gamblers. But apparently there are rules for Durocher and other rules for the rest of baseball.[6]

Rickey's comments created a sensation. Durocher was asked whether he agreed with them, to which he responded: "Where does MacPhail come off flaunting his company with known gamblers right in the players' faces? If I even say hello to one of these guys, I'd be called up before Commissioner Chandler and probably barred."[7]

By that point, the controversy had gone beyond a friendly rivalry. MacPhail demanded an investigation by the commissioner, who called for a hearing in Sarasota, Florida, on March 24, 1947.

During the investigation, Chandler called a number of witnesses, Durocher being last. Durocher admitted writing the articles in the *Brooklyn Eagle* and stuck to his quotations. In his book *Nice Guys Finish Last*, Durocher reported the events as follows:

> At the direction of the Commissioner, MacPhail stood up and read the column through from beginning to end.
>
> The moment he had finished, I said, "Well, Larry, as far as I'm concerned that's all baseball jargon. That's baseball talk, Larry. That's the way you and I have always talked."
>
> I said, "Look, Larry, I didn't mean anything derogatory about you. I worked for you, and you fired me . . . how many times? You must have fired me sixty times and we were always friends. Maybe I have needled you a little bit in there, but to me it was nothing personal. Larry, if you think it's personal, if you think I've done something wrong here, I will right now apologize to you. And I also will apologize publicly if you want me to. Because I don't want you as an enemy of mine. We've been friends too long."
>
> MacPhail just took the clipping he had been reading from and ripped it up into little pieces. He came up to the witness chair, put his arm around me and gave me a bear hug that practically lifted me out of the chair. "You've always been a great guy with me, and you always will be a great guy," he said. "Forget it buddy, it's over."
>
> I sat down. I'd been worried about nothing, just like everybody had said all along.[8]

If Durocher thought his troubles were over, however, he was wrong. The commissioner then questioned Durocher on clubhouse activities, including card playing (primarily gin rummy) and dice games. Durocher denied the dice games but admitted that he and the players occasionally played gin rummy and occasionally for small stakes. Durocher admitted running up winnings from pitcher Kirby Higbe, but he claimed that he forgave these debts when Higbe won games and never actually collected a cent.

With that, Chandler ended the hearing, warning all parties to keep silent. They were not to discuss the hearings with anyone, particularly the press.

The general consensus among Brooklyn management was that the hearing had gone well and the incident was closed. Speculating on what action might come, veteran sportswriter Dan Daniel predicted in the *Sporting News* that the likely outcome of the hearing was a ban on future columns by Durocher, as well as a ban on newspaper writing by other managers. The hearings were generally criticized by the press, and Chandler was roundly criticized for his order of silence.

On April 9 Chandler released a statement with the results of the hearing. Many of the participants—including the Brooklyn Baseball Club, Harold

Parrott, and Charlie Dressen—were fined and Durocher was suspended from baseball for a period of one year. Chandler's statement read in part:

> The incident in Havana, which brought considerable unfavorable comment to baseball generally, was one of a series of publicity producing affairs in which Manager Durocher has been involved in the last few months. Managers of baseball teams are responsible for the conduct of players on the field. Good managers are able to insure the good conduct of the players on the field, and frequently by their example can influence players to be of good conduct off the field.
>
> Durocher has not measured up to the standards expected or required of managers of our baseball teams. As a result of the accumulation of unpleasant incidents in which he has been involved, which the Commissioner construes as detrimental to baseball, Manager Durocher is hereby suspended from participating in professional baseball for the 1947 season.[9]

The suspension of Durocher caught everyone by surprise and brought mixed reactions. J. Roy Stockton of the *St. Louis Post-Dispatch* wrote, "suspension for a year seems an unfairly drastic penalty for Durocher." Ned Cronin of the *Los Angeles Daily News* commented, "regardless of the fact that from a moral standpoint Durocher probably will never do anything to forestall juvenile delinquency . . . he still is being made the fall guy in a game of back-biting between MacPhail and Rickey." Arthur Daily of the *New York Times* wrote, "to my mind, Leo Durocher is like the man who is hauled into traffic court for passing through a red light and then is sentenced to the electric chair." In contrast, Jimmy Powers of the *New York Daily News* wrote, "Chandler's decision was long overdue and too lenient. Landis would have barred Durocher for life long ago." Will Connolly of the *San Francisco Chronicle* wrote, "greatest thing that has happened to organized baseball in our generation; greater yet for the generation of kids coming up."

Despite appeals by the Dodgers and a strong emotional appeal by Yankees boss Larry MacPhail, Durocher's suspension stuck. By missing the 1947 season, Durocher missed a great pennant race, Jackie Robinson's debut in the major leagues, and a pennant for Brooklyn.

Looking back at the whole Durocher affair, it is hard to rationalize his suspension. It seems as if Durocher was indeed a scapegoat—the honesty of sports was attacked by the press, and Chandler, ever the politician, felt he had to do something. Given the range of controversies that Durocher was involved in—his associations with gamblers, his romance and later marriage to Laraine Day, the MacPhail controversy—Durocher was the closest thing baseball had to a villain. As a designated villain, Durocher was punished, and the punishment seemed to far outweigh the crime.

Why did Chandler suspend Durocher? In his book *Heroes, Plain Folks, and Skunks*, Chandler wrote the following:

> For a number of days I had been doing some serious thinking about what it would take to improve the atmosphere of the big leagues, what was really needed

to eradicate the odor of sleaziness that had so strongly crept in. I couldn't get Frank Murphy's letter out of my mind. If little kids couldn't go to the ball parks and look up to the players as their heroes and role models. . . What was organized baseball coming to?[10]

As it turned out, the Dodgers paid Durocher during his suspension, so he did not lose financially. The suspension was lifted after the 1947 season, and Durocher was able to finish his career.

In 1948 Durocher returned to the helm of the Dodgers, but it was clear that his situation with Brooklyn was no longer secure. During the season the New York Giants were looking for a new manager, and Giants owner Horace Stoneham received permission from Rickey to approach Durocher. Sensing that his days with the Dodgers were numbered, Durocher seized the opportunity and moved across town. He enjoyed great success with the Giants, leading them to the pennant in 1951 and the pennant and world championship in 1954.

Durocher later returned to the Dodgers as a coach, and in 1966 he took over the managerial reins of the Chicago Cubs. Later, he managed the Houston Astros.

Durocher went to his grave in 1991 with one great ambition unfulfilled: enshrinement in the Baseball Hall of Fame. Durocher was finally elected to the Hall of Fame in 1994. It was an honor long overdue him.

Chapter 12

The Denny McLain Incident

The reinstatement of Leo Durocher in 1948 ushered in another decade free of gambling scandals at the major league level. While the suspension of Durocher was questionable at best from the standpoint of fairness, it did serve notice to other players that Commissioner Happy Chandler, and his successors, would continue to guard the game in the best of the Landis tradition.

The next serious major league incident was uncovered on September 22, 1959. The incident involved Humberto Robinson, a pitcher for the Philadelphia Phillies.

Robinson was born on June 25, 1930, in Colón, Panama. He broke into the big leagues with the Milwaukee Braves in 1955, compiling 3-1 record in 13 appearances, with an ERA of 3.08. He bounced back and forth between the minor leagues and the major leagues for the next few years, appearing in one game with Milwaukee in 1956 and 19 games with Milwaukee in 1958.

In 1959 Robinson began the season with Cleveland and was traded in midseason to the Philadelphia Phillies. With the Phillies, Robinson appeared in 31 contests, winning two and losing four. Primarily a reliever, he started four games, completing one of them, and his ERA was a solid 3.33.

One of Robinson's four starts during the season was the second game of a September 22 doubleheader in Philadelphia versus the Cincinnati Reds. Just before the game began, Robinson, whose English was rather limited, told teammate Ruben Gomez that on September 21 he had been offered a bribe of $1,500 to throw the contest to the Reds. Gomez reported the information to Phillies manager Eddie Sawyer.

As it turned out, Robinson gave a stellar performance in the game. He went seven innings, striking out five men and giving up only three hits. He also hit a double and scored the first run of the game. Robinson was credited with the 3–2 victory over the Reds.

After learning of the incident, Sawyer reported it to Baseball Commissioner Ford Frick, who contacted the Philadelphia police. As a result, on September 24, Robinson appeared in municipal court before Judge Sydney Hoffman.

Denny McLain. McLain's suspension was the beginning of the end of a bright career. National Baseball Library & Archive, Cooperstown, N.Y.

Robinson testified that he had been offered the bribe by Philadelphia nightclub owner Harold Friedman. According to Robinson, Friedman told him that he had bet on the Reds to win the game and "wanted me to lose the game." Friedman was released on bond on a charge of attempted bribery of an athletic contest.

On September 28, a grand jury heard Robinson's testimony and indicted Friedman. Robinson was congratulated on his honesty and forthrightness in reporting the incident. The momentum at the hearing swung when it was revealed that Friedman had been under investigation by District Attorney Victor Blanc for operating a vice ring. Blanc revealed that he had a signed statement from an 18-year-old girl who claimed that she had "entertained" three National League players in Friedman's club. Commissioner Frick immediately ruled Friedman's Moon Glow café as "off limits" for major league players.[1]

After that, the incident quickly faded away. Robinson returned to the Phillies in 1960 but was less successful, with a record of no wins and four losses in 33 games. After that he faded from the major league scene.

All in all, the Robinson affair was a relatively minor matter: a small bribe offered to a relatively obscure pitcher toiling for a last-place team in a meaningless late-season contest. Major league baseball's next scandal, in contrast, involved one of the game's brightest stars, Denny McLain.

Dennis Dale McLain was a special player from the day he began his professional career. A high school star in the Chicago area, McLain received a $17,000 bonus to sign with the Chicago White Sox in 1962. In his first game, with Harlan, Kentucky, in the Appalachian League, McLain threw a no-hitter against Salem, striking out 16 batters. His next time out he struck out 16 batters again but lost the game on an error. After that impressive showing, McLain was promoted to Clinton of the Midwest League. With Clinton he struck out 93 batters in 91 innings but had a record of only 4-7.

The 1963 White Sox were overloaded with pitching. The staff featured such budding stars as Gary Peters, Juan Pizarro, and Joel Horlen, along with veterans Jim Brosnan, Hoyt Wilhelm, Ray Herbert, and Eddie Fisher. Unfortunately for the White Sox, they were also overloaded with young talent, including McLain, future basketball star Dave DeBusschere, and Bruce Howard. The rules at the time stated that only two of these bonus players could be protected on the major league roster, which meant that one of the three would have to clear waivers to remain with the organization.

The White Sox decided to keep Howard and DeBusschere, placing McLain on first-year waivers. Because of McLain's impressive performance in the minor leagues, the Detroit Tigers claimed him for the $8,000 waiver price.

McLain started the 1963 season with the Duluth-Superior team of the Northern League. After compiling a 13-2 record, he was promoted to Knoxville in the Sally League. While McLain enjoyed limited success at Knoxville, he was brought up to the major leagues by the Tigers when the rosters expanded in September. McLain pitched in three games for the Tigers, winning two games and losing one.

During the off-season, McLain married Sharon Boudreau, daughter of former Cleveland star and Hall of Famer Lou Boudreau. It appeared that this was an ideal baseball family in the making—the wife was the daughter of a Hall of Famer and the husband was a budding major league superstar.

After opening up the 1964 season with Syracuse in the International League, McLain was back in Detroit. Still learning how to pitch and how to throw a curveball, McLain struggled to a 4-5 record and a 4.05 ERA during the remainder of the 1964 season. In 1965 , however, McLain's career really began to take off. He had an impressive 16-6 record and an earned-run average of 2.62. The next year, McLain became a 20-game winner for the first time.

In 1967 McLain experienced a difficult year as he struggled to a 17-16 mark with a 3.79 earned-run average with the Detroit club, which barely lost the pennant to the Boston Red Sox during the "impossible dream" season. McLain, however, was about to take a major step toward stardom.

The year 1968 will be forever remembered as the year of the pitcher. Never in baseball annals had the efforts of batters been so anemic. In fact, Carl Yastrzemski led the American League in batting with a .301 average, the lowest average for a batting champion in the history of baseball. And Yaz had to rally during the final weeks in order to avoid winning the title with an average under .300. In the All-Star game that year, the National League won by a score of 1–0, the winning run scored by Willie Mays on a double play.

Two incredible pitching performances highlighted the season. In the National League, Cardinals star Bob Gibson led his team to the pennant with a 22-9 record and an incredible 1.12 earned-run average. In the American League, Denny McLain emerged as the league's top pitcher, becoming the first 30-game winner in baseball since Dizzy Dean in 1934. He posted a 31-6 record and a 1.96 earned-run average, leading the Tigers to the pennant. For this, McLain was awarded the league's Most Valuable Player Award, as well as the Cy Young Award.

McLain came back to earth the next year but still had an outstanding season with a 24-9 mark. His performance was good enough to earn him another Cy Young Award, but this time he shared the award with Baltimore Orioles star Mike Cuellar. There seemed little question that McLain had developed into one of the game's top pitchers, on his way to a Hall of Fame career.

Unfortunately, McLain's life off the field was not meeting with the same success as his life on the field. To the outside world, McLain was a colorful character with flamboyant habits. His hobbies included flying his own airplane and playing the organ professionally. In reality, he was a young man suddenly finding himself with success and money—and not knowing how to handle it.

One aspect of McLain's problems was financial. According to McLain, his relationship with Ed May was the cause of his financial difficulties. In 1969 McLain turned over the management of his business affairs to May, giving him the power to invest his money. While on a goodwill trip to Vietnam after the season, McLain's wife contacted him in a panic—they were behind on the mortgage and bills were not being paid, and she could not get in contact with Ed May. McLain returned to find his financial affairs in tatters. He was in debt over $400,000 and eventually had to declare bankruptcy.

McLain's real problems were tied to gambling. His involvement with gambling ultimately ruined his baseball career and had a major negative impact on the lives of McLain and his family.

The McLain gambling story first came into the public eye when an article entitled "Downfall of a Hero" broke in the February 3, 1970, issue of *Sports Illustrated.*[2] The article told of a horse race held on August 4, 1967, a man named Edward Voshen, who won more than $46,000 on the race, and his attempts to collect the money owed to him from a Flint, Michigan, bookmaking ring.

To make a long story short, when Voshen went to collect from the man he placed the bet with, Jiggs Gazell, who operated out of the Shorthorn Steakhouse in Flint, Gazell informed him that he could not pay more than $1,000 on the bet. Gazell was reportedly connected with the Syrian mob in Flint. While Gazell would not pay the bet personally, he told Voshen to see his partners, Pepsi-Cola Bottling executive Ed Schober and Denny McLain.

The story went on to chronicle McLain's involvement in the Flint bookmaking operation and the operation's ties to organized crime. According to the article, Voshen went to mobster Tony Giacalone for help in collecting the debt, and the mob boss agreed to arbitrate the dispute. According to the article, Giacalone did intervene, threatening McLain and Schober unless the debt was paid. The article stated that the mob boss brought his heel down on McLain's toes and dislocated them, hurting McLain's effectiveness during the Tigers' unsuccessful 1967 stretch drive. It was well known that McLain had dislocated toes at that time, but according to McLain, he had injured them himself.

The *Sports Illustrated* story had an ominous ending. On October 16, 1968, Ed Voshen was killed in an unexplained one-car traffic accident. Before his death, he had managed to collect only $1,000 of the amount owed to him by McLain's bookmaking firm.

According to McLain, parts of the article were correct—he had been gambling and had become a bookmaker, but "other than that, the story could have been written by Hans Christian Andersen. It was a fairy tale."[3]

McLain's story was that his gambling began in 1967 with his friend Ed Schober. McLain had come to know Schober well from his much-publicized addiction to Pepsi-Cola. McLain was consuming a case or more of Pepsi every day, and Schober wisely used the local hero to help promote his product.

According to McLain, Schober was a much heavier bettor than he was. McLain also explained that while he was betting on sports, he never made a bet on baseball either during or after his career.

McLain explained[4] that the idea of going into the bookmaking business came from Clyde Roberts, who ran the Shorthorn Steakhouse. McLain rejected the idea at first but allowed himself to be persuaded by the lure of easy money. Roberts employed Jiggs Gazell as the front man, and Roberts, Schober, and McLain were the backers. McLain borrowed $4,500, and the operation was in business.

According to McLain, the operation was a failure from the beginning. After sinking about $15,000 into the operation, McLain claimed that he withdrew his support. According to him, this was a number of weeks before the Voshen incident.

While McLain admitted being aware of Voshen's claim—in fact, he loaned around $10,000 to Schober to help pay off the claim—he stated that he was totally uninvolved. He categorically denied most of the claims in the magazine article, stating that he never met Giacolone. He especially denied the charge that his toes had been injured by the mob boss, instead explaining the injury was a combination of kicking a locker in anger and getting up during the night when his foot was asleep.

Shortly before the *Sports Illustrated* story, Tigers management had contacted the new baseball commissioner, Bowie Kuhn, to alert him that McLain was having financial problems. Kuhn asked baseball's security director, former F.B.I. man Henry Fitzgibbon, to investigate.

Once the *Sports Illustrated* story broke, the baseball investigation became an urgent matter. Reacting to the story and the evidence that Fitzgibbon had accumulated, Kuhn summoned McLain on February 19 and informed him that he was being suspended indefinitely, pending an investigation. The announcement created a national sensation, and McLain's future in baseball was in doubt.

On April 1, 1970, Kuhn announced the results of the investigation. McLain was suspended from baseball until July 1, 1970, and placed on probation. According to Kuhn:

> So far as we could determine, the grand jury had developed no evidence that McLain had been involved in baseball betting, directly or indirectly. Nor had we. He was plainly at fault in his endeavors to become a partner in the Flint bookmaking operation and in his associations with the operation's criminal element. But the evidence strongly suggested that he was more a dupe than anything else. For his stupidity and greed, and for the harm he had done to public confidence in baseball, he clearly deserved a suspension, but I could not find justification for a full season suspension, let alone a longer one.[5]

Kuhn was roundly criticized for being too lenient by giving McLain only a three-month suspension. Some of the strongest criticism came from Detroit-area sportswriters, whose relationship with McLain had never been good. Detroit writer Joe Falls summed up the feelings of many of his colleagues:

> I couldn't believe how easily the Commissioner let Denny off. Denny is a very lucky boy, and I sense that he knows it. In my opinion, Kuhn became the first Commissioner to compromise the standards of baseball.[6]

McLain, of course, felt just the opposite—he did not feel that the suspension was warranted, saying, "I've never done anything to hurt baseball." Despite his feelings, McLain took a low-key attitude, merely saying, "I'll be ready to pitch on July 1st."[7]

During his suspension, McLain continued to work out and stay in shape. His key goal was to get the financial side of his life back together. He had debts of $446,069.96 and assets of only $413. The Michigan Securities and Exchange Commission was looking into his paint company, Denny McLain Dyco International, accusing it of violating Michigan blue sky laws—in other words, illegally selling stock. Without his $90,000 baseball income (McLain's suspension was without pay), he was forced to file for bankruptcy.

McLain returned to the game right on schedule on July 1. A crowd of more than 53,000 was there at Tiger Stadium, and the game was covered as a national event. Unfortunately for McLain, his return was less than triumphant—he lasted only five and a third innings, giving up eight hits. He was not involved in the decision.

McLain continued to struggle on the mound, winning three games against five losses with a bloated earned-run average of 4.65. Sportswriters commented that he did not appear to be the same pitcher as he had been before the suspension.

On August 28 McLain pulled a "prank" on two sportswriters, Jim Hawkins and Watson Spoelstra. One at a time, he dumped buckets of icewater over the heads of the writers. While McLain later claimed it was a prank, there was little doubt that he was acting out of frustration for his poor performance and the constant abuse heaped on him by these two writers.

Tigers General Manager Jim Campbell was furious over the incident and suspended McLain indefinitely. It also came to light that McLain was carrying a gun, although he did not have a concealed-weapon permit. Given the fact that McLain was already on probation, Kuhn felt that he had no alternative but to suspend McLain for the balance of the season.

On October 9 Kuhn announced that McLain's suspension had been lifted. Tired of McLain's antics and worried that his career was on the downswing, the Tigers traded McLain to the Washington Senators in an eight-player deal that brought third baseman Aurelio Rodriguez, shortstop Ed Brinkman, and pitcher Joe Coleman to the Tigers. This trade was to be remembered as one of the best in Tigers history. McLain continued to struggle in 1971, compiling a record of 10 wins and 22 losses for a weak Washington team. In the spring of 1972, he was traded to the Oakland Athletics.

The former 30-game winner started the 1972 season with Birmingham in the Southern League. Although not particularly successful (McLain had a record of 3-3 with a 6.32 ERA with Birmingham), he was brought back to Oakland for five starts, winning one of three decisions. He was then traded to the Atlanta Braves, where he compiled a record of three wins and five losses.

McLain was invited to spring training with the Braves the next year, but his pitching failed to improve. On March 26, 1973, just three and a half years after winning his second straight Cy Young Award, Denny McLain was given his unconditional release. His major league baseball career had ended.

McLain's life went from bad to worse. A self-admitted hustler, McLain was always looking for a big deal—a way to make easy money. In the pursuit of this easy money, he was involved in a variety of business deals, all of which were failures. He went from the projection television business to a mortgage brokerage company and eventually back to bookmaking. Looking for the fast buck in the fast lane, he fell in with the wrong crowd, associating with a number of shady characters who were also involved in the drug trade.

McLain continued to go from business to business. On the legitimate side, he was a partner in a group of walk-in medical clinics. On the illegitimate side, he earned $160,000 by smuggling a fugitive from justice out of the country in his private plane.

The U.S. Justice Department began to investigate the group with whom he was traveling. The drug dealers and the gamblers began to turn state's evidence, naming their associates. As a result, on March 19, 1984, seven individuals, including McLain, were indicted on charges of racketeering, extortion and narcotics. McLain was facing up to 90 years in prison and a $90,000 fine.

McLain was charged with five specific counts. Count one charged him with racketeering and the collection of unlawful debts. Count two charged him with conspiracy to perform illegal activities. In count three, McLain was charged with extortion, a charge related to an alleged threat to a debtor if the debtor did not pay the money he owed. Count four charged McLain with possession of cocaine and intent to distribute, and count five charged him with conspiracy to import cocaine.

The details of the events leading up to this case and the trial could be an entire book (in fact, they form the bulk of the content in Denny McLain's book *Strike Out*). The net result of the trial was that, in 1985, McLain was found guilty on four of the five counts and sentenced to 23 years in prison. He would not be eligible for parole until November 13, 1992.

McLain appealed the case, and on August 7, 1987, the appeals court unanimously overturned his conviction. The judges called the trial "a classic example of judicial error and prosecutorial misconduct combined to deprive the appellants of a fair trial," and McLain was released from prison. Initially it appeared that he would be retried—the appeal claimed that McLain's trial was flawed but did not acquit him of the charges. Eventually, however, the government dropped the case.

Since getting out of prison, McLain has sought to put his life back together and has been writing, appearing at sports card shows, and working in the front office of a minor league hockey club. Most recently he has been on the air for a radio station in Detroit during the morning drive time.

McLain's story is indeed a sad one. If it were not for his gambling activities, McLain would not have been suspended from baseball in 1970. If he had not been suspended from baseball, would he still have lost his great pitching talent? The answer to this question will never be known. We are left only to speculate on what might have been.

Chapter 13

The Pete Rose Scandal

The Denny McLain incident was a tremendous shock to organized baseball. Until that time, those running the game felt confident that at least at the major league level, the game was free of the influence of gamblers, and the integrity of baseball was above question.

There were a number of reasons that this seemed to be a good assumption. For one thing, the stern actions taken in the past, including the overly severe punishment of Leo Durocher in 1947, certainly should have sent a message to all ball players that association with gambling or corruption would not be tolerated. In addition, players were becoming more worldly, better educated, and, perhaps most important, better paid. Given the increasing earning potential that baseball players had—on the field and from endorsements—the possibility of corruption seemed increasingly remote. More than at any other time in history, they had a great deal to lose if caught fixing games or even associating with the gambling element.

The McLain case showed that the setup was not foolproof. While McLain never threw games, he certainly was involved in activities that were not in the best interests of baseball. The McLain incident helped alert organized baseball to the fact that vigilance would always be required to keep the game above reproach.

The next incident of note occurred on July 22, 1972, and involved Cincinnati Reds pitcher Wayne Simpson. On that day, Simpson was offered $2,000 to throw a game he was pitching against the Pittsburgh Pirates later that night.

A native of Los Angeles, Simpson had broken into the big leagues with the Cincinnati Reds in 1970 in spectacular fashion. As a rookie, Simpson fashioned a record of 14 wins and three losses, with a 3.02 earned-run average. Named to the National League All-Star team, he appeared to have a bright future. Unfortunately, late in the year he developed arm trouble, which was to plague him throughout his career. Although he continued to pitch in the big leagues until 1977, he was never the same pitcher.

The 1972 Simpson incident was a very strange one. Simpson received the bribe offer over the telephone in his hotel room from a gambler whom he had never met. In addition to asking Simpson to throw the game, the caller

Pete Rose. Rose's guilt in betting on baseball games had not been officially resolved as of this writing. National Baseball Library & Archive, Cooperstown, N.Y.

requested that Simpson make Pirates first baseman Bob Robertson, who was struggling through a terrible year, look good in the sixth inning. When Simpson told the caller he would not throw the game, the caller said, "you'd better think about it." He then called Simpson's catcher, Johnny Bench, telling Bench to "remind Simpson what I told him."

Simpson immediately reported the incident, but he did not take it very seriously. The request to feed a fat pitch to Robertson in the sixth inning struck Simpson as particularly strange "because there was a chance Robertson might not even come to bat in the 6th inning." As it turned out, Simpson won the game by a score of 6–3. Bob Robertson did bat in the sixth inning and hit a single.

After Simpson reported the incident to manager Sparky Anderson, the Reds' manager advised Cincinnati General Manager Bob Howsam, who contacted the F.B.I. Nothing more came of the incident.

Baseball's increased vigilance toward gambling led to an extremely controversial decision by Commissioner Bowie Kuhn in 1979. Kuhn's decision led to the suspension of Hall of Famer Willie Mays from baseball that year, to be joined by fellow Hall of Famer Mickey Mantle in 1983.

Mays and Mantle were two of baseball's greatest stars, arguably the two greatest players during the 1950s and early 1960s. Both had tremendous all-around talent—they were great fielders, great hitters, and great base runners, and both had outstanding power. Mantle was the leading player on the perennial champions, the New York Yankees, and Mays led their crosstown rivals, the New York Giants, who in 1958 became the San Francisco Giants.

The honesty and integrity of both Mays and Mantle were beyond question. However, in 1979, Mays was offered a contract to do public relations for Bally's Park Place Casino in Atlantic City. Mays would not be involved in the gambling operations, but he would be entertaining the casino's large clients in activities such as meals and golf.

This was an extremely difficult situation for Kuhn both from a personal standpoint and a public-relations standpoint. On the one hand, Mays was one of the great stars of the game. At the same time, Kuhn felt that he had established a precedent when he earlier ordered Oakland A's owner Charlie Finley and three minority owners of the Atlanta Braves to divest themselves of their interest in the Parvin-Dohrmann Company, which owned three Las Vegas casinos. In addition, Kuhn had informed former Yankees owner Del Webb, whose company also owned casino operations in Las Vegas, that he would not support Webb's bid for the Chicago White Sox unless Webb divested himself of his casino interests.

On October 26, 1979, Kuhn sent the following telegram to Mays:

> I have been informed that you are about to sign a long-term contract with Bally, in which you are rendering services to promote that company's casino gambling interest. While I appreciate the motivations leading you to this association, it has been my view that such associations by people in our game are inconsistent with its best interests. Accordingly, while I am not happy at the prospect of losing your active participation in baseball, I must request that you promptly disassociate yourself from your contract with the New York Mets.[1]

Unfortunately, the financial aspects of the casino offer were much more lucrative than those that baseball was currently offering, so Mays chose to accept the offer from Bally. Therefore, Kuhn banned Mays from official association with the game.

The same situation happened in 1983 when Mickey Mantle accepted employment from the Claridge Hotel in Atlantic City. Again, financial considerations led Mantle to accept employment, and he also was banned from any official association with baseball.

Public sentiment was heavily against Kuhn and supportive of the former stars. Most writers and fans argued that Mays and Mantle were not actually associated with gambling, and they felt that Kuhn's judgment was far too harsh. The fact that the honesty of Mays and Mantle was above question certainly contributed to the negative publicity for Kuhn.

Kuhn weathered the criticism and stuck to his guns, and Mantle and Mays were not reinstated until 1986, when Kuhn's successor, Peter Ueberroth, reversed Kuhn's verdict. The move was a popular one with baseball fans throughout the nation.

The 1970s also introduced a new kind of scandal to baseball: drug-related scandals. A number of players, primarily on the Pittsburgh Pirates and Kansas City Royals, were publicly implicated for their involvement in the drug trade, and a number received suspensions from baseball. This led to a drug treatment policy agreed upon by the owners and the players union. Sadly, this has not prevented baseball from having problems with drug use. In 1992, multiple offender Steve Howe was permanently suspended for his continued involvement with drugs, although an arbitrator later reinstated him.

Drug-related scandals are beyond the scope of this book, so we will not discuss them in any detail. However, it is worth pointing out that in addition to the legal and moral issues of drugs, the people in the drug trade tend to be the same people as those involved in illegal gambling, and it is strongly in baseball's best interest to keep players as far away from this crowd as possible. In addition, distributing illegal drugs is a felony, and players involved in such activity leave themselves open to blackmail by underworld figures, which could lead to corruption in the game.

Baseball's next gambling scandal was the biggest and the most controversial since the 1919 Black Sox scandal. This scandal, which came to light in 1989, involved superstar Pete Rose, the man who broke Ty Cobb's record for the most base hits in a career, and a man who had come to symbolize the aggressive, rugged style of baseball that fans love.

Peter Edward Rose was born on April 14, 1941, in Cincinnati, Ohio. After graduating from high school, Rose signed with the Cincinnati Reds for a bonus of $7,000, and the promise of an additional $5,000 if he was able to reach the major leagues and stay for a period of 30 days.

The first stop in his professional career was with Geneva in the New York–Pennsylvania League. Playing hard all the time, which was the style that he would become known for, Rose had a good first year and batted .277. The next year Rose was with Tampa of the Florida State League. He had a much stronger second season, batting .331 in 1961. This earned him a promotion to Macon in the South Atlantic League, where in 1962 he batted .330.

In spring training of 1963, Rose's ability and his all-out hustle—which would earn him his nickname "Charlie Hustle"—impressed Reds manager Fred Hutchinson enough to give Rose a job with the Reds. Many scouts were still skeptical of Rose's ability, but he had a very good rookie season, batting

.273 and winning the National League Rookie of the Year Award. He followed
with a .269 average in 1964 and then really blossomed in 1965, hitting .312
with a league-leading 209 hits. Pete Rose had arrived as a baseball star.

Rose continued to improve every year. While not a dominating player like
Ty Cobb, Babe Ruth, or even Willie Mays, Rose was consistently outstanding.
In 1968 and 1969, he won back-to-back batting titles with averages of .335 and
.349. He won another National League batting crown in 1973. He left the Reds
after the 1978 season, signing with the Philadelphia Phillies as a free agent,
winning his fourth and final batting crown with them in 1981. In 1984 he moved
on to Montreal, by this time closing in on Ty Cobb's record of 4,191 career base
hits. By now Rose's skills were fading—after hitting .271 in 1982, he slumped
to .245 in 1983 and was hitting .259 when Montreal traded him to the Reds.
He became player-manager of the Reds, playing well during the latter part of
the season and hitting .365 in 26 games.

The 1985 season was probably the highlight of Rose's career. He managed
the Reds to a second-place finish and, more memorably, broke Ty Cobb's
record for base hits. All the same, his career was clearly on a downslide, as
he hit just .264 in 119 games. His last season as a player was 1986. He hit
a weak .219 in 72 games and once again brought the Reds home to a second-place finish. This final season left Rose with a career average of .303,
and he held the career record for most games played, most at-bats, and most
hits.

After ending his career as an active player, Rose continued as manager of
the Cincinnati Reds, guiding the club to second-place finishes again in 1987
and in 1988. During the 1988 season Rose got into a shoving match with umpire Dave Pallone and was suspended for 30 days by National League President Bart Giamatti. Rose was also fined $10,000 for the incident.

Most observers felt that Rose's punishment was excessive. While Rose was
certainly wrong to shove the umpire, most observers believed that both Rose
and Pallone had acted incorrectly. The incident created a great deal of ill will
between Rose and Giamatti; ill will that was to explode during the coming
months.

Bart Giamatti's path to a baseball career was by no means a usual one.
While traditionally baseball executives have come from the playing field, the
front office, or the press box, Giamatti made his mark as a professor of romance
literature at Yale University. Moving to the administrative side, Giamatti eventually became the president of Yale. A fanatical follower of baseball in general
and the Boston Red Sox in particular, Giamatti had become a high-profile
baseball fan, writing eloquently about his love for the game and the romance
of baseball.

When National League President Chub Feeney announced his retirement
in 1986, baseball began searching for a new president of the National League.
While the job of president of the National League was at one time a powerful

position, for example, in the days of William Hulbert, the advent of the commissioner of baseball and the commissioner's growing role in running all facets of baseball had made the league presidential jobs largely ceremonial ones. Since the job was for show anyway, baseball decided to pursue two high-profile candidates, Bart Giamatti and James Baker. They finally settled on Giamatti.

There is little question that Giamatti's appointment to the National League presidency was good for baseball's image. Giamatti was respected for his charm, intelligence, and wit, and there is no doubt that he added a touch of class to the game. While not a baseball man, he was a lifelong fan who loved the game and was very sincere in his desire to make sure baseball continued to be a wonderful game for the fans. His tenure as National League president was relatively uneventful. In fact, the only major decision Giamatti made was to suspend Pete Rose.

Peter Ueberroth had replaced Bowie Kuhn as commissioner of baseball in 1986. A well-thought-of businessman, Ueberroth had gained worldwide prominence for being in charge of the 1984 Los Angeles Olympic Games, one of the most financially successful Olympic endeavors in the history of the games. In a period of rising costs and stagnant revenues in the game of baseball, a businessman such as Ueberroth seemed like the right man to lead the game.

During his tenure, Ueberroth focused on promoting the game and expanded baseball's exposure and revenue from strong licensing agreements. Unfortunately, he also urged baseball owners to avoid bidding on free agents, an act that was later ruled by an arbitrator to be collusion, which cost baseball owners many millions of dollars.

After a few years in office, Ueberroth realized that he would never have the degree of control he would like to have over the owners. The politics of major league baseball are very tricky, since most of the baseball owners today are extremely wealthy individuals who are involved in professional sports more for ego than for the profit potential. Tiring of fighting with the owners, and suspecting that he might not be reelected, Ueberroth announced his intention to resign from office once a successor could be found. Ueberroth stated on a number of occasions that his ideal successor was close at hand—Bart Giamatti.

Giamatti was elected unanimously as the next commissioner of baseball. While Giamatti was an ideal choice for a league president—intelligent, well-respected, and with a high profile—he was a somewhat questionable choice for commissioner. With neither a strong sports background nor a strong business background, some wondered whether the owners were not merely trying to satisfy their own egos by having a certified intellectual running the game. At the same time, those who got to know Giamatti found him a charming man with a good sense of humor and an instinctive love for the game that they felt would help guide him over the rough roads of his learning experience.

In order to assure a smooth transition, baseball set up a complicated management team for the first half of 1989. Ueberroth was still technically

Bart Giamatti. Giamatti and Pete Rose clashed throughout Giamatti's time in baseball. *Courtesy of Transcendental Graphics.*

commissioner, but Giamatti was serving as commissioner-elect, actively getting his apprenticeship from his predecessor. In addition, Giamatti brought on board business executive Fay Vincent, who was slated to serve as deputy commissioner to Giamatti.

On February 20, 1989, Pete Rose appeared in the offices of major league baseball at 350 Park Avenue in New York to meet with Ueberroth, Giamatti, and Vincent. With Rose were his attorneys Reuven Katz and Robert Pitcairn. The reason for the meeting was a simple one. Ueberroth began the meeting by stating, "we have only one purpose here. We've heard rumors about your gambling. We don't want to hear about betting on basketball or football. Did you or did you not bet on baseball?"[2]

Rose knew that the answer to this question would determine his future in baseball.

As the reader will remember, in the aftermath of the Cobb-Speaker and Risberg cases in 1927, Judge Landis had issued a set of rules about baseball and gambling. Rule 21(d) states

> Any player, umpire or club or league official or employee, who shall bet any sum whatsoever upon any baseball game in connection with which the bettor has no duty to perform, shall be declared ineligible for one year.
> Any player, umpire or club or league official or employee, who shall bet any sum whatsoever upon any baseball game in connection with which the bettor has a duty to perform shall be declared permanently ineligible.[3]

Rose denied that he had ever bet on a baseball game. There were a good many questions asked, especially by Giamatti, but the net result was that no action was taken. When Rose asked what he should tell the media about this meeting, Ueberroth suggested, "tell them, I just needed some advice. Nothing ominous." Speaking to the press the next day, Ueberroth stated, "we asked him to come. We didn't order him. There's nothing ominous, and there won't be any followthrough."

Unfortunately for Pete Rose, this was far from true. On February 21, 1989, baseball launched a full investigation into Pete Rose's gambling activities. We do not really know what they expected to find, but we can assume that the scandal they uncovered far exceeded even their worst expectations.

Rose's involvement in gambling was not a recent development. As early as 1963, Pete was spending a great deal of his free time at the track, gambling on horses. Rose loved the excitement of all sports and felt that gambling made being a spectator even more exciting. And, unfortunately, he simply loved to gamble.

Before long, Rose began to supplement his legal gambling at the track with illegal gambling through bookmakers on horse races, football games, basketball games, and hockey games. Rose reportedly ran up debts with bookmakers—and rather than pay his debts, he simply moved on to another bookmaker. This was a pattern that he was to continue in later years.

Associating with gamblers and bookmakers was against baseball rules. Placing bets through bookmakers was certainly a violation of the rules. Owing money to bookmakers was a major violation, since it placed a ball player at the mercy of gamblers. Obviously, the danger was that the gamblers could use their leverage on the ball player to influence the outcome of games.

By the time of the Rose investigation in 1989, Rose had been gambling and associating with bookmakers for more than 20 years. So why had baseball officials never uncovered this? The answer appears to be that they had, but they chose to take no action.

In the early 1970s Baseball Commissioner Bowie Kuhn asked head of

baseball security Henry Fitzgibbon to launch a low-key investigation of Rose.
According to Fitzgibbon, he conducted an ongoing investigation of Rose from
1971 until Fitzgibbon retired in 1981.

Early in the investigation, Fitzgibbon became aware of Rose's gambling
problem. While there was no actual proof that Rose was betting illegally – no
testimony from gamblers or betting sheets existed at the time – there was little
question that there was a problem. Fitzgibbon talked with Rose regularly, warning him of the dangers of his activities. Unfortunately, Rose denied any wrongdoing and failed to heed the good advice he received from Fitzgibbon.

It also appears that the management of the Cincinnati Reds, and the
Philadelphia Phillies afterward were aware of Rose's gambling problems. Dick
Wagner, the general manager of the Cincinnati Reds during the 1970s,
reportedly told a group of Reds executives in 1978, "Pete's legs may get broken
when his playing days are over." Bill Giles, president of the Philadelphia
Phillies, the club that Rose joined after he left the Reds, was also aware that
Rose was gambling on professional sports, but he too took no action. In all
fairness, it should be pointed out that neither of these men had any idea that
Rose might have been betting on baseball, which is by far a more serious
offense.

On February 23, 1989, the commissioner's office retained John Dowd, a
Washington, D.C., attorney, to handle the investigation of the Pete Rose matter. A tough, hard-nosed attorney, Dowd had ten years of experience with the
U.S. Justice Department in Washington, where he ran a unit called Strike Force
18, which was in charge of prosecuting mob-related cases. Among his targets
during his Justice Department years was the internationally known gangster
Meyer Lansky.

Dowd had no problem quickly learning a great deal about Rose's gambling activities. Pete never bothered to cover his tracks, probably because
he was aware that baseball officials knew of his illegal gambling activities but
had chosen to take no action. Pete Rose was baseball's all-time hit king and
a great star. Perhaps he had come to feel that baseball would never take action
against him or that he was too big a star to be forced to live within baseball's
rules.

The evidence that Dowd uncovered went far beyond what was previously
known. Not only was Pete Rose involved in illegal gambling on professional
sports, but it soon became apparent to Dowd that during the 1985, 1986, and
1987 seasons, Rose had been betting on baseball games. More important,
Dowd felt that Rose had been betting on the Cincinnati Reds, the club for which
Rose served as player-manager. According to baseball rules, the penalty for
betting on games involving your own club was permanent expulsion from
baseball.

On May 9, 1989, Dowd issued a comprehensive report of his investigation.
According to the report, in 1978 Pete Rose befriended a young man named

Tommy Gioiosa. For the next eight years, Gioiosa became a constant companion to Rose. They talked together, spent time together, and watched sports together. In addition, starting in 1984, Gioiosa began "running bets" for Pete Rose. In other words, he acted as a middle man to place bets for Rose on professional sports. The man Gioiosa used to place bets for Rose, as well as for himself, was Ron Peters, a bookmaker in Franklin, Ohio. Gioiosa was introduced to Peters by James Eveslage, who became friendly with Gioiosa when both became members of Gold's Gym in 1986.

When Dowd approached Gioiosa, Tommy denied that he had been placing baseball bets for Pete Rose. Bookmaker Ron Peters, though, testified that he had taken bets from Gioiosa for Rose, and in a few cases directly from Rose, from late 1984 until 1986, when Peters stopped accepting Rose's bets because Rose owed him more than $30,000. Peters stated that Rose had bet on professional football, college basketball, and major league baseball, including games involving Rose's Cincinnati Reds. A key portion of Peters's testimony was the following:

> Q: And when he bet on baseball, did he bet on the Cincinnati Reds?
> A: Yes, he did.
> Q: And was this at a time that he was the manager of the Cincinnati Reds?
> A: Yes, sir.
> Q: Is there any doubt in your mind?
> A: Absolutely not.

In addition to his bets with Peters, the Dowd report states that in 1985 Rose began placing bets with a New York bookmaker through Mike Bertolini, a young man from Brooklyn who was involved in promoting baseball card shows. Bertolini refused to give evidence against Rose, but according to Dowd the New York bookmaker was known as "Val." It was later revealed that Val was actually Richard Troy, a bookmaker who was indicted on gambling charges twice in 1985 and who was reportedly connected with the Bonano crime family.

Rose and Bertolini began working together at baseball card shows. As the sports memorabilia industry boomed, more and more baseball card shows appeared across the country. One of the key attractions of these shows was to have a sports star (or, in the case of the major shows, a number of sports stars) available to sign autographs for a fee. Since Bertolini was involved in this business, he arranged for Rose to appear at shows, for which Rose collected lucrative fees. These fees helped support Rose's gambling habit, although Rose was losing at such a fast pace that Bertolini ended up loaning Rose a great deal of money. It was later revealed that Rose did not report a major portion of his income from card shows on his income-tax returns.

In 1986 Gioiosa introduced Pete Rose to Paul Janszen and Janszen's girlfriend Danita Marcum. Janszen and Rose soon became good friends, and when Rose and Gioiosa had somewhat of a falling out in 1986, Janszen replaced

Gioiosa as Rose's constant companion and as the man who placed Pete's bets.

Much of the evidence that Dowd uncovered against Pete Rose came from Paul Janszen. Janszen testified to Dowd that Rose had bet through Gioiosa on the 1986 National League playoffs between the New York Mets and the Houston Astros. Janszen also claimed that he placed bets for Rose with Steve Chevashore, a Florida bookmaker, initially on basketball and hockey, but later on professional baseball. In mid–April 1987, Chevashore directed Janszen to place Rose's bets directly with Val (bookmaker Richard Troy) in New York.

Dowd's report also states that in 1987 Rose fell behind on his gambling debts to the New York bookmaker Val, who refused to take any more bets from Rose. Dowd reported that Rose then asked Janszen to contact Ron Peters to place his bets. Peters informed Janszen that he was willing to take Rose's bets, but that Rose still owed him $34,000 from previous betting. Rose claimed that the debt had been paid – and without resolving this issue Janszen began placing bets through Peters.

Unlike Gioiosa and Bertolini, Janszen and Marcum were not at all reluctant to discuss Rose's gambling with Dowd. Below is one excerpt from Janszen's testimony in front of Dowd:

> JANSZEN: From maybe the third or fourth week in May, all through June, up until the All-Star break, Pete Rose bet through me with Ron Peters in Franklin, Ohio. I have phone numbers, tape recordings with Ron Peters.
> DOWD: He bet on?
> JANSZEN: Baseball, only baseball.
> DOWD: Including the Reds?
> JANSZEN: Yes, sir, every game.

This was supported by Marcum in the following testimony:

> DOWD: Did you bet on the Cincinnati Reds baseball team at the request of Pete Rose?
> MARCUM: Yes.
> DOWD: While he was Manager of the Cincinnati Reds baseball team?
> MARCUM: Yes.
> DOWD: And you placed those bets with Ron Peters?
> MARCUM: Yes. Not as many times as Val. Just a couple of times with Ron Peters.[5]

In addition to the testimony of Peters, Marcum, and Janszen, Dowd was able to obtain a number of documents that contributed to the case against Rose. The evidence included

- Three "betting sheets" from April of 1987. Two of the sheets listed bets placed on both major league baseball and NBA basketball, with the results indicated by the letter L or the letter W. The third sheet referred totally to college and professional football games. On March 16, 1989, these sheets were analyzed by Richard Casey, a retired F.B.I. agent and handwriting expert. Casey concluded that the sheets were written by Pete Rose.

- Paul Janszen's betting notebook. Janszen kept a notebook of the bets he placed for Pete Rose during April and May of 1987, and Janszen turned this notebook over to Dowd. The entries specified bets placed on various sports, including baseball. Handwriting analysis confirmed that Janszen had written the entries.
- Ron Peters's betting records. Dowd also received betting records that Ron Peters had kept during 1987. Peters claimed that he normally destroyed records like this, but he kept these because of his dispute with Rose over a $34,000 debt that Peters claimed Rose owed him. The records itemized bets placed by Janszen in Rose's name during the period, and they tied in with Janszen's testimony.
- Other documents were telephone records from Pete Rose's home phone, his car phone, Janzsen's home and car phones, Gold's Gym, phone logs maintained by the Cincinnati Reds to and from the clubhouse, and hotel bills from the Cincinnati Reds' 1987 road trips. Dowd also obtained Pete Rose's bank records, including cancelled checks and statements.

From this evidence, and a great deal more (the full report ran 225 pages and was backed by 2,000 pages of transcribed interviews and documents), Dowd concluded that "the testimony and the documentary evidence gathered in the course of the investigation demonstrates that Pete Rose bet on baseball, and in particular, on games of the Cincinnati Reds Baseball Club, during the 1985, 1986 and 1987 seasons."[6]

During the time that Dowd was conducting this investigation, Ron Peters approached *Sports Illustrated*, offering to sell the story of Pete Rose's betting on baseball. While the magazine declined to buy the full story, it did talk with Peters and subsequently uncovered a great deal of the Pete Rose scandal. When baseball officials learned that the magazine was preparing to publish the story, they decided to go public.

On March 20, a statement from the office of the commissioner of baseball revealed that an inquiry was being made "into serious allegations against Pete Rose." The next day, March 21, the *Sports Illustrated* story broke containing many of the details of the scandal.

The press release from major league baseball and the *Sports Illustrated* article served to increase the intensity of the investigation, and it also launched a firestorm of publicity. Baseball scandals were big news, but a scandal involving one of baseball's greatest players was enormous news.

At the time, the Reds were in spring training in Tampa, Florida. Rose was trying to prepare his team, which was coming off its fourth consecutive second-place finish, to challenge for the 1989 title. As soon as the story broke, Rose was swarmed upon by the press, followed night and day, and constantly asked questions about the gambling scandal.

All things considered, Pete Rose handled the pressure remarkably well. He continually denied the stories and was able to keep a sense of humor about the whole matter. As the days spread into weeks with no letup in the media circus, there is no question that the pressure on Rose was intense—but he continued to keep his head held high.

As mentioned earlier, Dowd's report was completed and submitted to the commissioner on May 9, 1989. On May 11 Bart Giamatti wrote to Pete Rose and informed him that the report had been completed. Giamatti informed Rose that pursuant to his power to investigate activity deemed to be "not in the best interest of the national game of baseball," he intended to hold hearings regarding the matter within two weeks. The Dowd report and the accompanying exhibits were forwarded to Rose.

The baseball man that Giamatti admired most was Judge Landis. In the case of the Black Sox, Judge Landis had never bothered to hold a hearing—he merely informed the players that they were on baseball's permanently ineligible list. Giamatti chose not to take this step, partially out of a desire to be fair to Rose by giving him a chance to answer the charges, and partially because he knew that any action relating to Pete Rose perceived as being arbitrary or unfair would be a public relations nightmare for baseball in general and the commissioner in particular.

With the body of evidence available, what could Pete Rose possibly say? Was there any doubt whether he was guilty? Did this mean the end of the road for Pete Rose?

As it turned out, the battle had a long way to go. Rose's lawyers blasted the report and the evidence it contained. While not denying that Peters, Janszen, and Marcum had made incriminating statements to Dowd, they raised grave questions about the reliability of these witnesses. Both Peters and Janszen had recently pleaded guilty to felonies, Peters's plea involving gambling and drug trafficking and Janszen's plea involving the sale of illegal steroids. Convicted felons are not the most reliable people in the world. In addition, both Janszen and Peters claimed that Rose owed them money. Peters's claim was based on the disputed 1985 gambling debts, and Janszen claimed that he and Rose fell out over money Rose owed Janszen.

Peters had another strong motive besides revenge for testifying before Dowd. Peters was awaiting sentencing on drug charges. (It is interesting that it was Janszen who helped point the finger at Peters, since cooperating with authorities led to a lighter sentence for Janszen as punishment for his own crimes.) During Peters's April 5 deposition before Dowd, the investigator stated that "in exchange for your full and truthful cooperation with the Commissioner, the Commissioner has agreed to bring to the attention of the District

Judge in Cincinnati, the fact that you were of assistance to us and that we believe that you have been honest and complete in your cooperation."[7]

In addition to all of this, the character reports on the witnesses, especially Peters and Janszen, were not particularly positive. In fact, an affidavit received from the lawyer of Ron Peters's ex-wife stated that "Ron Peters cannot separate truth from fantasy even if he wished to. If Mr. Peters would testify under oath that the sun will come up in the morning, I would take great pains to verify his testimony independently."[8]

Finally, the attorneys for Rose challenged Giamatti's rights and credentials to be considered an impartial observer. On April 18, Giamatti had written a letter to Judge Carl Rubin in Cincinnati, who was handling the Peters trial, stating that Giamatti was "satisfied Mr. Peters had been candid, forthright, and truthful with my special counsel." This letter, which had been drafted by Dowd, delivered on Dowd's promise to Peters that if Peters cooperated, the commissioner would send a letter to the judge. Peters's hope was that the judge would consider this cooperation in a positive light when sentencing Peters.

Unfortunately for Giamatti, Judge Rubin was highly offended by the unsolicited letter, stating "I don't believe that it is of any concern to me, zilch, what this man may have done with the Commissioner of Baseball. . . . I would not take this into consideration in sentence imposed upon Mr. Peters."[9] Rubin then made the letter public and sent it to Rose's lawyers, Reuven Katz and Robert Pitcairn, Jr.

Rose's legal team decided to make Giamatti's bias their point of attack. In his official response to the Dowd report, Pitcairn wrote

> In my opinion, [the Dowd report] is no more than the bellicose, repetitive arguments of a prosecutor who knows he cannot make his case but is trying to confuse the jury with speculative, tainted evidence. In fact, most of the information you describe as circumstantial evidence is not evidence at all and would never be admitted into evidence in a court of law. . . .
>
> What puzzles me is why you would engage in a hatchet job after you assured us repeatedly that you were conducting a fair and impartial investigation. The Report goes beyond mere bias on your part. It shows desperation to provide support for action Mr. Giamatti apparently wants to take. If this Report is your idea of fair play and natural justice, I feel sorry for you.[10]

A few days later, Pitcairn wrote to Giamatti demanding that the commissioner remove himself from the investigation because of his bias. Giamatti, of course, denied that he was in any way biased against Rose, or that he had made any decision regarding Rose's guilt or innocence. Rose's attorneys expressed their disappointment and requested a 30-day delay for the hearing, which Giamatti granted. A new date for the hearing was set for June 26.

On June 19 Rose and his lawyers filed a suit in the Court of Common Pleas of Hamilton County, Ohio, against Bart Giamatti. The suit asked the court to restrain baseball from holding its hearing on June 26 and asked for punitive damages against Giamatti for "his unfair and outrageous conduct."

On June 21 Giamatti responded by denying the charges, stating that he had reached no conclusion in the Rose case. He also expressed a desire for a quick resolution to the problem, stating, "major league baseball must move quickly to assure the public's confidence in the integrity of the game."[11]

The motions were heard before Judge Norbert A. Nadel in Cincinnati. In the three days of hearings that followed, Rose's attorneys assailed John Dowd for the way in which he conducted the investigation and Giamatti for being prejudiced against Rose, with Giamatti's letter to Judge Rubin being a prime piece of evidence. One of the witnesses for Rose was Sam Dash, who served as chief counsel to the Senate Watergate Committee. Dash testified that if during the Watergate hearings one of his investigators had given him a report like the one Dowd wrote, "I would have fired him."

While all this was going on, Rose continued as manager of the Reds. The Rose scandal was clearly a distraction, and the club was not playing up to expectations. It was rumored that unless Rose's lawyers were able to secure an injunction against baseball, Reds management would fire Rose.

On Sunday, June 25, Judge Nadel granted a temporary restraining order preventing baseball from holding a hearing for a period of two weeks. The judge stated that in his view, "the Commissioner of Baseball has prejudged Peter Edward Rose." He further added that if a hearing were to be held on June 26, it would be "futile, illusory, and its outcome a foregone conclusion." Nadel scheduled a hearing to consider Rose's attorneys' motion for a preliminary injunction for July 6. At the same time, baseball filed suit with the First Ohio District Court of Appeals to suspend Nadel's ruling.

Legal opinion was divided on whether Nadel was correct in his judgment. However, the decision was extremely popular with Nadel's constituents in Cincinnati.

At that point, preparations began for an all-out legal battle. On July 29, Rose's lawyers, led by Robert Stachler, went to Dowd's offices in Washington to take the deposition of Bart Giamatti in their lawsuit. The deposition would allow Rose's lawyers to probe Giamatti for information that they could use during a lawsuit, and what was perhaps more important, to see how Giamatti would stand up in court under rugged questioning.

Unfortunately for Giamatti, he could not hold up under close scrutiny. Giamatti was nervous and faltered a great deal during the questioning. Giamatti was a chain smoker—and Rose's attorneys knew that if Giamatti performed that poorly with access to his cigarettes, in court for many hours with no opportunity to smoke he would likely crumble.

The key focus of the deposition was the letter that Giamatti had written on behalf of Ron Peters. Giamatti described his signature on the letter as a "ministerial act." He reiterated that the opinion of Peters's honesty was that of

John Dowd and not Bart Giamatti's. In signing the letter, he was merely fulfilling Dowd's obligation to Peters, not actually passing judgment on whether Peters's testimony was correct.

In his excellent book *Collision at Home Plate*, James Reston, Jr., points out that Giamatti's deposition was a key turning point in the legal battle between Pete Rose and major league baseball. According to Reston, baseball's litigator stated after the deposition, "Giamatti cannot get on that witness stand. This case has got to be settled."[13]

For the next six weeks the legal machinations continued. As the ordeal went on, Giamatti showed signs of physical deterioration. The pressure led to his gaining weight and putting in longer hours. He desperately needed a rest, but he would not take one.

Rose also was beginning to feel the pressure. His mind was not on the game, and his team floundered in the standings. Also, Rose began to backtrack, admitting to the *Washington Post* that he had indeed bet illegally on sports through Gioiosa, Peters, and Janszen, but he had never bet on baseball. Rose admitted that most of the evidence against him was correct—all but the pieces that said he had bet on baseball games.

A great deal of the legal maneuvering was about which courts had jurisdiction over the lawsuit—the state of Ohio or the federal courts. Major league baseball was in favor of the federal courts, which they perceived as more impartial. Rose, of course, wanted the trial carried out in the state of Ohio courts, which he felt would give him a "home field advantage." On July 31, however, Rose lost an action to move the suit to the state court, and Giamatti responded by setting August 17 as the hearing date.

At that point each side had certain negotiating points. On the side of Rose was the fact that baseball did not feel that Bart Giamatti would hold up under testimony. In addition, the ongoing publicity from the scandal was bad for the game. Giamatti and the baseball hierarchy wanted the issue settled.

On baseball's side were strength of the evidence against Rose and the fact that long, drawn-out legal battles are quite expensive. Major league baseball had deep pockets; Pete Rose did not. One final factor in major league baseball's favor was that, even if it could not be proven that Rose bet on baseball, his involvement with gamblers was cause enough for a long suspension.

In August the two sides met to try to reach a settlement. Fay Vincent's first offer was banishment from baseball for 10 years. This was rejected because Rose's legal team, led by Reuven Katz, did not like the word *banish* and would accept no settlement in which it was concluded definitely that Rose had bet on baseball. Rose was still denying that he had bet on baseball, and whatever settlement was reached must allow Rose to continue this denial. Vincent countered with an offer of a seven-year banishment, which was also rejected.

Finally, the two sides found a compromise. It was agreed that Rose be put on the permanently ineligible list—but for infractions of Rule 21(f), which referred to misconduct that was not in the best interests of baseball, not Rule 21(d), which dealt with betting on baseball games. There would be no conclusive finding that Rose had bet on baseball, and Rose would have the right to appeal for reinstatement anytime after a period of one year.

On August 23, 1989, at a press conference in New York, Bart Giamatti announced the decision that Pete Rose was being placed on baseball's permanently ineligible list. In contrast to his poor performance during the deposition, Giamatti was marvelous at the press conference. He radiated a love for baseball and projected himself as the protector and symbol of baseball's integrity. He delivered his speech forthrightly and with great strength.

After the statement was read, the press began to ask questions. The first question, naturally, was whether Giamatti personally believed that Pete Rose had bet on baseball and whether Rose had bet on the Cincinnati Reds.

The negotiated agreement stated that the official findings on the Rose case would include no conclusion on whether Rose had bet on baseball. Giamatti, however, had a right to a personal opinion, and he responded, "in the absence of a hearing and therefore the absence of evidence to the contrary, I am confronted by the factual record of Mr. Dowd. On the basis of that, yes, I have concluded he bet on baseball."[14]

And so, finally, the investigation into the gambling activities of Pete Rose was complete. After long months of denial, and long months and many dollars spent on legal posturing, Rose was on baseball's permanently ineligible list. In addition, although Rose had fought so hard to deny that he had bet on baseball games, the commissioner of baseball stated that, in his opinion, Rose had bet on baseball. Rather than take the 10-year suspension or the seven-year suspension, Rose was permanently ineligible—and although he could apply for reinstatement after one year, there was no guarantee or promise that he would ever be reinstated.

The aftermath of the Rose affair was a sad one. Rose, of course, was out of a job as manager of the Reds. (Tommy Helms took over to finish out the season.) A year later, Rose pleaded guilty to filing false income-tax returns in 1985 and 1987, charges that related primarily to his failure to declare much of his income from baseball card shows, money that he had used to pay his gambling debts. Rose was sentenced to five months' imprisonment, one year of supervised release, 1,000 hours of community service, continued psychiatric treatment for his gambling addiction (after months of denying that he had a gambling problem, Rose finally admitted this fact), and a fine of $50,100.

The end for Giamatti was even more tragic. He fled to his cottage on Martha's Vineyard to rest and recover from the pressure-packed ordeal he had faced. Giamatti was in extremely poor health—he was overweight, chain-smoked, and practiced a horrible diet—and on September 1, 1989, one week after Rose's suspension, Giamatti died of heart failure. His deputy, Fay Vincent, was named to replace him as commissioner of baseball.

Pete Rose served his time in prison and is now back in society. He has moved to South Florida and is involved in a number of projects, including running a restaurant and having his own radio talk show. Rose hopes to be reinstated to baseball and has expressed an interest in working for the Florida Marlins baseball team.

Rose's most cherished goal has been election to the Baseball Hall of Fame. Rose had always hoped to become the first man to be unanimously elected to the Hall, and with his performance record that was not an impossibility. While few argued that Rose was as great a player as Babe Ruth, Ty Cobb, Joe DiMaggio, Willie Mays, Mickey Mantle, and Hank Aaron, he had broken baseball's all-time hit record and would have been a sure landslide winner in 1992, his first year of eligibility for the Hall of Fame. Unfortunately for Rose, shortly after his expulsion, the Hall of Fame passed a rule that no one on baseball's permanently ineligible list was eligible for Hall of Fame election. Rather than a landslide acclamation to the Hall of Fame, Rose received only protest votes, 41 write-ins, in 1992.

To date, there is no indication that Pete Rose will be reinstated anytime in the near future, but Rose's chances have improved now that Fay Vincent is no longer the commissioner. Vincent was intimately involved in the Rose case and had no doubts about Rose's guilt. Vincent was quoted as saying:

> He bet on baseball; we'll leave it at that. He bet on the Reds, too. There is just no doubt about that—the evidence was overwhelming. No one should kid themselves: Pete Rose bet on baseball.[15]

Should Rose be reinstated? There is a great diversity of opinion on this matter. The author will offer his opinion in the final chapter of this book.

The baseball establishment certainly hoped, and felt, that the Rose case, like the McLain case, was an aberration—a one-time incident. This was not to be the case.

The next baseball scandal occurred in 1991 when it was revealed that Lenny Dykstra, center fielder for the Philadelphia Phillies, had lost $78,000 playing high-stakes poker with Herbert Kelso. Dykstra was called to testify at Kelso's trial for running an illegal casino, conspiracy, money laundering, and perjury. Dykstra claimed that he had learned his lesson and that he would not engage in illegal gambling in the future. Because the gambling Dykstra was involved with was poker rather than betting on sports, he was merely placed on probation.

This was not to be the end of Dykstra's problems that year. A short time later Dykstra was driving under the influence of alcohol and was involved in a one-car auto accident. With him in the car was teammate Darren Daulton. Both received major injuries and missed a great deal of playing time during the year.

On August 20, 1991, it was revealed that two major league umpires were being placed on probation for the rest of the year for gambling activities. These gambling activities involved placing small bets on professional sports other than baseball. The names of the two umpires and the details of the case were not revealed to the public. Fay Vincent stated that "umpires are different from players. They're the authority figures. No public benefit is served if their mistakes or errors of judgement are disclosed."[16]

Naturally, many journalists were outraged by this attitude. Did the public not have a right to know about the details of the case? Otherwise, how could the baseball public be sure that baseball remains free from corruption?

In answering these questions, baseball deputy commissioner Steve Greenberg, baseball's deputy commissioner, stated that

> The public has a right to know when persons are removed from the field of play. Otherwise, it will not become public. There is no way that the Lenny Dykstra situation would have been handled publicly by the Commissioner's office if it had come to us in a non-public fashion.[17]

These comments by Greenberg will be discussed in the final chapter of this book.

The final scandal of 1991, and the final major league scandal that we will deal with, came in September when *Penthouse* magazine reported that former Chicago Cubs and Boston Red Sox manager Don Zimmer had bet $3,000 to $5,000 per week on football and basketball games when he was managing the Cubs. The author of the article, Jerome Tuccille, claimed that Zimmer had admitted that major league baseball had questioned him about his gambling activities. Zimmer's contention, however, was that while he had gambled, all his gambling had been of the racetrack variety, which was neither a violation of the law nor of baseball policy. More damaging, however, was Tuccille's claim that a gambler had told him that Zimmer once divulged that his starting pitcher in the next day's game had a sore arm and would not last long. Passing information on to gamblers for their use would be a clear violation of baseball law and would definitely call for action on the part of major league baseball.

Zimmer totally denied the accusations that he had been involved in illegal gambling. No additional evidence against Zimmer was forthcoming, and the case was closed.

Chapter 14

Minor League
Scandals Before 1930

While the major leagues represent the highest level of play and are of the greatest interest to fans and baseball historians, we should not forget the significant role that the minor leagues play in baseball history. The minor leagues have not only provided a training ground for the vast majority of baseball's great stars but have also produced many memorable moments in their own right. For example, the single-season records in professional baseball for runs scored, hits, doubles, home runs, RBIs, stolen bases, and strikeouts were set not in the major leagues, but in the minor leagues. Among the more amazing totals are Joe Bauman's record of 72 home runs with Roswell in the Longhorn League in 1954, Paul Strand's 325 hits with Salt Lake City in the Pacific Coast League in 1923, and Bob Crues's record of 254 RBIs with Amarillo in the West Texas–New Mexico League in 1948.

The first minor leagues were established in 1877, just one year after the birth of the National League. In 1877 three minor leagues were operating: the International Association, the League Alliance, and the New England League. It is generally felt that the International Association, which lasted only two years, was the best of these earlier leagues, featuring former stars such as Hall of Famer William "Candy" Cummings and future stars such as Hall of Famer Jim Galvin.

During the nineteenth century, minor league baseball generally lacked stability. Minor leagues came and went quite frequently, with some leagues lasting only a season or two. Some of these leagues are still in operation today, including the International League (which was originally known as the Eastern League), the Southern League, the Pacific Coast League, and the Texas League.

Because the minor leagues have never received the press coverage and attention of the major leagues, chronicling the gambling scandals throughout minor league history is a much more difficult job than doing so for the major leagues. Therefore, it is quite probable that at some point in the future, additional gambling scandals from the minor leagues will be uncovered by researchers. The next two chapters will discuss those scandals of which the author is aware.

The first gambling scandal in minor league history occurred in the International Association in 1878, the second year of the minor leagues. The scandal involved an umpire rather than a player.

The scandal occurred on June 12, 1878, in Buffalo, New York. Since the International Association did not have a regular roster of umpires, the procedure was for the home club to produce a list of choices for umpire, from which the visiting team would select the one that they wanted. On this day, the visiting Rochester team selected George Campbell to umpire the game.

The game was not a close one; Rochester won by a score of 15–3. The most controversial decision occurred in the third inning with Rochester leading 2–0. Buffalo mounted a rally, loading the bases on a single and two walks. After a forceout at home, Buffalo batter Steve Libby drove a ball down the third-base line, apparently scoring three runs. Umpire Campbell called the ball foul. While the fans roared in disapproval, the umpire's decision stood, and Buffalo was never able to climb back into the game.

The *Buffalo Express* ran a story the next day criticizing Campbell's performance. The paper stated, "if ever a defeat of a nine was helped by an umpire, that of Buffalo was yesterday."[1] A few days later, on June 18, the *Buffalo Express* broke a big story, accusing Campbell of selling out the game to gamblers.

The *Buffalo Express* claimed that the Buffalo club had hired two private detectives to investigate Campbell. According to baseball historian Joe Overfield, the man who resurrected this early scandal, the detectives discovered that umpire Campbell had agreed to make Rochester the winner for a sum of $200, which was paid to him by Rochester and Syracuse gamblers. The gamblers supposedly made $1,600 betting on the game.

Furious at the accusation, George Campbell filed a libel suit for $5,000 against *Buffalo Express* editor James N. Matthews. According to the legal papers filed in the suit, which were uncovered by Overfield, Campbell claimed that Matthews had published an article containing "false, malicious, scandalous and defamatory matter." Matthews's defense was quite simple—he was merely reporting a news story, and he believed that the charges against Campbell were indeed well founded.

After a long period of legal maneuvering, the trial date was set for April 20, 1888, in the Erie County courthouse. Matthews was there ready to defend himself—but neither George Campbell nor his attorneys appeared, resulting in a default judgment of $108.26 being rendered in favor of Matthews.

No official investigation was ever launched by the International Association, so we will never know with any certainty whether Campbell was guilty of the charges. Certainly, the fact that he failed to appear for the trial is not in his favor. The evidence appears to make a strong case against Campbell in this first minor league scandal.

The International Association disbanded after the 1878 season but reorganized itself as the National Association. The National Association's first season, in 1879, proved to be a difficult one in all respects. In addition to having financial problems, the league endured two gambling scandals.

The first gambling scandal involved the Capital City club of Albany, New York, one of two clubs in the circuit from the New York state capital. The Capital City club appeared to be a strong one, including such former major league stars as Tim Murnane, former Cincinnati Red Stocking Andy Leonard, and our old friend from the New York Mutuals, Dick Higham.

Capital City was expected to be one of the strongest teams in the league, but things did not turn out that way. The club got off to a bad start, playing poorly and losing games. According to a contemporary newspaper account, "the number of errors committed, and those too by the men who were receiving the highest salaries, led to but one conclusion, that something was rotten in Denmark."[2]

The bad publicity deprived the club of fan support, and on March 21 the club was disbanded, with the majority of the players being transferred to a newly formed team, the Rochester "Hop Bitters," named after a famous patent medicine of the day. Shortly after the Capital City club disbanded, Albany Alderman Thomas Cavanaugh formally charged that five members of the Capital City club were involved in game fixing. No formal action was ever taken on the charges against the players.

While the exact details of the scandal will probably never be known, the fact that Dick Higham was involved would suggest that the charges of game fixing were true. Higham had already been involved in game fixing in the major leagues, and he would soon fix games as an umpire, so there is little reason to suspect that he changed his ways during his minor league days.

Not long after the Capital City scandal, another scandal began to erupt, this one involving the Manchester club. Early in the season, Manchester fans began to suspect that the club was being controlled by gamblers and that the games were not being played on their merits. Therefore, interest in the club declined, attendance dwindled, and the Manchester club was forced to play its games away from home for lack of support.

The National Association continued for one more year, playing with only three clubs during the 1880 season. One of the clubs, Albany, disbanded on July 20, and when Rochester disbanded in early September, the league collapsed. Summing up the Association, baseball historian Henry Chadwick wrote, "It played fast and loose with the question of sustaining honest play."[3]

The setting for minor league baseball scandals then moved from the Northeast to the West Coast. While major league baseball did not reach the state until 1958, California was a hotbed for baseball teams as early as the 1860s. The great Cincinnati Red Stockings of 1869 journeyed to California, and by the 1870s there were many fine teams and talented players on the West Coast.

In the nineteenth century, California was still in many ways the wild, wild west. The discovery of gold around San Francisco in 1848 led to a large influx in population and the creation of a frontier life-style. Gambling and vice were prominent in California towns, so it is not a surprise that the gambling trade had an early hand in California baseball. Old-time baseball player William Shepard, who relocated from New Jersey to San Francisco in 1861, described the gambling situation as follows:

> I well remember a habit that gamblers among the spectators used to have, that surely savored of the wild and wooly west. Just as a fly-ball was dropping into a fielder's hand, every gambler who had bet on the nine at bat would discharge a fusillade from his six-shooter, in an endeavor to confuse the fielder to make him miss the ball.[4]

By 1880 the professional game reached California when the California League was formed. While a number of former and future major leaguers played ball in the California League, there can be no doubt that it was indeed a minor league. On the whole, the caliber of players was far below that of the National League at the time. The California League was successful all the same and was soon followed by the California State League.

The two leagues began to grow and flourish from a continuous flow of good players and the strong support of the fans in California. Unlike other minor leagues, these leagues did not join "organized baseball." In other words, they were outlaw leagues, not respecting the rules, regulations, and contracts of the other leagues in the country. Naturally, given the situation, organized baseball did not respect the rules, regulations, or contracts of the California League or the California State League.

From the very beginning, the California League was plagued by discipline problems, most notably drunkenness. Then, in 1883, a much more serious problem reared its head when seven players were expelled by the league for throwing games. Most notable of these players was Charlie Sweeney, star pitcher of the Niantics club. The *San Francisco Chronicle* reported Sweeney's actions as follows:

> The game was between the Niantics and Californians, and by the time the second inning was over it was evident to everybody that Charles Sweeney, who was pitching for the Niantics, was throwing the game. He was reproved, but still continued offending, and was therefore expelled from the League on account of insubordination and unprofessional conduct. One result of this expulsion is that Sweeney will never be able to play any League game in the city, and wherever he goes this black mark will stand on his record. Sweeney was expelled from the League about three weeks ago, but was taken back on probation, only to be ejected again and for good.[5]

Not all the *San Francisco Chronicle*'s predictions came true. Sweeney immediately found a job with Providence in the National League, finishing the

1883 season with a 7-7 record with that club. The next season he got off to an outstanding start with Providence, compiling a record of 17-8, including one nine-inning game in which he struck out a record 19 batters. Unfortunately, Sweeney did not react well to discipline, and when he was suspended for insubordination and drunkenness, he jumped to the St. Louis club of the Union Association, where he won 24 more games against only seven losses.

At that point Sweeney, a San Francisco native, was considered one of the up-and-coming stars of baseball, but his personal habits led to his downfall. Over the next three seasons in the major leagues, with St. Louis in the National League and Cleveland in the American Association, he had a combined record of 16-30. After assaulting one of his teammates with Cleveland, he was released and he then returned to California.

Sweeney's life went from bad to worse back in San Francisco. His drinking increased, and in 1894 he shot and killed an acquaintance in a San Francisco barroom. He pleaded self-defense, but he was convicted of manslaughter and sentenced to 10 years' imprisonment. While in prison he contracted tuberculosis, and by 1902 Sweeney was dead.

Another player expelled from the California League was San Francisco Stars pitcher Jimmy Mullee. On May 2, 1886, Mullee lost to Haverly by a score of 13–0 and was accused of throwing the game. Mullee apparently admitted not giving his best efforts, but he claimed that he was trying to foil a plot by two of his teammates and a local businessman to break up the team. As it turned out, the Stars were kicked out of the league and Mullee was blacklisted. Mullee continued his career for the rival California State League, and by 1887 he was back in the California League.

In 1890 scandal again erupted in the California League. In this case, the controversy revolved around a game between the Stockton and Sacramento clubs on the last day of the regular season. If Sacramento beat Stockton, they were assured of at least a tie for first place. If they lost, they were in danger of losing the race to San Francisco. Sacramento won the game, but it was widely suspected that the outcome had been prearranged and that Stockton had thrown the game.

The accuser in this case was Pete Meegan, who umpired the game. Meegan felt sure that the Stockton players were not playing up to their best efforts, and he told the players so. During the game he explained to both sides, "I'm perfectly willing for the Stocktons to lose, but you must play ball while I'm umpiring." According to the *Sacramento Bee*,

> The impression prevails among more than a few that it had been decided to have a close game, in order to please the audience, but that the contest was figured down to so fine a part that Holliday's hit and Meegan's refusal to declare it a foul, brought about a result neither expected nor desired.[6]

This last sentence refers to a close call on a ball hit by Stockton's Holliday, which Meegan ruled a fair ball. Meegan accused Stockton catcher Red Armstrong of giving away his signs to Stockton batters so they would know which pitch was coming. No action was taken as a result of this incident.

As baseball moved into the twentieth century, a general rise in gambling on games took place, which led to many problems in both the major and minor leagues. By 1904 it was rumored that the Southern League was a hotbed of corruption. Unfortunately, the minor leagues followed in the majors' footsteps, sweeping corruption under the rug. When pitcher Billy Phyle claimed that many games in the Southern League were not being played on their merits, no investigation was launched. In fact, Phyle, the honest player, was expelled and blacklisted from the league when he refused to appear before the National Board to substantiate his charges. Phyle's charges were substantiated by long-time umpire and manager Joe Cantillon, who publicly denounced the Southern League as a crooked organization. No attempt was made either to discipline Cantillon or to investigate his charges.

As was the case with the major leagues, during the following decade there were occasional rumblings of scandal in the minor leagues, but the rumors were never wholeheartedly investigated, and the stories soon faded away. Also as in major league baseball, corruption in the minor leagues was building to a climax.

In 1919 the Pacific Coast League (PCL) pennant race was fought down to the wire by the neighboring Vernon and Los Angeles teams. In the end, Vernon pulled ahead, winning the pennant by two and one-half games. Vernon's victory was in no small part due to their domination of the third-place Salt Lake team late in the season.

At the conclusion of the final Vernon–Salt Lake series, there were rumors that the games were not played entirely on their merits. The rumors failed to get wide circulation, and the story was forgotten for a while. In the winter of 1920, William H. McCarthy was elected the new president of the Pacific Coast League, replacing Alan Baum. McCarthy was aware of the rumors of corruption in the league, and he decided to do something about them.

The first battle in the war against corruption in the PCL came in early May 1920, when it was announced that two pitchers from the San Francisco club, Tom Seaton and Luther "Casey" Smith, had been given their releases. In a statement accompanying the announcement, Charlie Graham, president of the San Francisco club, stated that "rumors of the most serious nature have reached me regarding practices of the players and their associates, and whether they are true or not, it was decided for the best interest of the game that the two pitchers should be released from their baseball connections."[7]

Tom Seaton, born in 1887 in Blair, Nebraska, was a well-known former major league pitcher. A knuckleballer, Seaton broke into the big leagues with the Philadelphia Phillies in 1912, compiling a record of 16-12. During the next season he appeared on his way to stardom, leading the National League with 27 wins and 168 strikeouts. Seaton then jumped to the outlaw Federal League, turning in a 25-14 record with the Brooklyn Feds in 1914 and a 14-17 mark with Brooklyn and Newark in 1915.

After the Federal League disbanded, Seaton returned to the National League, landing with the Chicago Cubs for the 1916 and 1917 seasons. He was not particularly effective during those years, and he moved on to the Pacific Coast League. He ended his major league career with a record of 93 wins and 65 losses and a very respectable earned-run average of 3.14.

Seaton came to the Pacific Coast League with a somewhat questionable reputation. Rumors had followed him during his National League career that he may have been in partnership with gamblers. "Casey" Smith, however, had no such marks against his record, although he was involved in a recurring brawl with Oakland catcher Dan Murray throughout the 1917 season, a feud that was started by Murray's use of a racial slur (Smith was a Native American). Smith was liked and respected by the fans, partly because he had enlisted in the service during World War I.

McCarthy's next attack came on May 10, 1920, when he announced that "three known gamblers"—Roy Hurlburt, Martin Breslauer, and Nate Raymond—were being barred from all Pacific Coast League parks. In a statement, McCarthy blamed the growing corruption in baseball on the gambling influence, stating that "it means either the survival of baseball or gambling, and decent men could make but one choice. I would rather close every park than permit gambling to continue."[8] McCarthy was universally praised for his action and was promised the support of both the club owners and police in Pacific Coast League cities to get the gamblers out of the ball parks. Plainclothes detectives then moved into the parks and began arresting gamblers operating in the stands.

Although this was far from the end of the scandals for the Pacific Coast League that year, the next minor league gambling controversy of 1920 occurred in the Southern League and was a direct result of McCarthy's actions. Less than three weeks after Seaton and Smith had been released by San Francisco, Casey Smith was signed by the Little Rock, Arkansas, club of the Southern League. A few days later, the Little Rock club also signed Tom Seaton. When the contracts were submitted to Southern League President John D. Martin, he refused to approve them. Martin's stand was that the players were not eligible to play in the Southern League until they could get a clean bill of health. Martin suggested that the players, if they were not guilty of corruption, should demand a hearing from the Pacific Coast League and clear their names.

Little Rock club owner Bob Allen was furious at the decision and announced his intention to go to court. Since no definite accusations were ever made against Seaton and Smith, Allen and manager Norman "Kid" Elberfeld claimed that Martin had no authority to bar them from playing for Little Rock. In addition, Elberfeld stated that "there is another side of the story, and the players will be shown in a better light when it comes out."[9]

When Martin continued to hold firm to his refusal, Allen proceeded with his lawsuit. In a June 15 hearing in United States Court in Memphis, Tennessee, Allen asked for an injunction against Martin to restrain him from interfering with Little Rock's making use of the players.

At the same time, Allen announced that he would use Smith and Seaton while legal action was pending. He then announced that Smith would pitch in Atlanta on June 17. When the Little Rock club reached the Atlanta ball park, however, they found that it was locked up and the game had been canceled. Atlanta, along with the Mobile and Chattanooga clubs, announced that no games would be played with Little Rock as long as Smith and Seaton were in the lineup.

Manager Elberfeld was furious at this turn of events. The *Los Angeles Times* quoted Elberfeld as follows:

> The charges against the players is all hearsay evidence. In spite of our repeated request of the San Francisco club officials for full information as to the details of the case, we have received no reply. In justice to these players, the case should be investigated thoroughly. If they are proven true both men should be barred from baseball, but if unfounded, as they seem to be, Smith and Seaton have been done an injustice.[10]

The only response from the West Coast was a statement by San Francisco President Charles Graham that Smith and Seaton had been released "for the good of baseball."

During the next few days, negotiations heated up among the various club owners. The issue would be decided by a special board of directors meeting of the Southern League on June 21. Bob Allen agreed to abide by the result of this decision.

The decision of the board was that Smith and Seaton were ineligible, pending the results of the lawsuit. It was again suggested that the players approach the San Francisco club and ask for a full investigation. The board criticized the players for not having demanded an investigation by the Pacific Coast League after their releases, even though the players had said that they would do so.

While Allen was willing to go along with the decision for the time being, he was by no means pleased. Allen publicly charged that he had received letters citing a number of incidents in which Southern League players had been accused of corrupt behavior, with their only penalty being that they were traded to other clubs in the league. Allen questioned why, if Seaton and Smith were ineligible, action was not being taken against these players.

For their part, Smith and Seaton continued to watch the events carefully. They both turned down lucrative offers in industrial leagues because they wanted to stay in organized baseball. Furthermore, they indicated a willingness to sign an agreement not to sue the San Francisco club if the club would make all the charges against them public and give them a chance to defend themselves.

Meanwhile, scandals were beginning to spring up in other minor leagues across the country. In the Texas League, Beaumont catcher Ted Easterly was given his unconditional release. Easterly was a seven-year major league veteran, having played with the Indians, the White Sox, and the Kansas City Federal League club between 1909 and 1915. Easterly ended his major league career with a batting average of .300.

Normally, the release of a veteran player would not cause a great stir. In Easterly's case, however, the circumstances were extremely strange. Easterly was the Beaumont club's best player, leading the team in batting at the time he was released. Beaumont President O. G. Greeves refused to discuss the reasons for Easterly's release other than to say that he was let go "for the good of the club." Easterly countered by saying that the real reason for his release was club manager Joe Mathes's fear that Easterly was trying to get his job.

Shortly thereafter, Galveston manager Hunter Hill was fired. No specific reasons were given for Hill's release, but the implication was that there was corruption on the club. When asked about his release, Hill stated that the Texas League could "well occupy its time investigating some of the allegations of crookedness that have been hinted at."[11]

Next to be released by the Texas League was Shreveport second baseman Chick Knaupp. While Knaupp was not exactly the star of the team (he was hitting only .217 at the time of his release), rumors flew that this move was part of a quiet cleanup effort by the Texas League. The controversy spread to the Southern League when the Nashville club was allowed to sign Knaupp. Little Rock owner Bob Allen was outraged, demanding to know what the difference was between Nashville signing Knaupp and his attempt to sign Seaton and Smith. No answer was forthcoming.

More scandals emerged in the Texas League as the season wore on. Pitcher Bill Fincher of the pennant-winning San Antonio club claimed that he had been offered $1,000 to throw a game. It was also reported that an unnamed Texas League umpire had been rooming with a gambler who had attempted to fix Texas League games.

While no official public investigation was ever launched into any of these charges, there is no question that the ranks of the Texas League were becoming closed to players suspected of fixing games, and the league was moving to clean up corruption. In fact, in December 1920, when J. Doak Roberts took over as president of the Texas League, he ordered all club owners to file a list of gambling houses and known gamblers in their respective towns. He also notified all ball players that if anyone was caught at one of these establishments or found to be associated with any of the gamblers on the list, they would immediately be expelled from the league.

Also hit by the outbreak of scandal in 1920 was the Western Canada

League. The league played a split season, the first half ending on June 27, 1920, and the second half ending on September 6. The winners of each half then played a seven-game series for the league title.

The Regina team handily won the first half, while Calgary came on to win the second half. Calgary defeated Regina in the postseason series for the championship. Shortly after the series, Bill Speas of the Regina team, one of the league's best hitters, claimed that he believed some of his teammates had thrown the series to Calgary at the instigation of gamblers. (Regina had won the first three games of the series and then lost four straight.)

The scandals of 1920 extended to leagues that were not part of organized baseball. In June the Pocatello team, part of an outlaw league in Idaho, released two of their players, Art Forrest and Red Lynch. Forrest was charged by the club's management with "favoring" the opposition in a game against the Blackfoot team. While no specific charges were leveled against Lynch, it was revealed that both men had been barred from playing with any other club in the league.

Before the year was over, the Smith-Seaton case in the Southern League was finally settled when the United States courts upheld the right of league president Martin to ban the two players from playing in the Southern League.

The major scandal of 1920 in the minor leagues broke in August in the Pacific Coast League. While Pacific Coast League President McCarthy had taken his first steps toward cleaning up the league by banning certain gamblers and arranging for the release of Tom Seaton and "Casey" Smith, he knew that the league's corruption went deeper than just these two players. He continued his investigation, and by August he was ready to announce the results.

The first person to feel McCarthy's wrath was none other than the notorious Hal Chase. After being eased out of organized baseball, Chase had returned to his native California. He attached himself to the San Jose club in the outlaw Mission League, a league that played ball only on Sundays.

To supplement his ballplaying, Chase pursued his perennial sideline of game fixing. In late July, Chase approached Charles "Spider" Baum, a pitcher for Salt Lake in the Pacific Coast League, and told him that he had some friends willing to bet large sums of money on Pacific Coast League games, provided that they had the edge. Chase proposed that Baum throw some of the games he was pitching and offered to pay Baum $300 per game for doing so. Baum refused the bribe and reported the attempt to the league. Chase subsequently was banned from all PCL parks.

Below are key excerpts from McCarthy's statement banning Chase.

> Chase will not hereafter be permitted in any park in our league. It is unfortunate that no further punishment can be imposed. Certainly there is no punishment too severe, but perhaps the contempt of men and women who love baseball and believe in clean sport would prove sufficient penalty.
>
> The task of keeping baseball clean is not the easy one I'd hoped. Today's developments prove it. But I am determined, and my directors are determined,

that no matter what the sacrifice, baseball on the Pacific Coast is going to be clean and above suspicion.[12]

The following Sunday Chase showed up to play with his Mission League San Jose club as usual. In the meantime, the president of the Mission League had received word of Chase's Pacific Coast League shenanigans. He also banned Chase, and the umpire refused to let Chase play. When the San Jose club insisted on playing Chase, the game was entered as a San Jose forfeit to the Hollister club. That ended Chase's involvement with the Mission League.

At the same time that Chase was banned from attending Pacific Coast League games, it was announced that the Salt Lake club had unconditionally released outfielder Harl Maggert. Salt Lake President Lane announced that Maggert was released "because suspicions had been aroused and I cannot, in justice to myself or the Salt Lake club, permit him to continue with the club." Also at that time, PCL President McCarthy announced that Vernon first baseman William "Babe" Borton was being suspended as a result of the investigation that led to the release of Harl Maggert.

The 37-year-old Maggert was a longtime veteran of organized baseball. He began his career in 1906 with Fort Wayne, Indiana, of the International Association, moving on to Wheeling, Illinois, of the Central League in 1907. At the end of the 1907 season he appeared in three games with the Pittsburgh Pirates, but he was back with Wheeling in 1908. He then moved on to Springfield in the Connecticut League, and in 1909 he joined Oakland in the Pacific Coast League. Maggert spent the 1912 season in the majors with the Philadelphia Athletics, appearing in 72 games and batting .256. He returned to the Pacific Coast League with Los Angeles in 1913 and remained in that league with the Los Angeles, San Francisco, and Salt Lake clubs.

Ironically, Maggert was enjoying his best season in 1920. He was leading the league with a .370 average, by far the highest mark of his career.

Babe Borton was born in 1888 in Marion, Illinois. He broke into the major leagues with the White Sox in 1912, enjoying his finest season that year with an average of .371 in limited action. Midway through the 1913 season he was traded to the New York Yankees as part of the Hal Chase deal.

Borton drifted to the minor leagues and resurfaced in 1915 with St. Louis of the Federal League. With St. Louis he appeared in 159 games, batting .286. He led the Federal League in runs with 97 and in bases on balls with 92. When the Federal League folded, he joined the major league St. Louis Browns for one season and then moved back to the minor leagues.

In late July of 1920, Borton met with pitcher Ralph Stroud of Salt Lake in the Lankershim Hotel in Los Angeles and offered him $300 to throw a game to Borton's Vernon club. Stroud refused the offer and left the hotel. Just after this incident, Borton met with Maggert and paid him $300, which looked suspicious.

Despite the fact that he refused Borton's offer, Stroud pitched poorly and was knocked out in the first inning. After the game, Borton approached Stroud in the hotel lobby and handed him $300, saying, "You earned it." Stroud refused the money, insisting that he tried to win but had just had an off day.

In the statement announcing the release of Maggert, William H. Layne, president of the Salt Lake club, said the following:

> On Thursday of last week, ten days after this money had been paid, Maggert, the first man up to bat, deliberately provoked a quarrel with Umpire McGrew despite the protest and pleas of his teammates. There was no alternative but to remove him from the game. His suspension by the President was a certainty.
>
> I tried to give Maggert every opportunity to explain. I made the trip from Salt Lake for the express purpose. Last night I went to Oakland to visit him. This morning, President McCarthy, Dr. Charles Strub, President of the San Francisco club, and others, including myself, again urged him to give the full facts and information relative to the game, but the information was refused.
>
> I am sorry that the circumstances have aroused suspicion which, whether true or untrue, make it imperative to end Mr. Maggert's connection with the Salt Lake Club. I, therefore, unconditionally released him.[13]

While Maggert was given his unconditional release, Borton was merely suspended pending the results of the investigation. The Vernon club assured PCL President McCarthy that they would cooperate fully with the investigation against Borton. Vernon President Eddie Maier stated that "while Borton's play has been above suspicion, baseball is too big a thing to allow a few men throughout America to ruin it by crookedness and gambling. I believe that in the present instance, Mr. McCarthy will get to the bottom of this affair and make a clean sweep of those who have tried to dishonor the pastime."[14]

Both Borton and Maggert initially denied all charges. Borton denied that he had made the offer to bribe Stroud, and he and Maggert claimed that the $300 was money that Borton owed Maggert from a crap game. Borton and Maggert refused to reveal the names of others involved in the game. McCarthy replied that unless Borton was willing to give all the facts, he would refuse to hold a hearing and would instruct the Vernon club to release Borton.

For a few days it looked as if the impasse would continue, but Vernon President Maier intervened and persuaded McCarthy to come to Los Angeles to hold a hearing on the matter. Maier told McCarthy that Borton was prepared to give him full details of the case.

On August 11, three days after the hearing, Maier announced that Babe Borton was being given his unconditional release. Maier stated, "I would have taken this action last week were it not for the fact that Borton made charges recently involving members of the Vernon ballclub, members of other clubs, and owners of other Pacific Coast League clubs."[15]

The charges from Borton that Maier referred to launched a bombshell. According to Borton, Vernon players had bought the 1919 pennant by bribing players from Salt Lake, Portland, and Seattle to throw games that they played against Vernon. Borton claimed that a $2,000 fund was raised from contributions by 20 players on the Vernon team.

According to Borton, shortly before the end of the 1919 season, Vernon manager Bill Essick approached him, asking, "if I can get any of the Salt Lake players to lay down so we might win the pennant. I then told him I'd see what could be done." According to Borton, he agreed to pay Maggert $500, Bill Rumler $250, and Gene Dale $500. Borton also claimed that he later learned that another player on the Vernon club, whose name he refused to divulge, was also approaching players and had agreed to pay Eddie Mulligan of Salt Lake $350, Del Baker of Portland $100, Red Oldham of Portland $100, Elmer Rieger of Seattle $100, and Art Koehler of Portland either $50 or $100. The money supposedly came from the "Fan's Fund," money that the fans contributed to the players in appreciation for their fine play.

According to Borton, all the bribed players except Harl Maggert received their money promptly. Borton claimed that Maggert did not want his wife to know that he received that amount of money, so Borton held the money until 1920. Borton claimed that he gave Maggert $200 when Salt Lake visited Vernon on its first trip and the remaining $300 on July 27. This is the money that Maggert claimed to have won in a crap game.

After weighing the evidence for a few days, McCarthy announced that Borton's charges were "a mass of falsehoods," and that in spite of several days of painstaking investigation, he had been unable to verify them. "Concealed beneath the mass of lies there may be some truth. If there be, let me say there will be further investigations to develop it," McCarthy stated.[16]

At first, it looked as though the case would end there and that Borton's charges would be swept under the rug. McCarthy, however, was true to his word, and the investigation continued. Within a matter of days, McCarthy announced that he had thoroughly investigated Borton's charges and that there was some corroboration that Borton had indeed attempted to bribe players to throw games late in the 1919 season. McCarthy revealed that

> Yesterday, I received verification of Borton's statement made to me last Sunday that two drafts purchased by him at the Los Angeles Trust and Savings Bank had been sent to William Rumler and Gene Dale on October 18, 1919. The draft to Rumler was forwarded to him at Milford, Nebraska, and was for $250. The draft to Dale was forwarded to St. Louis, Missouri, and was for $500.
>
> I've already communicated with Rumler by wire. Dale is not under jurisdiction. My wire reached Rumler at Salt Lake yesterday morning.
>
> I felt that if Borton had been given an opportunity to explain and Maggert having been given the same chance, that Rumler was entitled to equal consideration.[17]

McCarthy concluded, despite Borton's testimony, that a ring of gamblers was behind the bribes, not the Vernon players. He based his conclusion on information received from W. H. Klepper, president of the Seattle club, and Seattle first baseman Rod Murphy.

Murphy's evidence was particularly significant. He claimed that Nate Raymond, a Seattle gambler and one of the men barred from Pacific Coast League parks, had offered Murphy $3,000 in August 1920 to throw games, and he gave the names of Harl Maggert and Babe Borton as "references." According to Murphy, Raymond said

> "Remember last year when some of the boys on Salt Lake sold out to Vernon?" I replied, "I remembered that it was common gossip." He said, "Rod, I was the man who put the deal through. It cost me $10,000, and I cleaned up about $50,000." I asked what players were involved. He said "Rod, to prove my truthfulness to you, I would mention two players. Ask Maggert and Borton how I treated them in our agreement."[18]

When McCarthy expelled Borton and Maggert, he believed that the only outstanding issue was to investigate Rumler. Dale was no longer in the Pacific Coast League, having moved on to the Texas League, and he cleared the other players that Borton accused of taking bribes.

The controversy was far from over, however. While the Salt Lake club accepted and believed that Maggert was guilty, they questioned the judgment on Rumler, who had led the Pacific Coast League in batting in 1919 with an average of .362. On August 12, the board of the Salt Lake City club met, and for their part, exonerated Rumler. The following is the statement issued:

> The Board of Directors of the Salt Lake Baseball Club in session this 12th day of August, 1920, after full deliberation and careful consideration of the charges preferred against player William G. Rumler as contained in the press dispatches from Los Angeles, finds that the evidence contained in the statement of William Baker Borton, former Vernon club member, does not involve player Rumler, and after full consideration of all phases of the alleged gambling affair, exonerates player Rumler from guilt.
>
> The Board finds that player Rumler did accept $200.00 sent to him in conformity with an agreement made early in 1919 and a long time before the present race and long before the present deplorable charges of corruption were made against coast league players.
>
> Sworn statements by player Rumler and catcher Byler of the Salt Lake club explained to our entire satisfaction that the transaction charged in the statement of Borton is irrelevant to the present upheaval in the coast league.
>
> We regret the aforementioned agreement was made with a player involved in the present difficulty yet, after a complete and thorough investigation, we are led to exonerate player Rumler from all blame.[19]

Much of the sympathy for Rumler was based on his amiability. Born in Milford, Nebraska, in 1891, Rumler appeared with the St. Louis Browns in the American League in 1914, 1916, and 1917, appearing in 138 games with a .251 batting average. Both his teammates and his employers liked him.

McCarthy stood firm against the ruling of the Salt Lake management. While granting Rumler a hearing, McCarthy stated that regardless of the action of the Salt Lake board, Rumler could not play unless McCarthy cleared him.

During the next few days, McCarthy's annoyances increased by leaps and bounds. Hal Chase announced that he was suing McCarthy for defamation of character, to which McCarthy replied, "I never knew he possessed such a thing." Salt Lake President Bill Layne and the Salt Lake club were unhappy with the suspension of Rumler, and rumors that there was more truth to Borton's suggestion of a master conspiracy to fix the 1919 pennant race kept resurfacing. In addition, Harl Maggert kept proclaiming his innocence, stating that while he had accepted the bribe from Borton, he had played his best. According to Maggert, "if the rest of the fellows are taking the money, I might as well get mine."

On August 14, Borton revealed more information, alleging that Vernon second baseman Robert Fischer was the other Vernon player who had helped fix games. In his statement, Borton named Eddie Mulligan, Red Oldham, Del Baker, Art Koehler, and Jack Farmer as players who had taken bribes.

Rumler's hearing with McCarthy was not a successful one as far as the player was concerned. On August 16 McCarthy stated, "I've today notified [Salt Lake president] Mr. W. H. Layne that player William G. Rumler is indefinitely suspended. His answer to the Borton charges is at least an admission that he gambled on games last season and bet on the Vernon club to win the pennant."

Rumler's defense had been that in actuality the $250 he received from Borton was a result of a bet. The bet, according to Rumler, was that if Salt Lake won the pennant, Rumler owed $250; if Vernon won the pennant, Borton owed Rumler $250. In effect, that meant that both Borton and Rumler were betting against their own teams, which in McCarthy's view was enough to justify expulsion, whether or not the other charges were true. Both Rumler and the Salt Lake management continued to insist that Rumler was innocent, but their cries fell on deaf ears. As far as McCarthy was concerned, the case against Rumler was closed.

While McCarthy had reached his conclusions about the guilty and the innocent, he continued to investigate. On August 26, he met with Eddie Mulligan, whom he had earlier exonerated, and Salt Lake second baseman Marty Krueg to discuss the incident further. No particularly shocking revelations were uncovered.

In Rumler's defense, he was able to obtain an affidavit from Salt Lake teammate Butch Byer, who claimed to have some recollection about a discussion between Rumler and Borton regarding the $250 bet on each other's team to win the pennant. McCarthy was firm, however, that even if Rumler's story was true, it still would result in his expulsion from organized baseball for a period of at least five years.

At that point baseball was through with the investigation—but the legal system took over. On September 1 Babe Borton filed a $50,000 libel suit against Vernon manager Bill Essick. Borton stated that Essick's claim (that Borton's statements regarding the complicity of Essick and other Vernon club members in the gambling fix were false) was made for the purpose of injuring Borton's reputation. On September 17, Bill Rumler also joined in the legal action, announcing that he was going to sue the Pacific Coast League.

Salt Lake President Bill Layne continued to protest that Rumler was innocent. McCarthy did not agree, and on September 30 the league's board backed McCarthy. While that ended Layne's involvement in the case, the hard feelings between Layne and McCarthy would continue for quite a while.

By the end of September, Maggert stopped protesting his innocence and began corroborating Borton's story of a slush fund put together by the Vernon club to bribe other teams to throw games in 1919. Maggert sent a letter to Borton, claiming that three members of the 1919 Vernon team had confessed to McCarthy the existence of a slush fund to buy the pennant. Maggert's letter was made public on September 29.

By early October, of course, the Black Sox scandal had erupted, and dishonest baseball players were a hot topic of conversation. At the urging of McCarthy and other baseball officials, a Los Angeles grand jury started an investigation into the Pacific Coast League scandal.

The grand jury probe was a long and thorough one. Most of the players on the Vernon team, along with those players accused by the league or by Babe Borton, were called on to testify. Borton was the first witness, and he repeated his story of a slush fund. His testimony was supported by Maggert but denied by all other witnesses.

During the investigation, new evidence came to light. Salt Lake player Edward "Tub" Spencer claimed that he had been offered $1,700 by Borton near the end of the 1919 season; Pat Singlin of Portland claimed to have been offered $100 by Borton; and Vernon pitcher Wheezer Dell claimed that he was offered $300 by Borton on July 26, 1920, to throw a game. Borton wasted little effort in denying the charges, although he claimed that the bribe to Spencer had been for $500 rather than $1,700.

On Borton's side, in addition to Rumler, Vernon player Al DeVormer submitted an affidavit claiming that he received less money than he had expected from the "Fan's Fund," which Borton claimed had been used to buy the 1919 pennant. DeVormer claimed that the fund had been $700 short and supported Borton's claim that the missing money had been used to bribe players.

The Vernon club management denied these claims. While the club admitted that the "Fan's Fund" was short, they claimed that it was because some of the pledges from fans had not been received, plus the fact that some of the checks had bounced.

Meanwhile, fresh evidence against Borton was uncovered. It was alleged that Borton had approached Oakland manager Howard in 1920, stating, "why don't you have pitcher Kramer cover up his curveball? We can tell every time he is going to throw it." It was also alleged that when Borton attempted to bribe Vernon pitcher Wheezer Dell in 1920, he stated that "all you need is to get a man on first base, and when they bunt you field the bunt and throw it a little hard to me. I'll let it get away, and nobody will be any the wiser."[20]

On December 11 the grand jury reached a verdict. After hearing all the evidence, the grand jury gave the Vernon club itself a clean bill of health but returned indictments against Babe Borton, Harl Maggert, Bill Rumler, and Nate Raymond. They were charged with conspiracy to commit a felony. All four then surrendered and were released on bail.

The defendants immediately asked that the charges be dismissed. On December 24, 1920, Judge Willis agreed with them, dismissing the indictments. The judge ruled that even if the charges were true, it amounted only to a breach of civil conduct and that the offense was in no way a felony. Judge Willis stated that while the charges against these men were reprehensible if they were true, they were not liable to a criminal prosecution. He further stated that this was not a technicality but a matter of law, and the case could not be remedied by a resubmission of the matter to a grand jury.

To a great extent, this was the same decision that was reached in the Black Sox trial in 1921. As was the case with the Black Sox, organized baseball proved capable of cleaning up its own house. On January 10, 1921, the National Association of Professional Baseball Leagues, the minor leagues' ruling body, banned Borton, Maggert, Rumler, and Dale from baseball. At the same time, the baseball establishment called on Congress to pass laws making the throwing of baseball games a felony actionable in the courts.

In 1929 Rumler was allowed to return to the PCL with the Hollywood club. None of the others who were suspended ever appeared in organized baseball again. Two of the men accused and exonerated—Del Baker and Eddie Mulligan—went on to long and respected baseball careers. Baker, a former major leaguer, continued playing in the minor leagues and later became a major league manager. In eight seasons, primarily with Detroit, he compiled a managerial record of 401 wins and 344 losses, including an American League pennant for his 1940 Detroit Tigers. Baker also spent a number of years as a minor league manager, major league coach, and special-assignment scout.

Eddie Mulligan, who had previously appeared in the major leagues with the Chicago Cubs, joined the White Sox for the 1921 and 1922 seasons. Ironically, his assignment was to replace Buck Weaver, who was expelled from baseball by Commissioner Landis. After his retirement as a player, Mulligan spent 20 years as president of the California League. Today he is remembered for his executive abilities, rather than as one of the players accused by Babe Borton of throwing games.

While Harl Maggert never again appeared in baseball, his son, Harl Maggert, Jr., was a professional ball player, making it to the major leagues with the

Boston Braves in 1938. The senior Maggert died on January 7, 1963, in Fresno, California. He outlived Borton, who died on July 29, 1954, in Berkeley, California. Bill Rumler returned home to Nebraska, passing away on May 26, 1966, in Lincoln.

As was the case with major league baseball, minor league baseball became extremely vigilant toward the gambling problem after the scandals of 1919 and 1920. Gamblers continued to be thrown out of minor league ball parks for a number of years. One alleged gambler, James Finnessey of Seattle, who was banned from Pacific Coast League parks, had the temerity to sue for $25,000 in damages. Judge Truax of the Washington state court threw the case out, ruling in favor of the Pacific Coast League.

In 1923 the possibility of scandal in the Pacific Coast League was raised again. Los Angeles manager Marty Krueg charged that his third baseman, Charlie Deal, had "laid down" on his job. Krueg traded Deal to the Vernon team for Red Smith, and the incident was regarded as an attitude problem rather than a gambling fix. No further investigation was undertaken.

And so ended a period of intense scandal in minor league baseball. Unlike major league baseball, in which the last alleged game-fixing incident occurred in 1924, minor league baseball was to experience a wave of corruption in future years. But as baseball moved into the depression years, it appeared that minor league baseball was safe and free of corruption.

Chapter 15

Minor League Scandals from 1930 to 1994

As was the case in the major leagues, the depression years were scandal-free in minor league baseball. It is interesting from a sociological standpoint that periods of major economic depression in the United States, such as the 1890s and the 1930s, have been relatively scandal-free for baseball.

As America emerged from the Great Depression, the problem of gambling scandals began to reappear in the minor leagues. The first of these scandals occurred in the Pacific Coast League in 1941, when a pitcher for the Los Angeles Angels, Julio Bonetti, was accused of receiving a large sum of money from a gambler.

Bonetti was born on July 14, 1911, in Genoa, Italy. He pitched parts of three seasons in the major leagues, compiling a record of four wins and 11 losses in 28 appearances with the St. Louis Browns in 1937 and a 2-3 record for the Browns in 1938. His lifetime earned-run average was an unimpressive 6.07, although some allowance must be made for the fact that he pitched in an era of high-scoring games.

In 1939 Bonetti joined the minor league Angels. He was an immediate success, compiling a record of 20 wins and five losses during the 1939 season. On August 10, 1939, Bonetti pitched a perfect game against Oakland, and later that season he compiled a streak of 64 consecutive innings without walking a batter. By the time 1941 came around, Bonetti was established as one of the better pitchers in the Pacific Coast League.

Bonetti's downfall occurred in June of 1941, when private detectives hired to track gambling activity in baseball witnessed his receiving a large sum of money from a well-known gambler. Bonetti's counterclaim was that as a great fan of horse racing and a frequenter of the track, he was given the payoff as winnings from his bets on horse races. Nevertheless, he was expelled from baseball.

Bonetti attempted to clear himself, even taking legal action. He was not successful, however, and the expulsion stood.

Jesse Levan. Levan was a central figure in the Southern League scandals of 1959.
Courtesy of National Baseball Library and Archive, Cooperstown, New York.

Bonetti maintained his innocence until the end. His case was never reopened, and Bonetti died with a clouded name on June 17, 1952, in Belmont, California.

During World War II, the number of minor leagues shrank dramatically. Severe manpower shortages arose from the fact that most players were in the service or otherwise occupied with war-related work, and the majority of minor leagues chose to suspend their operations until the war was over. Only ten minor leagues were active in 1943 and 1944, the number rising slightly—to 12—in 1945 when it became apparent that the end of the war was near.

The postwar period brought a massive increase in the number of minor leagues. Forty-two leagues were active in 1946, and by 1949 the number of minor leagues was up to a since-unequaled 59.

While the end of the war was great for the baseball business, postwar conditions also gave baseball cause for concern about corruption. It should be remembered that the most famous fixes in baseball history occurred just after World War I, and the same social conditions—a growing economy and an increase in gambling—were present as World War II ended. The gamblers were increasing their activities in sports: For example, unsuccessful attempts were made to bribe New York Giants football stars Merle Hapes and Frank Filchock and famous boxing middleweight Rocky Graziano.

By 1947 this state of affairs had the baseball establishment worried enough to take action. The National League voted that all gamblers, bookies, touts, and other "undesirable characters" be barred from ball parks. A system of photographing gamblers and cataloging their activity, developed by Yankee magnate Ed Barrow, was used as the model for the National League system. The American League expressed full sympathy with the National League's legislation, but it stated that since a variety of antigambling measures had already been taken by the clubs, additional legislation would be counterproductive.

The vigilance against gambling extended to baseball's minor leagues as well. George Troutman, who had only recently succeeded Judge William Bramham as president of the National Association, the ruling body of the minor leagues, had good reason to support these policies, since the minor leagues had been rocked by two major gambling scandals during the 1946 season.

The first occurred in the Sally League on August 3, and it involved Columbus, Georgia, outfielder Hooper Triplett. The 26-year-old Triplett was the younger brother of Coaker Triplett, a major league outfielder from 1938 to 1945. Hooper, considered a fine prospect in the Cardinals organization, had joined the Columbus team in May of that year after his release from the army. He had played with Columbus in 1940, winning the Sally League batting championship with a .369 mark and helping the club to the pennant. He was promoted to New Orleans in 1941 and played half the 1942 season with Columbus of the American Association and Rochester, New York, of the International League before entering the army.

After his return to civilian life in 1946, Triplett was enjoying a fine season in the Sally League, hitting .314 with 44 RBIs. His downfall occurred on the afternoon of August 3 in a Columbus bar. During the course of the afternoon, Triplett placed a bet of $20 that the visiting Columbia, South Carolina, team would defeat his Columbus Cardinals in the game that evening. Within hours of the time the bet was made, the man with whom Triplett placed the bet reported the incident to Columbus business manager Bing Devine, who was later to become general manager of the St. Louis major league organization. The informant demanded that he remain anonymous, telling Devine that he would deny everything if his name became public.

Devine immediately went to Cardinals manager Kemp Wicker, and they decided to remove Triplett from the game. In his only two appearances at the plate that evening Triplett had walked and struck out. He made no errors in the field and in fact had made an outstanding running catch of a foul ball in the second inning.

Triplett was suspended the next day for what was described as an "infraction of club rules," and the details of his case were sent to Sally League President Dr. E. M. Wilder. Wilder took quick action, fining Triplett $500 and suspending him indefinitely. The fine and suspension were approved at a meeting of the league's directors on August 11.

While Triplett admitted making the bet, he claimed that he meant no harm.

> I wasn't in complete control of myself. When some of the people around began talking about Columbia's chances, I falsely said I'd bet they would win. I took it as a joke then. Now I know it was one of the costliest, if not the costliest, joke I've ever made.[1]

Despite this explanation, however, Triplett never again played in organized baseball. Later that year, he was expelled for life by Judge W. G. Bramham, the National Association president.

The second minor league scandal of 1946, which was not publicized until early 1947, proved to be the biggest minor league scandal since the Pacific Coast League gambling scandals of 1919 and 1920. The scandal took place in the Evangeline League, a Class D league that was reactivated in 1946 and operated primarily in Louisiana.

The Evangeline League was one of the many leagues reactivated after World War II. The dominant team in the league throughout the year was the Houma, Louisiana, club, nicknamed the Indians. Houma, a small (population 30,000) fishing and refining community, was able to dominate the league by acquiring a number of veteran players from the Brooklyn Dodgers' Mobile, Alabama, farm club in the Southern Association. With the younger prospects returning from World War II, these veteran players had little hope of ever making the major leagues and were expendable.

The most outstanding of these veteran players was pitcher Bill Thomas. Thomas was born in 1905 in St. Louis and began his professional career in 1926 with Hanover, of the Blue Ridge League. He bounced from team to team in the ensuing years, and by 1946 he had fashioned a minor league record of 296 wins and 293 losses. His best season was probably in 1928, when he compiled a record of 15-9 with Wheeling, West Virginia, of the Mid-Atlantic League, with an earned-run average of 2.75. He later won 20 games in 1932 (against 16 losses) and again in 1939 (against 17 losses).

Thomas had the greatest year of his career with Houma in 1946, winning a league-leading 35 games against seven losses and compiling a 2.88 ERA. Those 35 wins were not only high for the Evangeline League, but for all of organized baseball.

With Thomas leading the way, the Houma team ran away with the pennant, finishing with a record of 92-38, a phenomenal .708 winning percentage. Second baseman Dwight Conroy led the league in hitting with a .372 average and first baseman Paul Fugit led the league in RBIs with 130. In addition, center fielder Lenny Pecou stole 53 bases to lead the circuit.

With such a strong team, it was widely expected that Houma would have no trouble in the league's postseason playoffs, and that proved to be the case. In the first round of the playoffs, Houma defeated fourth-place Alexandria, Louisiana, four games to one, losing only the fourth game of the series. In the second round, Houma defeated Abbeville, Louisiana, four games to one, losing only the first game. Bill Thomas again powered the team with a record of 5-0 in the playoffs.

Rumors of corruption began to surface during the playoffs. On October 1, in the second round of the playoffs, Evangeline League President J. Walter Morris called Judge Bramham to report that there were persistent rumors that some of the players were in league with gamblers, and as a result, some of the games were being manipulated. Judge Bramham was in the process of winding down his career in baseball. He was scheduled to retire in January 1947 and hand over the reins of the minor leagues to George M. Troutman. Bramham stated that one of his final actions would be to resolve the Evangeline League scandal. Bramham urged Morris to make a thorough investigation at the National Association's expense and report his findings. On October 4 Morris wrote to Bramham stating that the investigation was completed and he had reached the conclusion that there were no grounds for the rumors. Some of the league's team owners were not satisfied with the investigation, and Morris and Bramham agreed to intensify the investigation.

Among the charges that had reached the ears of Morris were that bookmakers were actively trying to raise $8,000 in bets for one of the Houma-Alexandria games, with the bookies betting on Alexandria despite the fact they were an inferior team racked with injuries. The $8,000 figure was supposedly the amount needed to make it worthwhile to pay off the Houma players to lose. When the $8,000 in bets was not raised, the Houma club won the game easily.

A meeting of the Evangeline League was held on October 23. At the meeting, I. N. Goldberg, owner of the Abbeville club, charged that Houma had intentionally lost the fourth game of their first-round series in the playoffs and the first game of the second round of the playoffs. Goldberg also charged that players on his Abbeville team had intentionally lost the fourth game of their series against Houma.

After months of investigating, Bramham announced his decision on Jan-

uary 25. Five players—Houma player-manager Paul Fugit, Houma third
baseman Alvin Kaiser, Houma center fielder Leonard Pecou, Houma pitcher
Bill Thomas, and Abbeville catcher Don Vettoral—were expelled from the
game. In addition, Bramham was highly critical of the way the Evangeline
League operated, disclosing the following charges:

- Employment of at least one player by a bookmaker.
- Contact by players with gamblers and bookmakers and schemes in
  which players were to share in winnings from bets on games.
- Suggestions to the players that they could make a lot of money by throw-
  ing games.
- Constant betting on horse races by players through bookies.
- Appearances by gamblers in the dugouts and clubhouses.
- Implication that stockholders of some of the clubs had connections with
  gambling houses.

Bramham's official statement admitted that the evidence against the named
players was circumstantial and documented the players' denial of the allegations. The statement nevertheless concluded that both Thomas and Vettoral
had made "contact with gamblers and bookies, and entreat[ed] them to make
bets on the results of games in which they would play and against their own
clubs." While Thomas admitted that he was approached by some gamblers who
were introduced to him by his roommate Babe Benning and teammate Al
Kaiser, Thomas stated that he had rejected the bookies' approach and offered
his career-long reputation and his record during the 1946 season as evidence.

Vettoral was also charged with arranging for the fourth game of the second
round of the playoffs to be fixed and with showing $600 in cash in a local bar-
room, bragging that he had earned it by manipulating games. Vettoral denied
all charges.

Kaiser and Pecou were accused of conspiring with Vettoral and with betting on horse races through bookies and being in constant company with these
bookies. They were also accused of arranging for a gambling scam by turning
a clock back 20 minutes in order to bet on a race that had already been run.
Thomas supported the allegations that Kaiser and Pecou were frequent com-
panions of gamblers.

Both Kaiser and Pecou maintained their innocence of the game fixing
charges. While both admitted placing bets on horse races and associating with
gamblers, they denied any corruption. In fact, Pecou stated:

> I never threw a game. I went to see Judge Bramham and pleaded guilty to hob-
> nobbing with gamblers, betting on horse races and so on, but I didn't throw any
> games. I did the things I pleaded guilty to and, if I am to be barred for that, I
> doubt if any ballplayer in the country can play. I see lots of them at the race
> tracks—big league and minor league players.
>
> When I signed a contract it said in there what I would do and couldn't do, and
> there wasn't anything in it about betting on horses.[2]

Fugit was accused of being the major character in the game fixing plot. It was alleged that during the games in question, Fugit played far off first base, drawing throws off the bag from the other infielders which allowed Alexandria's batters to reach first base safely. It was also alleged that Fugit had not run out ground balls he had hit and that he had committed errors intentionally. Pecou was also accused of lax play, allegedly allowing a fly ball to drop in front of him intentionally during one of the games in question.

While the charges against the players were admittedly circumstantial, there could be little doubt that widespread corruption existed throughout the Evangeline League. The league's fans and owners demanded further investigation in order to make the league corruption-free. The rest of the investigation continued for a while, but nothing else came of it. The Evangeline League continued to function for another decade, and no further action was taken against other players in the league.

All the expelled players continued to protest their innocence. Given the circumstantial nature of the evidence, and the fact that the league was widely believed to be full of corruption, it appears that these players were to a great extent made scapegoats. The case against Thomas was particularly weak, given his record of five wins against no losses during the playoffs.

After their expulsions, Fugit, Kaiser, and Vettoral left baseball behind and pursued other interests. Thomas and Pecou petitioned the National Association for reinstatement at six-month intervals, and on August 27, 1949, Troutman restored them to eligibility. Returning to Houma, the players participated in the tight pennant race of 1949, which culminated in Houma winning the Evangeline League pennant.

Thomas continued his remarkable career in the minor leagues until 1952. He had another outstanding year in 1950, when he compiled a record of 26-12 with three different clubs. He ended his career with 383 minor league wins, the highest total for a player in minor league history. He also lost 346 games and ended with a career earned-run average of 3.71.

As the reader has seen throughout the course of this narrative, baseball gambling scandals have tended to occur in clumps. Therefore, it should be no surprise that the 1947 season brought another gambling scandal to minor league baseball. The central figure in this new scandal was Al McElreath, an outfielder with Muskogee, Oklahoma, of the Class C Western Association.

Born in 1915, McElreath broke into organized baseball with Joplin, Missouri, in 1931. In the ensuing years he bounced from team to team in minor leagues across the country, appearing with as many as four teams in a single season. He finally found some stability in 1944 and 1945 with the Sacramento, California, team, moving down to Muskogee in 1946 when many of the younger players returned from World War II.

The primary charge against McElreath was that he had attempted to bribe one of his teammates to help him throw a game that Muskogee was playing against St. Joseph, Missouri, on May 4. According to the testimony that came out later, McElreath approached an unnamed teammate the morning of May 4 at the Robidoux Hotel in St. Joseph, stating that "we can make some good money if we throw one of the games." When the player declined to participate in the fix, McElreath reportedly stated, "I don't see why you won't do it, because they don't care anything about you." Muskogee was scheduled to play a doubleheader against St. Joseph that day.

McElreath's play during the first game of the doubleheader was extremely suspicious. Two incidents stood out, the first occurring in the fifth inning with Muskogee leading 5–1 and St. Joseph at bat. A fly ball was hit to McElreath in center field, and McElreath reportedly made "several false starts toward the ball," the result being that the ball dropped in safely a few feet behind him. All the runners scored, and the hitter was credited with a triple. The other suspicious play took place later in the game with McElreath at bat. McElreath signaled for a hit-and-run play, at which point the runner took off for second base, but McElreath failed to swing at the ball. McElreath admitted that he gave the hit-and-run signal but stated that he did not swing at the ball because "it was a bad pitch and the runner was safe." His teammates had a different version of the play; they stated that the pitch that McElreath did not swing at was a perfect one, which was backed up by the fact that the pitch was ruled a strike by the umpire.

The next day McElreath's teammate who had refused the bribe from McElreath reported the incident to his club. McElreath was released by the club a few days later. According to McElreath, manager Ray Baker told him he was being released to make room for players returning from the service.

On May 10 league President Thomas Fairweather turned the incident over to National Association President Troutman. On June 4, 1947, Troutman made the evidence public and announced that McElreath was being expelled from the game. McElreath responded angrily to the charges, calling them "a lie."

There was certainly some evidence that McElreath's expulsion was at least somewhat suspect. Although a number of his teammates testified against him, the official scorebook for the game showed some discrepancies in the case against McElreath. For example, the triple by Bill Cloud of St. Joseph in the fifth inning was well hit, traveling 400 feet, and the official scorer had felt that McElreath made a sincere effort to play the ball. In addition, the record shows that McElreath went two for five in the first game, with two runs scored and one run batted in. He fielded two chances in center field without an error. In the second game he had no hits in three at-bats but scored a run and made two putouts without an error. Despite the conflicting evidence, McElreath's expulsion stood. He never played in organized baseball again.

The next minor league scandal occurred less than a year later. This scandal involved Barney DeForge, pitcher-manager of the Reidsville, North Carolina, club in the Carolina League.

In May 1948 reports began to circulate that a "gambling coup" had been made by an out-of-town gambler in Winston-Salem's Southside Park on May 14. On that night, Winston-Salem had defeated the visiting Reidsville club by a score of 5–0. The Winston-Salem management immediately began an investigation into the rumors and informed the police.

Initially, little evidence turned up, and it looked as though the incident was closed. Then, in early June, National Association President George Troutman announced that player-manager Barney DeForge of the Reidsville club and Ed Weingarten, who was the principal stockholder and general manager, secretary, and treasurer of the Florence, South Carolina, club in the Tri-State League, and president of the Leaksville, Mississippi, club in the Blue Ridge League, were being placed on the permanently ineligible list. Troutman's statement, released on June 1 after an extensive investigation, revealed that DeForge and Weingarten had conspired with gambler W. C. McWaters to make sure that DeForge's Reidsville club lost their game to Winston-Salem on May 14 by at least three runs.

The events that took place during the game were certainly more than a little suspicious. At the beginning of the eighth inning, Winston-Salem was leading Reidsville by a score of 2–0. Then DeForge, who was noted for his fine control, put himself on the mound instead of starter Ted Abernathy. DeForge went on to issue four bases on balls that, along with a wild pitch, helped lead to three runs for Winston-Salem, bringing the final score to 5–0.

The suspicious nature of DeForge's pitching, along with persistent rumors of the gambling coup, kept the investigation alive. After much questioning, DeForge confessed to Troutman that he had, in fact, thrown the game. He stated that on May 10 he had met with Ed Weingarten in the Hotel Belvedere in Reidsville. Weingarten had introduced him to W. C. McWaters, a used-car dealer who was a professional gambler. McWaters had told DeForge that the opportunity existed for "making a lot of money by betting on baseball games," and it was agreed that McWaters would contact DeForge at the proper time.

According to the testimony of DeForge, McWaters contacted DeForge on May 14 and set up a meeting at the Robert E. Lee Hotel in Winston-Salem for that afternoon. At the meeting, McWaters instructed DeForge to make sure that Reidsville lost the game by at least three runs. After the game, DeForge met McWaters in the hotel lobby, at which time McWaters handed DeForge three $100 bills for his efforts. Weingarten totally denied DeForge's statements, but it was established that Weingarten had been a guest at the Belvedere Hotel on the day in question and that he and McWaters were seen in conversation in the hotel lobby during the day.

DeForge expressed his regret over becoming involved in the incident. A veteran minor leaguer, he began his career with Beatrice in the Nebraska State League in 1937, later playing with Dayton, Ohio; Durham, North Carolina; Birmingham, Alabama; Portsmouth, Virginia; and Montreal, Canada. After three

years in the service during World War II, he joined Natchez, Mississippi, in
the Evangeline League in 1947, serving as player-manager. When confronted
with the evidence, DeForge stated, "I don't know why I did it. I guess it was
just a weak moment. I thought I was being smart." The history of the
Evangeline League suggests the possibility that the seeds of his corruption were
sown during his membership in that league. The Evangeline League would
have been an excellent place to learn about baseball corruption.

After Troutman's action, the directors of the Blue Ridge League declared
that Weingarten's Leaksville franchise was forfeited. They decided that the
club would be operated by the league until new owners were found.

Baseball was powerless to take any action of its own against gambler
McWaters, who instigated the whole affair, but in the wake of the Black Sox
scandal, North Carolina had passed a statute making a bribe of a baseball
player, umpire, or official a felony. Upon conviction, the person in question
would be confined to the state penitentiary for a period of not less than one
year and not more than five years.

DeForge, Weingarten, and McWaters were all arrested in early June and
released on bond. DeForge cooperated fully with authorities, admitting his role
in the scandal and providing evidence against Weingarten and McWaters.

On June 14 Ed Weingarten was again arrested, this time in Florence, South
Carolina, after police raided a billiards parlor where an alleged baseball lottery
was being held. Weingarten was charged with taking part in the lottery and
released on bond. He failed to appear when his case was called, and his bond
was forfeited.

On June 24 DeForge, Weingarten, McWaters, and gambler Tom Phillips
were indicted in Forsyth County, North Carolina, and charged with conspiracy.
A trial date was set for July 7 but ended up being postponed because Weingarten became ill with a blocked kidney. The former clubowner lapsed into a
coma on July 5 and died on July 9 before a trial could be held. The trial was
rescheduled for September.

The legal process finally ended on October 23, when DeForge was found
guilty of throwing the May 14 game. In a surprising decision, the jury acquitted McWaters and Tommy Phillips. Judge Allen H. Gwin termed the acquittal of McWaters and Phillips "in its entirety unsatisfactory." He added "I have
no doubt that he [DeForge] met in Reidsville with Weingarten and McWaters."

At the urging of prosecuting attorney Walter Johnstone, Jr., county Sheriff
Ernie Shore, and Chief of Police John Gold, DeForge's one-year prison term
was suspended. DeForge's complete cooperation with authorities was given as
the reason for suspending his sentence. Judge Gwin placed DeForge on probation for five years and urged him to "rise above what has come out of this case."
DeForge replied, "I will sir."

Sheriff Ernie Shore was himself a former major league baseball player.

Shore pitched in the major leagues between 1912 and 1920, mostly with the Boston Red Sox, and compiled a lifetime record of 65 wins against 43 losses, with a fine earned-run average of 2.47. He was best known for his role in a game played on June 23, 1917, when he relieved Red Sox pitcher Babe Ruth, who was ejected from the game for protesting a walk to the first batter. The runner was caught stealing, and Shore retired the next 26 batters in a row to record a perfect game.

Fortunately for George Troutman, the DeForge affair marked the last minor league gambling scandal of the 1940s. In fact, this was the last incident to occur until 1959, when a new scandal broke out, this time in the Class AA Southern Association.

On July 3, 1959, Southern Association President Charlie Hurth announced that first baseman Jesse Levan and shortstop Waldo Gonzalez of the Chattanooga Lookouts were being suspended indefinitely. They were charged with failing to report a bribery attempt.

The 31-year-old Levan was a veteran of 13 years in organized baseball. The Reading, Pennsylvania, native had played briefly in the major leagues, appearing in two games with the Philadelphia Phillies in 1947, seven games with the Washington Senators in 1954, and 16 games with the Senators in 1955. All told, he came to the plate 35 times in the major leagues and compiled a lifetime average of .286. In the minor leagues, Levan had won batting titles in both the Inter-State League and the Florida International League. Levan was batting .337, the fourth-best average in the Southern Association, at the time of his suspension.

While Levan was a veteran, Gonzalez was a young player on his way up. A native of Cuba, the 24-year-old had been obtained earlier in the year from Houston and quickly developed a reputation as an outstanding fielder. He was weak with the bat, however, hitting only .179 at the time of his suspension.

Few details were initially released of the reason for the players' suspension. Southern Association President Hurth would only say that the two players had been approached by gamblers and asked to "tip off the opposing team" about which pitches were coming. Levan vigorously denied the charges, saying "there's never been a nickel exchanged, and I have no doubts but that everything will turn out all right." The case was turned over to National Association President George Troutman, who launched a full-scale investigation.

Unfortunately for Levan, everything did not turn out all right, and on July 29 he was placed on the permanently ineligible list. Waldo Gonzalez was suspended from organized baseball for a period of one year.

While there was no evidence that any games had actually been thrown, there is a good deal of testimony that Levan had attempted to fix games. Pitcher James Heiss of Chattanooga, a former major leaguer, testified that Levan approached him on two different occasions asking whether he wanted to "make a little money" by throwing easy pitches to opposing players. Heiss stated that he had told Levan on both occasions that he would take no part in any actions of this kind. Heiss's testimony was backed up by pitcher Tom McAvoy of Chattanooga, who testified that Levan approached him and inquired whether he "would like to throw a game." McAvoy stated that he assumed that Levan was joking and simply laughed and walked away. In addition, outfielder Sammy Meeks, a veteran of four seasons in the major leagues with Washington and Cincinnati, stated that earlier in the season, while he was acting as first base coach for the Mobile club, he was invited by Levan into a bar for a conference with a gambler. In the conference, Meeks said that he was told that he could help his team by watching shortstop Waldo Gonzalez who, by his actions, would tip off the catcher's signals for each pitch. Meeks also claimed that he was offered money to go along with the scheme. While rejecting the offer of the money, Meeks was happy to watch Gonzalez, since this would give an edge to his team.

On July 18, 1959, Meeks was released by the Mobile team, and on July 20 he signed with Chattanooga. Though Meeks was perfectly willing to have advance warning of pitches by the Chattanooga team while a member of the opposition, now that he was with Chattanooga, he found the situation clearly unacceptable. Meeks told the story to catcher Roy Holton, a close friend of Chattanooga manager Red Marion's. Holton promptly relayed the story to Marion, who contacted Chattanooga President Joe Engle.

The bulk of the evidence in the case was against Levan, which is why he was placed on the permanently ineligible list. The official reason for his expulsion was "admittedly acting as liaison for a gambler in a program that was designed to throw Chattanooga games." Both Levan and Gonzalez testified that Gonzalez had refused to pass the signs to Meeks, and hence Gonzalez was charged only with failure to tell of the bribe attempt and was given only a one-year sentence.

Surprisingly, no disciplinary action was taken against Sammy Meeks. According to Troutman, the reason for this was "because it is clear that the facts might never have been brought to light had Meeks continued to be silent after he became a member of the Chattanooga club." Troutman continued: "He, and all other players are warned that the desire to win games must yield to the supreme duty to report any activities of this kind, and the failure to do so will result in the future in permanent ineligibility." Hurth, Engle, Marion, and Holton were commended for the services they had rendered in the investigation.

The sentences caused quite an uproar in Chattanooga, where both Levan and Gonzalez were quite popular. The sentiment was typified by 13-year-old Chattanooga batboy Bo Short, who stated, "It's a shock. They were both my good friends, Jesse and Waldo. I can't believe it."

Young Short was particularly upset about Levan, who was his favorite player. "He showed me how to hold the bat, and taught me nearly everything I know. Last spring, when I went to the training camp, Jesse was always around to help me with my school work. He told me I had to study my lessons and do the right thing."

The penalties against Levan and Gonzalez did not close the incident. On July 28 sportswriter Bob Christian published a story in the *Atlanta Journal* claiming that Southern Association players had been cooperating with gamblers. Christian's source, who was not revealed, told him that players were deliberately fouling off pitches for the benefit of the gamblers who had made bets. Another story, out of Dallas, quoted a former Southern Association player as describing one of the league's parks as "nothing but a gambling casino."

These charges touched off a continuing investigation by the National Association. Troutman stated that steps were being taken to try to prove or disprove the accusations. Levan agreed to cooperate fully with the investiga tion. The wheels of justice continued to turn during the next few months, with no apparent results. Then, on November 13, the investigation reached a startling conclusion, when Troutman announced that former major league catcher Joe Tipton was permanently barred from future employment by any minor league club.

Joe Tipton was born on February 18, 1923, in McCaysville, Georgia. While a teenager, he left home to get a job with a company that had a baseball team. It was there that Tipton was discovered by professional baseball, and in 1940 he was signed to a minor league contract.

Tipton started in Class D ball in Appleton, Wisconsin. After a good year, he moved up to Class C, playing with Charleston, West Virginia, in the Middle Atlantic League. He then moved to Harrisburg, Pennsylvania, in the Inter-State League, where he continued to play well.

In 1942 Tipton joined the navy, wherein he remained for the duration of the war. Upon returning from the service, he moved on to Wilkes-Barre, Pennsylvania, in the Eastern League, where he led the league with a .375 batting average in 1947. After this outstanding season, Tipton graduated to the major leagues, serving as a backup catcher on the Cleveland Indians' world championship team in 1948.

Tipton's rookie season was to be the highlight of his big league career. The 1948 Indians were an outstanding team, featuring future Hall of Fame's player-manager Lou Boudreau and pitcher Satchel Paige. The club won the American League pennant, set an all-time attendance record, and defeated the Boston Braves in six games to win the world championship.

Shortly after the 1948 season, Tipton was traded to the Chicago White Sox for pitcher Joe Haynes. Haynes was the son-in-law of Washington Senators owner Clark Griffith, who had a deep-seated dislike for Indians owner Bill Veeck. Rather than see Haynes forced to play for Veeck, Griffith traded future Hall of Fame pitcher Early Wynn, whom Veeck coveted, and star first baseman Mickey Vernon to the Indians for Haynes, Eddie Klieman, and Eddie Robinson. This would go down as one of Bill Veeck's greatest trades.

Tipton had a difficult season in Chicago; his batting average dropped from .289 to .204. He was constantly feuding with White Sox manager Jack Onslow, and after the season he was traded to the Philadelphia Athletics for a young infielder, Nellie Fox. Fox went on to became a star with the White Sox, winning the American League's Most Valuable Player Award in 1959. This was considered one of the best trades ever made by the White Sox, meaning that Tipton had been involved in two of the most one-sided trades in major league history.

Tipton remained with Philadelphia as a backup catcher until mid–1953, when he was traded back to the Indians. In 1954 he moved on to the Washington Senators for his final major league season, ending up with a lifetime average of .236 in 417 games.

Tipton then drifted to the minor leagues, playing in the Southern Association between 1955 and 1957. In 1958 he was named player-manager of the Panama City team in the Alabama-Florida League, but after a month he retired from the game.

Tipton's expulsion was related to the charges that players were intentionally hitting foul balls to help gamblers. The way this program worked was that gamblers in the stands would bet with the fans that the next pitch would be a foul ball, which was a very safe bet given that the player had previously agreed to foul off the pitch. Since foul-ball hitting did not affect the outcome of the game, this was a much safer bet for gamblers and a much easier scheme in which to recruit players than throwing a game.

Once the investigation was launched, a number of players were investigated. The players all denied their involvement, and no further action was taken against them. Joe Tipton, though, who was out of baseball, came forward on his own to explain that on two occasions he had agreed to go along with the foul-ball scheme. Both these incidents occurred in 1957, when his Birmingham club was visiting Chattanooga. On one occasion, he was paid $50 by Jesse Levan, and on another occasion he received a $75 payment in the mail, according to his agreement with Levan to deliberately hit a foul ball during a time at bat.

Tipton also revealed that after he was released from Birmingham in early 1958, a Chattanooga gambler approached him to help recruit players for the foul-ball-hitting scheme, saying, "there is a lot of money in it." Tipton rejected these advances. Tipton also explained to Troutman that the foul-ball-hitting scheme was relatively widespread, taking place in Atlanta, Chattanooga, and Nashville.

The investigation also revealed more serious corruption in the Southern Association. Jesse Levan, hoping to gain eventual reinstatement, told of a meeting that he and several other players (their names were never released by organized baseball) had with a gambler early in the 1959 season, in which they discussed a proposition under which both games of a Chattanooga-Mobile doubleheader to be played that night would be lost intentionally, one by each team. Levan said the players later decided against the plan, and he informed the gambler of their decision. The players were interrogated on August 25, and all denied Levan's story.

The foul-ball scheme that Tipton admitted to participating in was nothing new in baseball. In fact, the late Baseball Hall of Fame historian Lee Allen, in his outstanding column "Cooperstown Corner" in the *Sporting News*, told the following story, related to him by former major league infielder Walter Kimmick:

> The strangest thing that ever happened to me in baseball was when I was a shortstop with the Phillies in 1926. This fellow—I'd seen him around the park—came to me under the stands and said, "Kimmick, can you hit foul balls?" "Sure I can," I told him. "I don't believe it," he said. "Well," I replied, "I guess I could hit ten in a row. Naturally, I wouldn't try it if there were men on base, but if I come up with nobody on, you just watch."
>
> "They told me later the fellow made $10,000 betting I would hit fouls," Kimmick said with a laugh. "He'd bet a thousand I'd foul the next pitch and let the money ride. I didn't know he was a gambler, so I hit one after another. But I never saw him after that."[3]

The net result of the investigation was that there was obviously corruption in the Southern Association, but everyone accused of corruption denied involvement, and the only person to come forward was Joe Tipton, who admitted participating in a foul-ball scheme that had absolutely no effect on the outcome of games. Despite all this, baseball needed a scapegoat, and that scapegoat was Joe Tipton. Therefore, despite the fact that he came forward with evidence, despite the fact that his "crime" was a relatively small one, and despite the fact that he was retired from baseball, Tipton was placed on minor league baseball's permanently ineligible list.

On a brighter note, the expulsion from the minor leagues had no effect on Tipton's standing with the major leagues. Tipton, who died in 1994, was able to draw his major league pension. A friendly and charming man, Tipton maintained contact with many of his former major league teammates and colleagues and seemed to hold no grudge against baseball for the unjust treatment that he was given by the National Association.

Minor league baseball was free of gambling scandals throughout the 1960s and 1970s. Then in 1981, a new scandal unfolded. While not in any way related to gambling, this new scandal did affect the outcome of games and therefore will be dealt with in this chapter.

On August 21, 1981, Angel Rodriguez, a 20-year-old catcher for the Alexandria, Virginia, Dukes in the Carolina League, was suspended, charged with tipping opposing Hispanic batters to upcoming pitches. While the parent Pittsburgh Pirates imposed a "gag rule" on members of the Carolina League club, an anonymous Alexandria pitcher was quoted as saying "I've no doubt he's guilty. I could think of at least 2 or 3 ball games we lost when a Latin player got the

winning hit in the ninth inning. With all the one-run games we lost who knows
what kind of season we might've had?"

While Rodriguez denied the accusations, the evidence against him was
substantial. Six of the eight Carolina League umpires felt that Rodriguez was
guilty. In fact, umpire Coleman Coffelt stated,

> I've been with Rodriguez for all three of his years. In the Gulf Coast League
> I told him to cut it out. So I told the skipper (Woody Huyke). Then I saw him
> do it again with Shelby (South Atlantic) and I told his skipper (Joe Frasina). I only
> saw him do it once this year, July 22 against Kinston.[4]

The actions of Rodriguez were reported to Carolina League President Jim
Mills on August 16 by umpire Spook Jacobs, son of the former major league
umpire of the same name. Mills quickly completed an investigation and suspended Rodriguez. The case was then turned over to Johnny Johnson, president of the National Association.

The investigation dragged on throughout most of the off-season, with Rodriguez continuing to claim his innocence. Finally, on February 3, 1982, Johnson
announced that Rodriguez was being suspended for a period of one year and
would be eligible to return to active duty on August 21, 1982. No other players
were cited in Johnson's report, but he promised tighter scrutiny in the future.

Johnson said he decided on a suspension of only one year "because he
never admitted any guilt. He still denies it. We were working on circumstantial
evidence. We had some limited evidence from other players that he offered
signs, but they all denied taking them."

Johnson's announcement was heavily criticized. Alexandria President
Eugene Thomas stated:

> Absolutely nothing was accomplished by this. He can be released by Pitts-
> burgh and play for somebody else in 1983. I'd be surprised if he's back with the
> Pittsburgh organization. I'll tell you one thing, he won't be coming back through
> Alexandria.
>
> I can't be very happy. He cost us the first half title. We traced him to nine
> games where a Latin player hitting below .240 beat us, and we finished 3½
> [games] out. We were 9-27 in one-run games [for the season] and usually you
> split those about in half.
>
> I thought they knew who the others were. There were about eight or nine of
> them. Maybe it was because the other boys involved were high draft choices. . . .
> It could be embarrassing . . . but I'm surprised that he got off so easy. A year
> suspension. I don't know if it is going to be a deterrent.[5]

Rodriguez did return to organized baseball, continuing in the minor
leagues until 1988, when he closed out his career with the Milwaukee Brewers
organization. Although at one time he was considered an outstanding prospect,
he never reached the major leagues, perhaps partially due to the pitch-tipping
incident.

It is worth touching on a few other gambling scandals which occurred outside of organized U.S. baseball. One such scandal occurred in Japan, when on October 8, 1969, it was revealed that Masayuki Nagayasu, a pitcher with the Nishitetsu Lions, had accepted bribes to throw easy pitches to opposing batters and tried to convince his teammates to participate in game throwing. He was banished for life from Japanese baseball.

This was not the only incidence of scandal in Japanese baseball. In his book *Baseball Babylon*, author Don Gutman relates the following story:

> In 1966, two members of the champion Yomiuri Giants were found guilty of consorting with a baseball betting gang called Uchikoshi-Kai. Around the same time, Shiegeo Hasegawa, a slugger for the Nankai Hawks, became deeply indebted to gangsters and told friends he feared for his life. Shortly after, he was found murdered. A committee of the Japanese Parliament opened up a full-scale investigation into baseball corruption in March 1970, and three pitchers were suspended for life.[6]

Scandal also occurred in Cuba. In 1978 18 players were charged with accepting money to throw games. These players were suspended from baseball for life. One of these players was Barbaro Garbey, who in 1980 joined the "Freedom Flotilla" to the United States. Garbey was quickly signed by the Detroit Tigers and allowed to play professional baseball.

Garbey reached the major leagues in 1984, playing third base and hitting .287 with Detroit's world-championship team. His average dropped to .257 with Detroit in 1985, and he returned to the minor leagues. His last hurrah in the majors was in 1988, when he hit .194 in 62 at-bats with the Texas Rangers.

Given the Cuban system of justice, it is hard to determine Garbey's guilt. Garbey did admit taking money, but he claimed that he was bribed to keep games close, not to lose the games. Other sources disagree, claiming that Garbey was involved in game fixing. Although Barbaro Garbey was never accused of any gambling-related activity in U.S. baseball, one would have to question the double standard in accepting a player who admitted working with gamblers.

Game fixing and attempts to fix games have cropped up through the years in the amateur and semipro leagues. Former major league pitcher Jim "Mudcat" Grant told of an incident during his boyhood in the Deep South, where a gambler in the stands threatened to shoot Grant if his team did not lose the game. Grant kept the game close, but walked the bases loaded in the ninth inning while clinging to a one-run lead. The team bus was started and brought to the stadium, and as his teammates ran for cover Grant threw a third strike past the opposing player. A bullet shattered the back window of the team bus as they were pulling away after their victory.

A recent example of a gambling scandal in the amateur ranks occurred in 1992, when 13 baseball players from the University of Maine were suspended by their team during an investigation into a sports gambling ring on campus.

While no game fixing was involved, the players were all implicated in placing bets on their team's games, and a sophomore outfielder was identified as serving as a bookmaker.

So ends our story of baseball's gambling and game fixing scandals. In our final chapter, we will discuss the situation in baseball today, review a few of the major injustices from the past, and make recommendations for action by the baseball establishment.

Chapter 16

Summing It All Up

The aftermath of the Pete Rose scandal brought out a wide diversity of opinion regarding the relationship between baseball and gambling. On one side, some feel that baseball's obsession with gambling is an anachronism. These people argue that no major league player has been expelled for game fixing since 1924 and that the gambling problems of Pete Rose were merely an addiction.

On the other side, many argue that baseball has been taking an increasingly lax attitude with regard to gambling, and the fact that Rose had been betting illegally for many years before the scandal became public demonstrates this fact. These people argue that there must be no connection between baseball and gambling, and that increased vigilance is necessary to protect the sport.

It is unlikely that gamblers could successfully fix a major league baseball game today. In contrast to the players of 70 years ago, today's players realize that they will be punished severely for engaging in corrupt activity. Even more important, the earning power of players is so high that it is hard to imagine anyone throwing away a career in which he will earn millions of dollars to get involved in a game fixing scandal. The amount of money it would take to fix a game today would be tremendous, and far more than a gambler could earn betting on fixed games.

At the same time, anyone who has ever studied human behavior knows that logic often has little to do with the way people live their lives. The fact that it would make little sense for a player to get involved in game fixing does not mean it cannot happen. Despite their wealth, a number of players live quite exotic life-styles, and some have run into severe financial problems from overspending. If a player had the chance to make a fresh start by manipulating the results of one game, who is to say that he would not be tempted?

Another worry for baseball is the involvement of players in drugs or illegal gambling. These illegal activities involve associating with a very dangerous crowd and leave players open to blackmail. Suppose that a major star – a player earning many millions of dollars a year through salary and endorsements – becomes involved in an illegal drug deal. If caught, the player could go to prison and squander his future earnings potential. It is not inconceivable that his associates—obviously not law-abiding citizens—might use the threat of exposure to blackmail the player to tamper with the results of a key game.

Most important, it is critical that baseball always protect the integrity of each and every game. As mentioned in our Introduction, the allure of baseball depends on the assumption that the players are giving their best effort each time they take the field. Incidents such as the Pete Rose scandal can lead to an erosion of this belief by fans and cause severe damage to the sport. To understand the real danger that baseball faces, one only has to look at boxing, which suffered a huge drop in popularity 30 years ago when it was learned that many fights were being fixed.

It would be unfair to say that baseball is ignoring the gambling issue. Baseball does have a full-time security director and conducts the "resident agent program," in which local police in each major league city are paid a small retainer by baseball to help keep gamblers away from the park. In addition, the FBI, at its own expense, sends agents to spring training camps to warn players about the dangers of gambling and the tools that a gambler might use to try to blackmail a player into fixing a game.

All this provides evidence that baseball does not ignore the problem of gambling. All the same, there is evidence that baseball does not take the problem as seriously as it should. The fact that many baseball officials were aware of Pete Rose's gambling long before taking action is one such piece of evidence. Also disturbing were the comments of Fay Vincent and Steve Greenberg in 1991 when word leaked that two umpires had been placed on probation for gambling. Both Vincent and Greenberg refused to reveal details of the scandal, saying it was a private matter. Greenberg also stated that incidents such as Lenny Dykstra's gambling would normally have been handled in a private fashion. Unfortunately, in the early part of this century baseball chose to handle all corruption issues in a "private fashion"—in other words, baseball swept these incidents under the rug. The result, of course, was widespread corruption, leading to the 1919 Black Sox scandal.

Baseball should intensify its efforts against the gambling interests. For example, part of a new basic agreement should be a rule that any form of illegal gambling by a player, umpire, or official—whether or not it pertains to baseball—would result in an automatic fine or suspension. This includes situations such as the Lenny Dykstra incident, which involved illegal poker games. Some might argue that a rule of this nature is too severe and infringes upon the rights of baseball personnel, but baseball today is a lucrative business, and it will continue to be a lucrative business only if the integrity of the game is unquestioned. Asking those who profit from baseball's popularity to give up the right to gamble illegally does not seem to be too great a sacrifice to ensure baseball's integrity.

Should baseball take any action to address past scandals? The official viewpoint of the last three commissioners has been that once punishment is dealt out, the book is closed on past scandals. Baseball has refused to hear repeated requests for reinstatement brought by friends and relatives of players such as Joe Jackson, Buck Weaver, and Phil Douglas. In fact, the only player on the ineligible list who seems to have a chance for a hearing is Pete Rose.

This official view is not the proper attitude for baseball to take. A major part of the appeal and romance of baseball is its long and rich history. Baseball fans are interested not only in watching games but in discussing baseball's past and looking at players and teams in historical perspective. For example, the question of who should be elected to the Baseball Hall of Fame arouses great interest among fans. In addition, as our "national pastime," baseball occupies an important place in our history and culture. One cannot merely study baseball's past glories while ignoring its problems, just as one cannot study world history without addressing the evils of wars, bigotry, and social strife.

In looking back at past scandals, we have identified a number of cases in which players involved in corruption were never officially punished. Among those were Mike McGeary, Jack O'Connor, and Hal Chase, none of whom were placed on baseball's ineligible list. We have also examined other cases in which players who have been put on the ineligible list may not belong there, including Joe Tipton, Phil Douglas, and Ray Fisher. Finally, there is the case of Pete Rose and the question of whether he should be reinstated.

No purpose would be served by going back in history to add names to baseball's ineligible list. Players such as Chase, McGeary, and O'Connor are long dead, and the fact that their actions are recorded in history would seem to be punishment enough. Those who wish to correct a past injustice, on the other hand, should have a one-time chance for a hearing. For example, if supporters of Joe Jackson feel they have sufficient evidence to clear his name, they should be given an opportunity to present their case to the baseball hierarchy, and a panel should be appointed to review the evidence. However, the burden of proof must be on those presenting the appeal. In other words, it is not enough to show that there was reasonable doubt that Joe Jackson was guilty; it must be proven that indeed he was innocent.

There are at least nine former major league players who merit a hearing. These are Jean Dubuc, Joe Gedeon, Benny Kauff, Ray Fisher, Buck Weaver, Joe Jackson, Phil Douglas, Jimmy O'Connell, and Cozy Dolan. Whether there are supporters or relatives who would like to petition to have the cases of these players or others reviewed remains to be seen.

There is also at least one case that represents such an obvious miscarriage of justice that the player's expulsion should be overturned without the formality of a hearing. We are referring to the case of Joe Tipton, who implicated himself by volunteering his participation on two occasions in intentionally hitting foul balls. This is not to say that Tipton did not do wrong—Tipton himself acknowledged that he made a mistake. But to put a man on the permanently ineligible list for this type of mistake, rather than giving him a fine and a suspension, makes no sense. An argument can also be made that Hooper Triplett, who made a bet against his team while intoxicated, falls into the same category.

In the case of Pete Rose, we believe that baseball was correct to impose a stiff punishment upon him. Simply by engaging in illegal betting on sports and dealing with bookmakers, he has caused harm to the integrity of the game, which cannot be tolerated. Furthermore, there is very strong evidence that Rose did indeed bet on baseball and on the Reds.

While we support a strong punishment for Rose, we feel that permanent expulsion is too harsh a penalty. While Rose behaved foolishly and his behavior hurt baseball, never was any question raised about Rose's honesty on the playing field or in the dugout. Our recommendation would be to reduce Rose's sentence from being permanently ineligible to being ineligible for a fixed period of time, perhaps the seven years that Fay Vincent offered to Rose's attorneys during the negotiations.

The final issue that we will address is membership in the Baseball Hall of Fame. While many of the players involved in scandals were stars—players such as Buck Weaver, George Hall, and Eddie Cicotte—of those on baseball's ineligible list, only Joe Jackson and Pete Rose had Hall of Fame–caliber careers. In addition, two others tainted by scandal—Hal Chase and Carl Mays—might appear to have strong Hall of Fame potential.

In regard to Jackson, we believe that baseball should give his supporters a hearing and a chance to clear his name. If it is indeed proven that Jackson was not in any way involved in the World Series scandal, he should be in the Hall of Fame. If Jackson agreed to take part in the scandal but then double-crossed the gamblers by playing up to the best of his ability, we would have a hard time arguing that this type of behavior merits a plaque in Cooperstown.

The Pete Rose issue is a fairly simple one. If Rose's punishment is changed from being permanent to having a fixed expiration, Rose should be eligible for the Hall of Fame when the penalty expires.

The decision on Chase is also a fairly simple one. Despite the fact that he is not on baseball's permanently ineligible list, Chase was involved in massive corruption throughout his career. To consider him for Cooperstown would be to cheapen the entire Hall of Fame and make a mockery of baseball's integrity.

While there are some grounds for suspicion against Carl Mays, the evidence against him is far from conclusive. Given that Judge Landis did not feel that the evidence against Mays merited any disciplinary action, keeping him out of the Hall of Fame based on suspicion would seem to be an injustice. His candidacy should be decided based on his playing career rather than the suspicions against him during the 1921 World Series.

The history of baseball gambling and game fixing scandals has been a long and often tragic one. Despite these scandals, baseball has survived and thrived and will continue to do so.

Chapter Notes

Titles are abbreviated. For full bibliographic information, please consult the Bibliography.

Chapter 1

1. Allen, *Hot Stove League.*
2. Goldstein, *Playing for Keeps.*
3. Chadwick Scrapbooks.
4. Orem, *Baseball.*
5. *New York Times*, 24 June 1869.
6. Chadwick Scrapbooks.
7. Chadwick Scrapbooks.
8. Chadwick Scrapbooks.

Chapter 2

1. Allen, *100 Years of Baseball.*
2. Moreland, *Balldom.*
3. Anson, *Ballplayer's Career.*
4. Chadwick Scrapbooks.
5. Chadwick Scrapbooks.
6. Orem, *Baseball.*
7. Orem, *Baseball.*
8. Chadwick Scrapbooks.
9. *Cincinnati Enquirer*, 28 June 1914
10. Tiemann & Rucker, *Nineteenth Century Stars.*

Chapter 3

1. Spalding, *National Game.*
2. Spalding, *National Game.*
3. Chadwick Scrapbooks.
4. Orem, *Baseball.*
5. Chadwick Scrapbooks.
6. *Louisville Courier Journal*, 31 May 1876.
7. Chadwick Scrapbooks.
8. Chadwick Scrapbooks.
9. Chadwick Scrapbooks.
10. Allen, *Hot Stove League.*
11. *New York Clipper*, 10 Nov. 1877.
12. *Louisville Courier Journal*, 4 Nov. 1877.
13. *Louisville Courier Journal*, 4 Nov. 1877.
14. Spalding, *National Game.*
15. *Sporting News*, 19 March 1890.
16. *Troy Record*, 18 June 1901.
17. *Sporting Life*, 16 Aug. 1890.

Chapter 4

1. Chadwick Scrapbooks.
2. Chadwick Scrapbooks.
3. Postal et al., *Jews in Sports.*
4. Orem, *Baseball.*
5. *Louisville Courier Journal*, 27 June 1882.
6. Chadwick Scrapbooks.
7. *Boston Daily Globe*, 23 Sept. 1883.
8. Allen, *Cincinnati Reds.*
9. *Sporting Life*, 23 June 1886.

10. *Sporting Life*, 23 June 1886.
11. *Sporting Life*, 23 June 1886.
12. *Sporting Life*, 23 June 1886.
13. *Reach's*, 1887.
14. Lansche, *Glory*.

13. *New York Times*, 20 May 1947.
14. Chase File, National Baseball Library.
15. *Sporting News*, 28 May 1947.

Chapter 5

1. Chadwick Scrapbooks.
2. Allen, *Hot Stove*.
3. *Sporting Life*, 25 March 1905.
4. *Sporting News*, 7 Jan. 1905.
5. Taylor File—National Baseball Library.
6. Taylor File—National Baseball Library.
7. Taylor File—National Baseball Library.
8. *Sporting Life*, 25 March 1905.
9. Allen, *National League Story*.
10. Allen, *National League Story*.
11. Seymour, *Golden Years*.
12. Stump, "Ty Cobb's Fight."
13. Cobb and Stump, *My Life*.
14. *Spalding Guide*, 1892.
15. *Sporting News*, 17 September 1917.
16. Interview with Joel Platt, Boca Raton, Florida, 1992.

Chapter 6

1. Lieb, *Baseball*.
2. Lieb, *Baseball*.
3. Lieb, *Baseball*.
4. Allen, *Reds*.
5. Chase File, National Baseball Library.
6. Heydler, "A Defense."
7. Hoie, "Hal Chase."
8. *Sporting News*, 17 June 1920.
9. *Sporting News*, 7 Oct. 1920.
10. Chase File, National Baseball Library.
11. *Sporting News*, 23 April 1947.
12. Ritter, *The Glory of Their Times*.

Chapter 7

1. Asinof, *Eight Men Out*.
2. *Spalding Guide 1920*.
3. *Spalding Guide 1920*.
4. *Spalding Guide 1920*.
5. *Spalding Guide 1920*.
6. Asinof, *Eight Men Out*.
7. Thorn and Palmer, *Total Baseball*.
8. Asinof, *Eight Men Out*.
9. *Baseball Digest*, June 1949.
10. Asinof, *Eight Men Out*.
11. Asinof, *Eight Men Out*.
12. Asinof, *Eight Men Out*.
13. Asinof, *Eight Men Out*.
14. Asinof, *Eight Men Out*.
15. Spink, *Landis*.
16. Gropman, *Say It Ain't So*.
17. *ABA Journal*, 1 Feb. 1988.
18. Asinof, *Eight Men Out*.
19. *Los Angeles Herald*, 3 Aug. 1921.
20. Ritter, *Glory*.
21. Ritter, *Glory*.
22. Green, *Forgotten Fields*.
23. *Sports Illustrated*, 17 Sept. 1956.
24. *Sports Illustrated*, 17 Sept. 1956.
25. *Baseball Digest*, April 1956.
26. *Sporting News*, 30 Dec. 1959.
27. Black Sox Scandal File, National Baseball Library.
28. Stein, *Ginger Kid*.
29. Interview with Ray Allen, Atlantic City, N.J., 1991.
30. Bennett, "Shoeless Joe."
31. Gropman, *Say It Ain't So*.
32. Gropman, *Say It Ain't So*.
33. Gropman, *Say It Ain't So*.
34. Gropman, *Say It Ain't So*.

35. Bisher, *Sport Magazine*, p. 84.
36. Farrell, *My Baseball Prank*.
37. Falls, *Baseball Digest*, Feb. 1966.
38. Chapin, *Sporting News*, 2 Sept. 1969
39. Lieb, *Sporting News*, 30 Dec. 1959.

Chapter 8

1. *Sporting News*, 31 March 1921.
2. Allen, *Reds*.
3. Lieb, *Baseball*.
4. Lieb, *Baseball*.
5. Clark, *Last Round*.
6. Clark, *Last Round*.
7. Gold and Ahrens, *Golden Era*.
8. *Sporting News*, 24 Aug. 1922.
9. Fowler, *Great Mouth Piece*.

Chapter 9

1. *Sporting News*, 4 Oct. 1924.
2. *Sporting News*, 4 Oct. 1924.
3. *Sporting News*, 19 Feb. 1920.
4. *New York World*, 11 Jan. 1925.
5. *New York World*, 11 Jan. 1925.
6. *New York World*, 11 Jan. 1925.
7. *New York World*, 9 Oct. 1924.
8. *Sporting News*, 21 Jan. 1925.
9. *Baseball Magazine*, December 1924.

Chapter 10

1. Alexander, *Ty Cobb*.
2. Spink, *Landis*.
3. Spink, *Landis*.
4. Cobb and Stump, *My Life*.
5. Cobb and Stump, *My Life*.

6. Dickson, *Baseball's Greatest Quotations*.
7. *Sporting News*, 27 Jan. 1927.
8. *Sporting News*, 6 Jan. 1927.
9. Spink, *Landis*.
10. *Sporting News*, 13 Jan. 1927.
11. Spink, *Landis*.
12. Spink, *Landis*.
13. Spink, *Landis*.
14. Spink, *Landis*.
15. Spink, *Landis*.
16. *Sporting News*, 20 Jan. 1927.
17. Spink, *Landis*.

Chapter 11

1. Reidenbaugh, *Cooperstown*.
2. *Sporting News*, 2 Dec. 1943.
3. *Sporting News*, 2 Dec. 1943.
4. *Sporting News*, 2 Dec. 1943.
5. *Sporting News*, 9 Dec. 1943.
6. *Sporting News*, 19 March 1947.
7. Durocher, *Nice Guys*.
8. Durocher, *Nice Guys*.
9. *Sporting News*, 16 April 1947.
10. Chandler and Trimble, *Heroes*.

Chapter 12

1. *Sporting News*, 7 Oct. 1959.
2. *Sports Illustrated*, 3 Feb. 1970.
3. McLain, *Strikeout*.
4. McLain, *Strikeout*.
5. Kuhn, *Hardball*.
6. *Sporting News*, 18 Apr. 1970.
7. *Sporting News*, 7 March 1970.

Chapter 13

1. Kuhn, *Hardball*.
2. Reston, *Collision*.
3. Spink, *Landis*.
4. Dowd, *Report to the Commissioner*.

5. Dowd, *Report to the Commissioner.*

6. Dowd, *Report to the Commissioner.*

7. Reston, *Collision.*

8. Reston, *Collision.*

9. Reston, *Collision.*

10. Reston, *Collision.*

11. Reston, *Collision.*

12. Rose and Kahn, *My Sport.*

13. Reston, *Collision.*

14. Reston, *Collision.*

15. *New York Post,* 9 Jan. 1992.

16. *New Orleans Times-Picayune,* 21 Aug. 1991.

17. *New Orleans Times-Picayune,* 21 Aug. 1991.

Chapter 14

1. Overfield, *100 Seasons.*

2. Pietrusza, *Major Leagues.*

3. Chadwick Scrapbooks.

4. Church, *Baseball.*

5. *San Francisco Chronicle,* 19 May 1883.

6. *Sacramento Bee,* 25 Nov. 1890.

7. *Sporting News,* 13 May 1920.

8. *Los Angeles Times,* 10 May 1920.

9. *Sporting News,* 3 June 1920.

10. *Los Angeles Times,* 18 June 1920.

11. *Sporting News,* 26 Aug. 1920.

12. *Los Angeles Times,* 4 Aug. 1920.

13. *Los Angeles Times,* 4 Aug. 1920.

14. *Los Angeles Times,* 5 Aug. 1920.

15. *Los Angeles Times,* 11 Aug. 1920.

16. *Los Angeles Times,* 11 Aug. 1920.

17. *Los Angeles Times,* 12 Aug. 1920.

18. *Los Angeles Times,* 4 Aug. 1920.

19. *Los Angeles Times,* 13 Aug. 1920.

20. *Los Angeles Times,* 25 Oct. 1920.

Chapter 15

1. *Sporting News,* 21 Aug. 1946.

2. *Sporting News,* 5 Feb. 1947.

3. *Sporting News,* 1 Feb. 1969.

4. *Sporting News,* 12 Sept. 1981.

5. *Sporting News,* 13 March 1982.

6. Gutman, *Baseball Babylon.*

Bibliography

Ahrens, Arthur. "Jack Taylor, King of the Iron Men." *Baseball Research Journal*, 1976.
————. "The Split Century." *Baseball Research Journal*, 1973.
Alexander, Charles. *Ty Cobb*. New York: Oxford University Press, 1984.
Allen, Lee. *The American League Story*. New York: Hill & Wang, 1962.
————. *The Cincinnati Reds*. New York: G. P. Putnam's Sons, 1948.
————. *The Hot Stove League*. New York: A. S. Barnes, 1955.
————. *The National League Story*. New York: Hill & Wang, 1961.
————. *100 Years of Baseball*. New York: Bartholomew House, 1950.
————. *The World Series*. New York: G. P. Putnam's Sons, 1969.
Anson, Adrian. *A Ball Player's Career*. Chicago: Era, 1900.
Asinof, Eliot. *Eight Men Out*. New York: Holt, Rinehart and Winston, 1963.
Axelson, G. W. *Commy*. Chicago: Reilly & Lee, 1919.
Bak, Richard. *Cobb Would Have Caught It*. Detroit: Wayne State Univ. Press, 1991.
Bartlett, Arthur. *Baseball and Mr. Spalding*. New York: Farrar, Straus & Young, 1951.
Bennett, Jay. "Did Shoeless Joe Jackson Throw the 1919 World Series?" *1992 Proceedings of the American Statistical Association Section on Statistics in Sports*. Alexandria, Va., 1992.
Blaisdell, Lowell. "Mystery and Tragedy: The O'Connell-Dolan Scandal." *Baseball Research Journal*, 1982.
Boren, Steve. "The Bizarre Career of Rube Benton." *Baseball Research Journal*, 1983.
Broeg, Bob, and William Miller. *Baseball from a Different Angle*. South Bend, Ind.: Diamond Communications, 1988.
Brown, Gene, ed. *The New York Times Encyclopedia of Sports*. New York: Arno, 1979.
Brown, Warren. *The Chicago Cubs*. New York: G. P. Putnam's Sons, 1946.
————. *The Chicago White Sox*. New York: G. P. Putnam's Sons, 1952.
Chadwick, Henry, Scrapbooks. New York Public Library, Albert Goodwill Spalding Collection, Rare Books and Manuscripts Division; Astor, Lenox and Tilden Foundations.
Chandler, Happy, with Vance Trimble. *Heroes, Plain Folks, and Skunks*. Chicago: Bonus, 1989.
Charleton, James, ed. *The Baseball Chronology*. New York: Macmillan, 1991.
Church, Seymour. *Baseball: The History, Statistics, and Romance of the American National Game from Its Inception to the Present Time*. San Francisco: Self-published, 1902.
Clark, Tom. *One Last Round for the Shuffler*. New York: Truck, 1979.
Cobb, Ty, with Al Stump. *My Life in Baseball—The True Record*. Garden City, N.Y.: Doubleday, 1961.

Costello, James, and Michael Santa Maria. *In the Shadows of the Diamond*. Dubuqe, Iowa: Elysian Fields, 1992.

Crepeau, Richard. *Baseball, America's Diamond Mind*. Orlando, Fla.: University Presses of Central Florida, 1980.

DeWitt's Baseball Guide, 1872–1880.

Dickson, Paul. *Baseball's Greatest Quotations*. New York: Harper-Collins, 1991.

Dowd, John. *Report to the Commissioner*. Cincinnati, OH: Official Shorthand Reporter, 1989.

Durocher, Leo. *The Dodgers and Me*. Chicago: Ziff-Davis, 1948.

_____, and Ed Linn. *Nice Guys Finish Last*. New York: Simon & Schuster, 1975.

Einstein, Charles, ed. *The Third Fireside Book of Baseball*. New York: Simon and Schuster, 1968.

Ellard, Harry. *Baseball and Cincinnati*. Cincinnati, Ohio: self-published, 1907.

Enright, Jim. *Chicago Cubs*. New York: Collier, 1975.

Eskenazi, Gerald. *Bill Veeck, A Baseball Legend*. New York: McGraw-Hill, 1988.

Farrell, James. *My Baseball Diary*. New York: A. S. Barnes, 1957.

Fowler, Gene. *My Great Mouthpiece: The Story of William Fallon*. New York: Covici, Friede, 1931.

Frick, Ford. *Games, Asterisks and People*. New York: Crown, 1973.

Frommer, Harvey. *Shoeless Joe and Ragtime Baseball*. Dallas, Tex.: Taylor, 1992.

Gold, Eddie, and Art Ahrens. *The Golden Era Clubs*. Chicago: Bonus, 1985.

Goldstein, Warren. *Playing for Keeps: A History of Early Baseball*. Ithaca, N.Y.: Cornell University Press, 1989.

Green, Paul. *Forgotten Fields*. Waupaca, Wisc.: Parker, 1984.

Gropman, Donald. *Say It Ain't So, Joe! The True Story of Shoeless Joe Jackson*. New York: Citadel, 1992.

Gutman, Dan. *Baseball Babylon*. New York: Penguin, 1992.

Hall, Alvin, ed. *1989 Cooperstown Symposium on Baseball and the American Culture*. Westport, Conn.: Meckler, 1991.

_____. *1990 Cooperstown Symposium on Baseball and the American Culture*. Westport, Conn.: Meckler, 1991.

Hanks, Stephen, et al. *150 Years of Baseball*. New York: Beekman House, 1989.

Harris, Stanley. *Playing the Game*. New York: Grosset & Dunlap, 1925.

Harshman, Jack E. "The Radbourn and Sweeney Saga." *Baseball Research Journal*, 1990.

Henderson, Robert. *Ball, Bat and Bishop*. New York: Rockport, 1947.

Heydler, John. "A Defense of the Hal Chase Affair." *Baseball Magazine*, December 1920.

Hilton, George. "The Evangeline League Scandal of 1946." *Baseball Research Journal*, 1982.

Hoie, Bob. "The Hal Chase Story." *Grandstand Baseball Annual*, 1991.

James, Bill. *The Bill James Historical Baseball Abstract*. New York: Villard, 1986.

Johnson, Lloyd, and Miles Wolfe. *The Encyclopedia of Minor League Baseball*. Durham, N.C.: Baseball America, 1993.

Karst, Gene, and Martin Jones, Jr. *Who's Who in Professional Baseball*. New Rochelle, N.Y.: Arlington House, 1973.

Katcher, Leo. *The Big Bankroll*. New Rochelle, N.Y.: Arlington House, 1958.

Krueger, Joseph. *Baseball's Greatest Drama*. Milwaukee, Wisc.: self-published, 1942.

Kuenster, John, ed. *From Cobb to "Catfish": 128 Illustrated Stories from Baseball Digest.* Chicago: Rand McNally, 1975.

Kuhn, Bowie. *Hardball, the Education of a Baseball Commissioner.* New York: Times Books, 1987.

Lanigan, Earnest. *Baseball Cyclopedia.* New York: Baseball Magazine, 1922.

Lansche, Jerry. *Glory Fades Away.* Dallas, Tex.: Taylor, 1991.

Levine, Peter. *A. G. Spalding and the Rise of Baseball.* New York: Oxford University Press, 1985.

_____, ed. *Baseball History.* Vols. 1–4. Westport, Conn.: Meckler, 1989–91.

Lieb, Frederick. *Baseball as I Have Known It.* New York: Coward, McCann and Geoghegan, 1977.

_____. *The Detroit Tigers.* New York: G. P. Putnam's Sons, 1946.

_____. *The Pittsburgh Pirates.* New York: G. P. Putnam's Sons, 1948.

_____. *The Story of the World Series.* New York: G. P. Putnam's Sons, 1949.

Lowenfish, Lee, and Tony Lupien. *The Imperfect Diamond.* New York: Stein and Day, 1980.

Luhrs, Victor. *The Great Baseball Mystery.* New York: A. S. Barnes, 1966.

McCallum, John. *The Tiger Wore Spikes.* New York: A. S. Barnes, 1956.

_____. *Ty Cobb.* New York: Praeger, 1975.

McLain, Denny, and Dave Diles. *Nobody's Perfect.* New York: Dial, 1975.

_____, with Mike Nahrstedt. *Strikeout: The Story of Denny McLain.* St. Louis: Sporting News, 1988.

Mann, Arthur. *Baseball Confidential.* New York: David McKay, 1951.

Minor League Baseball Stars. Vols. 1 and 2 Manhattan, Kan.: Society for American Baseball Research, 1978+1985.

Moreland, George. *Balldom.* New York: Baldham, 1914.

Murdock, Eugene. *Ban Johnson, Czar of Baseball.* Westport, Conn.: Greenwood, 1982.

_____. *Baseball Players and Their Times: Oral History of the Game, 1920–1940.* Westport, Conn.: Meckler, 1991.

Names, Larry. *Bury My Heart at Wrigley Field.* Neshkoro, Wisc.: Sportsbook, 1990.

Neft, David, Lee Allen, et al., eds. *The Baseball Encyclopedia.* New York: Macmillan, 1969.

Nemec, David, et al. *20th Century Baseball Chronicle.* New York: Beekman House, 1991.

Obojski, Robert. *Bush League.* New York: Macmillan, 1975.

Okkonen, Marc. *The Federal League of 1914–1915.* Garrett Park, Md.: Society for American Baseball Research, 1989.

Okrent, Daniel, and Steven Wulf. *Baseball Anecdotes.* New York: Harper & Row, 1989.

O'Neal, Bill. *The Pacific Coast League, 1903–1988.* Austin, Tex.: Eakin, 1990.

_____. *The Texas League, 1888–1987.* Austin, Tex.: Eakin, 1987.

Orem, Preston. *Baseball, from the Newspaper Accounts, 1845–1881.* Altadena, Calif.: self-published, 1961.

Overfield, Joseph. *The 100 Seasons of Buffalo Baseball.* Kenmore, N.Y.: Partner's Press, 1985.

Peterson, Harold. *The Man Who Invented Baseball.* New York: Charles Scribner & Sons, 1969.

Pietrusza, David. *Major Leagues.* Jefferson, N.C.: McFarland & Company, 1991.

Postal, Bernard, Jesse Silver, and Roy Silver. *Encyclopedia of Jews in Sports.* New York: Bloch, 1965.

Proctor, Donald. "The Black Listing of Ray Fisher." *Baseball Research Journal*, 1981.
Reidenbaugh, Lowell. *Cooperstown, Where Baseball's Legends Live Forever*. St. Louis: Sporting News, 1983.
_____. *The Sporting News, First Hundred Years*. St. Louis: Sporting News, 1985.
Reston, James, Jr. *Collision at Home Plate*. New York: Harper-Collins, 1991.
Ritter, Lawrence. *The Glory of Their Times*. New York: Macmillan, 1989.
Rose, Pete, and Roger Kahn. *Pete Rose: My Story*. New York: Macmillan, 1989.
Ryczek, William. *Blackguards and Red Stockings: A History of Baseball's National Association 1871–1875*. Jefferson, N.C.: McFarland & Company, 1992.
Selzer, Jack. *Baseball in the Nineteenth Century: An Overview*. Cooperstown, N.Y.: Society for American Baseball Research, 1986.
Seymour, Harold. *Baseball*. 2 vols. New York: Oxford University Press, 1960, 1971.
_____. *Baseball, The People's Game*. New York: Oxford University Press, 1990.
Shannon, Mike, ed. *The Best of Spitball*. New York: Pocket Books, 1988.
Shapiro, James. *My Baseball Diamond*. New York: A. S. Barnes, 1957.
Shatzin, Mike. *The Ballplayers*. New York: Arbor House, 1990.
Smith, Ira. *Baseball's Famous First Basemen*. New York: A. S. Barnes, 1956.
Smith, Robert. *Baseball in America*. New York: Holt, Rinehart and Winston, 1961.
Sokolove, Michael. *Hustle: The Myth, Life, and Lies of Pete Rose*. New York: Simon and Schuster, 1990.
Sowell, Mike. *The Pitch That Killed*. New York: Collier, 1989.
Spalding, Albert. *America's National Game*. New York: American Sports Publishing, 1911.
Spalding, John. *Always on Sunday*. Manhattan, Kan.: AG Press, 1992.
Spalding's Official Baseball Guides, 1877–1939. Chicago: A. G. Spalding, 1877–1939.
Spink, J. G. Taylor. *Judge Landis and 25 Years of Baseball*. New York: Crowell, 1947.
Sporting News Official Baseball Guide, 1982.
Stein, Irving. *The Ginger Kid: The Buck Weaver Story*. Dubuque, Iowa: Brown & Benchmark, 1992.
Stump, Al. "Ty Cobb's Wild Ten-Month Fight to Live." In *My Life in Baseball: The True Record*. Garden City, N.Y.: Doubleday, 1961.
Thompson, S. C. *All Time Rosters of Major League Baseball Clubs*. New York: A. S. Barnes, 1967.
Thorn, John, and Pete Palmer, eds. *Total Baseball*. New York: Warner, 1989.
Tiemann, Robert, and Mark Rucker, eds. *Nineteenth Century Stars*. Kansas City, Mo.: Society for American Baseball Research, 1989.
Turkin, Hy, and S. C. Thompson. *The Official Encyclopedia of Baseball*, 4th ed. New York: A. S. Barnes, 1968.
Veeck, Bill, and Ed Linn. *The Hustler's Handbook*. New York: G. P.Putnam's Sons, 1965.
_____, and _____. *Veeck—as in Wreck*. New York: G. P. Putnam's Sons, 1962.
Voigt, David. *American Baseball*. 3 vols. University Park, Penn.: Pennsylvania University Press, 1966, 1970, 1983.
Wallop, Douglas. *Baseball: An Informal History*. New York: W. W. Norton, 1969.
Wayman, Joseph, ed. *Grandstand Baseball Annual, 1991*. Downey, Calif.: self-published, 1992.
Zoss, Joel, and John Bowman. *Diamonds in the Rough*. New York: Macmillan, 1989.

Periodicals Consulted

ABA Journal
Baseball Digest
Baseball Magazine
Boston Daily Globe
Chicago Tribune
Los Angeles Times
Louisville Courier Journal
New Orleans Times-Picayune
New York Clipper
New York Post
New York Times
New York World

Palm Beach Post
Pittsburgh Post-Gazette
Sacramento Bee
San Francisco Chronicle
San Francisco Examiner
Sport Magazine
Sporting Life
Sporting News
Sports Collectors Digest
Sports Illustrated
Troy (N.Y.) Record

Index